WHAT TO DO
IN AN
EMERGENCY

WHAT TO DO
IN AN
EMERGENCY

Reader's
Digest

Published by The Reader's Digest Association, Inc.
London • Sydney • New York • Montreal

contents

🏃 ACCIDENTS AND INJURIES 79–120 »

🏠 HOUSEHOLD EMERGENCIES 121–162 »

📹 CRIMINAL ACTS 163–186 »

☢ PUBLIC EMERGENCIES 187–218 »

🚗 DRIVING EMERGENCIES 219–248 »

OUTDOOR INCIDENTS
249–276 »

TRAVEL EMERGENCIES
277–302 »

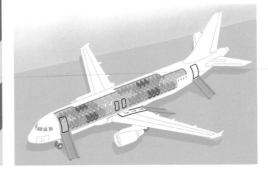

how to use this book

WHAT TO DO IN AN EMERGENCY assumes that you may have to deal with a difficult and dangerous situation without professional help. The instructions should enable you to minimise injury and damage and get effective help and support as swiftly as possible.

This book has been designed to help you to cope with a range of possible situations, some that all of us may face one day; others much rarer. The first three chapters focus on medical emergencies, including key life-saving techniques and critical signs. The next four chapters deal with problems arising in your home; as a result of crime; public emergencies such as fire, weather and bomb attacks; and crises while driving. The book aims to help prepare you even for emergencies that arise when you are abroad or in unfamiliar terrain, or faced with a dangerous animal. Finally, there are useful fixes to deadline-busting technology problems.

① PRECAUTIONS
Practical tips help you avoid potential hazards and prepare you for an emergency situation

② ASSESSMENT
Gives a clear order for evaluating the extent of the emergency and assessing resources

③ WARNINGS
Highlight dangers in the particular emergency that you should be aware of

④ ACTION
Step-by-step sequences with clear explanatory diagrams and photographs tell you exactly what to do to get on top of the emergency

⑤ TAKE CARE
Points out important safety information to ensure that you do not put yourself or others at further risk

⑥ LEARN MORE
A series of boxes give detailed additional information on particular points of interest

LIFE-SAVING FIRST AID

attending to a casualty

When dealing with someone who is injured, stay calm and follow a clear plan of action. Consider your own safety above all. Once you are sure that it is safe to do so, assess and treat the casualty and get appropriate help.

assessment

Check your own – and the casualty's – safety and then identify and treat conditions that are an immediate threat to life. The most important of these is unconsciousness – from whatever cause (see pages 14–17), next are conditions that affect breathing or blood circulation.

1 CHECK THAT IT IS SAFE TO APPROACH THE CASUALTY – if it isn't, call the emergency services and keep your distance but keep an eye on the casualty. Do not approach even if his condition worsens

2 CHECK THE CASUALTY'S SAFETY – only move someone if his life is in immediate danger (and if there is no risk of you injuring yourself)

3 ASSESS AND TREAT – deal with potentially life-threatening injuries or conditions, such as unconsciousness (see opposite) before attending to other conditions or injuries

4 GET APPROPRIATE HELP – you may need to call the emergency services or enlist the help of someone nearby

Getting help

Call for emergency help if a casualty is seriously injured and/or needs to be transported by stretcher. If a casualty requires hospital treatment, but he can walk or sit and his condition is unlikely to deteriorate, you can go by car or taxi. For other injuries, call the casualty's local doctor's surgery or the NHS advice line, or visit an NHS walk-in centre or NHS minor injuries unit.

Call 999 or 112 (also in EU) and state:
● Your telephone number, your exact location, including any landmarks, and the type of incident.
● The number of casualties, their approximate ages and a description of their injuries.
● Stay on the line to answer any questions and receive first-aid advice. The controller will also contact the police or fire service.

action

IS THE CASUALTY CONSCIOUS? Talk to the person. If he is conscious, he will respond by making a gesture or eye contact with you. If there is no response, gently shake his shoulders. If there is still no response, he is unconscious. Shout for help, and go to the next step.

He is unconscious

He is conscious

OPEN AIRWAY Tilt the casualty's head back and lift his chin to open the airway. See **Unconscious Adult** (pages 13–14).

CHECK AIRWAY Make sure that the airways are open and clear. Treat **Choking** (see page 24) or remove anything covering the mouth or that prevents normal chest movement.

CHECK BREATHING Look for chest movement and listen and feel for breaths for up to 10 seconds. See **Unconscious Adult** (pages 13–14).

CHECK BREATHING Monitor the casualty's breathing and check it is normal. Treat any condition that could be affecting his breathing, such as **Asthma** (see pages 42–43).

He is breathing normally

He is not breathing

CIRCULATION
Check and treat conditions that affect circulation, such as **Severe Bleeding** (see page 22) or **Burns** (see page 23).

GIVE CPR
Call the emergency services, then start **CPR** (see pages 16–17).

CIRCULATION Check and treat any conditions that affect circulation, such as **Severe Bleeding** (see page 22) or **Burns** (see page 23).

CHECK WHAT ELSE IT COULD BE If there is no life-threatening injury or illness, assess what else it could be (see pages 28–30). Call for emergency help if necessary.

PLACE IN THE RECOVERY POSITION
If safe to do so, place the casualty in the **Recovery Position** (see page 15) and call for emergency help. Monitor the casualty and then check for possible causes.

> **⚠ WARNING**
> If the casualty is a child or an infant under one year old, go straight to pages 18–19 as there are important differences in the way that unconsciousness is managed in children.

▶▶See also: MAKING FURTHER CHECKS p28 **13**

unconscious adult

An unconscious person has no muscle control in his throat so the tongue can fall back and block the airways, preventing breathing. He cannot cough or swallow so risks choking on fluid or vomit. Fast action can be life-saving.

✓ CHECK

Make sure the area is safe for you to approach.

⚠ WARNING

● If a person is not breathing, the heart can stop, so begin CPR immediately (see step 4).
● If the casualty is a child or baby, go to pages 18–19 as there are important differences in the way unconsciousness is managed in children.

👁 GET HELP

● Find out whether or not an unconscious casualty is breathing before you call the emergency services, as this is likely to be the first question you will be asked.
● If you are not alone, send someone to call for help as soon as you have checked breathing. Ask the person to come back and confirm that the call has been made.
● If you have help, when you place the casualty in the recovery position, one person can support his head while you roll him onto his side.

1 TILT HEAD Kneel next to the casualty – level with his shoulders – put one hand on his forehead in front of the hairline, then tilt the head back. His mouth will fall slightly open.

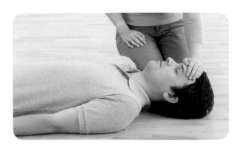

2 LIFT CHIN Place two fingers of your other hand on the point of the casualty's chin, then lift it. This action will lift the tongue away from the back of the throat, opening the air passage to the lungs.

3 CHECK BREATHING Put your ear as near as possible to the casualty's mouth and nose and look towards his chest. Listen for breathing sounds, feel for breaths against your face and look to see if the chest is moving. Do this for up to 10 seconds.

4 IF NOT BREATHING Call for emergency help. Start Cardio-pulmonary Resuscitation (CPR) (see pages 16–17). If you are in a public place, ask someone to fetch an AED machine (see page 17), which may correct the heart rhythm.

5 IF BREATHING NORMALLY Check for and treat conditions that affect circulation, such as severe bleeding (see page 22) or burns (see page 23). Call for emergency help. If possible, place the casualty in the recovery position (see opposite). Note any change in the casualty's condition while you are waiting for help.

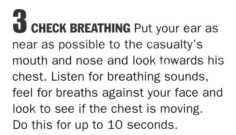

recovery position

If the casualty is breathing normally, place him on his side in the recovery position (unless you suspect serious back injury, see page 85). In this position his airway is open, fluid and/or vomit can drain and he cannot roll forward. Try not to leave a casualty, but you may need to go and call for help.

1 **POSITION ARMS AND LEGS** Remove anything bulky from the casualty's pockets. Ensure his legs are straight, then kneel beside him, level with chest. Place the arm nearest to you at a right angle to his body with the palm facing upwards. Pull his far leg up at the knee until his foot is resting flat on the ground. Lift his other arm, bring it across his body towards you and hold the back of his hand against his cheek.

2 **TURN THE CASUALTY** Grasp his raised knee with one hand and support the hand against his cheek with your other hand. Pull on the knee and gently roll the casualty towards you. Keep the casualty's head, back and neck aligned during turning. If you have help, one person can support the casualty's head while you roll him onto his side.

3 **ADJUST THE HEAD POSITION** Tilt his head back slightly to keep the airway open. The casualty's uppermost hand should be under his cheek to help maintain the correct position.

4 **ADJUST THE LEG AND ARM** Make sure the casualty's upper leg is at a right angle at his hip and knee, his lower leg and back align, and his lower arm is at a right angle at the shoulder and elbow.

5 **MONITOR CASUALTY** While you are waiting for help, monitor the casualty's level of consciousness, breathing and pulse and note any changes (see page 30). If normal breathing stops, begin CPR (see page 16).

▶▶See also: **BACK AND NECK INJURY** pp84–85

cardiopulmonary resuscitation (CPR)

If a person is not breathing, his heartbeat will stop. Do CPR (chest compressions and rescue breaths) to help circulation and get oxygen into the body. Early use of a machine called an AED (automated external defibrillator – see opposite) can restart a heart with an abnormal rhythm.

✓ CHECK

Open the airway and check breathing (see page 14). Do not begin CPR if a casualty is breathing normally.

☎ GET HELP

If you are not alone, send someone to call for help as soon as you have checked breathing. Ask the person to come back and confirm that the call has been made.

⚠ WARNING

● **DO NOT press on the ribs, the lower tip of the breastbone or the upper abdomen when giving chest compressions to a casualty.**
● **If the chest does not rise and fall with a rescue breath, adjust the head position and try again. DO NOT try more than twice before going on to repeat chest compressions.**

❓ WHAT NEXT

Continue giving CPR until emergency help arrives; the casualty starts to breathe normally; you are too tired to keep going. If normal breathing begins at any point, place him in the Recovery Position (see page 15) and await help.

1 POSITION YOUR HAND Make sure the casualty is lying on his back on a firm surface. Kneel beside him and place the heel of your hand on the centre of the chest.

2 INTERLOCK FINGERS Keeping your arms straight, cover the first hand with the heel of your other hand and interlock the fingers of both hands together. Keep your fingers raised so they do not touch the casualty's chest or ribcage.

3 GIVE CHEST COMPRESSIONS Lean forward so that your shoulders are directly over the casualty's chest and press straight down on the chest about 4–5cm. Release the pressure, but not your hands and let the chest come back up. Repeat to give 30 compressions at a rate of 100 compressions per minute.

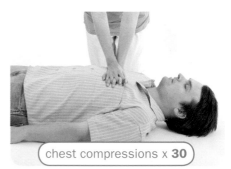

chest compressions x **30**

4 OPEN THE AIRWAY Move to the casualty's head. Tilt his head and lift his chin to open the airway again. Let his mouth fall open slightly.

5 **GIVE RESCUE BREATHS** Pinch the nostrils closed with the hand that was on the forehead and support the casualty's chin with your other hand. Take a normal breath, put your mouth over the casualty's and blow until you can see his chest rise.

rescue breaths x **2**

6 **WATCH CHEST FALL** Remove your mouth from the casualty's and look along the chest, watching the chest fall. Repeat steps 5 and 6 once.

7 **REPEAT CHEST COMPRESSIONS AND RESCUE BREATHS** Place your hands on the chest again and repeat the cycle of 30 chest compressions, followed by two rescue breaths. Continue the cycle.

chest compressions x **30**
rescue breaths x **2**

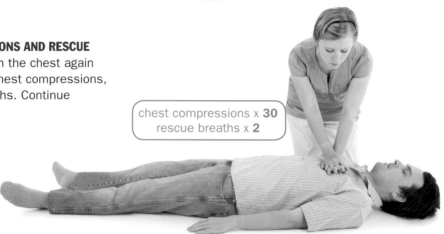

Using an automated external defibrillator (AED)

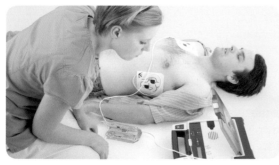

Give CPR while you wait for the AED. If there is no one available trained in its use, follow the machine's instructions.

1 **ATTACH PADS** Switch on AED. Position pads against the skin as shown on the pack.

2 **LISTEN TO MACHINE PROMPTS** Stand away from the casualty and make sure that no one is touching him while the AED is analysing. It will tell you as to whether or not a shock is advised.

● **IF SHOCK ADVISED** Make sure no one is touching the casualty and stand clear. Press the shock button; the casualty will 'jump'. Continue CPR for two more minutes, then the AED will re-analyse the casualty. Follow instructions. Leave pads attached if casualty recovers.
● **IF NO SHOCK ADVISED** Continue CPR for two more minutes, then the AED will re-analyse the casualty. Leave pads attached and keep following the AED's instructions.

▶▶See also: **UNCONSCIOUS CHILD** p18 • **UNCONSCIOUS BABY** p19

unconscious child

Use this sequence to treat a child aged between one year old and puberty. If a child stops breathing, the cause is more likely to be a breathing difficulty than a heart problem, so begin by giving rescue breaths to raise blood oxygen levels.

✅ CHECK

If the chest does not rise and fall with a rescue breath, adjust the head position and try again.

☎ GET HELP

● If you have help, ask the person to call the emergency services as soon as you know the child is not breathing.

● If you are on your own and the child is not breathing, carry out CPR for one minute before stopping to make the call for emergency help.

⚠ WARNING

DO NOT press on the ribs, the lower tip of the breastbone or the upper abdomen when giving chest compressions.

❓ WHAT NEXT

● Continue giving CPR until emergency help arrives and takes over; the child starts to breathe normally; you are too tired to carry on. If normal breathing begins, place the child in the recovery position and wait for emergency help.

● If there is an AED machine available (see page 17), it can be used on a child.

1 OPEN AIRWAY AND CHECK BREATHING

Tilt the child's head back and lift the chin. Put your ear next to her mouth: look, listen and feel for breaths for up to 10 seconds. If she is not breathing, go to step 2. **IF BREATHING NORMALLY** Place the child in the **Recovery Position**, as for an adult (see page 15).

2 GIVE RESCUE BREATHS
Tilt her head and lift her chin; let the child's mouth fall open slightly. Pick out any visible obstruction from the mouth – do not do a finger sweep. Pinch the nostrils closed, take a breath, put your mouth over the child's and blow steadily until you see her chest rise. Remove your mouth and watch the chest fall. Give the casualty five rescue breaths.

rescue breaths x **5**

3 GIVE CHEST COMPRESSIONS

Place the heel of ONE hand on the centre of the chest. With your shoulder directly over your hand, press straight down about one-third of the depth of the chest. Release the pressure, but not your hand; let the chest relax. Give 30 compressions at a rate of 100 compressions per minute.

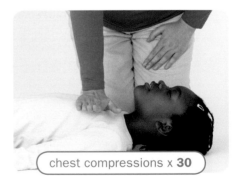

chest compressions x **30**

4 REPEAT RESCUE BREATHS AND COMPRESSIONS
Tilt the child's head, lift her chin and repeat rescue breaths – this time give TWO rescue breaths. Continue a cycle of 30 compressions followed by two rescue breaths.

rescue breaths x **2**
chest compressions x **30**

unconscious baby

Use this sequence to treat an infant less than one year old. Talk to the baby and tap the foot to assess consciousness; never shake a baby. If a baby's breathing stops, begin by giving rescue breaths. Place the baby on a firm surface before you start.

✅ CHECK

If the chest does not rise and fall with a rescue breath, adjust the head position and try again.

☎ GET HELP

● If you have help, ask the person to call the emergency services as soon you know the baby is not breathing.

● If you are on your own and the baby is not breathing, carry out rescue breaths and chest compressions (CPR) for one minute before stopping to make the call for emergency help.

⚠ WARNING

● **DO NOT press on the ribs, the lower tip of the breastbone or the upper abdomen when giving chest compressions.**

● **An AED cannot be used on an infant aged less than one year old.**

❓ WHAT NEXT

Continue giving CPR until emergency help arrives; the baby starts to breathe normally; you are too tired to carry on. If normal breathing begins, hold the baby in the recovery position (see right) and await emergency help.

1 OPEN AIRWAY AND CHECK BREATHING

Tilt the baby's head back and lift the chin. Put your ear next to the baby's mouth: look, listen and feel for breaths for up to 10 seconds. If she is not breathing, go to the next step. **IF BREATHING NORMALLY** Go to step 5.

2 GIVE RESCUE BREATHS

Tilt the baby's head slightly and lift the chin. Pick out any visible obstruction from the mouth and nose – do not do a finger sweep. Put your mouth over the baby's mouth and nose and blow steadily until you see the chest rise. Remove your mouth and watch the chest fall. Give five breaths.

rescue breaths x **5**

3 GIVE CHEST COMPRESSIONS

Place two fingers on the centre of the chest. With your shoulder over your hand, press straight down about one-third of the depth of the chest. Release the pressure, but not your hand; let the chest relax. Give 30 compressions at a rate of 100 per minute.

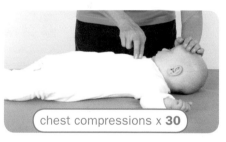

chest compressions x **30**

4 REPEAT RESCUE BREATHS AND COMPRESSIONS

Tilt the baby's head, lift the chin and repeat rescue breaths – this time give TWO rescue breaths. Continue a cycle of 30 compressions and two rescue breaths.

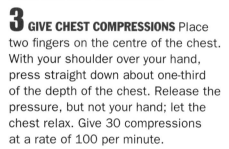

chest compressions x **30**
rescue breaths x **2**

5 IF BREATHING NORMALLY

Hold the baby with the head lower than the body in the recovery position. Call for emergency help and monitor the level of consciousness, breathing and pulse (see page 30) while waiting.

severe **allergic reaction**

A severe allergic reaction affects the whole body and can develop within seconds or minutes of contact with an allergen. Act quickly and call for help as the person urgently needs adrenaline (epinephrine). Help administer the autoinjector if the casualty has one.

✔ ASSESSMENT

Signs of severe allergic reaction include:
- Red, watery and puffy eyes
- General flushed appearance
- A red itchy rash, especially around the mouth and throat
- Swelling of mouth and throat, causing difficulty swallowing
- Difficulty breathing – chest may be tight and casualty may gasp for air
- Abdominal cramps and possible nausea and vomiting
- The casualty may be very agitated, frightened or experience a sense of impending doom

✖ GET HELP

If the casualty does not have an autoinjector, tell the emergency services when you make the call.

⚠ WARNING
- **If the casualty becomes very pale and the pulse is weak, lay her down with her legs raised above the level of her heart.**
- **If the casualty becomes unconscious, open the airway and check breathing (see page 14). Be prepared to begin CPR (see page 16).**

1 **CALL FOR HELP** Call for emergency help immediately and tell the ambulance controller that the casualty is having a severe allergic reaction. If there is a bee stinger still in the casualty, remove it immediately.

2 **GIVE MEDICATION** Find the casualty's autoinjector and give it to her. If she cannot use it, you can help her. Hold it with your fist, remove the grey safety cap and press the end firmly against the thigh through any clothing. Rub the area.

3 **SIT CASUALTY DOWN** Help her to sit down in whatever position she finds most comfortable for breathing. The best position is generally sitting upright with her back straight.

4 **MONITOR CASUALTY** Check her level of consciousness, breathing and pulse (see page 30) while waiting for emergency help. Make a note of any change in her condition. If the symptoms return, you can repeat the dose of adrenaline (epinephrine) every five minutes.

asthma attack

When a person has an asthma attack, the air passages narrow and the muscles tighten, making breathing difficult. In addition the mucus that lines the airway becomes sticky. The casualty will need prompt help to use her inhaler.

✔ ASSESSMENT

Signs of asthma include:
- Difficulty breathing, especially breathing out
- Wheezing and coughing
- Difficulty talking
- Blueness around lips and earlobes as condition worsens

☎ GET HELP

If this is a first asthma attack, or the casualty does not have an inhaler, call for emergency help straightaway.

⚠ WARNING

- **Make sure the casualty is using the reliever inhaler (blue) and not the preventer inhaler (brown or white) as this will not help during the attack.**
- **If the attack worsens and the casualty becomes unconscious, open the airway and check breathing (see page 14). Be prepared to begin CPR (see page 16).**

1 GIVE INHALER Help the casualty find her reliever inhaler (normally blue) and help her to take a puff from it. Tell her to breathe slowly and deeply while she does this.

give **1** puff of reliever inhaler

2 SIT CASUALTY DOWN Help her to sit down in whatever position she finds most comfortable for breathing. The best position is leaning forward slightly with her back straight. Do not let her lie down. If the attack does not improve after a few minutes, give her another puff from the inhaler.

3 CALL FOR HELP If breathing does not improve, the casualty's condition becomes worse, or she finds it difficult to talk because of her breathlessness and/or she is becoming exhausted, call for emergency help.

4 MONITOR CASUALTY Help the casualty to use her inhaler as necessary and monitor her level of consciousness, breathing and pulse (see page 30) while you are waiting for help. Make a note of any change in her condition.

▶▶See also: UNCONSCIOUS ADULT pp14–17 • UNCONSCIOUS CHILD p18 • ASTHMA ATTACK pp42–43

severe **bleeding**

When a casualty is bleeding profusely, it can be life-threatening as vital body fluids are lost from the circulatory system. It is vital to control the casualty's blood loss or he will lose consciousness and there is a risk that his breathing and heartbeat may stop.

⚠ TAKE CARE

Put on a pair of disposable gloves if you have them. Use latex-free gloves as some people are allergic to latex.

⚠ WARNING

● **DO NOT** use a tourniquet to control bleeding.
● If there is an object such as a piece of glass in the wound, press either side of it to control bleeding.
● **DO NOT** give the casualty anything to eat or drink as he may need to have an anaesthetic later.
● If the casualty becomes unconscious, open the airway and check breathing (see page 16). Be prepared to begin CPR (see page 18).

☎ GET HELP

Ideally get someone else to call the emergency services while you attend to the casualty.

❓ WHAT NEXT

● Monitor the casualty's level of consciousness, breathing and pulse (see page 30) while you wait for emergency help.
● Make sure that the bandage is not too tight. Press on a fingernail until it turns white. Release the pressure; colour should return straight-away. If it does not, loosen and reapply the bandage and check it every 10 minutes.

1 APPLY PRESSURE Place a dressing pad directly over the wound and press firmly. Remove or cut away clothing to expose the wound if necessary.

press against wound

2 RAISE AND SUPPORT Raise the injured limb so that it is higher than the casualty's heart; this will slow down the blood flow to the area.

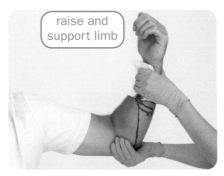

raise and support limb

3 LAY CASUALTY DOWN Help the casualty to lie down, while keeping the injured area raised and supported. Raise his legs above the level of his heart and support them on a chair. This reduces the risk of shock (see pages 38–39), a life-threatening condition that can develop after serious loss of fluids.

4 SECURE DRESSING WITH BANDAGE Tie a bandage around the dressing and limb to hold the pad in place and maintain pressure. Call for emergency help. If blood seeps through the dressing, cover it with another one, secured with a second bandage. If blood comes through the second bandage, take off both dressings and apply a new one.

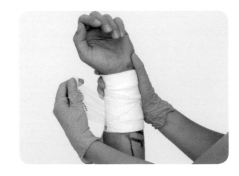

severe burns and scalds

This type of injury carries major risks: body fluids are lost from the circulatory system, and infection is likely because the body's protective layer is damaged. Your aim is to cool the burn as soon as possible to stop the burning process.

✓ ASSESSMENT

Establish the severity of the burn. There may be:
- Severe pain at the site of injury, although deep burns may be pain-free
- Blisters around the site of the injury
- Redness and swelling at the site of injury, or charred skin if the burn is severe

⚠ TAKE CARE

Put on disposable gloves if possible. Use latex-free gloves as some people are allergic to latex.

⚠ WARNING
- **DO NOT cover the burn with plasters.**
- **Never put ointments or gels on a burn.**
- **DO NOT give the casualty food or drink as he may need an anaesthetic later.**
- **If the casualty becomes unconscious, open the airway and check breathing (see page 16). Be prepared to begin CPR (see page 18).**

☺ GET HELP

Seek medical advice for any burn larger than 2.5cm. All deep burns or burns on children need hospital treatment.

❓ WHAT NEXT

Monitor the casualty's level of consciousness, breathing and pulse (**see page 30**) while you wait for emergency help.

1 COOL THE BURN Pour cool or tepid water over the burn for at least 10 minutes, or until the pain eases. Sit the casualty down and raise the injured area. Make her as comfortable as possible. Call for emergency help.

cool with water

2 REMOVE CONSTRICTIONS Remove or cut away any clothing or jewellery from the affected area while you are cooling it. Do not try to remove anything that is stuck to the burn.

3 PROTECT THE BURN Cover the burn, ideally with plastic kitchen film or a clean plastic bag. If you do not have either of these available, use a sterile dressing large enough to cover the burn or a clean, non-fluffy material such as a cotton pillowcase.

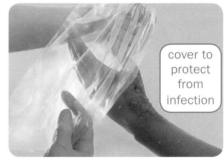

cover to protect from infection

4 LAY CASUALTY DOWN Help the casualty to lie down, while keeping the injured area raised and supported. Raise her legs above the level of her heart and support them on a chair. This reduces the risk of shock (see pages 38–39), a life-threatening condition that can develop after serious loss of fluids.

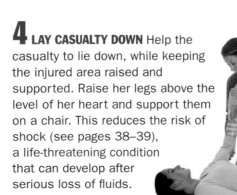

choking adult/child

An object lodged in a casualty's air passages can prevent him from breathing, speaking or coughing. If the casualty cannot clear the blockage by coughing, take fast action to intervene and call the emergency services.

✔ ASSESSMENT

● The casualty suddenly starts coughing and gasping for breath
● If the obstruction is partial, the casualty can speak, cough and breathe
● If the obstruction is complete, the casualty is unable to speak, cough or breathe
● **DO NOT** intervene until the obstruction is severe as the person may be able to clear the blockage by coughing

⚠ WARNING

Pick out anything obvious but don't sweep a finger around in the mouth. You're more likely to push the object back down the throat or damage the tissues in the throat.

❓ WHAT NEXT

● Continue the cycle of five back blows followed by five abdominal thrusts until the obstruction is clear or emergency help arrives and takes over.
● If the casualty loses consciousness go to page 14: the throat may relax, freeing the blockage.
● Anyone who has been given abdominal thrusts must be checked over by a doctor.

1 ENCOURAGE COUGHING Tell the casualty to cough and clear a mild obstruction himself if he can. Remove any obvious object from a child's mouth.

2 GIVE BACK BLOWS If the obstruction is severe, stand beside the casualty. Support his upper body and give five sharp back blows with the heel of your hand between the shoulder blades. Check mouth. A child may need you to remove any obvious object. If the mouth is still not clear, go to step 3.

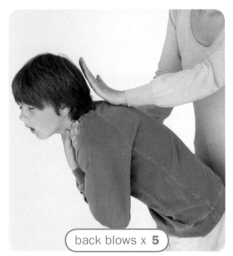

back blows x **5**

3 GIVE ABDOMINAL THRUSTS Place your arms around his body, with one fist against the abdomen. Grasp the fist with your other hand and pull inwards and upwards up to five times.

4 GET HELP Check the mouth. If necessary repeat steps 2 and 3 up to three times. If you have not been able to clear the obstruction, call the emergency services. Continue with the cycle of back blows and abdominal thrusts until help arrives.

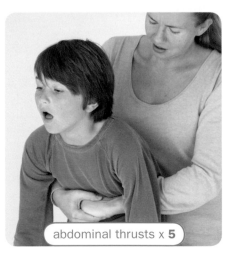

abdominal thrusts x **5**

choking baby

When an infant who is under one year old has a small object or piece of food lodged in the air passages, you will have to act very quickly to clear the obstruction. If the baby has stopped breathing, giving back blows and chest thrusts may dislodge the object.

✓ ASSESSMENT

● The casualty suddenly starts coughing and gasping for breath

● If the obstruction is partial, the baby can cough, but finds it difficult to make a noise or to cry

● If the obstruction is complete, the baby will not be able to make any noise or breathe

⚠ WARNING

Pick out anything obvious but don't sweep a finger around in the mouth. You're more likely to push the object back down the throat or damage the tissues in the throat.

❓ WHAT NEXT

● Continue the cycle of five back blows followed by five chest thrusts until the obstruction is clear or emergency help arrives.

● If the baby loses consciousness go to page 19: the throat may relax, freeing the blockage.

● A baby who has been given chest thrusts must be seen by a doctor.

1 GIVE BACK BLOWS If a baby can't breathe, lay her face down along the length of your forearm, supporting her head. Using the heel of one hand give five sharp blows between the baby's shoulder blades. Sit down and support a larger baby across your thigh.

back blows x **5**

2 CHECK MOUTH Turn the baby over so that her back is along your forearm. Cradle her head with your hand. Keeping her head as low as possible, look in the mouth and remove any obvious object. If the mouth is not clear, go to step 3.

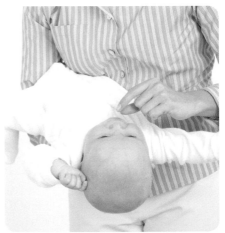

3 GIVE CHEST THRUSTS With the baby along your forearm, support her head and rest your arm against, along or across your thigh. Place two fingers a finger's breadth below the nipple line. Press sharply inward and upward up to five times. Check the mouth again.

4 GET HELP Repeat steps 1 to 3 up to three times. If the mouth is still not clear, take the baby with you and call the emergency services. Continue with the cycle of back blows and mouth checks until help arrives.

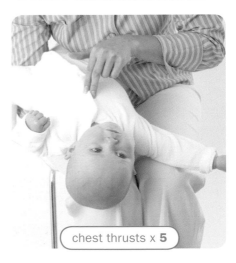
chest thrusts x **5**

▶▶See also: **DIFFICULTY BREATHING** pp40–41

heart attack

A person who is having a heart attack needs urgent medical help because there is a risk that the heart will stop. Your aim is to comfort, support and monitor the casualty while you are waiting for the emergency services to arrive.

✓ ASSESSMENT

Signs of a heart attack include the following:

- Vice-like chest pain that does not ease when the casualty rests. Pain often extends down one or both arms and up towards the jaw
- Breathlessness, possibly gasping for air
- Rapid, weak and irregular pulse
- Pale, grey, clammy or sweaty skin
- Discomfort high in the abdomen. Nausea and vomiting
- Feels faint and dizzy and may collapse

⚠ WARNING

If the casualty becomes unconscious, open the airway and check breathing (see page 14). Be prepared to begin CPR (see page 16).

1 MAKE THE CASUALTY COMFORTABLE

Reassure the casualty, sit him in a half-sitting position and make him as comfortable as possible. Loosen clothing at his neck, chest and waist. Raise his knees slightly and place cushions underneath them; this eases any strain in the heart.

2 CALL FOR EMERGENCY HELP

Call the emergency services and tell the ambulance controller that you suspect a heart attack.

3 GIVE MEDICATION

If the casualty suffers from angina (see page 32), he may have medication for this – let him take it. If he is fully conscious, give him one full-dose (300mg) aspirin tablet. Tell him to chew it slowly so that it dissolves and can get into the bloodstream as quickly as possible.

4 MONITOR CASUALTY

Monitor his breathing and pulse as well as his level of consciousness (see page 30), while you are waiting for emergency help. Make a note of any change in his condition.

stroke

If you suspect that someone is having a stroke, use the FAST test – check Face, Arms, Speech and know when it is Time to call for emergency help. If the person fails any one of the face, arm or speech tests, call the emergency services.

✅ ASSESSMENT

Signs of a stroke include sudden onset of:

- Weakness on one or both sides of the body that affects face, arms and/or legs
- Speech problems, difficulty understanding and/or confusion
- Loss of sight or blurred vision
- Sudden severe headache
- Collapse

☎ GET HELP

Tell the emergency services that you have assessed the casualty using the FAST test and you supect a stroke.

⚠ WARNING

- **DO NOT give anything to eat or drink as the casualty may not be able to swallow and could choke.**
- **If the casualty becomes unconscious, open the airway and check breathing (see page 14). Be prepared to begin CPR (see page 16).**

1 CHECK FACE Look at the casualty. Do you notice any facial weakness? Ask her to smile. If she has had a stroke she may only be able to smile on one side. The other side of her face may droop.

2 CHECK ARMS Ask the casualty if she can lift her arms. If she has had a stroke she may only be able to lift one arm – on the same side of the body that she can smile.

3 CHECK SPEECH Talk to the casualty. Can she understand what you are saying and can she speak clearly? If the casualty has had a stroke her speech may be impaired and she may not understand you.

4 CALL FOR EMERGENCY HELP If the answer is yes to any **one** of these assessments, suspect a stroke. Call for emergency help immediately. Reassure the casualty and monitor her breathing and pulse as well as level of consciousness (see page 30) while you are waiting for help.

▶▶See also: **UNCONSCIOUS ADULT** pp14–17 • **SUSPECTED STROKE** pp34–35   **27**

making **further checks**

If you have established that a casualty does not have a life-threatening injury or condition but are not sure what is wrong, carry out a methodical assessment. Also assess him if his condition has stabilised and you want to check for other problems.

DETAILED ASSESSMENT Establish what happened (the history) and listen to what the casualty tells you about how he feels (his symptoms). Look, listen and feel for other possible injuries that you can see (the signs). Do not move the casualty.

What is the history?

What are the symptoms?

What are the signs?

ASK WHAT HAPPENED How far did he fall and how did he land? Was anyone else involved? The point of impact can indicate likely injury.

LISTEN CAREFULLY Try not to interrupt the casualty when he talks. He may be able to say what happened. Ask for as much detail as possible.

CHECK THE SKIN Check the colour and temperature of the casualty's skin – is it pale or flushed, grey or bluish, hot or cold, clammy or dry?

TALK TO WITNESSES They may be able to give additional clues about the casualty's injury – this is especially important if a casualty is not fully conscious.

IS HE IN PAIN? If so, ask him to describe it. Where does it hurt? Is it a dull ache, a stabbing pain, or vice-like pain? Does anything improve it or make it worse?

ASSESS VITAL SIGNS Is he fully conscious? Listen to his breathing – is it normal or laboured, noisy or quiet? Check his pulse – is it fast or slow, weak or strong?

FIND OUT HIS MEDICAL HISTORY Is the casualty taking any medication? Is he allergic to anything? He may be wearing or carrying medical identification. When did he last eat or drink?

OTHER SYMPTOMS Ask the casualty to describe any other symptoms he's experiencing such as tingling, loss of feeling, dizziness, nausea and thirst. Again, find out if anything makes it worse.

MAKE A COMPARISON Make a physical check. See how the affected side of the body compares with the unaffected side – note any deformity or swelling. Is the casualty able to move normally?

assessment

Carry out a head to toe examination of the casualty to identify less obvious injuries. Start by checking general symptoms and signs – level of consciousness, breathing and pulse (see page 30). Complete the examination before you start treating her.

HOW TO CHECK THE CASUALTY FROM HEAD TO TOE

PART OF BODY	WHAT TO LOOK FOR
Head and neck, nose, eyes, ears, mouth and face	• Feel the scalp to check for bleeding and check for any swelling or depression that may indicate skull fracture. Do not move the head if you suspect neck injury. • Speak into each ear – can the casualty hear you? Is there any bleeding? Watery blood coming from the ears could be a sign of head injury. • Check the eyes – is there anything on the coloured part of the eye? Do the pupils (black centre) react to light? Different-sized pupils can indicate head injury. • Watery blood from the nose could result from head injury. • Bleeding from the mouth could result from a wound; soot around the mouth can indicate burns to the airway. Check lip colour. Leave well-fitting dentures in place. • Look at her face and check the skin colour and temperature – cold, clammy skin can indicate shock; hot, dry skin could indicate fever or heatstroke.
Chest, abdomen and back	• Listen to breathing sounds and ask the casualty if breathing causes her any pain. Feel both sides of the ribcage. Does the chest expand evenly on both sides? • Tenderness or a rigid abdomen may indicate an internal wound. • Feel as far along the spine as you can. Do not move the casualty. Suspect a back injury if she is in pain or is unable to move her arms or legs.
Shoulders and arms	• Feel across collarbones, shoulders and down arms as far as the fingers. Can she move her hands or fingers? Look for bracelets warning of a medical condition. Check for needlemarks and the skin colour of the fingertips.
Hips and pelvis	• Carefully feel both sides to check for fracture. Check clothing for signs of incontinence or bleeding as this may indicate internal injury.
Legs and feet	• Compare both legs for any signs of swelling, bruising or deformity. Ask the casualty if she can move her legs. If there is no obvious injury, ask her to raise her legs one at a time. • Compare her feet. Look at the skin colour of her feet and toes.

monitoring the casualty

A casualty's level of consciousness, breathing and pulse together give an indication of how the body is responding to an illness or injury. Assess all three when you carry out your detailed examination of a person and repeat the checks regularly (about every 10 minutes) while you wait for help. Make a note any changes as this helps the medical team decide on the best treatment.

assessment

LEVEL OF CONSCIOUSNESS

Between being conscious and unconscious there are several stages – any change can indicate deterioration or improvement.
● **ALERT AND AWAKE** The casualty's eyes are open and questions are answered normally
● **RESPONDS TO VOICE** The casualty is not fully conscious, but can respond to commands
● **RESPONDS TO PAIN** He is not very responsive, but aware of pain. Do not try to cause pain
● **UNCONSCIOUS** The casualty does not respond at all to any stimulus (see page 13)

BREATHING

An adult normally breathes about 12–18 times per minute, but children breathe about 20–30 times a minute
● Watch and time the number of breaths a person takes in one minute. For a child it may be easier to put one hand on the chest and count breaths
● Listen to the quality of the casualty's breaths – are they quiet or unusually noisy; difficult or easy or deep or shallow?
● A casualty with breathing difficulties may find it difficult to talk, so do not insist on this

How to check a pulse

Each heartbeat sends a wave of pressure along the arteries (the vessels that take blood to the tissues of the body). This is called the pulse – it can be felt where an artery is close to the surface of the body.
● The heart pumps blood around the body. It normally beats 60–80 times a minute in an adult, and faster – up to 120 times a minute – in babies and children.
● The easiest points to check the pulse are at the wrist (radial pulse) in adults and children, or the upper arm in babies (brachial pulse).
● Place the pads (not the tips) of your fingers on the pulse point and, using a watch, count the number of beats in a minute.
● You can also check the pulse at the neck (the carotid pulse) by placing two fingers between the windpipe and the large neck muscle, although it is more difficult to find the carotid pulse.
● While you count the beats, try to be aware of the quality of the pulse – is it regular or irregular and is it weak or strong?

● **ADULT OR CHILD**
Place three fingers in the wrist crease on the thumb side (radial pulse).

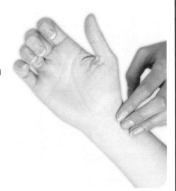

● **FOR A BABY**
Press two fingers on the inner side of the upper arm (brachial pulse).

MEDICAL EMERGENCIES

potential heart attack

A heart attack is caused by an obstruction of the blood supply to the heart muscle (usually by a blood clot in the coronary blood vessels). The outcome depends on how much of the muscle is affected and how quickly help can be given. If you think someone is having a heart attack, always call for emergency medical help rather than waiting to see if the symptoms subside.

assessment

These are the common signs and symptoms of a heart attack. A casualty will experience some, but not necessarily all. If the pain subsides with rest, it could be angina (see below).

Suddenly feels faint or dizzy

ADDITIONAL SYMPTOMS
- Fear – feels sense of impending doom
- Pale, grey (ashen), clammy or sweaty skin
- Nausea and vomiting
- Rapid, weak and irregular pulse
- Collapses – often without warning
- Possible loss of consciousness

Severe chest pain – persistent and vice-like, spreading up to the jaw and down one or both arms – which does not subside when the casualty rests

Breathlessness – casualty may be gasping for air

Discomfort high in abdomen – may feel like severe indigestion

Angina

If the pain subsides after the person rests for a few minutes, it is likely that it is an angina attack. This is a long-term condition in which the coronary (heart) arteries are narrowed, so that the heart muscle cannot get enough blood to meet its demands. Someone diagnosed with angina will have been given medication for use in an attack.

- **REASSURE** Keep the casualty calm; sit her down.
- **ASSIST WITH MEDICATION** Help the casualty to find her medication – usually a tablet or spray. If necessary, help her to take it.
- **KEEP WATCH** The attack should ease within a few minutes. If the pain does not ease or the person has no medication, treat as a heart attack.

GET HELP If you suspect a heart attack, call for emergency help and state that it is for a heart attack casualty. Or get someone else to make the call and stay with the casualty.

TIME TO ACT A casualty is three times more likely to survive if he receives advanced medical help within an hour of having a heart attack.

WATCHPOINT If a casualty is suffering from an angina attack (see box, opposite) but has no medication to hand, call for emergency help immediately. Treat as described below.

action

A CONSCIOUS CASUALTY

1 **EASE STRAIN ON HEART** Make the casualty as comfortable as possible, in a half-sitting position, with his head and shoulders well supported and knees bent to ease strain on the heart. Loosen clothing at the neck, chest and waist.

2 **CALL FOR EMERGENCY HELP** Keep bystanders away from the casualty.

3 **GIVE ANGINA MEDICATION** If the casualty has medication for angina (see opposite) help him to take it. Keep him calm and encourage him to rest.

4 **GIVE ASPIRIN** If the casualty is fully conscious, give him a full-dose (300mg) aspirin tablet. Tell him to chew it slowly so that it dissolves and is absorbed into the bloodstream more quickly when it reaches the stomach. Aspirin helps to break down blood clots, minimising muscle damage.

5 **MONITOR CASUALTY** Regularly check and make a note of consciousness, breathing and pulse.

AN UNCONSCIOUS CASUALTY

1 **OPEN AIRWAY** Check for breathing (see page 14) and be prepared to begin CPR (see pages 16–17) as the heart may stop.

2 **SEND FOR AED** Ask someone to bring an AED (automated external defibrillator – see page 15), if possible, while you treat the casualty. AEDs can deliver a shock to correct an abnormal heart rhythm called ventricular fibrillation – the cause of some heart attacks. The machines are found in most public places – shopping centres and train stations, for example.

3 **OPERATE AED** An AED is simple to use. Attach the pads, as indicated on the machine, then the machine will talk the operator through the process. An AED will only deliver a shock if the casualty's condition indicates that it is necessary. If you have attached an AED to a casualty leave the machine switched on at all times, and leave the pads attached, even if the casualty recovers.

what next?

● Wait for the emergency services. The earlier a person receives advanced medical help, the greater the chances of survival. There is a risk that the heart may stop, so the emergency team will bring resuscitation equipment.

● Diagnosis will be confirmed at the hospital with an electrocardiogram (ECG) and blood tests. Advanced care may include a short stay in an intensive care unit and treatment with drugs or even surgery. The aim is to minimise pain, restore the blood supply to the damaged heart muscle and prevent complications.

● Hospital treatment for a heart attack will be followed by a period of rehabilitation.

▶▶See also: **UNCONSCIOUS ADULT** pp14–17

suspected stroke

Also known as a brain attack, a stroke occurs when the blood supply to part of the brain is cut off or reduced because of a ruptured blood vessel or a clot in one of the blood vessels that supplies the brain. The effects will depend on the part of the brain that is affected. The sooner a casualty receives hospital treatment, the better the chances of recovery.

assessment

Damage to the brain caused by a stroke affects bodily functions. This can be most obvious in facial expressions, arm movement and speech. If you notice any one of these symptoms, call for emergency help immediately:

Facial weakness – noticeable on one side

Speech problems – inability to speak clearly

Arm weakness – noticeable on one side

ADDITIONAL SYMPTOMS
● Sudden dizziness or complete collapse
● Weakness or even loss of movement down one or sometimes both sides of the body
● Sudden severe headache, without previous head injury or other cause
● Sudden blurred vision or loss of sight
● Sudden confusion and difficulty understanding
● A stroke that results from a burst blood vessel may be accompanied by signs of serious head injury or Compression (see page 82)

THE 'FAST' TEST
A quick test to help check for the most obvious signs of a stroke, FAST requires an assessment of three specific symptoms. If the casualty fails any one of these tests, call for emergency help.
● Facial weakness: Can the person smile? Does his mouth or eye droop?
● Arm weakness: Can the person raise both of his arms together?
● Speech problems: Can the person speak clearly and understand what you say?

MINI-STROKE
A transient ischaemic attack (TIA), often called a mini-stroke, happens when the brain's blood supply is interrupted for a few minutes. Symptoms are similar to a stroke (such as weakness on one side of the body, visual disturbance and slurred speech), but they disappear within 24 hours. If a TIA occurs, call for emergency help as there is a risk of a more serious stroke in the future.

GET HELP If you suspect a stroke, make a 'FAST' assessment (see below) and call for emergency help. Prompt action can help to prevent further damage to the brain.

WATCHPOINT If you suspect a TIA or mini-stroke (see box, opposite) get emergency help. Although the symptoms only last for a few minutes, a full stroke could follow.

action

1 F – CHECK HER FACE

Look at the casualty. Do you notice any facial weakness? Ask her to smile. If she has had a stroke, she may only be able to smile on one side; the other side of her face may droop.

2 A – CHECK HER ARMS

Ask the casualty if she can lift both of her arms. If she has had a stroke, she may only be able to lift one arm – on the same side of the body that she is able to smile.

⚠ WARNING

● If the casualty becomes unconscious, open the airway and check for breathing (see page 14). Be prepared to begin CPR (see page 16).
● Do not give the casualty anything to eat or drink as she could choke and/or the object or fluid can enter the lungs, which leads to further complications. About 50 per cent of stroke casualties have difficulty swallowing (known as dysphagia) afterwards.

3 S – CHECK SPEECH

Talk to the casualty. Can she understand what you say and can she speak clearly? If she has had a stroke, **her speech may be impaired and she may not understand you.**

4 T – TIME TO CALL FOR EMERGENCY HELP

If the casualty fails any one of these tests, suspect a stroke and call for emergency help immediately. Reassure the casualty. Check and make a note of her level of consciousness, breathing and pulse (see page 30). Re-check these regularly until help arrives.

what next?

● Diagnosis will be confirmed in hospital with brain scans and blood tests. A stroke caused by a blood clot will be treated with drugs that break up the clot, to limit the extent of the brain damage, and minimise the risk of further strokes.
● All stroke patients are given a swallow test in hospital and will only be allowed to drink and eat normally when they can swallow properly.
● After a stroke, the dead brain cells will not recover, but the cells around the injured area may start functioning as any swelling goes down. Most recovery happens in the first few months but, depending on the area affected, people can continue to recover for several years.

feeling faint

Fainting is caused by a temporary reduction in the supply of blood to the brain. It can be a reaction to pain, exhaustion, stress, a sudden drop in blood pressure (the pressure at which blood is pumped around the body), or lack of food (low blood sugar). A person may feel dizzy and light-headed or pass out, but will recover as soon as the brain's blood supply is restored.

assessment

These are the common signs and symptoms of a faint. A casualty will experience some of them, but not necessarily all. Once the blood supply to the head is restored, recovery should be rapid.

- Casualty complains of feeling weak and dizzy and may also feel sick
- Skin is very pale and feels cold and clammy
- Slow pulse that quickly returns to normal as soon as the casualty lies down
- Sudden collapse, possibly followed by a brief loss of consciousness – once this happens, the casualty's head and heart are on the same level so that the blood supply is restored more easily

 **WARNING**

Repeated fainting attacks should be investigated. Isolated episodes of fainting are not normally anything to worry about.

POSSIBLE CAUSES

REASON	WHAT YOU SHOULD DO
Has been sitting or standing still for a long time, especially in a hot, stuffy atmosphere	Tell the casualty to move her legs and feet to encourage circulation. Take her to a cooler place and/or open a window.
Has not eaten for a few hours and/ or has diabetes	Low blood sugar causes fainting, so give the casualty something sweet to eat. If she has diabetes, tell her to see her doctor as her insulin dose may need to be reviewed.
Is reacting to pain	Fainting is a common reaction to pain. A person in pain may be able to take normal pain relief if there is no obvious injury or serious illness that requires medical treatment. If treatment is needed, do not give the casualty anything to eat or drink in case an anaesthetic is needed later.
Is reacting to emotional stress	Fainting is a common reaction to stress or emotional shock. As the casualty recovers, talk and offer reassurance.
Is pregnant	Fainting in pregnancy is common as hormone changes can cause blood vessels to relax, which can lower blood pressure. Advise her to see her midwife or doctor for a check up.
Is reacting to medication	Some prescription medications can cause low blood pressure and this can lead to fainting; tell the casualty to seek medical advice as the dose may need to be adjusted.
Is particularly tired, short of breath and very pale	Tell her to call her doctor. She could be anaemic (a condition in which the body has too few red oxygen-carrying blood cells).
Has a history of heart disease	Seek medical advice, especially if the pulse was very slow or fast before she fainted. Call the emergency services if in doubt.

GET HELP If the casualty does not recover straight away, or the condition worsens, call for emergency help.

TIME TO ACT If a person passes out completely, try to guide her as she falls so that she does not hurt herself, provided there is no risk of you injuring yourself.

action

1 LIE THE CASUALTY DOWN If a person starts to feel faint, help her to lie down on the floor – if possible on something to protect her from the ground. If you are out of doors, make sure she is in the shade.

2 RAISE HER LEGS Kneel beside her hips, raise her legs and rest them on your shoulder (or place them on a chair) to help improve the blood flow to the brain. Look at the casualty's face – the skin colour should return to normal quite quickly.

3 ENSURE SUPPLY OF FRESH AIR Fan her face to cool her down. If you are inside, ask someone to open the window to improve air flow.

4 SIT CASUALTY UP GRADUALLY Once the casualty starts to feel better, help her to sit up slowly. If she feels faint again, help her to lie down for a bit longer.

5 IDENTIFY CAUSE Try to find out why she collapsed (see opposite). If she has not eaten and is fully conscious, give her something to eat. If she is a known diabetic, treat as described on page 58.

⚠ WARNING

● If the casualty does not make a rapid, complete recovery, call for emergency medical help. Open the airway and check breathing (see page 14).
● If a person feels faint, do not sit her on a chair with her head between her legs – if she faints, she will fall off the chair and could injure herself.
● If a woman is pregnant, she should not lie flat on her back, as the weight of the baby in the uterus can compress the blood vessels, restricting blood flow back to the heart. Help her to lie down with her head low but tell her to lean towards one side. Place a cushion against her back, if necessary. Raise her legs as high as you can.
● Do not give the casualty anything to eat or drink unless she is fully conscious.

what next?

If a person is prone to fainting, advise her to see her doctor for further investigation. The doctor will want to know how often the person faints, whether she experiences any other symptoms at the same time and whether there is a family history of fainting episodes. The doctor will assess her and may carry out tests – for example, blood analysis or an ECG (electrocardiogram) to try to identify the cause. Treating an underlying condition, such as anaemia (low red blood cells), heart disease or diabetes, can often prevent further problems.

▶▶See also: **SHOCK** pp38–39 • **HEAT-RELATED ILLNESS** pp48–49 • **DIABETIC EMERGENCY** pp58–59

shock

Medical, as opposed to emotional, shock is a life-threatening condition that develops if the circulatory system fails to provide sufficient oxygen-rich blood to the heart and brain. Severe bleeding (external or internal) is the most common cause, but it can also follow fluid loss from burns, vomiting or diarrhoea, or be the result of a severe allergic reaction or heart failure.

assessment

Signs of shock worsen as the circulatory system fails. Suspect shock after, for example, severe Bleeding (see pages 96–97), but also if any of the following occur with no obvious wound:

- Rapid pulse at first, which becomes weaker. By the time half the blood is lost from the circulatory system (about three litres in an adult), you may not be able to feel the pulse at the wrist
- Profuse sweating with cold, clammy skin
- Fast, but shallow, breathing
- As circulatory system fails or fluid loss worsens, skin becomes grey-blue (known as cyanosis). This is evident at the ears, lips, inside the mouth and at the fingertips. If you press a fingernail then let go, the healthy pink colour will not return quickly
- Casualty will become weak and feel dizzy. He may feel nauseous and may even be sick
- Casualty will begin to feel very thirsty
- As the oxygen to the brain reduces, the casualty will feel restless and may be aggressive. He will be yawning and gasping for air. **Eventually he will become unconscious and his heart may stop**

SIGNS OF INTERNAL BLEEDING

Severe internal bleeding can develop after a blow to the body that does not break the skin or it can also be spontaneous, for example as the result of a burst ulcer.

- Signs of shock (see above) but no obvious injury
- Bruising on the skin that matches the pattern of clothes and worsens as the area swells
- Casualty may tell you that the abdomen or chest feels swollen, as if there is extra fluid inside
- Bleeding from body openings (see below)
- Sudden collapse and loss of consciousness some time after an injury
- Information from the casualty or a bystander that indicates possible internal injury

BLEEDING FROM BODY OPENINGS

BODY OPENING	APPEARANCE AND POSSIBLE CAUSE
Ears/Nose	Bright red blood in the ear is likely to be caused by injury to the outer part of the ear or ear-drum. Bright red blood from the nose results from a ruptured blood vessel in the nose. The watery blood that appears after a head injury is fluid from around the brain mixed with blood from the ear and nose.
Mouth	Coughed-up bright red, frothy blood indicates bleeding in the lungs. Dark-reddish blood that looks like coffee grounds comes from the digestive system.
Anus	Fresh bright red blood comes from the lower part of the intestine or bowel. Darker, tar-like stools indicate injury further up the digestive system.
Urethra	Reddish urine, with possible clots, indicates possible bleeding from the kidneys, ureters, bladder or urethra.
Vagina	Fresh or dark-red blood could be a sign of menstruation, but it could also be caused by infection, a miscarriage, childbirth or sexual assault.

 ▶▶See also: UNCONSCIOUS ADULT/CHILD/BABY pp14–19

GET HELP If you suspect shock, call the emergency services or ask someone else to make the call while you look after the casualty, following the steps below.

TIME TO ACT Shock is life-threatening – suspect it if you notice any of the symptoms or signs detailed opposite even if there is no obvious injury.

WATCHPOINT If the casualty has a suspected broken leg, do not raise the affected leg, but raise the other leg, if possible.

action

1 TREAT OBVIOUS CAUSE Treat severe bleeding by applying direct pressure to the wound (see pages 96–97). Cool any burns (see pages 112–113). Raise and support the injury.

2 LIE CASUALTY DOWN Reassure the casualty and tell him not to move unnecessarily. Help him to lie down on a rug or blanket. Do not put anything under his head, leave it low. Raise and support his legs as high as you can above his heart, for example rest his feet on a chair.

3 LOOSEN CLOTHING Loosen any tight clothing, especially around his neck, chest and waist, that could restrict blood circulation around the body.

4 KEEP THE CASUALTY WARM Cover him with a blanket or coats. Do not warm him with a hot-water bottle or electric blanket (see Warning, right).

5 CALL EMERGENCY HELP Call the emergency services. Tell the controller that you suspect shock, and give as much information as you can about the possible cause.

6 MONITOR CASUALTY Check and note the level of consciousness, breathing and pulse (see page 30). Re-check regularly until medical help arrives. If the casualty is thirsty, moisten his lips with a clean damp cloth.

⚠ WARNING

● Do not warm the person with direct heat. The aim of treatment is to keep vital organs supplied with blood. If you put a hot-water bottle on the casualty's skin, blood will be drawn to the surface of the body and away from the centre where it is needed.
● Do not give the casualty anything to eat or drink as he may need an anaesthetic at the hospital.
● If the casualty loses consciousness, open the airway and check his breathing (see page 14). Be prepared to begin CPR (see pages 16–17).

Understanding medical shock

If a person reacts to an emotional situation, he is described as being in 'shock'. Medical shock is different. It develops when the circulatory system fails for two main reasons: there may not be enough fluid in the body to be circulated (after bleeding) or the heart is not functioning normally so cannot pump enough blood around the body.

▶▶See also: **WOUNDS AND BLEEDING** pp96–97 • **BURNS AND SCALDS** pp112–113

difficulty **breathing**

Breathing problems are serious and must be treated as emergencies. Every part of the body needs oxygen to survive – brain cells start to die after only three minutes without it. If the body is not receiving enough oxygen, through injury or illness, a potentially fatal condition called hypoxia results. If the cause is not treated, breathing (and the heartbeat) may stop.

assessment

Depending on how long the casualty has been in difficulty, you may notice any of these symptoms:

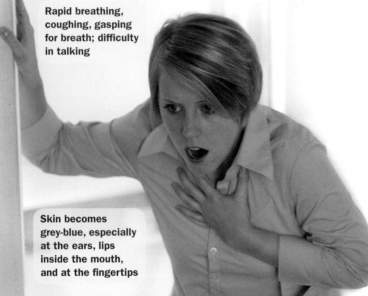

Rapid breathing, coughing, gasping for breath; difficulty in talking

Skin becomes grey-blue, especially at the ears, lips inside the mouth, and at the fingertips

Inability to think clearly

ADDITIONAL SYMPTOMS
- **If the airway is blocked, the casualty will not be able to cough or make a sound**
- If there is a constriction around the casualty's neck, blood vessels in the face and neck may be prominent
- An obvious cause, such as a plastic bag near the face or a chest injury that prevents normal breathing
- Casualty complains of feeling sick and may even vomit
- Possible loss of consciousness

POSSIBLE CAUSES

REASON	WHAT HAPPENS
Blocked airway	Anything that covers the mouth, constricts the casualty's windpipe or blocks the airway (see pages 80–81) can prevent oxygen from entering the body. Swelling within the airways after smoke inhalation (see pages 44–45) or allergic reaction (see pages 54–55) will restrict breathing.
Unable to move chest	Crushing (see pages 102–103), for example if buried in sand, will prevent normal movement of the chest so the casualty cannot breathe in or out. Injury to the ribcage can also prevent normal movement (see pages 94–95).
Insufficient oxygen in the air (fumes)	Poisonous fumes (see pages 44–45) can prevent the body from taking up any oxygen in the air.
Illness	Long-term conditions such as asthma or allergy can affect breathing, as can an infection such as pneumonia, croup or bronchiolitis.
Head injury	Any injury that affects the part of the brain or nerves that control respiration can restrict breathing.

medical emergencies

▶▶See also: UNCONSCIOUS ADULT/CHILD/BABY pp14–19 • CHOKING pp24–25 • ASTHMA pp42–43

GET HELP Your aim is to help the casualty to restore normal breathing as soon as possible. Help him into fresh air or to take medication, and call the emergency services.

TIME TO ACT If an infant less than a year old has a bad cough and high fever, it may indicate a viral lung infection called bronchiolitis. Seek medical advice.

WATCHPOINT If you are treating a casualty known to have asthma let her use her inhaler (see pages 42–43). If she has no medication, call the emergency services.

action

1 REMOVE OBVIOUS OBSTRUCTION Remove anything that is covering the person's mouth and/or nose or that prevents normal chest movement. Treat choking if necessary (see page 80–81).

2 CALL EMERGENCY HELP Call the emergency services even if the casualty appears to have recovered completely.

3 OBSERVE THE CASUALTY Check and make a note of the casualty's level of consciousness, breathing and pulse (see page 30). Re-check regularly until the emergency services arrive.

Hanging and strangulation

An incident that leads to compression of the windpipe prevents air getting to the lungs. It might also result in serious neck injury.

1 REMOVE CONSTRICTION Remove the cause of strangulation as quickly as you can. If the casualty has a tight constriction around the neck, cut as near to the knot as possible using shears or scissors. Slide the shears under the rope or tie and cut towards you – away from the casualty's neck.

2 SUPPORT THE CASUALTY'S WEIGHT Support the body as the ligature is removed. You may need help as the casualty could be very heavy, especially if he is unconscious.

3 CALL EMERGENCY HELP Call the emergency services, or ask a helper to make the call. Check and make a note of the level of consciousness, breathing and pulse (see page 30). Re-check until medical help arrives.

 WARNING

If the casualty becomes unconscious, open the airway and check for breathing (see page 14). Be prepared to begin CPR (see pages 16–17).

what next?

All casualties who have experienced breathing difficulties must be assessed at a hospital even if they appear to have recovered. It is important to make sure that there is no permanent damage and confirm the cause. If a person was rescued from water there may be water in the lungs, which can cause irritation and swelling several hours later.

 SAFETY FIRST WITH CHILDREN

● Make sure you keep all plastic bags locked away out of reach of children.
● Secure all curtain pulls, tie-backs and blind cords out of a child's reach.
● If a young child wants to wear a tie, use the ready tied type with a quick-release fastening.
● Remove strings from jacket or sweatshirt hoods.
● Do not give toys with very small parts to young children. All soft toys should be suitable for young children with securely affixed details.
● Stay with your child when she is eating. Never let her run around while she is eating or drinking.
● Remove ribbons that are not securely fastened from clothes or soft toys.

Always check the safety labels on toys.

▶▶See also: **INHALING FUMES** pp44–45 • **ALLERGIC REACTION** pp54–55

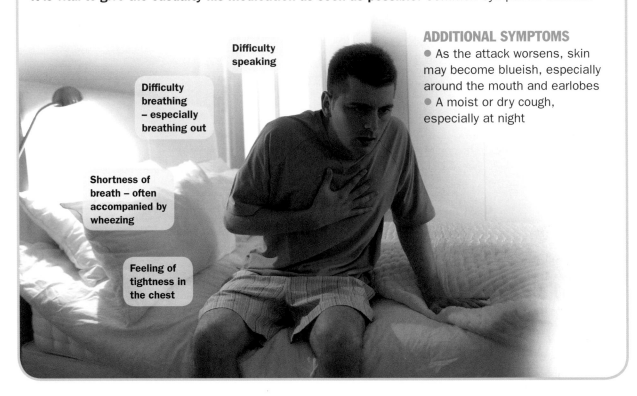

asthma attack

Exposure to certain triggers causes breathing difficulty in people who suffer from asthma, a chronic (long-term) disease. During an asthma attack, the muscles around the airways in the lungs contract, causing the airways to narrow. The amount of mucus that lines the air passages increases. Asthma cannot be cured, but it can be controlled with medication.

assessment

Symptoms are often worse at night and people have different patterns to their attacks. **It is vital to give the casualty his medication as soon as possible**. Common symptoms include:

Difficulty speaking

Difficulty breathing – especially breathing out

Shortness of breath – often accompanied by wheezing

Feeling of tightness in the chest

ADDITIONAL SYMPTOMS
- As the attack worsens, skin may become blueish, especially around the mouth and earlobes
- A moist or dry cough, especially at night

Croup

This is an infection, often viral, that causes breathing difficulty and wheezing in young children. It can be alarming but there is rarely any long-term effect. It is sometimes confused with asthma but there are a number of critical differences. The child often has a fever, there will be a barking cough and the child has more difficulty breathing in. It is likely to occur at night and is normally relieved by creating a moist atmosphere. Seek medical advice if the symptoms persist or are very severe.

1 SUPPORT THE CHILD Sit the child on your lap, supporting her chest. Stay calm, reassure her and encourage her to relax and breathe steadily.

2 CREATE STEAMY ATMOSPHERE If possible, take the child into the bathroom and run hot water into the bath to create steam. Keep her on your lap and well away from the water.

3 CALL MEDICAL HELP If the child's condition does not improve or worsens, call for help.

GET HELP Asthma attacks can be life-threatening. If this is a casualty's first asthma attack, or she does not have an inhaler with her, call for emergency help straight away.

TIME TO ACT Make sure the casualty is using her reliever inhaler (blue) and not her preventer inhaler (normally brown or white) as the latter will not help in an attack.

WATCHPOINT Common triggers are contact with an allergen, such as pollen, dust, fur and/or some medications. Foods such as milk, eggs or nuts can be triggers.

action

1 GIVE INHALER

Help the casualty to find his reliever inhaler (normally blue) and help him to take a puff from it. Tell him to breathe slowly and deeply. If he has a spacer, he should use it to take the medication.

2 SIT CASUALTY DOWN
Help him to sit down in whatever position he finds most comfortable for breathing. The best position is generally leaning forward slightly with his back straight. Do not let him lie down. The attack should ease after a few minutes – if it does not improve, give him another dose from his inhaler.

3 CALL FOR HELP
If breathing does not improve, the casualty's condition is worse or he finds it difficult to talk because of breathlessness, and/or he is becoming exhausted, call for emergency help.

4 MONITOR CASUALTY
Help the casualty to use his inhaler and monitor his level of consciousness, breathing and pulse while you wait for help. Note changes in his condition.

WARNING
If a casualty becomes unconscious, open the airway and check breathing (see page 14). Be prepared to begin CPR (see page 16).

Treating children

Asthma often develops in childhood and many children grow out of it. The condition is managed in the same way but young children will need help taking their medication.

1 ADMINISTER MEDICATION INTO A SPACER
Young children find it difficult to use an inhaler. A 'spacer' with a mouthpiece or mask can be used to deliver the medication. Place the inhaler into one end of the device and 'squirt' the medication into it.

2 GIVE SPACER TO THE CHILD
Let the child put the mouthpiece in his mouth, or mask over his face if it has one. Tell him to breathe normally.

what next?

● If this is the first attack, hospital assessment is necessary. Two main types of medications are prescribed: reliever and preventer inhalers. Relievers (bronchodilators) give immediate relief for the symptoms of an attack. Preventer inhalers, normally taken every day, treat the underlying inflammation, helping to reduce symptoms.

● The person may be referred to an allergist to help identify what triggers the attacks.

● A personal plan of asthma management will be prepared. Regular medical check-ups are needed to ensure that the medication is effective.

▶▶See also: UNCONSCIOUS ADULT pp14–17 • UNCONSCIOUS CHILD p18 • DIFFICULTY BREATHING pp40–41

inhaling fumes

The inhalation of fumes can be life-threatening as they reduce the amount of oxygen available to the body. A casualty needs urgent medical help, but rescue should only be carried out by someone wearing protective breathing apparatus.

GET HELP Never enter a fume-filled room or building even if there are casualties. Call for emergency help. Ask for the fire brigade and tell the controller there are fumes.

assessment

Any casualty will have very low levels of oxygen in his body. Symptoms vary depending on the gas or vapour inhaled and how long a person is exposed to it. General symptoms include:

- Rapid breathing – the casualty may cough, gasp for breath and find it difficult to talk
- Skin becomes grey-blue (called cyanosis) – this is especially noticeable at the ears, lips, inside the mouth and at the fingertips
- Inability to think clearly – as oxygen levels fall, the casualty will become increasingly restless and anxious, and possibly aggressive
- The casualty may complain of feeling sick and may even vomit

DANGEROUS FUMES

FUMES	SOURCE	SYMPTOMS
Smoke	Fires – as fire uses oxygen to burn, smoke contains very low oxygen levels. Smoke may also contain toxic gases given off by other materials as they burn.	Noisy breathing, coughing, hoarseness, black or grey saliva (spit) and fluids in the lungs. Skin colour may range from grey-blue to cherry-red. As the condition worsens, the casualty may lose consciousness or stop breathing. The heat may burn nose hairs and there may be burns in the throat and inside the nose.
Carbon monoxide (CO)	Colourless, odourless gas that is a by-product of incomplete burning of any fossil fuel. For example, exhausts, gas fires, faulty gas boilers or water heaters and paraffin heaters.	Mild symptoms are headache, nausea, vomiting, drowsiness and poor co-ordination. In more moderate or severe cases there may be confusion, unconsciousness, chest pain and shortness of breath.
Solvents	Lighter fuels, glues, paints, cleaning fluids, camping gas canisters and aerosol sprays.	General symptoms of fumes, plus headaches and possible loss of consciousness. Solvent use can cause the heart to stop (cardiac arrest). The casualty may also have an obstructed airway as a result of breathing solvents from a plastic bag.
Carbon dioxide (CO_2)	Environmental gas, produced naturally and through human activities. It can accumulate in deep enclosed spaces, such as wells. High concentrations can occur in places that are crowded and have poor ventilation. The gas is normally odourless but can be detected at very high concentrations.	General symptoms of fumes, plus headache, breathlessness, a dramatic increase in breathing and pulse rate, tinnitus and impaired vision. Eventual unconsciousness.

 ▶▶See also: UNCONSCIOUS ADULT/CHILD/BABY pp14–19

action

1 **CALL THE EMERGENCY SERVICES** Do not enter a room or building if you suspect fumes. Call the emergency services and ask for the fire brigade. Tell the controller that there are people in the building.

2 **HELP THE CASUALTY AWAY FROM THE FUMES** If the casualty is able to get away from the source of the fumes or the building, stay outside and help him to safety. Never enter the building yourself.

3 **TREAT ANY INJURY** Help the casualty to sit down. Assess his injuries and treat any burns (see page 113). He may have inhaled smoke and there could be burns to the mouth, throat and windpipe (airways). Loosen any clothing around the neck and chest to help breathing.

4 **MONITOR THE CASUALTY** Check and note his level of consciousness, breathing and pulse (see page 30). Re-check regularly until medical help arrives.

 TAKE CARE

Make sure that everyone in your house knows how to escape if there is a fire. Install smoke detectors on every floor of your home. If they are battery operated, check them every week to ensure that they still work.

 WARNING

If a casualty becomes unconscious, open the airway and check breathing (see page 14). Be prepared to begin CPR (see page 16).

what next?

● The casualty may be given oxygen by the medical emergency team and taken to hospital. People with moderate symptoms who receive early treatment tend to recover completely from the experience.
● Blood tests will be carried out to assess the casualty's blood oxygen levels and to find out whether any toxic gases are present in the blood.
● Burns in the airways need hospital treatment. Fluid can collect in the lungs after smoke inhalation, causing noisy breathing, so an X-ray and other tests will be needed.

Preventing carbon monoxide poisoning

While you can smell and see smoke, carbon monoxide (CO) is a colourless, odourless, highly toxic gas. Depending on the concentration, **CO gas can render a person unconscious within hours**. There are several ways to reduce the risk of exposure.

● **SERVICE ALL APPLIANCES REGULARLY** Appliances should be checked at least annually. Carbon monoxide can accumulate if solid fuel appliances, such as gas fires, boilers or water heaters, are badly maintained or faulty.
● **INSTALL DETECTOR ALARMS** Put them in every room where there is a fossil fuel appliance. Choose alarms that give visual and audible warnings when there is a build-up of the gas.
● **CHECK DETECTORS** If the detector alarms are battery operated, check them once a week to ensure that they are still working.

hypothermia

When the core body temperature falls below 35°C (95°F), the body shuts down the blood supply to the surface blood vessels to keep vital organs such as the heart supplied with blood. This leads to a condition known as hypothermia.

TIME TO ACT It is important to prevent body temperature dropping too low. If a casualty receives prompt medical help, mild to moderate hypothermia can usually be reversed.

assessment

Symptoms and signs of hypothermia are the same whatever the cause or age of the casualty. You may also see signs of frostbite on the casualty's fingers and toes (see opposite).

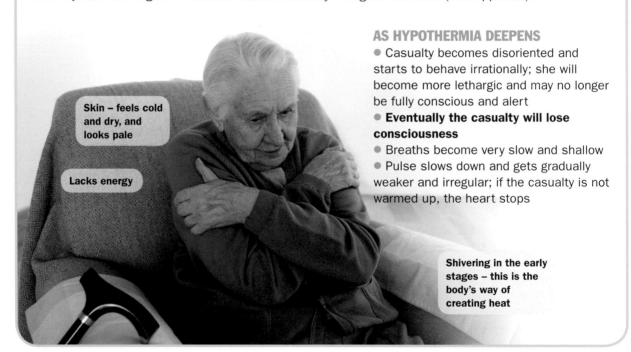

Skin – feels cold and dry, and looks pale

Lacks energy

Shivering in the early stages – this is the body's way of creating heat

AS HYPOTHERMIA DEEPENS
- Casualty becomes disoriented and starts to behave irrationally; she will become more lethargic and may no longer be fully conscious and alert
- **Eventually the casualty will lose consciousness**
- Breaths become very slow and shallow
- Pulse slows down and gets gradually weaker and irregular; if the casualty is not warmed up, the heart stops

action

1 WARM UP GRADUALLY If you are inside, start to warm the room, or move to a warmer room. Remove any wet clothes. Wrap her up in several layers of blankets to trap heat. Put a hat on her head.

2 GIVE WARM DRINK AND FOOD Provided the casualty is fully conscious, give her a warm (not hot) drink and a high-energy food such as chocolate for fast energy. You may need to help her.

3 GET EMERGENCY HELP Call the emergency services as soon as possible. Check and make a note of her level of consciousness, breathing and pulse (see page 30) regularly until help arrives.

Treating a baby

Young babies have very under-developed temperature control mechanisms, so can become hypothermic relatively quickly in a cold room. A baby will become very floppy, but may have bright pink skin. Her skin will feel very cold. She will not want to eat or drink.

1 WARM UP GRADUALLY Either warm the room or take the baby into a warmer room. Wrap the baby in warm blankets. Keep her head covered with a hat or the blanket, but leave her face exposed. Cuddle her so that you are using your own body heat for warmth.

2 GET HELP Either call the emergency services or take the baby to hospital if you can keep her warm. Check level of consciousness, breathing and pulse (see page 30).

 TAKE CARE

● Only start to warm someone up if there is no risk of her becoming cold again.
● Warm a person gradually to prevent blood from being diverted away from the core of the body towards the skin, as this forces cold blood back to the major organs, and can cause a heart attack.
● A healthy adult or older child can be warmed up in a bath if he can climb in and out unaided and there is no risk of him becoming cold again.

 WARNING

● Do not warm up an elderly person in a bath as this may send cold blood to the heart or brain too suddenly, and may cause a stroke or heart attack.
● Do not warm a casualty with direct heat, such as a hot-water bottle, or put him beside an electric fire.
● Do not give him alcohol, as this dilates the blood vessels, decreasing the body's ability to retain heat.
● Do not rub or massage the person as, in severe hypothermia, there is a risk of heart attack.
● If a casualty becomes unconscious, open the airway and check breathing (see page 14). Be prepared to begin CPR (see page 16).
● Signs of a stroke (see page 34) or heart attack (see page 32) can be masked by signs of hypothermia in an elderly person.

frostbite

The extremities, usually the fingers and toes, can literally freeze if exposed to severe cold. Tissues can be permanently damaged if treatment is not given quickly.

assessment

● Casualty may have pins and needles in affected areas; later he may have no feeling
● Skin may be waxy, pale and feel cold and hard
● Skin may turn from white to mottled blue/grey

action

1 STOP AND FIND SHELTER Get the casualty into a shelter. Do not warm the affected area unless there is no risk of re-freezing. Do not remove her gloves or shoes if she is likely to have to walk any further.

2 WARM UP GRADUALLY Tell the casualty to put her hands in her armpits to warm them up gently using her own body warmth. She can put her feet in your armpits to warm them up.

3 PLACE AFFECTED PARTS IN WARM WATER Once you are inside, remove the casualty's gloves or shoes and place her hands or feet in warm water. Try to remove rings or jewellery (do not force this though). Dry the affected area and wrap it in a loose, dry, non-fluffy bandage.

4 GET MEDICAL HELP The casualty should be taken to hospital. If she is in pain, she can take the recommended dose of her normal pain relief tablet, such as paracetamol or ibuprofen.

 TAKE CARE

As the skin is warmed up, it may become bright red, feel hot and be very painful. If the tissues are damaged, the affected area may turn black because of a lack of blood supply to the area.

heat-related illness

Heat exhaustion occurs in hot, humid surroundings when a person sweats profusely and loses a lot of fluids and body salts. Heatstroke is a medical emergency that occurs when the body's temperature regulation system fails and cannot cool the body. Both conditions need medical help, but heatstroke is life-threatening if untreated.

assessment

For **heat exhaustion**, the symptoms and signs are:

- Casualty complains of feeling hot but may look pale and will be sweating
- Will have a headache and may feel faint
- Skin feels cool and clammy
- May feel sick and vomit
- Signs of dehydration, such as cramps especially in the leg muscles (see pages 50–51)
- Breathing and pulse may be rapid and gradually become weaker

Symptoms for **heatstroke** are as follows:

- Severe headache
- Casualty complains of feeling very hot, but will not be sweating
- Skin looks flushed and feels hot, but will be dry
- Body temperature above 40°C (104°F)
- Breathing may be rapid and shallow but pulse will appear strong and bounding
- **Casualty will become confused and will rapidly lose consciousness**

 WARNING

A person who is already unwell, particularly if he has vomiting or diarrhoea, is more likely to suffer from heat exhaustion.

 TAKE CARE

Heatstroke develops if the body temperature rises to about 40°C (104°F), or lower if the environment is very humid. Take precautions in a heatwave. Stay out of the sun in the middle of the day – between 11am and 3pm. Wear light cotton clothing and a hat. Have plenty to drink (see page 50) and avoid alcohol and caffeine.

IS IT HEAT EXHAUSTION OR HEATSTROKE?

ACTION	HEAT EXHAUSTION	HEATSTROKE
Look at skin colour	Pale	Flushed
Feel the casualty's skin	Cool and clammy	Hot and dry
Check the pulse	Rapid and weakening	Strong and bounding
Check level of consciousness	Fully awake and conscious	Rapidly deteriorating level of consciousness

action

HEAT EXHAUSTION

1 MOVE THE CASUALTY INTO SHADE Help him into a cooler shady place – inside if possible. Lay him down and loosen any tight clothing. Raise his legs to help increase blood flow to the brain.

2 GIVE WATER Give the casualty sips of water – do not let him drink too much too quickly (see page 51). You can give him water containing oral rehydration salts or isotonic drinks to help replace some of the salts he has lost through sweating. Do not add salt to the water. Cool his skin with cold water.

3 MONITOR THE CASUALTY Check and make a note of his level of consciousness, breathing, pulse (see page 30) and body temperature (see page 62). Re-check regularly until he recovers. Advise him to stay in the shade and to see his doctor even if he appears to recover quickly.

 WARNING

• If a casualty with a heat-related illness does not improve quickly and you notice any of the signs of heatstroke, call for emergency help straight away.
• If a casualty becomes unconscious, open the airway and check breathing (see page 14). Be prepared to begin CPR (see page 16).

HEATSTROKE

1 GET HELP Call for emergency help. Move the casualty to a cool room and help him to sit down and remove as much clothing as you can.

2 COOL THE CASUALTY Soak a large sheet or towel in cool water and wrap it around the casualty. Pour more cool water over the sheet or towel to keep it cool. An alternative to this method is to shower or sponge with cool water. Fan his face if possible and open a window to ensure a supply of fresh cool air.

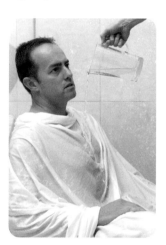

3 CHECK TEMPERATURE Cool the casualty until his body temperature has fallen below 37.5°C (99.5°F), then wrap him in a dry sheet if you have one.

4 MONITOR THE CASUALTY Check and make a note of his level of consciousness, breathing, pulse (see page 30) and body temperature (see page 62). Re-check regularly until medical help arrives. If his body temperature begins to rise again, re-start the cooling process. Provided the casualty is fully conscious, give him water to drink.

what next?

Most people who suffer from heatstroke make a full recovery with prompt treatment. The very young and the elderly are more likely to suffer complications. Medical treatment aims to continue the cooling process.

▶▶See also: UNCONSCIOUS ADULT/CHILD/BABY pp14–19 • DEHYDRATION pp50–51

dehydration

This condition develops when a person does not drink enough water to replace body fluids lost through sweating or through vomiting and diarrhoea. It is important to help the casualty to rehydrate as soon as possible to avoid severe dehydration.

WATCHPOINT A person who is unwell and is vomiting and/or has diarrhoea may become dehydrated. Give him plenty to drink. Give water or water containing rehydration salts.

assessment

Symptoms of dehydration start to become apparent when the body loses only about 1 per cent of its fluid. For mild to moderate dehydration, you may notice some or all of the following:

Feels unusually tired

Urine darker and/or smaller quantities and less frequent than normal

Mouth, lips and eyes feel dry

Headache

Feels thirsty

Dizzy or light-headed on standing up

Muscle weakness and possible cramps

If fluid loss is 5 per cent or greater:
- Heat-related illness
- Increasing thirst and irritability
- Decreased sweating
- Urination may cease
- Pulse and breathing rate increases, but gradually weakens
- If untreated, the casualty may develop seizures, and could lose consciousness.

⚠ **WARNING**

In addition to the above symptoms, in babies and children the skin may be very pale. In young babies, the fontanelle (soft area of the scalp) will be sunken and they shed few or no tears when they cry.

Staying hydrated

Water is lost mainly through sweating and urinating. The amount of water in the body is regulated to control the levels of compounds, such as salts, in the blood.

- **MAKE SURE YOU DRINK ENOUGH** The average person should drink about 2.5 litres of water a day. Drink more than this in hot weather, if you are exercising or working in extreme heat and/or humidity for long periods. The amount needed depends on body weight, temperature and the type of activity. You should consume enough fluids to produce clear urine.
- **DRINKING TOO MUCH WATER** Heavy sweating can lead to water intoxication if too much water is consumed too quickly and the body salts become too diluted (known as hyponatraemia). **This can cause the brain to swell, leading to confusion or collapse.** Even someone resting in extreme heat risks water intoxication if he drinks a large amount of water over a short period.

1 GIVE FLUIDS Sit the casualty down. Give her plenty of water to drink and tell her to drink it slowly. Water is sufficient, but you can also give her water containing oral rehydration salts, or isotonic drinks. Do not give her anything to eat as this may dehydrate her even more.

2 TREAT MUSCLE CRAMPS Stretch and massage the affected muscles to relieve the cramp (see below).

3 MONITOR CASUALTY Advise the casualty to rest, and monitor her condition. She should start to feel better. If she does not improve, or she deteriorates, get medical advice.

⚠ WARNING
- Do not add salt to the casualty's water.
- If a casualty becomes unconscious, open the airway and check breathing (see page 14). Be prepared to begin CPR (see page 16).

Treating muscle cramp

Muscles may go into spasm or jerk involuntarily as a result of exercise, dehydration and/or heat exhaustion. Muscle cramps can be very painful. The aim of treatment is to stretch the muscles to reverse the effect and relieve the cramp.

- **CRAMP IN THE THIGH MUSCLES** Help the person to lie down. If the cramp is in the front of the thigh, bend the knee to stretch the muscles, then rub the front of the leg. If cramp is in the back of the thigh, straighten the leg, then massage the back of the leg.

- **CRAMP IN THE CALF MUSCLES** Sit the person down. Hold his foot and flex his ankle, pointing his toes upwards to stretch the calf muscles. Massage the back of the calf.

- **CRAMP IN THE FOOT** Help him to stand on the foot and lean forward to stretch the affected muscles on the underside of the foot. Massage the foot firmly.

▶▶See also: **HEAT-RELATED ILLNESS** pp48–49 • **VOMITING** p72 • **DIARRHOEA** p73

sunburn

Damage (burning) caused by over-exposure to the ultraviolet (UV) rays in sunlight is called sunburn. Two main types of UV rays cause damage to skin: UVB rays are responsible for the majority of sunburn and can lead to skin cancer; UVA rays penetrate deeper into the skin causing ageing, but contribute much less towards sunburn.

assessment

Most sunburn is caused by exposure to bright sunlight, but it can also occur on overcast days, especially at high altitudes, or from sitting under a sun lamp.

MILD SUNBURN
- Itchy skin, especially in the days after the initial exposure, which eventually peels
- Skin very sore to touch, and may feel 'tight' as it begins to heal

SEVERE SUNBURN
- Possible fever
- Blisters
- Swelling
- There may also be symptoms of heat-related illness (see pages 48–49), such as headaches, dizziness, and nausea

Skin looks red and feels tender and hot even after initial cooling

Sun protection

When skin is exposed to sunlight, it produces a pigment called melanin to provide some protection from UV rays. The less melanin in the skin, the less the skin is protected. People with fair skin naturally have lower levels of melanin than those with darker hair or skin.

- **COVER UP** Wear clothes that cover the shoulders (sun-proof clothing is ideal), a hat that protects the neck and sunglasses.
- **STAY IN THE SHADE** Do this as much as possible, but always when the sun is at its peak – between 11am and 3pm.
- **ALWAYS USE SUNSCREEN** Use cream with a sun protection factor (SPF) of at least 15 and reapply it at least every two hours and immediately after swimming. For very pale skin, use SPF 50. Make sure children are well protected (see right) as their skin is more delicate than an adult's.

action

1 **MOVE CASUALTY TO THE SHADE** Give the casualty a towel or light cotton clothing to cover affected areas and help into the shade.

2 **COOL THE BURNED AREA** Tell the casualty to cool his skin by sponging it with lukewarm water or by having a tepid shower. For a large area of skin, he may want to cool the area by soaking in a cool bath.

what next?

● Mild sunburn can be treated at home. Advise the person to stay out of the sun, either inside or in the shade, and to keep the area covered with light (preferably cotton) clothing until the skin has healed. The casualty's skin may also flake or peel after a few days. This is the body's way of protecting itself: the skin cells have been damaged and are at risk of becoming cancerous, so the body sheds them.
● Adults may take one of their usual painkillers such as paracetamol or ibuprofen to relieve discomfort. A child can be given appropriate doses of children's paracetamol or children's ibuprofen.
● A casualty with severe burns will need to be assessed at a hospital. As with any burn, there is a risk of fluid loss and infection (see pages 112–113).

3 **DRINK WATER AND FLUIDS** Make sure the casualty drinks plenty of fluids to replace the fluid lost through sweating and to cool down. Do not let him drink alcohol because it will dehydrate him further.

4 **APPLY CREAMS**
For mild sunburn, tell the casualty to apply a moisturising lotion or aftersun lotion. Aftersun lotions help to cool and moisturise the skin, which helps prevent the 'tight' feeling that can develop as the skin heals, but they do not provide protection from the sun. Calamine lotion may also relieve itching and soreness.

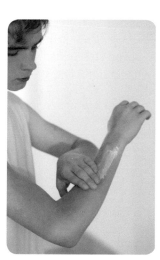

⚠ TAKE CARE
Do not touch blisters caused by sunburn, treat as for burns. Cool the burned area with water until the pain eases. Cover the blister with kitchen film or a non-fluffy dressing and take the casualty to hospital.

Check for moles

Regularly check your skin for moles. They are formed by a collection of skin pigment cells called melanocytes. Most are normal and harmless, but in a few cases they can develop into malignant melanoma, an aggressive form of skin cancer. If new moles develop or existing moles and/or freckles change, for example grow or start to bleed, consult a doctor to test for skin cancer.

allergic reaction

Any allergic reaction, including the most extreme form, occurs because the body's immune system reacts inappropriately in response to the presence of a substance that it wrongly perceives as a threat. There may only be mild itching, a skin rash, wheezing or sneezing, or, more rarely, a whole-body reaction – anaphylaxis.

assessment

Symptoms of allergy are commonly mild, but **a severe allergic reaction is life-threatening** and occurs within seconds or minutes of exposure to the allergen. In a severe allergy, many of the features of mild allergy are present, but more pronounced. Look out for the following signs or symptoms:

MILD ALLERGIC REACTION

- Red, itchy rash, possibly blotchy with raised red areas of skin (hives)
- Swollen, puffy hands and feet
- Sneezing and possible wheezing
- History of mild allergy
- Possible abdominal pain and/or vomiting
- Itchy, watery eyes, often reddened

SEVERE ALLERGIC REACTION

- Initially, generalised flushed appearance to the skin, possibly all over the body
- Swelling of the mouth and throat
- Difficulty breathing and possible asthma attack in a susceptible casualty, who may gasp for air
- Difficulty swallowing, which gradually worsens
- The casualty feels a sense of impending doom and may become very agitated, confused and frightened
- Casualty feels weak as blood pressure drops, and skin becomes pale; possible collapse

Understanding anaphylaxis

Also known as anaphylactic shock, anaphylaxis is an extreme and severe allergic reaction that affects the entire body. The reaction between the allergic antibody (IgE) and the allergen triggers the sudden release of body chemicals, including histamine, from cells in the blood and tissues. These chemicals act on blood vessels causing swelling anywhere in the body, especially the lungs, which results in breathing difficulties. Blood pressure falls and the circulatory system can fail, leading to shock (see pages 38–39).

- **ADRENALINE** A drug called adrenaline (also known as epinephrine) can reverse the effects of anaphylaxis if given quickly, constricting the blood vessels, relaxing the smooth muscles in the lungs, improving breathing, stimulating the heartbeat and reducing the swelling.

- **AUTOINJECTOR** Anyone who is susceptible to having a severe allergic reaction should carry an autoinjector (epipen) – a preloaded syringe containing adrenaline. There are different types and the person will normally know how to use it. If the casualty is unable to deliver the medication, follow the instructions on the autoinjector. The technique is also shown on the opposite page.

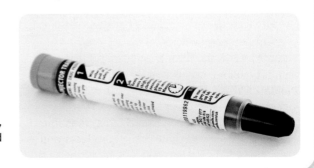

GET HELP A severe allergic reaction is life-threatening. Occasionally a serious reaction to a known allergen takes several hours to develop. If in doubt, call for emergency help.

TIME TO ACT Asthma attacks are often triggered by an allergic reaction. If a casualty does not have her asthma medication with her, call for emergency help immediately.

WATCHPOINT Common triggers of mild allergy are dust, pollen, pet fur and foods. Regular doses of antihistamine can help reduce symptoms. Seek medical advice.

action

MILD ALLERGY

1 ASSESS CASUALTY Ask the casualty about any known allergy. Ask if medication, such as an asthma puffer, is normally carried.

2 REMOVE THE TRIGGER If possible, remove the casualty from the trigger – for example take her inside if she is allergic to pollen or remove a bee stinger immediately (see page 322).

3 TREAT SYMPTOMS Let her take her normal medication if she has any. Seek medical advice if you are in any doubt about her condition.

 WARNING

If the casualty becomes pale and weak, treat for shock (see page 39). Help her to lie down and raise and support her legs.

Managing serious allergy

● **ALWAYS CARRY MEDICATION**
Anyone susceptible to severe allergic reactions will be prescribed a pre-loaded adrenaline injection kit (see left).
● **CARRY MEDICAL ID** Wear an ID tag or bracelet and, if possible, carry a card.
● **AVOID KNOWN TRIGGERS** Common allergens include foods, such as peanuts, tree nuts (almonds, walnuts, cashews, Brazils), sesame seeds or oil, fish, shellfish, dairy products and eggs. Non-food causes include wasp or bee stings, latex, penicillin and other drugs.

SEVERE ALLERGIC REACTION

1 CALL FOR HELP Call for emergency help immediately, telling the ambulance controller that the casualty is suffering from a severe allergic reaction and the cause if known. If there is a bee stinger, remove it immediately (see page 322).

2 GIVE MEDICATION Find the casualty's adrenaline (epinephrine) autoinjector and give it to him. If he cannot use it, you can help him. Hold it with your fist, remove the grey safety cap and press the end firmly against the thigh. The medication can be given through clothing. Rub the area.

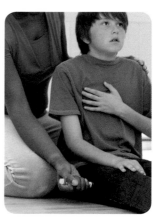

3 MAKE CASUALTY COMFORTABLE Help the casualty to sit down in whatever position he finds most comfortable for breathing. The best position is sitting upright with his back straight. Do not lie him down. His condition should start to improve.

4 MONITOR CASUALTY Check his level of consciousness, breathing and pulse (see page 30) while waiting for emergency help. Note any change and tell the emergency services. If he starts to deteriorate, treat as for shock (see pages 38–39). Lay him down with his head low and raise and support his legs.

5 REPEAT MEDICATION If his symptoms return, give adrenaline (epinephrine) again every five minutes, until medical help arrives.

▶▶See also: UNCONSCIOUS ADULT/CHILD/BABY pp14–19 • SHOCK pp38–39 • ASTHMA ATTACK pp42–43

drug and alcohol poisoning

Poisoning can result from an excess intake of alcohol or overdose of prescription, over-the-counter or recreational drugs. The effect will vary according to the drug. Some trigger hyperactivity and/or hallucinations in which the casualty starts to 'see things'; others depress the bodily functions, in particular the nervous system, so carry a risk of unconsciousness.

assessment

Drugs act on the brain and nervous system and change a person's level of consciousness or mood. A casualty may take more than one type of drug, which can complicate symptoms.

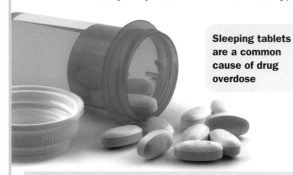

Sleeping tablets are a common cause of drug overdose

- Evidence of alcohol or drug near the casualty, or from people nearby
- Casualty may be very drowsy
- Enlarged or unequal-sized pupils (the black part of the eye)
- Nausea and/or vomiting
- Level of response may be reduced
- The casualty may lose consciousness

TYPES OF DRUGS

DRUG GROUP	POSSIBLE EFFECTS
Alcohol	Depresses the central nervous system, causing a flushed, moist face, deep and noisy breathing, strong pulse; later shallow breathing and a weak, fast pulse. Possible unconsciousness.
Anaesthetics, such as the recreational drug, ketamine	High doses suppress normal brain and breathing functions, causing drowsiness, shallow breathing, hallucinations and possible unconsciousness.
Depressants and sedatives, such as sleeping tablets, barbiturates and tranquillisers	Casualty is sedated and becomes increasingly drowsy; shallow breathing with weak, irregular or an abnormally fast pulse; drowsiness leads to unconsciousness and the heart may stop.
Narcotics, such as heroin and morphine	Drowsiness, leading to unconsciousness, shallow breathing with weak, irregular or fast pulse, and the heart may stop.
Hallucinogens, such as LSD and mushrooms	Agitation if the casualty has a 'bad trip', excitable, shaking hands, profuse sweating and possible unconsciousness.
Pain relievers	Nausea and vomiting, abdominal pain, drowsiness and possible unconsciousness. In addition, for aspirin overdose – rapid breathing, ringing in the ears, fever, sweating, disorientation and seizures. Paracetamol overdose symptoms develop gradually – jaundice and serious liver damage can develop days later.
Solvents, such as cleaning fluids which give off fumes	Headaches, ringing in the ears, hallucinations, nausea and vomiting, possible unconsciousness.
Stimulants, such as amphetamines (Ecstasy/ MDMA) and cocaine	Excitable and/or irrational behaviour, hands may be shaking, dilated pupils, profuse sweating, possible symptoms of heatstroke.

GET HELP If a casualty is losing consciousness, call for emergency help as soon as possible. Ideally, get someone else to make the call while you look after the casualty.

TIME TO ACT If you are unsure what drugs a casualty has taken, look for containers nearby to help you identify the drugs or ask any witnesses.

WATCHPOINT Do not touch needles found near a casualty as there is a risk of infection; they must be disposed of hygienically. Inform the paramedics when they arrive.

action

ALCOHOL POISONING

1 MAKE CASUALTY COMFORTABLE If the casualty is fully conscious, help him into a comfortable position. Wrap him in a blanket to protect him from the cold. Alcohol dilates the blood vessels so there is a risk of hypothermia (see page 46).

2 TREAT ANY INJURIES Check the casualty for injuries, treating anything you find. If he has fallen, assess him for signs of head injury (see page 82).

3 MONITOR CASUALTY If the casualty is conscious, monitor him until you are certain he has recovered. **If he loses consciousness, call for emergency help.** Check his level of consciousness, breathing and pulse (see page 30) while waiting for emergency help. Make a note of any change.

Possible complications

Symptoms and signs of drug or alcohol misuse can mask other conditions such as head injury (see page 82), stroke (see page 34) or hypoglycaemia (see page 58).

● **HYPOTHERMIA** If a casualty is outside in the cold there is a risk of hypothermia, especially after drinking alcohol.
● **HEAT-RELATED ILLNESS** A casualty who has taken stimulant drugs and collapsed after dancing in a hot atmosphere is at risk of heatstroke (see pages 48–49).
● **HIDDEN INJURY** If he has fallen, he may have a head injury. Look for signs of bleeding, especially if there has been a fight.

DRUG POISONING

1 MAKE CASUALTY COMFORTABLE If the casualty is fully conscious, help him into a comfortable position. Ask him what he has taken; bear in mind that he could become unconscious at any point.

2 CALL FOR EMERGENCY HELP Tell the controller that you suspect drug poisoning, giving any further information you have.

3 TREAT INJURIES If a casualty has had a fall, assess and treat any injuries.

4 MONITOR CASUALTY Check the level of consciousness, breathing and pulse (see page 30) while waiting for emergency help. Note any changes.

5 KEEP SAMPLES If a casualty vomits, try to preserve a sample or show the paramedics when they arrive as this can help the medical team to identify what the casualty has taken.

 WARNING
● If the casualty becomes unconscious, open the airway and check for breathing (see page 14). Be prepared to begin CPR (see page 16). If he is breathing, place him in the recovery position as he may vomit.
● Never try to make a person vomit in an attempt to clear the drug out of his system.

 TAKE CARE
Any casualty who is intoxicated may become belligerent and difficult to treat. In this case call for the emergency services. Watch from a safe distance until he allows you to help.

diabetic emergency

A diabetic can develop hyperglycaemia (raised blood sugar) or hypoglycaemia (low blood sugar). Giving sugar will be life-saving if blood sugar is low, and is unlikely to do harm if sugar levels are raised. Diabetics usually know how to control their condition but even long-term diabetics may be susceptible to an attack.

assessment

Suspect low blood sugar if a casualty is known to have diabetes and has missed a meal or has recently taken a lot of exercise. Some or all of the following symptoms may be present:

RAISED BLOOD SUGAR (HYPERGLYCAEMIA)

This is more likely to develop over several days or even weeks and the symptoms may include:
- Extreme thirst
- Frequent urination, especially at night
- Weight loss
- Itchy skin
- Wounds that heal more slowly than usual
- In the later stages, the casualty will become very drowsy, **which will lead to unconsciousness – this is an emergency**

 WARNING

If you know that a casualty has diabetes and he fails to respond to sugar, or his condition begins to deteriorate, call the emergency services straight away.

LOW BLOOD SUGAR (HYPOGLYCAEMIA)

This can occur if the blood sugar–insulin balance is incorrect. A person with diabetes often recognises the warning signs:
- Feels shaky and weak
- Skin is pale and feels cold and clammy
- Confused, irritable and behaving irrationally
- Rapid, but full and bounding pulse; casualty may tell you that his heart is pounding
- Casualty will quickly lose consciousness if he is not given some sugar

 TAKE CARE

A person who has recently been diagnosed with diabetes is more susceptible to a 'hypo' attack, especially while he is becoming used to balancing his sugar–insulin levels.

Understanding diabetes

Diabetes is a condition in which the body cannot control the level of glucose (sugar) in the blood. Insulin helps to remove glucose from the blood so it can be converted into energy. Diabetes develops either because an organ called the pancreas does not produce insulin (Type 1 diabetes), or because the body's cells are unable to use it (Type 2 diabetes). The condition can result in raised blood sugar levels (hyperglycaemia) or low blood sugar (hypoglycaemia), both of which are serious.

- **TYPE 1 DIABETES** This is a life-long condition that usually begins in childhood or early adulthood. People with Type 1 diabetes need to have insulin every day, normally via a syringe or an insulin pen.
- **TYPE 2 DIABETES** This is the most common type. It is associated with obesity, and is more common in the over 40s but can develop in much younger people. Type 2 diabetes is controlled by monitoring a person's diet, controlling weight and exercising. Oral tablet medication is often needed and some people also need insulin.

action

HYPERGLYCAEMIA

1 **CALL EMERGENCY HELP** If a casualty collapses and you suspect hyperglycaemia, open the airway and check breathing (see page 14). Call for emergency help.

2 **MONITOR CASUALTY** If he is breathing place him in the recovery position (see page 17). Check and note his level of consciousness, breathing and pulse (see page 30).

3 **RE-CHECK CASUALTY** Continue to re-check the casualty regularly while you are waiting for medical help to arrive.

what next?

● A person with suspected diabetes will be given a full medical examination at the hospital to assess his general state of health.
● If diabetes is confirmed, a medical team will work with him to plan a care programme, which will include advice on diet and exercise. A diabetes specialist nurse will demonstrate any equipment needed to help manage the condition.

HYPOGLYCAEMIA

1 **SIT CASUALTY DOWN** Reassure the casualty and help him to sit down on a chair or on the floor if he is feeling faint.

2 **GIVE SUGAR** Provided the casualty is fully conscious and alert, give him a sugary drink, such as fruit juice, or some glucose tablets. People who have diabetes often carry a dose of glucose concentrate or have some sugary food in their pocket as a precaution.

3 **CHECK RESPONSE** If the casualty improves quickly after eating or drinking something, follow this with some slower-release carbohydrate food, such as a cereal bar, a sandwich, piece of fruit, biscuits and milk or the next meal if it is due.

4 **FIND MEDICATION** Help the casualty to find his glucose testing kit and medication and let him check his glucose levels and take his insulin if required. Stay with him until he recovers completely. It is important to seek medical advice if you are at all concerned about the casualty.

seizures

A seizure is caused by a burst of excess electrical activity in the brain, which results in a brief disruption in the messages that pass between brain cells. Seizures can result from epilepsy, but in young children they can be triggered by a fever.

GET HELP If a seizure lasts five minutes or more, or a casualty has a series of seizures without regaining consciousness, get help. This is a medical emergency.

assessment

Seizures range from brief absences to episodes of convulsing and losing consciousness. The pattern is similar whatever the trigger.

FEBRILE SEIZURE IN YOUNG CHILD

A young child's temperature control system is not fully developed. Fever can trigger a febrile seizure.
● Child has a raised temperature
● Collapse followed by seizure
● History of febrile seizures with previous illness

MAJOR SEIZURE

Symptoms typically follow this pattern:
● Sudden collapse
● Casualty becomes rigid and may arch her back
● Convulsive movements begin – these may affect one or both sides of the body
● Breathing becomes difficult – casualty may clench her jaw. Blood or blood-stained saliva may appear at the mouth (she has probably bitten her lips or tongue). Do not be tempted to put anything in her mouth. There may also be signs of lost bowel or bladder control
● Eventually, the muscles relax and breathing returns to normal
● Casualty will wake up, but may be dazed
● Casualty is likely to fall into a deep sleep, after which she may not be aware of anything that has happened

ABSENCE SEIZURE

● The person may appear to be daydreaming or switching off. **She will be briefly unconscious** and totally unaware of what is happening around her
● Possible unexplained actions, such as lip smacking or rubbing hands

action

FEBRILE SEIZURE IN YOUNG CHILD

1 **PROTECT CHILD** Do not restrain the child, place padding such as pillows around her to prevent her injuring herself, for example, from falling off the bed.

2 **COOL THE CHILD** Seizures result from a raised body temperature. Cool the child by removing the bedclothes. Remove clothing, though you may have to wait for convulsive movements to stop before you can do this. Open a window if possible but do not let the child get too cold.

3 **CALL FOR MEDICAL HELP** Call for help. Place the child in the recovery position (see page 15) when the seizure stops. Check and note the level of consciousness, breathing and pulse (see page 30). Re-check regularly until medical help arrives.

 TAKE CARE
● Do not cool a child by sponging with water. This can make surface blood vessels contract and conserve body heat, causing temperature to rise.
● If a child has had a febrile seizure, she is likely to have another one if she has a fever again; this does not mean she will develop epilepsy.

MAJOR SEIZURE

1 CLEAR A SPACE Try to break the casualty's fall. Remove any objects or furniture from around the casualty, or place padding against her so that she cannot injure herself.

2 PROTECT THE CASUALTY'S HEAD Place cushions or rolled towels or blankets around the casualty's head to protect her further.

3 CHECK FOR EPILEPSY INFORMATION Once the convulsive movements have stopped, check the casualty's arms, neck or pockets as she may be wearing a medical ID bracelet (see page 55) or necklace or have a card that describes her condition and normal seizure pattern.

4 PLACE IN RECOVERY POSITION If she falls asleep, open the airway and check breathing. Place her in the recovery position (see page 15). Make a note of how long the convulsions lasted.

5 MONITOR THE CASUALTY Check and make a note of her level of consciousness, breathing and pulse (see page 30) and re-check regularly. Stay with her until she wakes up. Call the emergency services if you are in any doubt about the casualty.

When to call for help

Call the emergency services if:

- You know that it is the casualty's first seizure.
- The seizure continues for longer than five minutes.
- She remains unconscious for longer than 10 minutes after the convulsions.
- One seizure follows another without her regaining consciousness in between.
- The person is injured during the seizure.
- You are concerned about the casualty's condition and believe that she needs urgent medical attention.

 TAKE CARE

If a person is having a seizure:
- Do not restrain her or attempt to 'bring her round'.
- Do not try to put anything in the person's mouth during the seizure.
- Stay calm, do not frighten her by making abrupt movements or shouting.
- Assume the casualty is unaware of what is happening, or what has happened.
- Do not give her anything to eat or drink until she has fully recovered.

ABSENCE SEIZURE

1 HELP CASUALTY TO SAFETY Sit the casualty down somewhere quiet. Make sure she cannot hurt herself, for example by walking into a road. If she is inside, clear a space around her.

2 CHECK FOR EPILEPSY INFORMATION The casualty may be carrying a card or wearing a bracelet (see page 55) that describes her condition.

3 REASSURE CASUALTY Stay with the casualty until you are certain that she has fully recovered – be aware that an absence seizure can be followed by a major seizure. Calmly reassure her and explain anything that she has missed.

▶▶See also: **UNCONSCIOUS ADULT/CHILD/BABY** pp14–19

fever

Normal body temperature is 37°C (98.6°F). A fever is defined as a body temperature that rises above normal for any length of time and is one of the mechanisms the body uses to fight infection. Most fevers are caused by minor infections, such as colds and flu, and resolve as the cause disappears. In some instances, a fever is a sign of a more serious illness.

assessment

A fever can normally be treated at home with pain relief and rest, but there are some instances where medical advice is necessary. Symptoms will include:

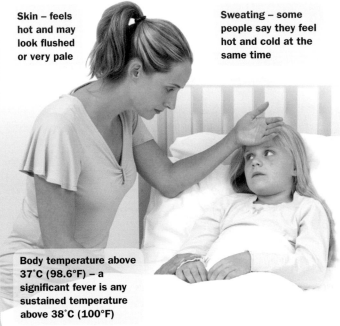

Skin – feels hot and may look flushed or very pale

Sweating – some people say they feel hot and cold at the same time

Body temperature above 37°C (98.6°F) – a significant fever is any sustained temperature above 38°C (100°F)

ADDITIONAL SYMPTOMS
● Casualty feels generally unwell and may complain of aches and pains
● Headache

WHEN TO SEEK MEDICAL ADVICE
● For an adult or child who is coughing up green, brown, grey or rusty-coloured phlegm (spit or catarrh); develops breathing difficulties; or who develops symptoms of Meningitis (see pages 64–65)
● If a person is elderly
● If the patient is a child and has lower back pain; pain or difficulty when passing urine; has been vomiting or suffering from diarrhoea for more than 24 hours and sooner if the child has both; has had a vaccination in the last 10 days and/or has a very high temperature and is prone to febrile seizures (see pages 60–61)

Fever warning signs in a baby

SEEK MEDICAL ADVICE IF A BABY:
● Has a raised temperature.
● Has a Seizure (see page 60).
● Becomes very pale, especially if the skin is blotchy (see page 64).
● Has breathing difficulties – quick, difficult or grunting breathing, or unusual breathing patterns.
● Is very hard to wake or unusually drowsy.
● Is coughing up green, brown, grey or rusty-coloured phlegm (spit or catarrh).
● Refuses feeds, keeps vomiting up feeds or has watery diarrhoea for more than eight hours. If the

baby has both vomiting and diarrhoea, seek medical advice sooner.

CALL EMERGENCY SERVICES IF A BABY:
● **Has a hoarse cough with noisy breathing**, is wheezing or cannot breathe through the nose.
● Is unusually hot, cold or floppy.
● Cries in an unusual way, or for an unusually long time, or seems to be in pain.
● If a newborn baby develops jaundice (looks yellow) when she is more than a week old, or develops jaundice over two weeks after birth.

GET HELP Raised body temperature can also be a sign of Heatstroke (see pages 48–49), a life-threatening condition that can occur in hot weather.

TIME TO ACT If a fever develops after travelling to a country with a high risk of infectious disease, seek urgent medical advice.

WATCHPOINT If an elderly person with a fever becomes confused, it can be a sign that a pre-existing condition has worsened, so seek urgent medical advice.

action

1 KEEP CASUALTY COOL Advise the casualty to rest and avoid strenuous activity. Keep her cool. She should not wear too many clothes or use too many bedclothes. It is important to keep the room at a comfortable temperature, and make sure that fresh air is circulating.

2 OFFER MEDICATION Let the casualty take the recommended dose of her usual pain relief medication, such as paracetamol. Give a young child the recommended dose of paracetamol or ibuprofen syrup. Do not give a baby less than three months old paracetamol or ibuprofen unless you have been advised to do so by your doctor.

3 GIVE DRINKS Make sure that the casualty drinks enough fluid to replace fluid lost through sweating and to prevent dehydration. To keep her hydrated, water is best but warm drinks can be soothing.

4 MONITOR CASUALTY Check her temperature every few hours. Seek medical advice if her condition deteriorates, she develops new symptoms and/or the fever lasts for four days or more.

 WARNING

• Don't give aspirin to a child who is less than 16 years old as it can trigger a rare but life-threatening condition called Reye's syndrome.
• A raised temperature in a child, especially aged under four, can result in a seizure (see page 60).
• Seek urgent medical advice if body temperature remains very high **and the person becomes lethargic and delirious**.
• Do not give ibuprofen to pregnant or breastfeeding women, and use with caution and on medical advice for anyone with asthma, a history of stomach ulcers, indigestion, kidney disease or anyone who is taking blood-thinning medication, such as warfarin.

Measuring body temperature

You can assess whether a person's skin is hot or cold by putting your hand against an exposed area, commonly the forehead. But to obtain an accurate reading use a thermometer.

● **DIGITAL THERMOMETER**
For an adult, or a child over the age of seven, place the thermometer under the tongue and leave it in place until it beeps; it takes about a minute. The reading will appear in the window. For a younger child, put the thermometer under the armpit; remember the reading will be about 0.6°C (1°F) lower than the oral measurement.

● **EAR SENSOR THERMOMETER**
Place the disposable cover over the sensor and put the tip of the thermometer in the ear. It will give a reading in about a second. This thermometer can be used while a person is asleep.

suspected meningitis

Meningitis is the term for inflammation of the meninges, the membranes around the brain and spinal cord. Meningitis can be caused by a virus or bacteria. Bacterial meningitis is more serious as the same bacteria is responsible for septicaemia (blood poisoning), which often occurs simultaneously. Without immediate hospital treatment, it can be fatal.

assessment

Symptoms can appear in any order, and may not all be present. They can develop over one to two days, or in a matter of hours. Watch for symptoms that appear suddenly and worsen quickly.

INITIAL SYMPTOMS
- Flu-like illness with high temperature
- Hands and feet feel cold; pain in the limbs
- Pale, blotchy skin
- Vomiting

AS THE CONDITION DEVELOPS
- Headache, possibly severe, with neck stiffness (less common in the very young)
- Stomach cramps or diarrhoea
- Eyes may become especially sensitive to light (less common in very young children)
- Rapid breathing – possibly breathlessness
- The casualty may become difficult to wake
- A blank staring expression
- Casualty may be confused and delirious
- Septicaemic rash may appear (see below)
- Possible seizures

IN BABIES AND TODDLERS
The following symptoms may also be present:
- Refusing to eat or feed
- Dislike of being handled
- High-pitched, whimpering cry
- Floppy, listless and unable to stand
- Blank, staring expression and unresponsive
- Tense or bulging fontanelle (the soft spot on top of the head)

⚠ WARNING
The organisms responsible for bacterial meningitis also cause septicaemia (blood poisoning), an even more dangerous condition.
This condition can appear with or without meningitis. Seek medical advice immediately if you notice any of the following symptoms:
- Fever; cold hands and feet.
- Limb, joint and muscle pain.
- Pale, blotchy skin.
- A rash (but do not wait for this to appear).

Checking for a rash

A septicaemic rash starts as red or brown pinprick marks, which can develop into larger red or purple blotches, or blood blisters, as the condition worsens. Press a glass against a rash. If it is septicaemia, you will see the marks through the glass (all other rashes fade when pressed).

GET HELP If a casualty's condition is deteriorating and you suspect meningitis, call the emergency services immediately, even if the person has already seen a doctor.

TIME TO ACT If you have been in close contact with someone who has developed meningitis, consult your doctor for advice.

WATCHPOINT A localised infection anywhere in the body could release meningitis-causing bacteria into the bloodstream, which can travel to and infect the meninges.

action

1 MONITOR THE SYMPTOMS Treat a Fever (see page 63). Watch the casualty carefully – it is easy to think that non-specific symptoms such as fever and vomiting are due to less dangerous illnesses.

2 SEEK MEDICAL ADVICE If the casualty has a flu-like illness plus any of the symptoms opposite, such as a headache, stiff neck, or his eyes are sensitive to light, seek medical advice. Do not wait for a rash to appear.

3 DO THE GLASS TEST If you see any sign of a rash, check it by pressing the side of a clear drinking glass firmly against the skin (see box, opposite). If the spots do not fade, it could be a sign of meningitis-related septicaemia. On darker skin, check for the rash on lighter areas, such as the palms of the hands, the fingertips or the soles of the feet. The spots or rash may fade at first, so keep checking.

4 CALL EMERGENCY HELP If someone is very ill, obviously getting worse and/or has a rash, call the emergency services immediately, even if you have already spoken to a doctor. If there is likely to be a delay, take the casualty to hospital yourself.

5 MONITOR CASUALTY Keep the casualty cool and reassure him – do not let him get too cold. Reassure him and check and make a note of any change in his level of consciousness, breathing and pulse (see page 30) while you are waiting for help.

what next?

● If a person has suspected bacterial meningitis and/or septicaemia, he will be admitted to hospital and given antibiotics. Diagnosis will be confirmed by blood tests and analysis of cerebrospinal fluid through a lumbar puncture.
● Anyone who has been in direct, prolonged close contact with the infected person may be given a short course of antibiotics as a precaution.

Understanding meningitis

Meningitis is caused by different organisms including bacteria, viruses and fungi.

● **BACTERIAL MENINGITIS** Most cases of bacterial meningitis and septicaemia are caused by germs that live naturally – and in most people harmlessly – at the back of the throat. Septicaemia (blood poisoning) is caused when the bacteria enter the bloodstream and multiply uncontrollably. The bacteria that cause meningitis and pneumonia are the most common in the developed world. They survive outside the body for only a few seconds and are spread by prolonged close contact, sneezing and kissing.
● **VIRAL MENINGITIS** This is more common than bacterial meningitis. It can make a person very ill, but most recover in two weeks. It can be caused by a number of viruses, including herpes simplex, chickenpox and mumps.
● **PROTECTION WITH IMMUNISATION** Children can be vaccinated against certain types of bacterial meningitis as part of the national immunisation programme. However, although they give excellent protection, they do not prevent all forms of the disease. There is as yet no vaccine for one of the most serious – meningitis B.

infected wound

Infection occurs when disease-causing micro-organisms (germs) enter the body and multiply. Any break in the skin allows bacteria to enter the body, increasing the chance of infection. Check daily for signs of infection; any wound that does not start to heal within **48 hours** is at risk. Early diagnosis can reduce any danger to the injured person's overall health.

assessment

Suspect infection if you notice any of the following symptoms or signs:

- The wound and surrounding skin feels hot
- The area around the injury is swollen
- Yellow pus in the wound and/or redness around the wound – there may be red 'trails' leading away from the wound
- Swollen lymph glands in the armpit or groin
- Raised temperature (see page 62) and the casualty may feel generally unwell

action

1 REMOVE OLD DRESSINGS Take off the old dressings and dispose of them hygienically. Carefully clean around the wound with soap and water or alcohol-free antiseptic wipes.

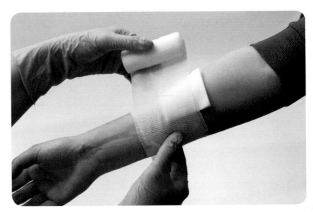

2 COVER THE WOUND Place a sterile dressing over the infected wound and secure it with a bandage. Raise and support the injury, for example in a sling (see pages 90–91) if necessary.

3 SEEK MEDICAL ADVICE Tell the person to arrange an appointment with his doctor as a course of antibiotics may be needed, or take him to hospital.

Understanding infection

- **INFECTION SOURCES** Germs can enter the body via the cause of injury, for example a dirty knife. Alternatively they can come from a person's clothing, hands or breath. There may also be tiny particles of dirt or dead tissue in a wound.

- **WOUND CARE** Good hygiene reduces risk. Wash your hands thoroughly with soap and water before treating a casualty. If water is unavailable, use alcohol gel. Wear disposable gloves – ideally nonlatex gloves as many people are allergic to latex. Bleeding naturally flushes out most, if not all, the dirt but you should always carefully wash around the wound as well to remove dirt from surrounding skin.
- **TETANUS IMMUNISATION** Tetanus is a very serious disease resulting from micro-organisms found in soil and manure. It is rare in the UK as most people are protected against this infection through immunisation (see page 101).

 WARNING

If an injured casualty becomes unwell, has a raised body temperature, is shivering and is becoming weak and lethargic, take him to hospital yourself or get emergency help.

sudden hearing loss

Most hearing loss is gradual and age-related but a number of conditions can result in sudden loss of hearing over a matter of days or even hours. In many cases, the cause is an ear infection or wax blockage that can be treated easily. Consult a doctor or hospital if sudden hearing loss occurs without an obvious cause in one or both ears.

assessment

Temporary hearing problems can result from:

● Blocked nose as a result of a severe cold or hay fever – this can cause a build-up of mucus against the ear-drum, especially in children
● Pressure change during take off and landing when flying
● Brief exposure to loud noise, such as music, which can leave a loud ringing in the ears for a few hours. A sudden, very loud noise such as an explosion can damage the ear-drum
● Infection of the outer or inner ear
● Build-up of wax in the ear canals
● Ménière's disease – a serious disorder in which excess fluid collects in the inner ear, resulting in severe dizziness
● Head injury

 WARNING

If sudden hearing loss follows a Blow to the Head (see page 82), call for emergency help immediately.

Protecting hearing

Persistent exposure to loud noise can cause permanent hearing loss, but there are steps that can be taken to prevent damage to ears.

● **WEAR EAR PROTECTION** Wear ear plugs or ear defenders if exposed to sustained loud noises at work and get hearing checked regularly.
● **KEEP SOUND LEVELS LOW** Make sure the sound level of headphones is low enough to be able to hear a conversation above them.
● **LIMIT LISTENING TIME** Restrict listening to personal stereo systems to about an hour at a time.

action

1 **REASSURE CASUALTY**
If the deafness results from a change in pressure after flying, tell the casualty to hold his nose and blow through his nose until he feels his ears 'pop'. If he has a cold or hay fever, hearing will return when he recovers. Ringing in the ears after exposure to loud noise should stop in a few hours.

2 **SEEK MEDICAL ADVICE** Arrange for the casualty to see his doctor for any other cause. If he cannot contact his doctor, take him to hospital.

3 **TREAT EARACHE** If the casualty is in pain, suggest he takes a dose of paracetamol medication. Give him a hot-water bottle wrapped in a towel to hold against the ear to help soothe the pain.

what next?

● The casualty's doctor may prescribe a course of antibiotics as treatment for an ear infection or burst ear-drum. The doctor will arrange a follow-up appointment to check that the infection has responded. A burst ear-drum will normally heal by itself.
● If the cause cannot be identified, a casualty will be referred to a specialist for tests to assess the cause and measure the degree of hearing loss.

sudden **vision problems**

Vision problems can develop following an injury to the eye or head. They can also result from disorders of the nervous system or of the eyes. Age-related deterioration is the most likely cause of vision problems and these can develop gradually or suddenly. Any sudden change should be investigated, as early treatment can prevent permanent loss of sight.

assessment

If a person is suffering from sudden vision problems, there may also be evidence of injury. As well as a reduction of vision, a person may experience the following symptoms:

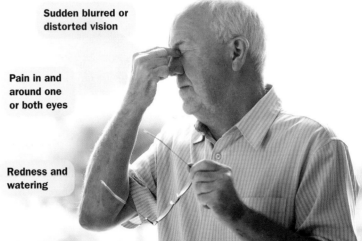

Sudden blurred or distorted vision

Pain in and around one or both eyes

Redness and watering

ADDITIONAL SYMPTOMS
- Difficulty focusing or colours may appear faded
- Burning or gritty sensation in the eyes
- Sudden appearance of 'floaters' in the eye – these are spots that appear to be 'on' the eye
- Partial loss of field of vision
- Obvious eye injury

SYMPTOM FINDER

SYMPTOMS	POSSIBLE CAUSES
Red itchy eyes, with yellow pus-like discharge	If vision is restored when the discharge is cleaned away, it may be conjunctivitis, an infection of the conjunctiva (the membrane that covers the eyes). Seek medical advice as treatment may be needed.
Sudden onset of double vision	Bleeding into the brain after a stroke or head injury, or it could be a symptom of a disorder of the nervous system. Call for emergency help.
Flashing lights and spots in front of the eyes	If this precedes a headache, it could be a migraine (see page 74). If it occurs with no warning, it could be a detached retina at the back of the eye (see box, right). Call for emergency help.
Blurred or double vision	Vision can be affected by diabetes-related disorders, some prescription drugs, ingestion of poisons and clouding of the eye lens (cataracts). Seek medical advice or take the casualty to hospital if severe.
Blurred or distorted vision with pain in one or both eyes	Glaucoma, a condition caused by excess fluid in the eye that results in a build-up of pressure in the eyeball. Seek medical advice.

GET HELP If a casualty experiences problems with his vision after a blow to the head, call the emergency services without delay.

TIME TO ACT Call for emergency help immediately if a casualty (adult or child) complains of sudden loss of sight in one or both eyes.

WATCHPOINT Regular eye tests for adults and children can detect signs of deterioration before more general symptoms of vision problems appear.

action

1 REASSURE CASUALTY The casualty is likely to be very frightened if there is loss of vision.

2 TREAT ANY INJURY
If the eye is injured, help her to lie down and support her head. Give her a pad to hold over the injured eye. If the casualty has splashed chemicals in her eye (see page 117).

3 SEEK MEDICAL ADVICE Advise the casualty to call her doctor, or make the call for her. If you are in any doubt about her condition, take her to hospital or call the emergency services.

Detached retina

The retina is the innermost layer at the back of the eye. It contains millions of light receptors that convert the image formed by the eye's optical system into impulses that are carried along the optic nerve to the brain. The retina can become detached from its underlying layer and may be torn. This causes sudden full or partial loss of vision, rather like a curtain falling over part of the eye.

● **TAKE CASUALTY TO HOSPITAL This is a serious condition that can lead to blindness** if it is not diagnosed and treated very quickly. The tear can be repaired surgically, which can restore vision and prevent further deterioration.

Snow blindness

The surface of the eyes can be damaged by over-exposure to ultraviolet (UV) light. This can be caused by the glare of sunlight on snow, concrete or water and can be prevented by wearing UV-protecting sunglasses.

1 ASSESS SYMPTOMS The casualty will experience a gritty feeling and excruciating pain in the eye. His eyes may be red and watering.

2 TAKE CASUALTY TO HOSPITAL Give him clean pads to hold against his eyes if there is likely to be any delay.

3 REST THE EYES The casualty will be advised to wear sunglasses and stay out of the sun until his eyes have healed.

what next?

● The casualty will be assessed at the hospital by a medical team. The tests that are carried out will depend on the symptoms.
● A basic sight test, known as a Snellen test, is used to assess a person's vision. The test involves reading letters from a chart that become progressively smaller on each line.
● The casualty may be referred to a specialist for additional eye tests. If a head injury is suspected, imaging tests, such as an MRI scan, may also be given to ascertain the underlying cause.
● Treatment depends on the findings. Some conditions such as glaucoma may respond to drug therapy. Other conditions, such as vision problems following a head injury, will almost certainly require surgery.

▶▶See also: CHEMICALS IN THE EYE p117 • EYE INJURY p118

severe abdominal pain

Most abdominal pain is short-lived and is caused by a minor ailment such as indigestion or mild food poisoning. Severe abdominal pain can result from injury or be a sign of a more serious disorder affecting the digestive system, urinary system or, in women, of the reproductive system. Persistent or severe abdominal pain needs prompt medical attention.

assessment

Pain anywhere in the abdomen may be localised or general. Find out as much detail as you can as it helps the medical team. Ask the casualty when she last ate or drank something.

SYMPTOMS

- Possible fever and/or generally feeling unwell
- Bleeding (internal or external) if pain results from an injury
- Bloating or distended abdomen

- Vomiting and/or diarrhoea – if together and either prolonged or severe
- Urinary problems
- Symptoms and signs of **Shock** (see page 38)

IS IT SERIOUS?

SIGNS	QUESTIONS TO ASK
Pain	Has this happened before? Where is the pain (see right)? Is it concentrated in one area or has it spread? If so, where? Is it mild, moderate or severe – ask the casualty to give it a score out of 10. Is the pain continuous or intermittent and has it changed or moved? When and where did it start? Does movement, breathing or coughing make it worse (or better)?
Bleeding	Where is the bleeding? Is blood loss slight or severe? Are there signs of internal bleeding (see page 38)?
Vomiting	How many times has the casualty vomited and when did it start? Does she feel better after vomiting? What does the vomit look like? Does it contain dark reddish blood that looks like coffee grounds (see page 38)?
Diarrhoea	How often do the bouts of diarrhoea occur? Does the casualty feel better after going to the toilet? Is there blood in the faeces?
Urine	When did the casualty last urinate and was it normal? Was it painful? Is the urine normal or cloudy? Does it smell unusual and/or contain blood?
Additional symptoms	Does the casualty have a Fever (see page 62)? Is she restless or tired, or is she too weak to move? Could she have food poisoning or has she been in contact with anyone who has gastroenteritis? Is the casualty a woman of child-bearing age? Does she have a history of menstrual pain? Could she be pregnant?

Top

Upper right

Upper left

Middle

Lower right

Lower left

Lower centre

GET HELP If a child is in severe, constant pain that lasts for an hour or more and/or her tummy is distended (bloated) call the emergency services.

TIME TO ACT If the casualty's pain is severe, he is vomiting and has a fever, call the emergency services. Treat for Shock (see pages 38–39) and monitor him until help arrives.

WATCHPOINT If you suspect serious illness or injury, do not give the casualty anything to eat or drink (including pain relief medication) as he may need an anaesthetic later.

action

1 **MAKE CASUALTY COMFORTABLE** Sit or lie her down. She may be most comfortable if she is propped up with pillows. Give her a bowl if she is feeling sick.

2 **GIVE A HOT WATER BOTTLE** Wrap a hot water bottle in a towel and give it to the casualty to hold against her stomach.

3 **SEEK MEDICAL ADVICE** If you are in any doubt about the casualty's condition, seek medical advice. Make a note of her level of consciousness, breathing and pulse (see page 30). If her condition deteriorates, call the emergency services.

 WARNING

Call the emergency services immediately if there is an obvious abdominal wound or if the pain lasts more than four hours in an adult (one hour in a child) and is accompanied by ANY of the following:
- Severe vomiting and/or diarrhoea.
- Blood-stained vomit.
- Swollen and tender abdomen.
- Swelling in the groin or scrotum.
- Casualty feels faint and confused.
- Fresh, bright red blood from the anus or dark, tarry stools.
- Blood in the urine.
- Severe pain and heavy bleeding in early pregnancy could be a sign of miscarriage or a life-threatening ectopic pregnancy in which the foetus develops outside the womb (see page 78) and requires urgent medical treatment.

Appendicitis

Appendicitis is an inflamed appendix. The appendix is a small blind-ended tube attached to the first section of the large intestine. It is situated on the lower right-hand side of the abdomen.

- **IS APPENDICITIS SERIOUS?** Appendicitis can be serious. It is a common cause of abdominal pain, especially in children. The appendix can become inflamed, swollen and infected. This can lead to gangrene (tissue death) in the wall of the appendix, which may burst as a result.
- **DIAGNOSIS AND TREATMENT** The pain usually begins in the centre of the abdomen. Over a period of hours it worsens and becomes most intense in the lower right-hand side. The casualty needs to be admitted to hospital for surgery. **If the appendix bursts, the pain may suddenly stop, but this can lead to the life-threatening infection, peritonitis** (inflammation of the membranes lining the abdominal cavity and covering the organs).

what next?

- A doctor will conduct a physical examination and ask the patient about the pain. Blood tests and X-rays or other imaging tests may be carried out to confirm a diagnosis.
- If the cause of the abdominal pain is still uncertain, endoscopic (internal camera) investigation may be needed. Further treatment will depend on findings.
- Some casualties will need to be admitted to hospital for further investigation and, depending on the findings, may require surgery.

▶▶See also: **SHOCK** pp38–39 • **VOMITING** p72 • **DIARRHOEA** p73 • **WOUNDS AND BLEEDING** pp96–97

vomiting

Caused by irritation of the digestive system, vomiting can result from a viral or bacterial infection or parasites. If prolonged, it can cause dehydration and the risk is greater when diarrhoea and vomiting occur together.

assessment

Most cases of vomiting are mild, but if symptoms are severe, the person is young, elderly or has another illness, hospital treatment may be needed. Any of the following symptoms can occur:

- Feeling of nausea
- Vomiting, possibly with diarrhoea
- Stomach pains
- Fever
- Known history of eating or drinking apoisonous or contaminated substance (see page 114)

 TAKE CARE

- Nausea, vomiting and tiredness are common during early pregnancy.
- Infections such as gastroenteritis can be highly infectious, so personal hygiene is very important.
- If you are concerned, tell the casualty to seek medical advice, as a few infections need treatment with antibiotics.
- Tell the casualty to avoid alcohol.
- Anyone whose work involves handling or preparing food must take leave until he is free of symptoms.

WARNING

- Call for emergency help if the casualty begins to show signs of Dehydration (see page 50).
- If dehydration is severe, there is a risk of shock developing (see page 38).

Vulnerable people

For elderly people, young children and babies, the effects of prolonged vomiting and diarrhoea can have serious health consequences. They are at a greater risk of becoming dehydrated than young, healthy adults.

ELDERLY PEOPLE

- Most elderly people can be treated at home. Make the casualty comfortable and treat as opposite, but monitor the casualty for signs of dehydration as this can be fatal.
- Give the casualty plenty of water to drink, on its own or with rehydration salts. Some types of rehydration salts are not suitable for people with a kidney condition. Always check the packet instructions.

- If the vomiting in an elderly person is severe, prolonged and/or accompanied by diarrhoea, call for medical advice. **If the casualty shows signs of dehydration, he may need to be taken to hospital for treatment**.

BABIES AND YOUNG CHILDREN

- If a baby is breastfed, advise the mother to keep breastfeeding to replace lost fluid. A baby who is bottle-fed, should be given water or water with rehydration salts.
- Call for medical advice if a baby or young child keeps vomiting most of his feeds or has watery stools; vomiting or diarrhoea lasts more than eight hours in a baby (or 24 hours in a young child); there are signs of dehydration, such as sunken eyes and/or fontanelle in a baby. If a baby or young child is vomiting and has diarrhoea, call for medical advice even sooner as the risk of dehydration is greater.

action

1 MAKE COMFORTABLE Reassure the casualty and make him as comfortable as possible. Give him a cloth to wipe his face.

2 GIVE SIPS OF WATER Give the casualty water after he has been sick. Tell him to sip the water slowly as he may vomit again.

3 BUILD UP FLUIDS Gradually build up the amount of fluid he drinks. Water is sufficient, but you can give him water containing rehydration salts (follow the packet instructions) or unsweetened fruit juice.

4 INTRODUCE FOOD GRADUALLY When the casualty is beginning to feel hungry again, give him small amounts of easily digested foods. Try plain pasta, rice or bread for the first 24 hours. If vomiting persists or recurs or there are other symptoms, such as diarrhoea, seek medical advice.

Food poisoning

Eating food or drink that is contaminated with bacteria or the toxins that it produces can cause food poisoning. Some bacteria, commonly Campylobacter, *E. coli* and salmonella, multiply fast in food in warm, damp conditions. The more bacteria are present, the higher the chance of infection and illness. Most bacteria are destroyed by thorough cooking; food poisoning can result from eating undercooked foods.

● **REPORTING INCIDENTS** Food poisoning can affect a whole group if they have all eaten the same contaminated food. Severe cases should be reported to the local health authority so that the source can be identified.
● **WHEN TO SEEK ADVICE** Most cases of food poisoning clear up within a few days without medical treatment. Seek medical advice if the vomiting or diarrhoea lasts for more than a few days or the condition worsens, there is blood in the stools, the diarrhoea contains yellowish or greenish mucus or the affected person is elderly, pregnant, or a baby or young child.

diarrhoea

If a casualty passes watery stools more than three times a day, he has diarrhoea. As with vomiting, it is generally a symptom of an infection, such as food poisoning.

assessment

Diarrhoea usually clears up in a couple of days and is not serious. There is a risk of dehydration if diarrhoea persists.

● Acute diarrhoea comes on suddenly, and can last for one to 10 days. It is most likely to be the result of an infection – such as food poisoning or gastroenteritis
● If a casualty has chronic diarrhoea that lasts for more than two weeks, it is most likely to be the symptom of a long-term condition such as irritable bowel syndrome
● Diarrhoea may accompany vomiting or it may occur on its own

action

1 GIVE SIPS OF WATER Give him water to drink to replace some of the lost fluids and tell him to sip it slowly. He should aim to drink about 200ml of fluid after every loose stool.

2 BUILD UP FLUIDS Gradually build up the amount of fluid that he drinks. Water is sufficient, but you can give him water containing rehydration salts. Avoid sports drinks or sugary drinks as the sugar content can make diarrhoea worse.

3 INTRODUCE FOOD GRADUALLY When the casualty is beginning to feel hungry again, give him small amounts of easily digested foods. Offer foods such as plain pasta, rice or bread for the first 24 hours. If diarrhoea persists or recurs or there is blood in the stools, seek medical advice.

severe headache

A headache is a common complaint, often due to stress or tension, but a sudden severe headache following a blow to the head can indicate a potentially life-threatening injury (see page 82). It can be a sign of serious illness such as Stroke (see page 34), of Meningitis (see page 64), of Carbon Monoxide Poisoning (see page 45) or of a condition such as migraine.

assessment

When a casualty has a sudden severe headache, establish the cause to eliminate serious injury or illness. Any or all of the following symptoms may indicate a potentially serious condition:

Sudden headache – especially after a blow to the head

Sensitivity to light

Stiff neck

Fever

Possible abdominal pain and vomiting

⚠ WARNING
A headache can appear hours or days after a blow to the head.

action

1 USE A COLD COMPRESS Sit the casualty down and give her a cold pad to hold against her head. This can soothe a headache and should reduce swelling and bruising if she has had a blow to the head.

2 GIVE PAIN RELIEF If the casualty is prone to tension headaches or suffers from migraine, let her take her usual pain relief or migraine medication. Don't ever give aspirin to a child under 16 years old as it can trigger Reye's syndrome, a rare but potentially life-threatening condition.

3 MONITOR THE CASUALTY Signs of serious head injury may not be immediately apparent. Monitor her condition. Get emergency help if you notice any of the symptoms above or she begins to deteriorate.

Understanding migraine

A migraine is a severe headache that is often accompanied by other symptoms. The person may experience an 'aura' comprising flashes of light or blind spots, difficulty in focusing and may see things as if through a broken mirror. Attacks can be triggered by emotional, physical, dietary, environmental and medicinal factors. A migraine attack can last from four hours to three days. Some people experience migraine attacks several times a week, others only occasionally. The casualty may be more comfortable in a darkened room.

⚠ WARNING
If the person becomes unconscious, open the airway and check breathing (see page 14). Be prepared to begin CPR (see page 16).

panic attack

This is a sudden bout of extreme anxiety that can be brought on by a strong fear of something (phobia) or an emotional upset. Some people have a history of panic attacks, but in others an attack can come on with no apparent warning. A panic attack is often accompanied by hyperventilation and/or an abnormally fast heart rate.

assessment

Panic attacks can cause concern, but they usually subside fairly quickly. You may notice that the casualty has some or all of the following symptoms:

- Signs of unnaturally fast breathing, such as hyperventilation or overbreathing
- A very fast pulse rate
- Feeling of tension that causes a headache or feeling of chest tightness
- The casualty may be very apprehensive and may even have a fear of dying

 TAKE CARE

Do not restrain someone who is having a panic attack, and **never attempt to slap the person to 'snap her out of it'.**

action

1 REMOVE THE CAUSE Try to find out the cause of the casualty's fear and separate her from it. Either remove it from her or move her away from it.

2 BE FIRM Try to calm the casualty by talking firmly but kindly and calmly to her. Explain that she is having a panic attack and keep others away.

3 ENCOURAGE HER TO BREATHE CALMLY Breathing more slowly will help to calm her and will stop her hyperventilating (see right). Try to encourage her to copy your breathing pattern.

4 MONITOR CASUALTY Stay with her until she has recovered. If she has a history of panic attacks, advise her to seek help to learn how to control them.

 WARNING

Do not ask a casualty to rebreathe her air from a paper bag as this can cause low blood oxygen levels.

Hyperventilation

A panic attack may be accompanied by hyperventilation – a state in which a casualty is overbreathing (breathing unnaturally fast). If it persists, the casualty breathes in too much oxygen and exhales carbon dioxide too quickly before the body can use it to regulate breathing.

- **HELP CASUALTY TO BREATHE SLOWLY** Help her regain control of her breathing. The out-breath should be longer than the in-breath. Ask her to copy your breathing pattern.
- **LONG-TERM HELP** If a person is susceptible to panic attacks and overbreathing, advise her to talk to her doctor as this is potentially harmful.

unexpected childbirth

Childbirth is a completely natural process that can be lengthy, especially with a first baby. There is usually plenty of time to get a woman to hospital, or for help to arrive. It generally happens around the 40th week of pregnancy, but about two weeks either side is normal. A pregnant woman is likely to be more anxious if labour starts unexpectedly.

assessment

If a woman goes into labour, offer her reassurance while you wait for the emergency services or help to deliver the baby.

- Find out the expected delivery date
- Ask if she has her maternity notes – these will have important contact details and medical notes

The following signs will tell you how far labour has progressed:
- Possible contractions – these last up to a minute and come at intervals of five to 20 minutes initially, becoming closer as the labour progresses. Note the length of each contraction and the time taken between the beginning of one contraction to the start of the next
- Rupture of the membrane around the baby can cause fluid to gush out (the waters breaking). Once this happens, there is an increased risk of infection as the baby's protective layer has gone

The stages of labour

Labour has three distinct stages. The first prepares the woman's body for the birth. The baby is born in the second stage. The afterbirth (placenta) is delivered in the third stage.

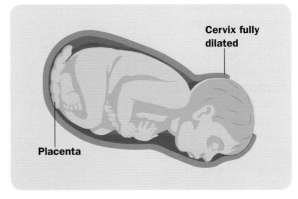

Cervix fully dilated

Placenta

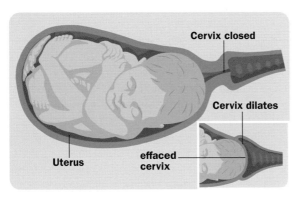

Cervix closed

Cervix dilates

Uterus

effaced cervix

- **FIRST STAGE** This stage of labour can last several hours, although it may be shorter in second and later pregnancies. The uterus begins contractions, which help to press the baby's head against the cervix. The cervix gradually opens and 'thins' until it is 10cm in diameter. During this stage, a plug of mucus will be expelled. In addition, the water around the baby (amniotic fluid) may gush out.

- **SECOND STAGE** When the cervix is fully dilated (open) the woman's contractions change and she will feel a desire to push the baby out – this is a sign that the baby is about to be born. This stage normally lasts anything from 10 minutes to an hour, but can be longer.

- **THIRD STAGE** Ten minutes to half an hour after the baby is born, the third stage begins. The uterus contracts again. The placenta, known as the afterbirth, comes away from the wall of the uterus and is expelled from the body along with the umbilical cord.

TIME TO ACT If the labour is premature, tell the emergency services so they can arrange to take the woman to a hospital that has neonatal facilities for the baby.

action

1 CALL EMERGENCY HELP Tell the controller the mother's due date, the place where she was expecting to give birth and the stage of labour she has reached.

2 DURING FIRST STAGE Listen to the woman and reassure her. She may be very worried, especially if the labour is earlier than expected. Help her into a comfortable position and encourage her to breathe slowly and steadily.

3 TIME HER CONTRACTIONS Make a note of the length and the frequency of her contractions. These will get stronger and more frequent. If she is uncomfortable, she may ask you to massage her back with the heel of your hands. If she is very hot, cool her face and neck with a damp sponge or cloth.

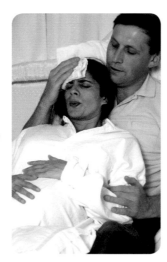

4 DURING SECOND STAGE If the woman tells you that she wants to push, this is a sign that the second stage has started. Ask her to remove any clothes that could interfere with the birth. Find a sheet to put underneath her and keep the area clean. Support her, but do not interfere with the birth.

5 WRAP THE BABY As soon as the baby is born, give her to her mother. Wrap them both in a towel and/or blanket. The baby will be very slippery so handle carefully. Do not cut the cord. Monitor both the mother and baby while you wait for help.

6 DURING THIRD STAGE Soon after the birth, contractions will recommence and the mother will deliver the afterbirth. Let this happen naturally (it can take up to 30 minutes). Do not interfere and do not cut the cord. The doctor and midwife will need to check that the afterbirth is complete.

Premature labour

About one baby in 10 in the UK is born before the 37th week of pregnancy. If it is close to 37 weeks, the birth may proceed as normal, **but it is vital to get the mother to hospital**. Some labours start earlier for a number of reasons. If contractions begin well before the baby is due, it may be possible for doctors to stop them with drugs. The mother will also be given steroid injections to help the baby's lungs, so she can breathe properly after the birth.

 WARNING
● If the umbilical cord is around the baby's neck as she emerges try to ease it over the head to prevent strangulation. Do not pull on the cord.
● If the baby does not cry or make a sound after being born, do not slap her. Open the airway and check breathing (see page 14). Be prepared to begin CPR if she is not breathing (see page 16).
● If the bleeding is profuse after the third stage, or the mother is in any pain, keep her warm and lie her down with her legs raised and supported as there is a risk of shock developing (see pages 38–39).

suspected miscarriage

A miscarriage is the loss of a foetus at any time during the first 23 weeks of pregnancy, but most happen during the first 12 weeks. As a miscarriage can happen without warning, and may result in serious blood loss, treat it as an emergency. The loss of a pregnancy can have a serious emotional impact, so the woman will need reassurance and support.

assessment

Miscarriage is very common, especially in the first 12 weeks of pregnancy. Symptoms may be similar to a normal menstrual period.

Vaginal bleeding – occasionally severe

Abdominal pain and low backache – similar to period pain

Possible severe cramping pains – similar to labour pains

ADDITIONAL SYMPTOMS
- In some cases, bleeding may be slight and develop over a few days
- Blood clots may be passed
- **If blood loss is severe or has been prolonged, symptoms of shock may be evident** (see pages 38–39)
- The casualty may say she has passed some tissue during the bleeding
- The casualty may become very distressed

action

1 REASSURE THE WOMAN If you suspect that a pregnant woman is having a miscarriage, arrange for some privacy. Help her to lie down in a comfortable position. Make sure she has a sanitary towel, or a small, clean towel, if she needs one. Do not give her a tampon. Assess the level of bleeding.

2 CALL FOR HELP If bleeding is slight, advise her to call her doctor or midwife. If bleeding is severe, call the emergency services or take her to hospital.

3 MONITOR THE CASUALTY Check and make a note of her level of consciousness, breathing and pulse (see page 30). Check regularly until medical help arrives. If the woman becomes very weak and/or collapses, treat as for shock. Raise and support her legs and cover her with a blanket to keep her warm.

 TAKE CARE
- Preserve any tissue that a woman passes and give it to the medical team attending her.
- All bleeding in pregnancy should be assessed by a midwife and/or doctor. Bleeding during pregnancy does not necessarily mean the woman is having a miscarriage. Occasional light bleeding in the first 12 weeks of pregnancy is not uncommon; many women go on to have a healthy pregnancy.

WARNING

If a newly pregnant woman complains of very severe abdominal pain, particularly if it is one-sided, call the emergency services, or take her straight to the hospital. This could be an ectopic pregnancy (when the foetus is developing outside the womb), which is a medical emergency.

ACCIDENTS AND INJURIES

choking

If a small object 'goes down the wrong way', it can block the airway and cause muscle spasm. This can be life-threatening as the air passages that lead to the lungs become partially or totally blocked. Elderly people are at particular risk as they often have difficulty chewing food. Young children are also apt to put small objects in their mouths.

assessment

If the casualty can still cough, do not intervene as there is a risk that the obstruction could get into the lungs. There may be another cause for the cough so ask the casualty if choking is the reason. Look out for the following symptoms of breathing difficulty:

- Casualty suddenly starts coughing, gasping for breath and has difficulty talking
- Skin becomes grey-blue (known as cyanosis). This is especially noticeable at the ears, lips, inside the mouth and fingertips (see page 40)

 WARNING

Act quickly to clear the obstruction or the casualty will lose consciousness. If the casualty becomes unconscious, open the airway and check breathing (see pages 14–19). The throat will relax, which may free the blockage or open up the airway for rescue breaths.

ADULT AND CHILD (AGED 1 TO PUBERTY)
- If the airway is partially blocked, the casualty will be able to speak, cough and breathe
- If the airway is completely blocked, the casualty will not be able to talk, cough or breathe

BABY (0–12 MONTHS)
- If the airway is partially blocked, the baby can cough but will find it difficult to cry or even to make a noise
- If the airway is completely blocked, the baby will not make a sound and will stop breathing

 SAFETY FIRST WITH YOUNG CHILDREN
- Keep toys with small pieces out of reach of very young children – check the CE label for suitability.
- Do not give a young child small, hard or chewy sweets or nuts.
- Stay with your child while he is eating.
- Make sure your child is sitting down whenever he is eating and/or drinking.
- Purée or mash food for a baby until he learns to chew properly.
- When a young child starts wanting to feed himself, give him soft or well-cooked foods to eat.
- Remove fruit pips.
- Do not leave a baby alone with his bottle or drink.

 TAKE CARE
Elderly people who are infirm need special attention at mealtimes. Make sure that they are seated, give them small spoonfuls of food and check that their mouth is completely clear when the meal is finished.

Stay with a young child at mealtimes and help him to eat.

action

ADULT/CHILD

1 **CLEAR A PARTIALLY OBSTRUCTED AIRWAY** Tell her to cough and clear an obstruction herself if she can.

2 **GIVE BACK BLOWS** If the airway is completely blocked, help her to bend forwards and support her upper body. Give five sharp back blows between the shoulder blades with the heel of your hand, then check her mouth.

3 **GIVE ABDOMINAL THRUSTS** If she is still choking, place your arms around her body, with one fist against the abdomen. Grasp the fist with your other hand and pull inwards and upwards up to five times. Check her mouth again.

4 **GET EMERGENCY HELP** If necessary, repeat steps 2 and 3 up to three times. If the obstruction has not been cleared, call the emergency services. Continue with the back blows and abdominal thrusts until help arrives or the casualty loses consciousness.

⚠ WARNING

● Check the person's mouth after every set of back slaps and abdominal thrusts or chest thrusts. Pick out anything obvious. **Don't sweep a finger around the mouth** to look for an object as you may push it further down the throat or damage the tissues.
● Anyone who has been given abdominal thrusts or chest thrusts must be seen by a doctor.

BABY

1 **GIVE BACK BLOWS** If a baby cannot breathe, lay her face down along your forearm, supporting her head. Using the heel of one hand, give her five sharp blows between her shoulder blades.

2 **CHECK MOUTH**
Turn the baby over onto your other arm. Cradle her head in your hand and keep it as low as possible. Look inside her mouth. If the mouth is not clear, go to step 3.

3 **GIVE CHEST THRUSTS** Keeping the baby along your forearm, support your arm along or across your thigh. Place two fingers a finger's breadth below the nipple line and press sharply inward and upward up to five times.

4 **GET EMERGENCY HELP** Repeat steps 1 to 3 up to three times. If the mouth is still not clear, take the baby with you and call the emergency services. Continue back blows and chest thrusts until help arrives. If the baby loses consciousness, prepare to give CPR, see page 19.

▶▶See also: **UNCONSCIOUS ADULT/CHILD/BABY** pp14–19

blow to the head

Any blow to the head is potentially serious. A comparatively minor bump could affect a person's level of consciousness. Brain tissue or blood vessels inside the skull could also be damaged but the effects may not be apparent. A person may appear to be fine, then develop a headache or collapse later on. Anyone with a head injury may also have a spine injury.

assessment

Stay with a casualty who has sustained a head injury. Assess her carefully. In particular, watch for any change in her condition. Signs of potentially serious injury to look out for include:

Mild headache initially that becomes progressively worse, or sudden severe headache

No recollection of recent events and/or the incident

ADDITIONAL SYMPTOMS
- A brief period of unconsciousness after a blow to the head
- Serious wound to any part of the face or head
- Depressed area of the skull following an injury indicates a possible skull fracture. There may also be watery blood leaking from the nose or ear
- Breathing becomes noisy and/or slow
- Slow, but strong pulse
- Pupils (the black part of the eyes) become unequal in size
- Casualty becomes drowsy; **she may become unconscious**

Confusion and uncharacteristic behaviour; she may become very irritable

⚠ TAKE CARE
- Do not let a casualty go home on her own after a head injury.
- Do not give any alcohol. Seek medical advice if the casualty needs to take prescription medication.

The risks of head injury

- **CONCUSSION** A blow to the head can cause the brain to be shaken within the skull – known as concussion. This shaking causes a temporary disturbance in the brain, which can result in the casualty becoming unconscious for a short time. The casualty normally recovers completely but may not remember what happened. However, a more serious brain injury – Compression (see right) – could develop later.

- **COMPRESSION** Compression injury results when there is a build-up of pressure against the brain within the skull. This can follow a severe blow to the head that results in skull fracture. But, for example, it can be caused by bleeding between the brain and the skull after an apparently minor blow, swelling within the brain, a stroke or a brain tumour. Symptoms may be apparent immediately or may develop hours or even days later. It is life-threatening; the casualty will deteriorate and almost always needs surgery.

GET HELP It is always better to be safe – seek medical advice even if the casualty appears to be unharmed by the blow to the head.

TIME TO ACT A person who is injured on the sports field should rest and must not be allowed to 'play on' even if he claims to have recovered.

WATCHPOINT If the casualty needs medical treatment, do not give him anything to eat or drink as he may need an anaesthetic. If he is thirsty, moisten his lips with water.

action

1 SIT CASUALTY DOWN Assess the casualty's level of consciousness. If he is fully conscious, help him to sit down, ideally on the floor, so that he cannot fall. Make him comfortable.

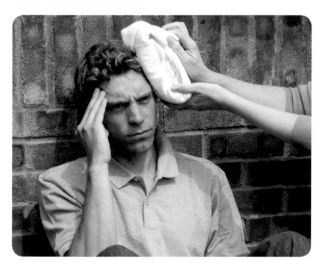

2 PLACE COLD PACK ON INJURY Give him a pack of ice (wrapped in a cloth) to place against the injury. If the person was knocked out, even if only for a very short time, seek medical advice.

3 MONITOR CASUALTY Tell the casualty to rest quietly. Stay with him. If he does not recover completely within half an hour, or begins to deteriorate at any point (see opposite), call the emergency services at once. If a casualty remains conscious, make sure that someone stays with him for at least 24 hours after the injury.

 WARNING
If the casualty is not fully conscious, help him to lie down and place him in the recovery position. Call the emergency services. Check for likely Back or Neck Injury (see pages 84–85).

If there is a scalp wound

● **APPLY DIRECT PRESSURE** Place a sterile pad over the wound and apply pressure directly over it. Help the casualty onto the floor into a half-sitting position so that her head is positioned above her heart.

● **BANDAGE** Secure the pad with a bandage wrapped around the head to maintain pressure on the wound (see also Wounds and Bleeding, pages 96–97). Take the casualty to hospital or call for emergency help.

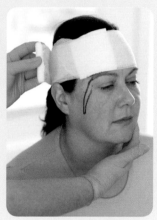

what next?

Severe head injuries always require treatment in hospital. The casualty will be assessed by the medical team and diagnosis will be confirmed with brain scans. Surgery may be required. Further treatment will depend on the severity of the injury.

 TAKE CARE
Children are particularly prone to head injuries as they have high energy levels and little sense of danger. To protect a child from head injuries when cycling, he should always wear a cycling helmet.

back and neck injury

The column of bones (vertebrae) in the back and neck supports the body and protects the delicate spinal cord. A back or neck injury can fracture one or more of the vertebrae or injure the muscles. Serious injury can damage the spinal cord, which could result in permanent loss of movement to any part of the body below that point.

assessment

If a person falls awkwardly onto his head, back or neck, suspect spine injury until you are told otherwise. **It is safer to immobilise him than risk permanent injury by moving him.** Look for:

Fall from a height – for example, off a ladder, down the stairs or from a horse

Severe pain in the neck or back

Signs of head injury

ADDITIONAL SYMPTOMS
- Feeling of heaviness in the limbs, or inability to move or feel them
- Inability to move or feel any part of the body
- Signs of loss of bladder control
- Possible irregularity along spine

⚠ WARNING
- Do not move the casualty unless his life is in immediate danger.
- If the person is unconscious, do not tilt the head to open the airway, use the jaw thrust (see box, opposite). Then check his breathing.

After a traffic incident

- **ASSUME THERE IS A NECK INJURY** The type of incident will give you an indication of the likely injury. In a car accident, the force of the collision may have propelled the casualty's body forwards and then back, resulting in a whiplash injury.
- **SUPPORT THE HEAD** Sit behind the casualty if possible and place a hand on each side of her head, without covering her ears (see right). Maintain this support until help arrives.
- **GET HELP** Ask someone to call the emergency services while you stay with the casualty.

action

1 CALL EMERGENCY HELP Reassure the casualty and ideally ask someone else to call the emergency services while you support the head.

2 IMMOBILISE CASUALTY Kneel or lie behind her head, place your elbows on your knees or on the ground. Leaving her head in the position you found her, place your hands on either side of her head to support it. Be careful not to cover her ears as she needs to hear you talking to her.

3 GET EXTRA SUPPORT Ask someone to get some rolled blankets, towels or coats and place them on either side of the casualty's head for additional support until the emergency services arrive.

4 MONITOR CASUALTY Stay at her head and ask your helper to check and make a note of her level of consciousness, breathing and pulse (see page 30). Re-check regularly until medical help arrives.

Opening the airway of a neck injury casualty

If a casualty with suspected back or neck injury is not breathing, do not tilt the head to open the airway, as it is important to keep her back and neck in a straight line. Instead, use a technique called the jaw thrust.

- **SUPPORT CASUALTY'S HEAD** Resting your elbows on your knees or on the ground, place your hands on either side of her head and keep it in line with her body.

- **PUSH THE JAW UPWARDS** Place your fingertips on either side at the angle of the lower jaw and 'push' it upwards (towards the ceiling) and forwards.
- **CHECK BREATHING** Look, listen and feel for signs of breathing for no more than 10 seconds (see page 14). Be prepared to begin CPR (see pages 16–19).

▶▶See also: **UNCONSCIOUS ADULT/CHILD/BABY** pp14–19 • **BLOW TO THE HEAD** pp82–83

injured **lower limb**

An injury to the pelvis or lower limb – thigh, knee and lower leg – is most commonly caused by a fall on a hard surface. Sprains and broken bones are most common, while an injury to the pelvis or thighbone may lead to internal bleeding and shock.

WATCHPOINT Do not give the casualty anything to eat or drink as he may need treatment requiring an anaesthetic when he reaches hospital.

assessment

Always compare the injured and the uninjured legs when assessing the severity of an injury. It is always safer to treat the injury as a break. Signs and symptoms to look out for include:

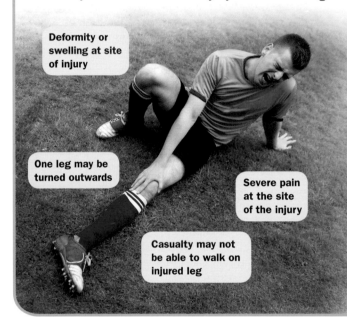

Deformity or swelling at site of injury

One leg may be turned outwards

Severe pain at the site of the injury

Casualty may not be able to walk on injured leg

ADDITIONAL SYMPTOMS
● One leg may be shorter than the other; this is most likely following a fractured thigh as the large muscles contract around the bone ends
● Possible shock if a large bone, such as the thigh, is broken (see pages 38–39).

⚠ WARNING
● Do not allow a casualty with a lower limb injury to walk. He must be taken to hospital on a stretcher. Call the emergency services as soon as possible.
● Avoid unnecessary movement as the broken bone ends can damage any blood vessels or nerves alongside the injured area.

Folding triangular bandages

Folded lengthwise, these bandages can be used to provide support to an injured lower or upper limb. Narrow-fold bandages can also be used to help maintain pressure to control bleeding if you do not have a roller bandage. Open triangular bandages are used as slings, but do not exert enough pressure to control bleeding.

1 LAY BANDAGE FLAT
Lay the bandage out on a flat surface with the longest edge facing you. Bring the top point down to touch the base.

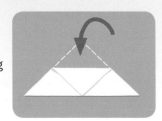

2 BROAD-FOLD BANDAGE
Fold the bandage in half again to make a broad-fold bandage used to 'splint' an injured limb to an uninjured part of the body.

3 NARROW-FOLD BANDAGE Fold the bandage in half again. This narrow bandage is used to tie the feet and ankles together.

action

LEG INJURY

1 SUPPORT INJURED LEG
Do not let the casualty walk. Hold the joints above and below the site of the injury. Ask a helper to put rolled blankets or towels either side of the injured leg.

2 CALL EMERGENCY HELP Ideally ask someone to make the call while you reassure the casualty and support the injured leg.

3 WHEN HELP IS DELAYED Provide extra support to the injured leg by immobilising it. Place soft padding between the legs and bring the uninjured leg to the injured one. Secure the feet and ankles using a narrow-fold bandage (see box, opposite) tied

securely in a figure of eight to prevent further movement. If you have help, ask the other person to do this for you while you support the joints.

4 ADD THREE MORE BANDAGES Slide three Broad-fold bandages (see box, opposite) under the natural hollows of the knees and ankles. Move the bandages into position: the first **A** around the knees, the second **B** above the fracture site and the third

C below it. You must avoid the fracture site. The photograph above shows a fractured lower leg. Tie Reef Knots (see box, right) against the uninjured leg or over the padding in the centre.

⚠ WARNING

● If there is a wound at the site of the break, or a bone is exposed, cover it with a piece of gauze, then build up padding either side of the bone until it is higher than the bone. Secure with a bandage.
● If the injury is near the ankle then, instead of a figure-of-eight bandage, use two narrow-fold bandages – one around the leg and one around the feet.
● If the injury is near the upper thigh, position the bandage above the injury so that it is around the hips, avoiding the fracture site.
● Stop bandaging if doing so causes the casualty discomfort. Immobilise the limb with rolled coats, blankets or cushions and wait for medical help.
● Always check the circulation in the limb beyond the bandages (page 93). If it is restricted, loosen the bandages and reapply or support as above.

Tying a reef knot

A reef knot is used for tying bandages. It lies flat so that it is comfortable as well as secure.

1 RIGHT OVER LEFT
Take the right-hand end over the left-hand end and pass it underneath.

2 LEFT OVER RIGHT
Then pass what is now the left-hand end over the right-hand end and under.

3 PULL TIGHT Pull the ends gently to tighten the knot.

4 TO UNDO THE KNOT
Hold the strands on one side of the knot (either both of the blue or both orange). Sharply pull both ends away from each other at the same time. Slide the straight section out of the knot.

PELVIC INJURY

1 HELP CASUALTY TO LIE DOWN **Do not let the casualty walk.** Help him to lie down on his back if he is not lying down already. Carefully slide some folded towels, a cushion or a rolled coat under his knees to raise them slightly. Stop if this causes the casualty any discomfort.

2 IMMOBILISE LEGS Place soft padding between the knees and ankles. For extra comfort, slide a folded triangular bandage (see Narrow-fold Bandage, page 86) under his ankles. Tie the bandage in a figure of eight around his feet and ankles to immobilise the legs and secure with a reef knot tied against the soles of his shoes.

3 IMMOBILISE LEGS Tie a second triangular bandage (see Broad-fold Bandage, page 86) around the knees for additional support.

4 CALL EMERGENCY HELP The casualty needs to be transported in the treatment position. Monitor him while you are waiting. Keep his head low to minimise the risk of shock as there may be severe internal bleeding following a pelvic injury.

 WARNING

A casualty with a leg injury must be taken to hospital on a stretcher. Call the emergency services as soon as possible.

 TAKE CARE

Do not move the casualty unless his life is in immediate danger. Even then the legs must be immobilised and supported beforehand.

KNEE INJURY

1 HELP CASUALTY TO LIE DOWN **Do not let the casualty walk.** Help her to lie down on her back with her knee in a comfortable position, probably slightly bent. She is likely to be in severe pain. Support the knee with pillows or rolled coats.

2 FOR EXTRA SUPPORT Wrap some soft padding, such as cotton wool, around the knee and, if possible, secure it with a roller bandage that extends from mid calf to mid thigh. Stop immediately if this causes further pain.

3 CALL EMERGENCY HELP The casualty needs to be transported on a stretcher in the treatment position (steps 1 and 2 above). Monitor the casualty while you are waiting for help to arrive.

Additional support

Occasionally it may be necessary to provide additional support to a casualty who has a thigh injury – if for example you have to wait a long time for help. In this instance it can help to place a splint along the outside of the body.

• **SUITABLE MATERIALS** Use something sturdy but not too bulky – a fence post, broom handle or walking stick are ideal. The splint needs to extend from the casualty's armpits to the feet. For additional comfort, place padding between the object and the limb before securing it.
• **SECURING THE SPLINT** Place the padding against the injured side and position the splint. Secure it using seven folded triangular bandages. Slide them under the natural hollows of the body and move them into position. Tie the first, a narrow-fold bandage (see page 86) around the feet and ankles, then tie six broad-fold bandages as follows: the first around the knees, then around chest, pelvis, above and below the fracture site, and, finally, a bandage around the lower legs.

injured **upper limb**

Normally, considerable force is needed to break a bone, but force can also pull a joint out of place (dislocation), injure the bands of tissue, called ligaments, that hold a joint together (sprain) or tear or strain a muscle. If in doubt, treat this kind of injury as a break, as broken bone ends can damage surrounding tissues.

assessment

Unless you can see a bone end in a wound, it is impossible to know if a bone is broken without an X-ray. If any of the following symptoms are present, immobilise the injured limb and take or send the person to hospital:

- Deformity or swelling at the site of injury; compare injured and uninjured arms
- Pain increased by movement
- Casualty may be unable to bend the arm
- If the casualty is supporting the arm and leaning towards the injured side, suspect injury to the collarbone or shoulder
- If one shoulder looks flatter when compared with the opposite one, the joint may be dislocated
- Possible wound near the broken bone
- Bone end may be protruding

 TAKE CARE

- If there is a wound, cover it with a dressing to protect it from infection and control bleeding by applying direct pressure (see pages 96–97). If the bone is visible, press either side of the wound. Immobilise the joints above and below the wound, then raise and support the arm.
- Always immobilise the injury before transporting a person to minimise the risk of further injury.

Improvising slings

A sling can be improvised by using a scarf folded in half diagonally. Depending on the site of the injury you may also be able to use the casualty's clothing.

- **JACKET 'SLING'** If the casualty is wearing a jacket, undo the fastenings. Ask the casualty to support the injured arm and fold the lower half of the jacket up over the injured arm, making sure the elbow is supported. Secure the hem of the jacket to the top half with a safety pin. This is ideal for an injured forearm, wrist or hand as it provides the most support.
If the casualty has an upper arm injury, partially unbutton or unzip the jacket and slide the hand

into the jacket opening. Secure the zip with a safety pin. Do not use this 'sling' for a casualty who has a forearm or wrist injury as it does not provide sufficient support.
- **SLEEVE 'SLING'** Help the casualty to support the arm on the injured side in the most comfortable position, across the chest. Pin the sleeve cuff to the opposite side of the shirt or jacket. This can be useful for a shoulder or upper arm injury – do not use it if the casualty has a wrist injury.
- **BELT 'SLING'** Use a belt or long scarf folded into a thin strip. Fasten or tie into a loop, slip over the casualty's head and twist once to form a figure of eight. Slip the lower loop over the casualty's wrist. Do not use if the casualty has a wrist injury.

▶▶See also: **SHOCK** pp38–39 • **WOUNDS AND BLEEDING** pp96–97

action

SHOULDER/COLLARBONE

1 **SUPPORT ARM WITH AN ELEVATION SLING** Help the casualty to support the injured arm so that her fingers are touching the opposite shoulder. Place a triangular bandage over the arm with the longest edge parallel to her uninjured side **A** and the top point at her shoulder **B**. Tuck the longest edge under her injured arm.

2 **SECURE SLING AT THE SHOULDER** Carry the lower point around the casualty's back and up to the shoulder to meet the other point **C**. Tie the ends in a reef knot just in front of the collarbone.

⚠ WARNING
● Any casualty with a suspected fracture or a dislocated joint must be taken to hospital for treatment. You can take the casualty yourself if you have transport.
● Always immobilise the injury before transporting the casualty. This minimises the risk of further injury and is more comfortable for the casualty.

3 **SECURE THE CORNER** Twist the corner of the bandage at the elbow **D** until it fits the elbow snugly and tuck in the end to secure the sling.

4 **TAKE TO HOSPITAL** If possible take the casualty to hospital yourself, or call the emergency services if you have no transport.

⚠ TAKE CARE
● For comfort, place a broad-fold bandage (see page 86) around the injured arm and upper body. Tie the knot against the chest on the uninjured side.
● Check the circulation in the thumb (see page 93) after securing the sling. If it is restricted, loosen the sling and reapply, or simply support by hand.
● Do not give the casualty anything to eat or drink as he may need an anaesthetic later.

Children and the elderly

● **CHILDREN AND BABIES** Children's bones are still growing so are softer than an adult's. As a result, the force that might break an adult's bone may cause a child's bone to partially break on one side and bend on the other, like a twig. This is known as a greenstick fracture. The injury needs to be treated in the same way as any other break.
● **ELDERLY PEOPLE** Conversely, the bones of an elderly person are more fragile and it can take comparatively little force to break a bone.

ARM INJURY

1 **SUPPORT ARM** Gently place the casualty's arm across her body. Encourage her to support it herself, help her if necessary. Help her to sit down.

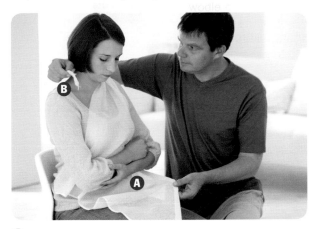

2 **IMMOBILISE WITH AN ARM SLING** Carefully slide a triangular bandage between the casualty's arm and her chest so that the longest side is along the uninjured side **A**. Take the top corner around the back of the casualty's neck to the front of the shoulder on the injured side **B**.

3 **PROTECT INJURY** Wrap soft padding – a small towel for example, around the site of the injury for extra support. Bring the lower part of the triangular bandage **C** up over the arm and tie a reef knot just over the hollow in front of the shoulder.

4 **SECURE** Twist the excess fabric **D** at the elbow so that the sling fits around it, then tuck the end into the fabric. The weight of the arm in the sling will hold it in place.

5 **TAKE TO HOSPITAL** If possible take the casualty to hospital yourself, or call the emergency services if you have no transport.

INJURY NEAR ELBOW

1 **SUPPORT ARM** If the injury is near the elbow the casualty will not be able to bend his arm. Help him to sit down and support his arm in the position that feels most comfortable. Tell him to avoid unnecessary movement. If one or more bones are broken, the jagged ends could damage the blood vessels or nerves around the joint.

2 **PROTECT ARM** Wrap soft padding around the outside of the joint – a small towel is ideal.

3 **IMMOBILISE THE INJURY** For additional comfort, tie two broad-fold bandages, (see page 86) or large scarves around the arm and body. Place one bandage above the elbow and the other around the forearm.

4 **CHECK THE CIRCULATION** Check the pulse at the wrist and loosen the bandages if there is no pulse.

5 **TAKE TO HOSPITAL** If possible take the casualty to hospital yourself or call the emergency services if you have no transport.

⚠ WARNING

If there is a wound, cover it with a dressing to minimise the risk of infection and bandage it in place. If there is a bone sticking out of the wound, loosely drape a piece of gauze over the top. Place padding on either side and bandage over the top.

wrist and hand injury

A typical wrist and hand injury results from a fall onto an outstretched hand, when a bone in the forearm is broken at the wrist. Known as a colles fracture, it is most common in the elderly. Wrists may also be sprained, and the small bones in the wrist, hand or fingers may be injured through crushing, in which case bleeding can be profuse.

assessment

It is difficult to tell whether the wrist is sprained or a bone is broken without an X-ray. **If in doubt, always take the casualty to hospital.** Look for:

- Severe pain at the site of injury, increased by movement
- Swelling, and later bruising, around the injured area
- Open wound and bleeding following a crush injury (see pages 102–103)

 **TAKE CARE**

- Cover a wound with a sterile dressing to protect it from infection and control bleeding by applying direct pressure (see pages 96–97). If the bone is visible, press on either side of the wound
- If a casualty's hand has been crushed and is still trapped, free it only if you know the incident happened recently (see page 102).

action

1 SUPPORT ARM Gently place the casualty's arm across her body. Encourage her to support it herself. Help her to sit down. If the casualty has injured her hand, treat any wounds (see page 96).

2 IMMOBILISE FOREARM IN AN ARM SLING Slide a triangular bandage between the casualty's arm and her chest so that the longest side is parallel with the uninjured side. Take the top corner around the casualty's neck to the front of the shoulder on the other side.

3 PROTECT INJURY Place soft padding around the site of injury for extra support. Bring the lower part of the bandage up over the arm and secure the sling in front of the shoulder (see page 91).

4 TAKE TO HOSPITAL If the casualty is uncomfortable, provide extra support by securing the arm to the body with a broad-fold bandage (see page 86). You can take the casualty to hospital or call the emergency services if you have no transport.

 WARNING

- If there is a wound on the hand, treat any bleeding (see page 96), raise the hand and support it with an elevation sling (see page 90).
- After immobilising the arm, check for a pulse at the wrist. If there is no pulse, remove the sling and support the injury by hand and/or cushions.

sprained ankle

A sprain occurs when one or more of the ligaments have been stretched, twisted or torn – it is the most common ankle injury. In a minor sprain, some of the fibres within the ligament are stretched. In more serious sprains, the ligament may be torn. Minor sprains can be treated at home. Serious sprains need medical attention and may even require surgery.

assessment

A sprained ankle is a common injury and the pain can be excruciating. If in doubt, take a casualty to hospital for an X-ray. Look for:

● With a severe injury, the casualty may not be able to bear weight on the leg
● Pain in and around the joint – the casualty may feel faint with the pain
● Swelling, and later bruising, around the joint

 TAKE CARE

Use **RICE** to remember treatment steps
R – Rest
I – Ice
C – Compression
E – Elevation

action

1 REST LEG The casualty should stop the activity that caused the injury. Help her to sit down and rest the ankle. Support it in a raised position.

2 COOL WITH ICE Cool the injury to reduce pain and swelling. Make a cold compress (see page 108). Ideally wrap a bag of ice or frozen peas in a cloth and place it on the ankle. Do not put ice straight onto the skin as it will cause a cold burn. Leave the ice in place for about 20 minutes.

3 COMPRESSION Leave the compress in place if it is small or wrap a layer of soft padding, such as a roll of cotton wool, around the ankle. Apply pressure with a compression support or compression bandage to help limit swelling. This should extend from the toes to the knee.

4 ELEVATE ANKLE Raise and support the ankle so that it is higher than the hip to prevent swelling. Advise the casualty to rest the ankle. **If you suspect serious injury, take the casualty to hospital.**

5 CHECK CIRCULATION Make sure that the bandage is not too tight. Press on a toenail until it turns white, then let go: the colour should return quickly. If it does not return, the bandage is too tight; remove it and reapply. Re-check every 10 minutes.

 TAKE CARE

Reapply the cold compress over the bandage every two to three hours. Remove the bandage at night and do not sleep with an ice pack on the injury.

▶▶See also: **INJURIED LOWER LIMB** pp86–88 • **SEVERE BRUISING** pp108–109

chest injury

A framework of bones called the ribcage surrounds and protects the organs of the chest as well as major blood vessels. The chest may be injured by an external force from a fall or traffic incident or even during an assault. It is important to immobilise the injured side as if a rib is broken, the bone end could pierce a lung, blood vessel or the chest wall.

assessment

Anyone with a suspected rib injury should be assessed at hospital. Sometimes the ribs are not broken, but there is bruising of ribs or nearby muscles. Rib fractures may (but don't always) show on a chest X-ray. If a rib fracture is suspected, the main purpose of the X-ray is to look for complications rather than to diagnose the fracture itself.

SYMPTOMS AND SIGNS OF CHEST INJURY
- Possible chest wound near site of injury
- Pain in one or both sides of the chest worsened by movement, breathing or coughing
- Swelling and deformity at site of injury may indicate a fractured rib
- Wound on the chest caused by fractured rib or injury that pierces chest wall, such as stabbing
- Evidence of bruising on injured side

Is it serious?

A chest injury is potentially serious as it can cause breathing difficulties. If a wound penetrates the chest wall, air can enter and a lung could collapse. The following are emergencies:

- **GASPING FOR BREATH** Symptoms of breathing difficulty (see page 40): person may be coughing, gasping for breath and find it difficult to talk. Skin becomes grey-blue (known as cyanosis). This is especially noticeable at the ears, lips, inside the mouth and at the fingertips.
- **FLAIL CHEST** Normal chest movement may be reversed over the damaged area on the injured side. This is known as flail chest.

- **RAPID BREATHING** Breathing may become fast and shallow; the casualty appears frightened, while struggling to breathe.
- **WOUND TO CHEST WALL** This can be caused by a broken rib or an injury that pierces the chest wall.
- **COUGHING UP BLOOD** If a lung is injured, the casualty may cough up bright red frothy blood and tell you there is a crackling sound. You may see blood bubbling from a wound and hear air being sucked in and out of it.
- **GOES INTO SHOCK** Symptoms and signs of shock may be evident (see page 38).

GET HELP If a casualty develops breathing difficulties after sustaining a chest injury, call the emergency services straight away.

TIME TO ACT Do not give the casualty anything to eat or drink as he may need treatment requiring an anaesthetic later at the hospital.

WATCHPOINT A broken or bruised rib usually heals in about four weeks. Good pain relief, such as paracetamol or ibuprofen, helps the person to breathe and cough more easily.

action

IF THERE IS A WOUND

1 PLACE IN HALF-SITTING POSITION Help the casualty to sit on the floor. Place a sterile pad against the wound and ask the casualty to hold it against him. Lean him towards the injured side and support him with cushions.

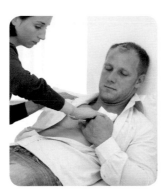

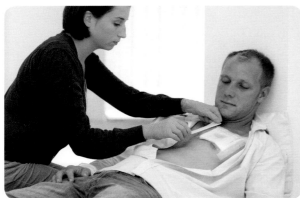

2 COVER WOUND Place a sterile dressing over the wound. Cover the dressing with a sheet of polythene or kitchen foil, secured with tape on three sides only. This allows air to escape from the chest but also prevents more from being sucked into the wound. The covering should be taut.

3 CALL EMERGENCY HELP Call the emergency services. Check and make a note of the casualty's level of consciousness, breathing and pulse (see page 30). Re-check regularly until medical help arrives. If the person needs to be put in the recovery position, place him on his injured side as this helps to stabilise the chest wall.

NO EXTERNAL WOUND

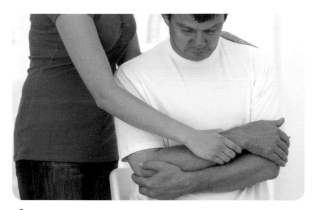

1 SUPPORT ARM ON INJURED SIDE Tell the casualty to support the arm on the injured side; help him if necessary. Encourage him to sit down. Support the arm in a sling (see page 91) to stabilise the chest wall and minimise the risk of further damage.

2 TAKE TO HOSPITAL You can take the casualty to hospital yourself or call the emergency services if you have no transport.

 TAKE CARE
If there is a wound, protect yourself and the casualty by wearing nonlatex disposable gloves.

 WARNING
If a casualty becomes unconscious, open the airway and check breathing (see pages 14–19). If he needs to be placed in the recovery position, roll him onto his injured side as this helps to stabilise the injured chest wall and enables the uninjured lung to work normally.

▶▶See also: **UNCONSCIOUS ADULT/CHILD/BABY** pp14–19 • **SHOCK** p38

wounds and bleeding

A wound is a break in the skin that allows blood to escape from the body. Bleeding is potentially serious as fluid is lost from the circulatory system. Bleeding from the smallest blood vessels – the capillaries – is usually minor. However, if the larger vessels, the arteries and veins, are damaged, significant life-threatening blood loss can result very quickly.

assessment

The principles of first aid are the same whatever the site of blood loss. Blood loss is faster when a larger vessel is damaged.

- Blood loss from an artery is often bright red and, if a major vessel is damaged, blood may be spurting from the wound in time with the heart beat
- Blood loss from a vein will be darker red and, if a larger vein is damaged, may gush profusely
- In some parts of the body, nerves and tendons can run very close to blood vessels and may be damaged. As a result the casualty may experience loss of movement or feeling

 TAKE CARE

- **Always wear nonlatex disposable gloves if you have them** to protect yourself and the casualty from infection.
- Always seek medical advice if a person who is taking a blood-thinning medication (anticoagulants) for a medical condition has a minor injury as he will bleed more profusely.
- Apply pressure directly over an injury or on either side if there is an object stuck in the wound (see page 100). Never use indirect pressure as it will cut off the blood supply.

 WARNING

- If signs of shock appear (see page 38), call the emergency services immediately. Make a note of the casualty's level of consciousness, breathing and pulse (see page 30). Re-check regularly until medical help arrives.
- If blood seeps through a dressing, cover it with another one, secured with a second bandage. If blood comes through the second bandage, you may not be applying pressure at the right point. Take off both dressings and apply a new one.

action

SEVERE BLEEDING

1 APPLY DIRECT PRESSURE Place a sterile wound dressing or clean pad against the wound and press firmly. Remove or cut away clothing to expose the wound if necessary.

2 RAISE AND SUPPORT INJURY Raise the injured part so that it is higher than the casualty's heart. This will slow down the blood flow to the area.

3 TREAT FOR SHOCK Help the casualty to lie down, while keeping the injured area raised and supported. Raise and support her legs above the level of her heart, on a chair for example. This reduces the risk of shock (see pages 38–39). Keep the legs straight and rest her ankles or heels on the chair to prevent blood pooling in her legs.

4 BANDAGE Tie a bandage around the dressing. Support an arm in a sling (see pages 90–91) for extra support. Call the emergency services.

WOUND ON THE PALM

1 COVER WOUND WITH DRESSING PAD Place a large sterile dressing pad into the palm of the casualty's hand, preferably the type with a bandage attached. Ask her to clench her fist tightly over the pad to apply pressure. Raise and support her hand.

2 SECURE DRESSING Wind the bandage around the casualty's clenched fist, leaving the thumb exposed. Secure the bandage over the top of the fingers to maintain pressure. Check the circulation in the thumb (see page 93).

AT INNER ELBOW OR KNEE

1 BEND ARM OR LEG Place a sterile dressing pad over the injury and bend the arm or leg over it to apply pressure. Raise the injured part to slow down the blood flow further.

2 CHECK CIRCULATION As raising the affected limb and applying pressure to the wound can severely reduce the blood supply to the rest of the limb, check the circulation in the lower arm or leg every 10 minutes, releasing the pressure if necessary.

 WARNING

● If the casualty becomes unconscious, open the airway and check for breathing (see pages 14–19). Be prepared to begin CPR (see page 16).
● Do not give the casualty anything to eat or drink as he may need an anaesthetic later.

Varicose veins

Veins in the legs have one-way valves that prevent back flow of blood as it returns from the tissues to the heart. If these valves fail, blood pools in the veins, resulting in varicose veins. The veins are often near the surface and can burst following a relatively minor knock, causing life-threatening profuse bleeding.

BLEEDING FROM VARICOSE VEINS

1 RAISE INJURED LEG Help the casualty to lie down on the floor and raise his leg as high as you can – this will immediately slow down the bleeding. Ideally, rest the leg on your shoulder.

2 APPLY DIRECT PRESSURE Keeping the leg raised, place a sterile dressing pad over the wound and press firmly until the bleeding is under control.

3 SECURE DRESSING If necessary, place another dressing and bandage over the first one. Bandage dressings firmly in place. To ensure the bandage is not too tight, check circulation in the foot (see page 93). If necessary, loosen the bandages and reapply.

4 CALL EMERGENCY HELP Call the emergency services as the casualty needs to go to hospital in the treatment position. Keep the leg raised until the medical team arrives.

 TAKE CARE

If a casualty is wearing elastic-topped stockings, remove them. Releasing the grip stops the bleeding.

gunshot wound

A gunshot can cause a life-threatening puncture wound. In addition to the entry wound, there may be an exit wound. A bullet can also bounce around inside the body, resulting in a deep pathway of damage within the body.

WATCHPOINT Do not give the casualty anything to eat or drink as he may need treatment that requires an anaesthetic. If he is thirsty, moisten his lips with water.

assessment

An entry wound on one side of the body that lines up with an exit wound on the other side does not mean that the bullet followed a straight path and internal damage could be erratic. The following are possible effects of a gunshot wound to look for:

- Possible entry wound and exit wound if a bullet passes through the body – it can be difficult to tell which is which, but this does not affect treatment
- Internal bleeding along the path of the bullet
- Severe external bleeding
- Sign of penetrating chest wound (see page 95)
- Internal organs may be damaged and protruding from the abdomen (see opposite)
- Signs and symptoms of shock may be evident (see page 38)
- Possible breathing difficulties, especially if the lungs are affected

 TAKE CARE

- Do not risk your own safety (see box, below).
- Wear nonlatex disposable gloves if you have them to protect yourself and the casualty.

 WARNING

If the casualty becomes unconscious, open the airway and check for signs of breathing (see pages 14–19). Be prepared to begin CPR (see page 16).

action

1 CALL EMERGENCY HELP Ask a helper to call emergency services and tell them it is a gunshot wound. Ambulance control will alert the police.

2 CONTROL BLEEDING Apply direct pressure over a sterile dressing to control bleeding (see page 96); bear in mind that there might be a second wound. Raise and support the affected part. If the wound is on the abdomen, position the casualty as shown in steps 2 and 3 (see opposite).

3 TREAT FOR SHOCK Help the casualty to lie down, keep his head low and raise and support his legs. If the wound is to the abdomen, position as step 3, opposite. Reassure him and make him as comfortable as possible.

4 SEAL CHEST WOUND If there is a chest wound, seal it on three sides with a dressing and foil or polythene (see page 95) to prevent air from being sucked into the wound.

5 MONITOR CASUALTY Check and make a note of the level of consciousness, breathing and pulse (see page 30). Re-check often until medical help arrives.

Safety at a crime scene

- **STAY SAFE** Any situation that involves a gun or stabbing is potentially dangerous. Do not approach the casualty unless you are certain that you are not putting your own life at risk. If you are not sure, call the emergency services and move to a safe distance. If possible, stay nearby as you may be needed as a witness.
- **PRESERVE ANY EVIDENCE This is a crime scene**. It is important that it is preserved so that the police can gather the evidence they need. If you have to move anything to help the casualty, tell the emergency services what you have done when they arrive.

stab wound

Stabbing causes a deep puncture wound. On the abdomen, a knife wound can pierce vital internal organs and damage major blood vessels. A casualty needs urgent medical help as these injuries can be life-threatening.

WATCHPOINT Do not give the casualty anything to eat or drink as he may need treatment that requires an anaesthetic. If he is thirsty, moisten his lips with water.

assessment

Your aim is to arrange to get the casualty to hospital as soon as possible, but if you are at a crime scene **remember that your own safety is paramount**. The effects of a stab wound are:

- Severe internal and external bleeding
- Penetrating chest wound (see page 95)
- Internal organs may be damaged and protruding from the abdomen
- Signs and symptoms of shock may be evident (see page 38)

 TAKE CARE

Wear nonlatex disposable gloves if you have them to protect yourself and the casualty.

 WARNING

- Do not risk your own safety (see box, opposite).
- If the casualty becomes unconscious, open the airway and check for signs of breathing (see pages 14–19). Be prepared to begin CPR (see page 16).
- If the abdominal contents are visible, do not touch them. If possible, cover to prevent them becoming dry. Use plastic kitchen film or, if not available, a sterile wound dressing or clean pad.

action

1 CALL EMERGENCY HELP Ask a helper to call emergency services and tell them that a person has been stabbed. Ambulance control will automatically alert the police.

2 CONTROL BLEEDING Apply direct pressure and, if possible, raise the affected part to help control bleeding (see page 96). If the wound is on the abdomen, help the casualty to lie down with his head low. Place a sterile dressing on the wound and press firmly against it.

3 RAISE CASUALTY'S KNEES To ease the strain on the abdomen, bend his knees slightly and place towels, cushions or rolled-up coats underneath them.

4 TREAT FOR SHOCK Help the casualty to lie down with his head low (see shock, pages 38–39). If necessary, raise and support his legs.

5 MONITOR CASUALTY Check and make a note of the level of consciousness, breathing and pulse (see page 30). Re-check often until medical help arrives.

▶▶See also: **SHOCK** pp38–39 • **CHEST INJURY** pp94–95 • **WOUNDS AND BLEEDING** pp96–97

glass wound

Broken glass causes incised wounds with clean-cut edges. This type of wound can bleed profusely. By acting quickly to give first aid you can reduce the amount of blood lost before taking the casualty to hospital.

WATCHPOINT Do not give the casualty anything to eat or drink as she may need an anaesthetic. If she is thirsty, moisten her lips with water.

assessment

The wound will need prompt attention, as well as stitches to help healing. Expect to find the following signs if there is a glass wound:

- There could be several wounds – treat the most severe first
- Possible bright red arterial bleeding at the wrist if a person has put an arm through the glass
- Symptoms of shock (see pages 38–39)
- Shards of glass on or embedded in a wound

 WARNING

Do not remove anything that is embedded in the wound as it could be plugging the wound and preventing additional blood loss.

⚠️ **TAKE CARE**

- Wear nonlatex disposable gloves if you have them to protect yourself and the casualty.
- Do not press down on the object as it will worsen the injury.
- Sweep up the broken glass, after helping the casualty, to prevent further injury.
- Dispose of the glass safely: wrap it in layers of newspaper and tape up the parcel.

action

1 MOVE CASUALTY Remove the person to safety away from the broken glass. Pick off any loose shards of glass.

2 CONTROL BLEEDING AND TREAT FOR SHOCK Apply direct pressure over a sterile dressing or clean pad and raise injured area to control bleeding (see page 96). Help the casualty to sit or lie down and raise the limb above the level of the heart.

3 IF GLASS IS EMBEDDED Do not remove the glass from the wound. Press either side of the piece of glass, pushing the edges of the wound together.

4 PROTECT WOUND Drape a piece of gauze loosely over the glass. Place padding either side of the piece of glass (roller bandages make excellent padding). If possible, build up the padding until it is higher than the glass.

5 SECURE PADDING Use another bandage to secure the padding. If you can build the padding up high enough, bandage over the top of the object, as shown here. If not, bandage securely on either side of the object.

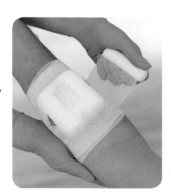

6 TAKE TO HOSPITAL You can take the casualty to hospital yourself or call the emergency services if you have no transport or if a stretcher is required.

gravel graze

The greatest danger from this type of wound is infection from bacteria in the gravel and soil. Bleeding may be controlled easily with direct pressure and elevation. Medical attention will be needed for a large or small graze where dirt has become embedded in the wound. There is a risk of tetanus infection with any dirty wound.

assessment

Points to note when checking the casualty:

- The wound may be extensive and/or the bleeding severe
- The wound may be very dirty. Dirt may be plugging the bleeding, which may start only after all the dirt has been washed off

 WARNING
Do not try to remove anything embedded in the wound (see opposite). Seek medical advice.

The danger of tetanus

Tetanus is a potentially fatal bacterial infection that can develop when a particular bacterium (germ) found in soil enters your body via a wound or an animal bite. The risk is greatest if the wound is deep or there is manure in the soil, but even small wounds, such as a prick from a thorn, can cause tetanus.

Tetanus infection is rare in the UK because many people are vaccinated against it as part of the national immunisation programme. Four doses are given before school age and one between ages 13–18. These five doses give lifetime immunity. If the wound is dirty, seek medical advice if the casualty has never been immunised or is unsure how many injections have been given in the past.

 TAKE CARE
Tell the casualty to seek medical advice if a fever develops, the wound fails to heal, swelling or redness develops, or it feels hot as this may mean that the wound has become infected (see page 66).

action

1 CONTROL BLEEDING Apply direct pressure over a sterile wound dressing or clean pad and raise the injury to control the bleeding.

2 WASH WOUND Once the bleeding stops, remove the pad. Keep the injury raised and rinse the wound under cold running water to wash away any loose dirt. If there is no running water, use alcohol-free antiseptic wipes. Pat it dry.

3 CLEAN AROUND WOUND Gently place a fresh sterile dressing over the wound. Carefully wipe dirt from around the injury – you can use clean gauze pads. Use a separate pad for each stroke. Pat the area dry.

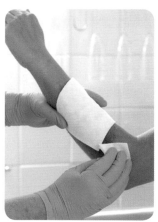

4 DRESS WOUND Cover the affected area with a plaster or a sterile wound dressing if the injury is extensive. If it has been thoroughly cleaned, the graze should heal on its own.

5 GO TO HOSPITAL All large wounds need medical attention, as does any wound with gravel embedded in it. Carefully cleaned minor injuries should heal naturally. Ask the casualty whether she has been immunised against tetanus (see box, left); if not, she should tell the hospital team or her own doctor.

▶▶See also: **INFECTED WOUND** p66 • **WOUNDS AND BLEEDING** pp96–97

crush injury

A crush injury occurs when a body part is squeezed between two heavy objects. It can follow an earthquake or explosion, or a traffic incident and the casualty may suffer internal and external bleeding, broken bones and shock.

GET HELP If a casualty is trapped, call the emergency services immediately. Tell them what has happened; they will bring specialist cutting and lifting equipment.

assessment

Your approach will depend on the cause of the crushing and how long the casualty has been trapped. Do not guess when the incident took place, ask the casualty and bystanders.

⚠ WARNING

Do not attempt to remove the weight from a casualty if you do not know how long ago the crushing incident occurred. Call for emergency help immediately.

⚠ TAKE CARE

● **Make sure that you are not putting yourself in any danger by approaching the casualty**.
● If you are releasing the casualty, ensure that you can lift the cause of crushing without injuring yourself or without putting yourself in danger.
● Protect yourself and the casualty with nonlatex disposable gloves if you have them.

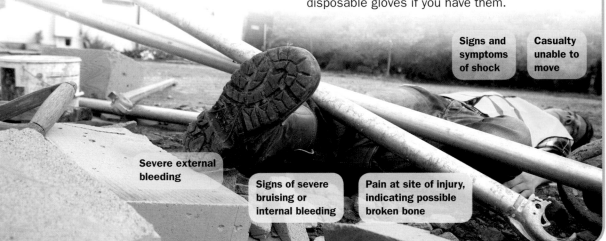

Signs and symptoms of shock

Casualty unable to move

Severe external bleeding

Signs of severe bruising or internal bleeding

Pain at site of injury, indicating possible broken bone

Dangers of crush injury

If a person is trapped for any length of time, there are two serious risks.

● **SUDDEN ONSET OF SHOCK** When a limb is crushed, circulation beyond the point of impact is likely to be completely cut off. If the weight is removed, fluid floods into the area, which can overwhelm the circulatory system, causing shock to develop (see page 38).

● **CRUSH SYNDROME** While circulation to an area is restricted by crushing, toxic substances can collect in the affected tissues. If the weight is removed, these substances are suddenly released back into the circulatory system, which can cause potentially fatal kidney failure.

action

YOU KNOW THE INCIDENT OCCURRED RECENTLY

1 RELEASE CAUSE OF CRUSHING Release the affected part of the body if you can and it is safe to do so.

2 TREAT ANY INJURY Support any suspected broken bones. If there is a wound, apply pressure over a sterile dressing or clean pad, and raise and support the area to control bleeding. Then, to minimise the risk of shock developing, help the casualty to lie down with her legs raised and supported.

3 CALL EMERGENCY HELP Call the emergency services. Check and make a note of the casualty's level of consciousness, breathing and pulse (see page 30). Re-check often until medical help arrives.

YOU DO NOT KNOW WHEN THE INCIDENT OCCURRED

1 CALL EMERGENCY HELP Do not remove the object which is crushing the casualty. Leave her in the position in which you found her and call for emergency help.

2 REASSURE CASUALTY Talk to the casualty and make her as comfortable as you can.

3 MONITOR CASUALTY Check and note her level of consciousness, breathing and pulse (see page 30). In addition, check the pulse in the trapped limb if you can reach it safely.

impalement

If a person becomes impaled on an object, moving the casualty (or the object) can worsen the injury and cause increased pain.

assessment

Find out how and when the person became impaled and which body part is affected. Look out for:

- Signs of external or internal bleeding
- Symptoms and signs of shock

 TAKE CARE
- Make sure that you are not putting yourself in any danger by approaching the casualty.
- Protect yourself and the casualty by wearing nonlatex disposable gloves if you have them.

action

1 CALL FOR HELP Do not move the casualty or attempt to remove the object. Ask someone to call the emergency services. Provide as much information as possible.

2 SUPPORT CASUALTY Make the person as comfortable as you can; support the body by hand or with cushions, if possible, to ease discomfort.

3 REASSURE CASUALTY Tell him that help is on the way. Check and make a note of the level of consciousness, breathing and pulse (see page 28). Re-check regularly until medical help arrives.

 WARNING
- Do not give the casualty anything to eat or drink as an anaesthetic may be needed later in hospital.
- If the casualty becomes unconscious, open the airway and check breathing (see pages 14–19). If he is breathing and placing him in the recovery position is difficult, maintain the head tilt and chin lift position (see page 14) to keep his airway open.

amputation

Fingers and toes – and even larger body parts such as arms – that are partially or completely severed in an accident can sometimes be reattached. It is vital to preserve the amputated part. The medical team will assess the extent of the damage.

WATCHPOINT Do not give the casualty anything to eat or drink as he will need an anaesthetic later in hospital. If he is thirsty moisten his lips with water.

assessment

There are various complications associated with amputation of a body part, depending on the extent of the injury. The first-aid treatment is always the same – check for:

- Severe external bleeding (see page 96) and possibly internal bleeding (see page 38)
- Symptoms and signs of shock may be evident (see pages 38–39)

 TAKE CARE

- Wear nonlatex disposable gloves if you have them to protect yourself and the casualty.
- Tell the medical team if the casualty is taking a blood-thinning medication (anticoagulants) as they will bleed more profusely.

Care of severed part

- **WRAP IT UP** Do not wash or rinse the part. Put the part in a polythene bag or wrap it in plastic kitchen film to keep it clean and prevent it from drying out. Wrap a soft cloth or towel around it.
- **PUT IT IN ICE** Place the wrapped part in a container full of ice (crushed is ideal). Make sure that the ice does not touch the surface of the part. Mark the package with  the casualty's name and time of the incident. Give the package to the emergency services.

action

1 CONTROL BLEEDING Place a sterile wound dressing or clean pad on the wound, apply direct pressure and raise the affected area. Secure the pad with a bandage.

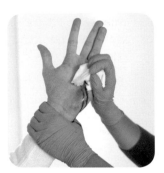

2 TREAT FOR SHOCK Keeping the injured area elevated, help the casualty to lie down on the ground. Raise and support his legs.

3 CALL EMERGENCY HELP Ask a helper to call emergency services and **tell the ambulance controller that it is an amputation.**

4 MONITOR CASUALTY Check and make a note of his level of consciousness, breathing and pulse (see page 30). Re-check regularly until help arrives.

5 PRESERVE THE PART Keep the part clean. Wrap it and place it in ice if possible (see box, left).

mouth wound

Wounds in the mouth are mostly minor and look worse than they are because they bleed profusely. They are often the result of a casualty biting her own tongue and/or lip during a fall. In some cases, a tooth may be knocked out. Prompt first aid can prevent a casualty inhaling blood, which could cause breathing difficulties.

assessment

Most mouth wounds can be treated at home, although those that are more severe may need the attention of a doctor or dentist. These are indicated by:

- Severe bleeding from lips or inside the mouth
- History of recent tooth extraction or any other facial injury
- Loss of tooth

 WARNING
- If bleeding has not stopped after half an hour, or it restarts, take the casualty to hospital.
- If a casualty has suffered a blow to the head, watch for signs of serious injury (see pages 82–83).

 TAKE CARE
Wear nonlatex disposable gloves if you have them to protect yourself and the casualty.

action

1 SIT CASUALTY DOWN Help her to lean forward so that she does not inhale blood accidentally.

2 PLACE PAD AGAINST INJURY Give the casualty a pad to hold against the injury. If the wound is on the lips or inside the cheek, tell her to pinch the pad over the injury between her finger and thumb.

3 FOR BLEEDING TOOTH SOCKET Roll up a small piece of gauze and place it in the gap. Tell the casualty to bite on the pad to apply pressure.

4 CHECK THE MOUTH After 10 minutes, check the mouth. If the injury is still bleeding, tell her to re-apply pressure for another 10 minutes. Advise her to spit out any blood in her mouth.

5 CHECK TOOTH If a tooth has been knocked out, preserve it (see box, right). Take the casualty to a dentist or hospital for possible re-implantation.

Care of knocked-out tooth

An adult, or second, tooth can often be re-implanted if it is not damaged. Do not wash the tooth however dirty it appears to be. Take the casualty to a dentist or hospital where they can assess the possibility of replanting the tooth as well as damage to the bone or gum.

- **KEEPING THE TOOTH SAFE** Once bleeding has stopped and as long as the person is fully conscious, tell her to put the tooth in the empty socket. If she cannot do this, tell her to put it in the side of her mouth against her cheek, taking care not to swallow it.
- **PRESERVE IN MILK** If it is not safe to put the tooth in the casualty's mouth, put it in a container of milk – not water.
- **CHILDREN'S TEETH** A child's milk (first) tooth cannot be replaced, but second teeth can be re-implanted. Preserve the tooth as described above and take the child to the dentist with the preserved tooth.

animal or human bite

Bites carry a serious risk of infection as mouths are full of bacteria. The force of the bite can cause bruising and lacerated wounds and can carry germs deep into the tissues. If the wound is small, you can clean it yourself. Large, severe or deep bites may require surgery as underlying structures, such as tendons or nerves, are likely to be damaged.

assessment

Seek medical advice for all but the most minor bites, especially bites to a hand. Symptoms and signs include:

● Bruising caused by crushing from the teeth
● Puncture wounds in the pattern of the jaw
● Severe lacerations
● Symptoms and signs of shock may be evident (see pages 38–39) if the blood loss is severe
● Tingling or loss of feeling and movement if the tendons or nerves are damaged

⚠ WARNING

Animal bites (particularly dog bites) that occur outside the UK carry the risk of rabies, which can be passed to humans. Antirabies treatment may need to be given immediately.

Safety with dogs

● **CHILDREN AND DOGS** Children are often the victims of dog bites. Never leave a young child alone with a dog. The defensive reaction of an irritated dog is to bite, even when the child bothers it unintentionally. A loved family pet can be as serious a threat to a child as an unknown dog.
● **DEALING WITH AN AGGRESSIVE DOG** Do not run away from the dog. Use anything at hand, such as a stick, to protect yourself and others. Back away slowly until you can get to safety.
● **WARD OFF AN ATTACKING DOG** Do whatever you can to stop an attack (see pages 304–305).
● **REPORTING A DOG BITE TO THE POLICE** You should report an incident with an aggressive dog to the police, who may prosecute the owner under the Dangerous Dogs Act.

action

1 MOVE CASUALTY TO SAFETY If the casualty is bitten by an animal, move to a safe place away from the animal. If it is a dog, shut in a separate room.

2 CONTROL BLEEDING Place a sterile wound dressing or clean pad on the wound, apply direct pressure and raise the affected area.

3 WASH SMALL BITES If the bite is small, wash the area thoroughly with soap and water if available, or alcohol-free cleansing wipes. Gently pat dry with gauze swabs, then cover with a sterile dressing secured with a bandage (see page 96).

4 TAKE TO HOSPITAL If the wound is severe or deep, take the casualty to hospital or call the emergency services. The casualty may need surgery. A course of antibiotics may be prescribed to prevent infection.

5 MONITOR CASUALTY If she becomes generally unwell with a high temperature within a week of a bite, advise her to seek medical advice urgently, especially if the wound was treated at home. Find out if the casualty has been immunised against Tetanus (see page 101).

⚠ TAKE CARE

Wear nonlatex disposable gloves if you have them to protect yourself and the casualty.

severe nosebleed

Nosebleeds are fairly common, especially in children. They usually happen as a result of a minor injury, nose picking or blowing the nose. Very occasionally, nosebleeds can be a sign of underlying illness or injury.

WATCHPOINT If a nosebleed continues for more than 30 minutes or follows a blow to the head, seek medical advice. Monitor the casualty for any change in the condition.

assessment

Very rarely a nosebleed can be life-threatening, especially in older people. Seek medical advice if you notice any of the following:

- Frequent nosebleeds (more than one a week); this can be a symptom of high blood pressure
- Persistent nosebleeds in a person who is on blood-thinning medication such as warfarin
- Thin watery blood from the nose following a blow to the head (see page 82), which can indicate a possible skull fracture

- Frequent nosebleeds accompanied by bleeding gums as well as bruises that develop for no apparent reason

 TAKE CARE

Wear nonlatex disposable gloves if you have them to protect yourself and the casualty.

action

1 SIT CASUALTY DOWN Help the casualty to sit down. Tell her to lean forward (she should not lean back) so that the blood can drain.

2 PINCH THE NOSE Tell the casualty to breathe through her mouth and pinch the soft part of her nose to help reduce blood flow. She can lean over a sink or give her a bowl so that she can spit out any blood; swallowing it can make her sick. Advise her not to sniff, swallow or cough as it can disturb the clots that are forming.

3 CHECK NOSE After 10 minutes release the pressure and check the nose. If it is still bleeding, pinch the nose again for another 10 minutes.

4 OFFER A COLD COMPRESS Give the casualty an ice or cold pack (see page 108) to hold against the bridge of her nose to help reduce the blood flow.

5 CHECK NOSE AGAIN Once bleeding has stopped, let the casualty clean around her nose with a damp cloth. Tell her not to blow her nose and to avoid strenuous activity for up to 12 hours.

Helping a young child

A very young child may not be able to pinch her nose for long enough. Help her to sit forward and pinch her nose for her. Reassure her, get her to spit into a bowl and wipe her face.

▶▶See also: **BLOW TO THE HEAD** pp82–83

severe **bruising**

A bruise is a closed wound in which bleeding from damaged blood vessels is trapped in the tissues, causing bluish-black discoloration. Depending on the force of the blow, there may be additional injuries. Bruising may not appear immediately.

GET HELP Call the emergency services if you suspect serious internal injury. Internal bleeding may be identified only by signs of shock (see page 38) that develop with no visible bleeding.

assessment

Bruising is most commonly the result of bleeding from the smallest blood vessels (the capillaries) and in some instances appears a few days after an injury. If a large blood vessel is damaged, swelling will be more severe. Signs of severe bruising include:

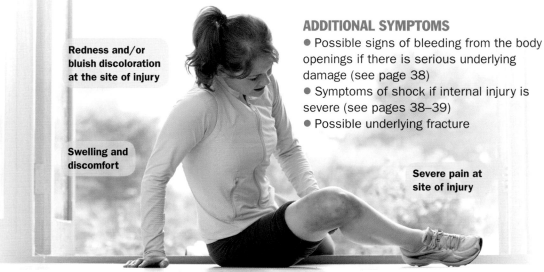

Redness and/or bluish discoloration at the site of injury

Swelling and discomfort

ADDITIONAL SYMPTOMS
- Possible signs of bleeding from the body openings if there is serious underlying damage (see page 38)
- Symptoms of shock if internal injury is severe (see pages 38–39)
- Possible underlying fracture

Severe pain at site of injury

 WARNING

- If unexplained bruises occur easily or for no apparent reason, especially if accompanied by frequent nosebleeds or bleeding gums, seek medical advice.

- A person taking a blood-thinning medication (anticoagulant), such as warfarin, for a medical condition is at risk of severe bruising because the medication can prevent clotting.

Making a cold compress

Cooling an injury with ice slows down the metabolism within the tissue, reducing bleeding, muscle spasm and inflammation (and therefore pain), so aiding recovery. Place a cold compress on an injury for 10–20 minutes at a time – don't leave it for any longer. Repeat this procedure every 2–3 hours; it is most effective in the first 48 hours after injury. Never put ice directly onto the skin because it can cause a cold burn.

- **MAKING AN ICE PACK** Fill a plastic bag with ice cubes or crushed ice. Seal the bag, then wrap it in a hand towel or dishcloth. Alternatively, you can use a bag of frozen peas or sweetcorn as it will mould well to the shape of the body.
- **MAKING A COLD PACK** If you do not have any ice, soak a small towel in cold water and wring it out, then place it over the injury. Keep it cool by dripping cold water over it at regular intervals.

action

1 REST THE INJURY Tell the casualty to stop his current activity and rest. Raise the injury, as this reduces blood flow to the area.

2 COOL THE INJURY Place a cold compress (see box opposite) over the injury. Leave it in place for up to 20 minutes.

3 COMFORTABLE SUPPORT Tell the casualty to keep the injury raised and to est the affected part. Wrap padding around the injury and apply a compression bandage if the pain is severe (see page 93).

4 ELEVATE THE INJURY Rest and support the injury in a raised position to minimise swelling. Apply a sling to an arm injury if necessary (see page 91).

⚠️ WARNING

- If several small bruises subsequently form around a large one, and the casualty has not had any other accidents, he should seek medical advice immediately to find out whether his blood is clotting as it should.
- Seek medical advice if the bruise is accompanied by swelling and severe pain and the person is taking a blood-thinning medication (anticoagulant).

black eye

A black eye develops when blood and other fluids collect in the space around the eye; resulting in swelling and the typical dark discoloration.

assessment

Most black eyes heal on their own and the eye itself is not injured. Sometimes the bruising signifies a more serious eye injury and there is a risk of long-term damage. Signs that cause concern are:

- Fluid leaking from the eye
- **Casualty complains of blurred vision** in the affected eye
- The affected eye appears to be a different shape from the other one

action

1 SIT CASUALTY DOWN Tell the casualty to stop her current activity and rest.

2 COOL THE INJURY Give the casualty a cold compress (see box opposite) to hold against the affected area for 10–20 minutes.

3 MONITOR CASUALTY Check and make a note of her level of consciousness, breathing and pulse (see page 30). Make a note of any change in her condition.

4 TAKE TO HOSPITAL If the casualty's condition deteriorates, or there is serious injury to the eye, take her to hospital or call the emergency services.

▶▶See also: EYE INJURY p118

electrical injury

Contact with domestic low-voltage electricity or lighting is often the cause of an electrical injury, usually a burn. The electrical current needs breaking before help can be given. If the casualty has been thrown by the current, there may be a fracture; if unconscious, the heart may stop. An incident with high-voltage electricity, such as power cables, is often fatal.

assessment

Assess the extent of the casualty's injuries – in particular, check to see if there is more than one burn. Symptoms to note are:

● Superficial, partial or full-thickness burns (see pages 112–113). There may be a second burn (an exit burn) where the electric current left the body
● Internal injury along the path of the electricity
● Symptoms and signs of shock if burns are severe (see pages 38–39)
● Signs of upper and lower limb Injury (see pages 86–91) or possibly back and neck Injury (see pages 84–85) if the casualty was thrown by the electrical current
● Casualty may be unconscious

⚠ WARNING
● **Do not touch a casualty who remains in contact with the source of electricity.**
● Do not touch a casualty with wet hands.
● Do not go within 18m of a person who has been struck by high-voltage electricity unless the authorities have officially told you that the supply has been switched off.
● Do not approach a casualty who is found near a high-voltage power line or overhead cable. Call the emergency services and keep any bystanders away.

⚠ TAKE CARE
Wear nonlatex disposable gloves if you have them to protect yourself and the casualty.

How to break the contact with electricity

If a casualty is still in contact with the cause of the injury, you too will sustain an electric shock if you touch him. Low-voltage alternating current (AC) can cause muscle spasm so the person will still be grasping the appliance that caused the electric shock.

● **TURN OFF THE MAINS SUPPLY** First, try to turn off the electric current. This can normally be done by switching the supply off at the mains. If successful you can approach the casualty.

● **MOVE THE SOURCE AWAY FROM THE CASUALTY** If you cannot find the mains switch, remove the source from the casualty using a length of wood, which is nonconductive. Stand on a thick book, such as a telephone directory, a stack of newspapers or some similar dry insulating material. Use the wood to push the object away from contact with the casualty.
● **PULL THE CASUALTY AWAY** If neither of the first options is successful, stand on the insulating material. Loop a rope around the casualty's legs and attempt to pull him clear.

TIME TO ACT Electric current can cause a casualty's breathing and heartbeat to stop. If the casualty is unconscious, be prepared to begin CPR.

WATCHPOINT Check electrical appliances regularly; this is especially important in an elderly person's home. Old appliances can be a fire risk.

action

1 BREAK ELECTRICAL CONTACT Assess the area carefully before you approach to make sure the casualty is no longer holding the electrical appliance (see box, opposite).

2 COOL BURNS Stop the burning process. Hold the injury under cool running water for at least 10 minutes, or until the pain eases. Remove the casualty's watch, jewellery or any tight clothing that might restrict swelling. Do not remove anything that is stuck to the wounds.

3 COVER BURNS Cover the burns to protect them from infection and further fluid loss. Use plastic kitchen film, laid along the burn – do not wrap it around a limb. Cover a hand or foot with a plastic bag. Tape it closed, making sure the tape is on the plastic not the skin. If you do not have either of these, use a sterile wound dressing or clean, non-fluffy cloth, such as a cotton pillowcase.

4 TREAT ANY OTHER INJURIES Attend to any other injuries, such as fractures, that the casualty has sustained in the incident. Watch the casualty for signs of shock and treat as necessary.

5 CALL EMERGENCY HELP Call the emergency services. Monitor the casualty while you are waiting. Check and make a note of the level of consciousness, breathing and pulse (see page 30). Re-check regularly until help arrives.

⚠ WARNING

If the casualty becomes unconscious, open the airway and check for breathing (see pages 14–19). Be prepared to begin CPR (see page 16).

⚠ TAKE CARE

● If you have young children in the home, put safety covers into unused electrical sockets.
● Do not overload sockets or extension leads.
● Use extension leads with 'gangs' of sockets rather than single socket adapters to reduce the risk of overloading a socket.
● Always use adapters and extension leads that have circuit breakers.
● Fix wires to the skirting board; never let them trail across the floor.
● Check wiring regularly; throw away appliances with cracked or damaged flexes.
● Make sure that appliances have sealed plugs.
● Keep electrical appliances away from water. Never touch appliances with wet hands.
● If a plug becomes warm when an appliance is switched on, it is faulty and should be replaced.

▶▶See also: **UNCONSCIOUS ADULT/CHILD/BABY** pp14–19 • **SHOCK** pp38–39 • **BURNS AND SCALDS** pp112–113

burns and scalds

Burns are caused by dry heat (fire or smoke), chemicals or electricity and scalds by wet heat (hot water or steam). The skin is the body's natural infection barrier and is made up of several layers. Any break in the skin allows fluid to escape and germs to enter. As burns may affect large areas and/or several layers of skin, serious fluid loss and infection can result.

assessment

Assess the extent and depth of the burn (see box, below). While you examine the casualty, start to cool the injury to stop the burning. Check for:

Redness and swelling around the site of the injury

Severe pain, although deep burns can be painless

Fluid-filled blisters

Raw patches of skin

ADDITIONAL SYMPTOMS
- Pale waxy-looking skin – this indicates a deep burn
- Soot around the mouth and burned nose hairs if the casualty has inhaled hot smoke
- Breathing difficulties may develop (see pages 40–41)
- Symptoms and signs of shock (see pages 38–39)

 TAKE CARE
- Wear nonlatex gloves if you have them to protect yourself and the casualty.
- Never put ice, iced water or any creams or greasy substances, such as butter, on a burn.
- **If you don't have cool water, you can use a cool liquid such as milk.**
- Do not let the person become too cold as there is a risk of Hypothermia (see pages 46–47).
- Do not use adhesive dressings on a burn as the injury may be larger than you think.

 WARNING
If the casualty becomes unconscious, open the airway and check for breathing (see pages 14–19). Be prepared to begin CPR (see page 16).

Depth of burns

- **SUPERFICIAL BURNS** These are burns that affect only the surface of the skin, characterised by redness and swelling. Sunburn is a prime example.
- **PARTIAL-THICKNESS BURNS** These are burns to the top layer of the skin and fluid (plasma) will escape from the body. And, if the skin is not broken, blisters form. The skin will be raw and the burns are very painful.
- **FULL-THICKNESS BURNS** The damage affects all the layers of the skin. These burns may be relatively pain-free as the nerves in the skin may be damaged. Blood vessels, muscle and fat beneath the skin will also be damaged.

GET HELP For all serious burns, ask someone to call the emergency services while you cool the burn. The paramedics will have specialist burn dressings in their medical kit.

TIME TO ACT Call the emergency services immediately if there is any sign of burns to the mouth or air passages – this can be life-threatening.

WATCHPOINT If the casualty needs hospital treatment, do not give her anything to eat or drink as she may need an anaesthetic. If she is thirsty, moisten her lips with water.

action

1 COOL THE BURN Stop the burning process by running cool water over the burn for at least 10 minutes, or until the pain eases. If possible, sit the casualty down and keep the injured area raised.

2 CALL EMERGENCY HELP Make the casualty as comfortable as possible. Call for emergency help if required (see box, right).

3 REMOVE CONSTRICTIONS Skin damaged by burning swells very quickly, so remove or cut away any clothing or jewellery from the affected area while you are cooling it. Do not remove anything that is stuck to the burned area.

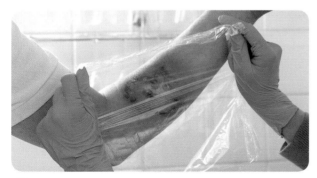

4 COVER BURN Cover the burn to protect it from infection and further fluid loss. Ideally, cover it with plastic kitchen film or a polythene bag. If these are not available, use a sterile dressing or clean, lint-free cloth, such as a cotton pillowcase. Lay the film along the burn rather than wrapping it around a limb. Cover a hand or foot with a plastic bag. Tape it shut, with the tape on the plastic and not the skin.

5 TREAT FOR SHOCK Help the casualty to lie down while keeping the injured area raised and supported. Raise his legs above heart level and support them on a chair. Cover with a blanket to keep him warm.

6 MONITOR CASUALTY Check and note his level of consciousness, breathing and pulse (see page 30). Keep monitoring until the emergency services arrive.

When to seek medical help

If in doubt, seek medical advice, and always if a burn is larger than 2.5cm. Take a casualty to hospital or call the emergency services for any of the following:

● **BABY OR YOUNG CHILD** For any burn on a baby or young child.
● **LARGE AREA OF BURNS** For partial-thickness burns that are larger than the casualty's hand.
● **BLISTERING** For burns with blisters or full-thickness burns.
● **FULL-THICKNESS BURNS** All deep burns need medical treatment, however small.
● **BURNS TO THE AIRWAY** For burns in the airway following inhalation of fumes of smoke. The tissues of the mouth and throat swell quickly, blocking the airway and preventing breathing.
● **BURNS AROUND A LIMB** Any burn that extends all the way round a limb, even if superficial.
● **ELECTRICAL OR CHEMICAL BURNS** See electrical injury (pages 110–111) or chemical burns (pages 116–117).
● **OTHER INJURIES** If there are other injuries that need attention, or if the person feels unwell.
● **PRE-EXISTING CONDITION** If the person has a pre-existing medical condition, such as heart disease, diabetes, a disease that affects the immune system or is pregnant.

▶▶See also: **UNCONSCIOUS ADULT/CHILD/BABY** pp14–19 • **SHOCK** pp38–39

accidental **poisoning**

The most common method of poisoning is by swallowing (ingestion). Many cases occur as a result of swallowing poisonous household products, which also cause burns. Most casualties are children, but the elderly are also at risk. Poisoning can also result from an accidental or, occasionally, deliberate overdose of over-the-counter, prescription or recreational drugs.

assessment

Symptoms and signs will depend on what the person has swallowed, so it is important to establish the cause. Look for:

Burns or blisters at the mouth if the poison is a corrosive substance

Abdominal pains – these can be severe

Empty containers, berries or leaves near the casualty

ADDITIONAL SYMPTOMS
- Vomiting and/or diarrhoea – this may be bloodstained
- Signs of breathing difficulties
- Possible Seizures (see page 60)
- Casualty may not be fully conscious, and **may lose consciousness at any time**

⚠️ TAKE CARE
- If the victim has swallowed a chemical, protect yourself from contact with it by wearing rubber gloves and protective clothing.
- Use a protective mask if an unconscious casualty has burns on the lips and you have to give rescue breaths.

POISONOUS SUBSTANCES

TYPE	WHAT TO WATCH OUT FOR
Cosmetics and creams	Make-up, creams and cleansers can be poisonous if swallowed.
Medicines	Overdoses of prescription drugs and over-the-counter medications, such as cough medicines, paracetamol, aspirin and ibuprofen (see also page 56).
Household chemicals	Bleach, carpet-cleaning products and dishwasher detergent can cause burns; soap, furniture polish and other household products are also poisonous.
Plants	Many plants are harmful, especially deadly nightshade, wild arum lily berries, yew, holly berries, laburnum, lupins, delphiniums and foxgloves.
Garden chemicals	Weedkiller can cause burns; slug pellets and fertilisers are also poisonous.

GET HELP Accidental poisoning can be life-threatening. If in any doubt, call the emergency services as soon as possible.

TIME TO ACT Never attempt to induce vomiting, especially if the substance is corrosive. Anything that burned the gullet on the way down, will burn it again on the way back up.

WATCHPOINT If you are not sure what the casualty has swallowed, give samples of vomit to the attending medical team; this can help to identify the substance.

action

1 IDENTIFY POISON If the casualty is conscious and able to talk, ask her what she took. If she is not fully conscious, look around for clues. Try to rouse the person and then encourage her to spit out anything that is in her mouth.

2 CALL EMERGENCY HELP Call the emergency services. Tell the control officer and the ambulance crew what the casualty has swallowed, when she took it and how much you think she took. Give them the container that the substance came in.

3 SOOTHE BURNED LIPS If the casualty has swallowed a corrosive poison, it may have burned her lips. Let her take small sips of cool milk or water to soothe the burns, but get her to spit it out.

4 WIPE AWAY VOMIT If the casualty vomits, wipe her mouth clean, but do not give her anything to eat or drink. Help her to lean forward so that fluid can drain from her mouth safely.

5 MONITOR CASUALTY Monitor the casualty's condition. Check and make a note of any change in her level of consciousness, breathing and pulse (see page 30) while you are waiting for help to arrive.

Safety with poisons

● **POISONOUS PLANTS** A surprising number of garden plants have poisonous berries, leaves or roots. If you have young children, consider fencing the plants off or even digging them up.
● **MEDICATION** Keep all medicines out of reach of children, preferably in a locked cabinet. Make sure that bottles have child-resistant caps. If a person is on regular medication but finds it difficult to remember which tablet to take and when to do so, consider putting pills in an automatic dispenser box to reduce the risk of an accidental overdose.

what next?

Treatment will depend on what the casualty has swallowed. Blood tests may be needed to identify the poison. Medical staff will want to know the person's age, estimated weight, whether she has any existing medical conditions and if she is on medication.

 WARNING

If the casualty becomes unconscious, open the airway and check for breathing (see pages 14–19) and be prepared to begin CPR (see page 16).

chemical on skin

Contact with chemicals can result in very severe burns, which need urgent medical attention. Try to determine which chemical has caused the injury as the information will help the medical team to decide on the most appropriate treatment.

GET HELP Some chemicals give off dangerous fumes, which can cause breathing difficulties, so do not put yourself in any danger. Call the emergency services.

assessment

Assess the injury while you wash the chemical. Some burns may not be immediately apparent. Check for:

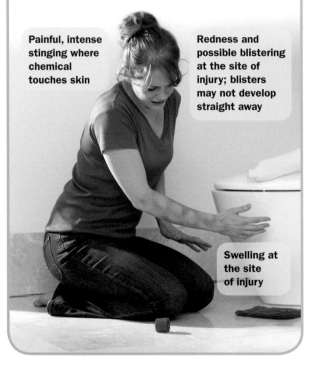

Painful, intense stinging where chemical touches skin

Redness and possible blistering at the site of injury; blisters may not develop straight away

Swelling at the site of injury

⚠ TAKE CARE

- Protect yourself from contact with the chemical by wearing rubber gloves and protective clothing.
- Check the label on the chemical. Some spills need to be notified to the local authority.

⚠ WARNING

- The casualty may develop Breathing Difficulties (see pages 40–41).
- If the casualty becomes unconscious, open the airway and check for breathing (see pages 14–19) and be prepared to begin CPR (see page 16).

action

1 MOVE CASUALTY TO SAFETY If the casualty is inside, move her to safety. Make sure that the area is well ventilated and any fumes are dispersed.

2 RINSE AFFECTED AREA
Pour water onto the burn for 20 minutes or longer – time this to ensure that you treat the injury for long enough. Pour the water away from yourself so that no chemical is washed onto your skin.

3 ALLOW WATER TO DRAIN SAFELY Make sure that the contaminated water can drain away safely; raise a casualty's foot if necessary so that the water does not run over unaffected areas.

4 REMOVE CONTAMINATED CLOTHES Help the casualty to remove any clothing that has become contaminated with the chemical while you are washing the area.

5 COVER BURN Cover the burn to protect it from infection and further fluid loss. Ideally cover it with plastic kitchen film or a plastic bag. Lay the film along the burn rather than wrapping it around a limb. If you do not have either of these, use a sterile wound dressing or lint-free cloth, such as a cotton pillowcase.

6 TAKE TO HOSPITAL You can take the casualty to hospital or call the emergency services depending on the extent of the injury. Treat casualty for shock if necessary (see page 38). Monitor the casualty's condition. Check and make a note of her level of consciousness, breathing and pulse (see page 30).

Safety at home

- **STORING CHEMICALS** Keep cleaning chemicals, dishwasher detergent and washing powder out of reach of children – do not keep them under the sink.
- **USE SAFETY CATCHES** Put safety catches on all cupboards containing chemicals. Choose chemicals with safety tops and leave them in their original bottles. Always keep garden chemicals in a locked shed.

- **USING CHEMICALS** Never combine chemicals (for example, toilet cleaner and bleach) when you are cleaning as they can give off dangerous fumes. Do not put potentially toxic chemicals down in the parts of the garden where children and pets are playing or where they might play.
- **POTENTIALLY DANGEROUS HOUSEHOLD CHEMICALS** Caustic chemicals such as drain cleaner, some weed killers, bleach and paint stripper, need special care as they can cause burns. Many other chemicals, such as kitchen cleaner, polish, washing powders and conditioners, can cause an allergic reaction in some people. Always follow the instructions on the bottle, including the best course of action to follow in case of an accident.

what next?

- At hospital, the burn will be assessed, and treatment will depend on the chemical involved. If the burn is severe, the casualty will be referred to a specialist and may need to be admitted to hospital.
- The injury will be cleaned and dressed with a sterile gauze or dressing.
- The casualty will be offered pain relief.

chemical in eye

The severity of the burn depends on the substance involved and for how long it was in contact with the eye. A casualty who cannot see is likely to panic.

assessment

Damage is usually limited to the front part of the eye, but there is a risk of internal injury. Try to identify the chemical.

OTHER SYMPTOMS
- Pain – possibly severe – and redness
- Watering and irritation; it may feel like there is something in the eye
- Inability to open the affected eye; eyelids may go into spasm
- Swollen eyelids
- Blurred or lost vision is a sign of a serious burn. Glaucoma – increased pressure inside the eye – can occur, though its onset may be delayed by hours or days

action

1 PROTECT YOURSELF Put on protective gloves to protect yourself from contact with the chemical.

2 RINSE EYE Hold the casualty's head under lukewarm running water for at least 10 minutes to wash out the chemical and prevent further damage. The affected eye should be lower than the good eye to prevent the chemical running into them both. If he cannot open his eye, gently hold the eyelids open.

3 COVER EYE Give the casualty a sterile or clean pad to hold over the injured eye.

4 TAKE TO HOSPITAL Take the casualty to hospital or call the emergency services. Tell the medical team what substance caused the injury.

eye injury

Eye injuries are usually the result of a scratch or graze caused by grit or a contact lens. Most injuries affect the transparent outer layer of the eye (cornea), which covers and protects the coloured part of the eye (iris) and lets light into the hole in the centre (pupil). These injuries need medical attention as they can result in temporary or permanent loss of sight.

assessment

Eye injuries are potentially serious as the casualty's sight can be damaged. Examine the eye very carefully. Small, loose pieces of dust can often be picked off by the casualty or rinsed off. The following are signs of serious injury:

- Severe pain in and around the eye
- An accident where the eye has been scratched by a thorn or small foreign body, such as a stone thrown up by a lawnmower
- Foreign object on the coloured part of the eye
- Obvious wound, especially if there is fluid leaking from the eye

 WARNING

- Do not try to remove anything that is sticking to the coloured part of the eye.
- **Call the emergency services if the casualty experiences a sudden loss of vision** as a result of the injury.

action

1 SUPPORT CASUALTY'S HEAD Tell the casualty to keep her head as still as possible. Help her to lie down. Kneel behind her head and support her head on your lap to prevent unnecessary movement.

2 COVER THE EYE
Give the casualty a sterile wound dressing or clean pad to hold over the affected eye. Tell her not to move her eyes; if she moves the good eye the injured one will also move.

3 REASSURE THE CASUALTY Keep the casualty as calm as you can. Do not give her anything to eat or drink as treatment requiring an anaesthetic may be needed when she reaches hospital.

4 TAKE TO HOSPITAL Try to keep the casualty in the treatment position (see steps 1 and 2 above) on the way to hospital. You can take her to hospital or call the emergency services if you have no transport.

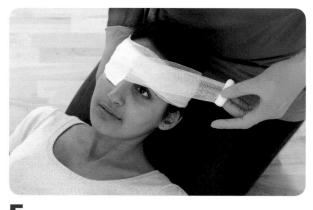

5 BANDAGE THE EYE If you have to wait a while for transport, the casualty may be more comfortable if you secure the dressing with a bandage.

what next?

- A superficial eye injury that does not penetrate the eye membrane will usually take 24–72 hours to heal, depending on the size of the abrasion. The injury may be treated with eye drops to prevent infection.
- The casualty will be referred to an eye specialist if her vision is affected, if the eye socket or eyeball is injured, or if there is damage to the retina at the back of the eye.

items in ear or nose

Children often put small objects into the nose or ear. Sharp items can easily damage the lining of the nose or structures of the ear, while the acid in small batteries could even cause burns. If an object is not removed, it could lead to internal injury and possible infection. A sharp object in the ear may pierce the ear-drum, leading to possible deafness.

assessment

Look into the nose or ear with a torch. If you see anything, take the casualty to hospital. You may also notice the following symptoms:

IF THE OBJECT IS IN THE EAR
- Temporary deafness
- Casualty will feel movement if it is an insect and may be very frightened. You may be able to see the insect float out (see below)

IF THE OBJECT IS IN THE NOSE
- Pain if a sharp object is lodged in the nose
- Difficulty breathing through one nostril
- Swelling on one side of the nose
- Possible smelly discharge if the object has been there for some time

action

ITEM IN EAR

1 TAKE TO HOSPITAL If the person has an object in his ear or an insect is stuck, take him to hospital. Take him yourself if you have transport or call the emergency services if you have no transport.

2 REASSURE THE CASUALTY Keep the casualty as calm as you can on your way to the hospital. Do not give him anything to eat or drink as treatment requiring an anaesthetic may be needed.

ITEM IN NOSE

1 REASSURE THE CASUALTY Tell the casualty to breathe through the other nostril or his mouth. Keep him as calm as possible. Do not let him poke inside his nose to try to release the object.

2 TAKE TO HOSPITAL You can take the casualty to hospital yourself or call the emergency services if you have no transport. Do not give the casualty anything to eat or drink as an anaesthetic may be needed when he reaches hospital.

Insect stuck in the ear

If an insect flies or crawls into a person's ear, it may be possible to float it out. Put a towel around the casualty's shoulders, tilt his head so that the affected ear is uppermost and gently pour tepid water into the ear. As the ear is flooded the insect should come to the surface. If this does not work, you should take the casualty to hospital.

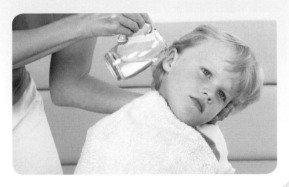

what next?

Hospital staff will assess the injury and use special instruments to remove the object. This may need to be done under an anaesthetic, especially if the casualty is a child.

acute backache

Back pain can be very uncomfortable, but it is not usually serious. It is more common in people who are between 30 and 55 years of age. Lower back pain – a pain or ache on your back between the bottom of your ribs and the top of your legs – is the most common and if it doesn't go away after a few days, it is a potential emergency.

assessment

Most back pain is caused by sprained ligaments or muscle strain but it can result from a ruptured or prolapsed (slipped) disc. If the main nerve at the base of the back is pinched or irritated, pain can spread down one leg (sciatica).

History of back problems

Sudden onset of pain after manual work, heavy lifting or bending awkwardly

Pain that spreads down into the buttocks and thigh (sciatica)

action

1 **KEEP THE CASUALTY MOVING** Advise him to stay active and continue with his usual activities. While bed rest may provide some temporary relief from symptoms, it can actually make the injury worse. Keeping the injured area mobilised, on the other hand, normally promotes healing.

2 **GIVE PAIN RELIEF** The casualty can take the recommended dose of his usual pain relief medication, such as paracetamol. A cold compress may also provide some relief (see page 108).

3 **SEEK MEDICAL ADVICE** If back pain persists or recurs frequently, the casualty should seek medical advice so that a correct diagnosis can be reached and appropriate treatment given.

what next?

● Acute (short term) back pain usually improves with physical activity. Recommended exercises for back pain include walking and gentle stretching.
● Chronic (long term) back pain usually requires a combination of self-help techniques, medical treatment and manipulation therapies.

 WARNING

Immobilise the casualty, treat as for Back and Neck Injury (see pages 84–85) and seek urgent medical advice if:
● **The backache follows a fall or head injury.**
● There is numbness or tingling in either leg.
● You can feel any deformity along his back or neck.
● There is loss of bladder and bowel control or he is unable to pass urine.

HOUSEHOLD EMERGENCIES

caught in a **blazing house**

The Fire and Rescue Service is called to around 60,000 UK house fires each year. Nearly 500 people are killed and more than 11,000 injured in fires in the home. In a house fire there is no time to think about what to do and smoke fumes can be disorientating. Survival depends on split-second decisions, effective precautions and an escape plan that everyone knows by heart.

action

FIRE IN HOUSE

1 RAISE THE ALARM AND GET OUT If you smell smoke or your smoke alarm is activated, shout to alert all those in the house. Get everyone together and follow your escape plan (see page 125). If you do not have one, get everyone out of the building quickly by the safest route and tell them where to meet.

2 DO NOT DELAY Do not waste time investigating how the fire was started or attempting to rescue any valuables or personal treasures.

3 CHECK DOORS Before opening an internal door, check the top of the door and the handle with the back of your hand. If the door is warm, do not open it – there is fire on the other side.

⚠ WARNING

Do not stop to call the emergency services. The Fire and Rescue Service recommends that you get out of the building first, then phone from a mobile, or neighbour's, phone.

> Despite the increasing use of flame-retardant materials, many homes contain a lot of flammable materials that can fuel a fire and cause it to spread rapidly.

GET HELP The Fire and Rescue Service is there to help. Do not attempt to tackle the fire yourself. Get out, stay out and call the emergency services without delay.

WATCHPOINT Keep door and window keys in an easily accessible place in the room where they are used. Everyone, including visitors, should know where the keys are located.

TIME TO ACT Install smoke alarms and draw up your fire escape plan now (see page 125). If in doubt, the Fire and Rescue Service can advise you.

4 OPEN CAREFULLY If the door is cool, stand behind it and brace your foot against the bottom before opening it a crack to look out. Your foot will stop the door from being forced open by the pressure of any hot gases. Open the door slowly and make sure no smoke or fire blocks further progress. If you cannot move forward, take refuge (see page 124).

5 CLOSE DOORS As you leave, close all doors and open only the doors that you need to go through; then close them behind you. This will help to prevent the fire from spreading.

6 KEEP LOW If there is smoke, keep close to the ground where the air will be cooler and cleaner. Visibility will also be better. Cover your nose and mouth with a damp cloth if possible.

7 DO NOT GO BACK Once you and the other occupants are outside, check everyone is safe. Stay outside and phone for help – never go back.

 WARNING
Summon pets such as dogs and cats as you leave the building but do not search for them; never go back for them. Stay out of your home until the Fire and Rescue Service tells you it is safe to return.

ESCAPE ROUTE BLOCKED

1 GET INTO ONE ROOM If you cannot get out of the house, get everyone into a refuge room. If possible, choose a room with a window that faces the road. Take a mobile phone or a landline handset with you.

2 KEEP FIRE AND SMOKE OUT Put bedding, rugs or a rolled-up carpet across the bottom of the door to block dangerous fumes.

3 GET ATTENTION Open a window and shout for help. Wave white or light-coloured fabric as a flag. If you have a phone, call the emergency services; if not, shout to someone outside to do it for you.

■ **TRAPPED IN AN ATTIC ROOM** A converted attic room will have a fire-resistant door, so shut the door and put fabric across the base to block fumes. Building regulations require that loft or attic rooms have skylights that can be accessed as a fire escape, often with a roll-out ladder. Exit with the ladder immediately. If there is no ladder, remain in the room, but hang a flag out of the skylight and call for help, stating where you are.

■ **TRAPPED IN A HIGH-RISE** If you live in a high rise, it is essential to be aware of escape routes. Follow the fire evacuation route. If the exit is blocked, remain in a refuge room and signal for help as above. If the window is sealed, break it at one corner, and push out the glass with a blunt instrument. Never use balconies or lifts in a fire, as you may get trapped.

NO ACCESS TO DOORS

 WARNING

If you cannot escape, it is highly recommended that you follow the 'Escape Route Blocked' action (see page 123). Only as an absolute last resort should you attempt to escape through a window.

1 OPEN WINDOW Choose a window with clear access from inside, and a safe place to drop on to. If you are unable to open a window, use a heavy object to break the glass at a bottom corner. Knock out the glass and cover sharp edges with bedding to protect yourself as you climb through.

2 CUSHION THE GROUND Drop bedding and rugs out of the window to cushion your fall.

3 LOWER YOURSELF OUT

Do not jump out of the window. Lower yourself down over the window sill to arm's length and drop to the ground. If you are alone with a child, lower her out first, holding her by her wrists then drop her to the ground. Do not leave first and expect to catch her, as she may be too scared to drop alone. Lower a baby to the ground cradled in a duvet.

■ **USE AN ESCAPE LADDER** For an isolated room or attic, a roll-out escape ladder can be a life saver. They are stored ready for use and can be fixed over a window sill (see page 123). If you have no ladder, make your way to your refuge room (see page 125) before your exit is cut off.

 TAKE CARE

Establish a bedtime routine so the house is safe overnight. Unless an appliance is designed to remain on permanently, such as a freezer, unplug it. Make sure all candles and smoking materials are extinguished, and place fireguards in front of open fires. Make sure exits are clear, and that door and window keys are accessible. Close all internal doors.

Smoke alarm

Install a smoke alarm on every storey of your home, positioned in hallways or on landings. Do not install in or directly outside the kitchen. You are twice as likely to die in a fire if you do not have a smoke alarm that works.

CHOOSING AN ALARM

● Ionisation alarms detect small fast-burning fires, such as chip-pan fires. An optical alarm detects slow-burning fires, such as smouldering furniture. Install at least one of each type, or invest in a combined alarm. Interconnected alarms will raise the alarm at all other points if smoke is detected.

● Most smoke alarms use a 9V battery. Standard batteries should be replaced every 12 months. Mains-operated smoke alarms, with a battery back-up in case of power failure, must be fitted by a qualified electrician.

● A 'hush' facility desensitises the alarm if it is triggered accidentally. During the 8 to 10 minutes that this will last, the alarm is still able to detect a fire.

● Some alarms are fitted with a light which comes on as the alarm sounds, in case damage to electrical wiring affects the house lighting.

● A slowly pulsing small light is visible when the alarm is on, and will flash more rapidly when the alarm sounds.

MAINTAINING THE ALARM

● All smoke alarms have a manual test facility. Press the button weekly to check the alarm, or shine a torch beam over those with a torch test facility.

● Most alarms will 'chirp' for the last 30 days of battery life. Change the battery immediately.

for next time...

DRAW UP AN ESCAPE PLAN

1 **INVOLVE EVERYONE** Plan together as a household when drawing up your fire escape plan. Consider any special arrangements for the very young or elderly.

2 **PLAN ROUTE A** The best escape route is the one you normally use for getting in and out of the house. Keep it clear of obstructions.

3 **PLAN ROUTE B** An alternative escape route should be agreed and kept unobstructed, in case the first choice is blocked by the fire.

4 **CHOOSE THE REFUGE** In case both escape routes are blocked, decide which room is best for your 'refuge'. Ensure the room can be accessed by all members of the household, especially considering anyone with mobility difficulties, and has a window that opens, facing onto a road. You will need a telephone and spare blankets or rugs.

5 **MAKE KEYS ACCESSIBLE** Identify where door and window lock keys are to be kept and make sure everyone, including visitors, knows where they are.

6 **MEETING POINT** Ensure every member of the family is familiar with what should happen after they have escaped, such as meeting at a rendezvous point and contacting emergency services.

7 **DISTRIBUTE THE PLAN** Put the plan somewhere prominent, such as on the fridge door. Conduct a fire drill to walk through the plan.

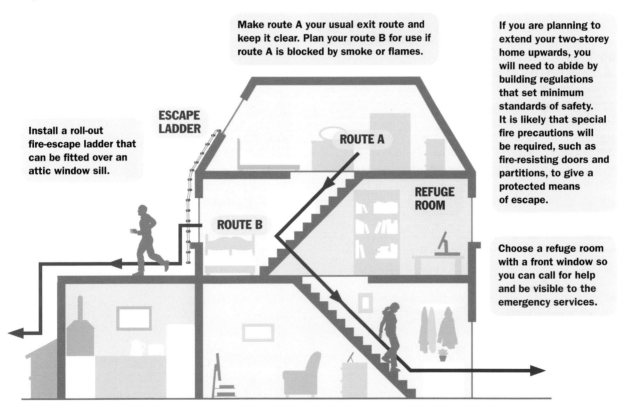

Make route A your usual exit route and keep it clear. Plan your route B for use if route A is blocked by smoke or flames.

If you are planning to extend your two-storey home upwards, you will need to abide by building regulations that set minimum standards of safety. It is likely that special fire precautions will be required, such as fire-resisting doors and partitions, to give a protected means of escape.

Install a roll-out fire-escape ladder that can be fitted over an attic window sill.

ESCAPE LADDER

ROUTE A

ROUTE B

REFUGE ROOM

Choose a refuge room with a front window so you can call for help and be visible to the emergency services.

■ **CHILDREN** Even small children should know that they must alert the household if they smell smoke or hear the smoke alarm. **All children old enough to understand should know how to contact the Fire and Rescue Service** and know their address by heart. Make sure they know only to call 999 in an emergency, and never in play.

■ **PLAN FOR RESTRICTED MOBILITY** If there are elderly people and people with disabilities in your home, consider them in your fire-escape plan. You can ask the Fire and Rescue Service to visit you to provide safety advice and fit specialised smoke alarms.

cooking fires

Nearly 20 people are killed or injured every day by accidental household fires that have spread from the kitchen. The most common sort are fires caused by deep-fat frying, known generically as 'chip pan' fires. These account for around 20 per cent of all fires in the UK that are attended by the Fire and Rescue Service.

action

CHIP PAN FIRE

1 LEAVE THE PAN ON THE HOB Do not attempt to move a burning chip pan.

2 TURN OFF THE HEAT Only do this at the hob if it is safe to do so. If you have to reach across the fire to do this, turn off the appliance at the power source (see Watchpoint, opposite).

3 GET OUT Leave the kitchen and close the door. Get everyone out of the house, ring the emergency services and wait to be told when it is safe to return.

 WARNING
Never use water on an oil fire as it can cause a fireball. Do not use a fire extinguisher as it may spread the flames.

The tea towel technique

Serious injuries are caused every year by people attempting to put out a chip pan fire, which is why the Fire and Rescue Service advise you not to attempt to extinguish the flames, but to evacuate the area and call them.

As used by professionals, the correct technique is to extinguish a chip pan fire by covering the pan with a damp tea towel, rolling it over the flames away from yourself, to cut off the supply of oxygen. A fire blanket (see box, opposite) can be used to put out the fire.

precautions

SAFE DEEP-FAT FRYING
● Consider oven or microwave chips instead.
● Heat oil just enough to crisp a piece of bread or potato, or use a thermostatically controlled electric deep-fat frying pan. If oil is overheated, it smokes first, then ignites. Never leave the pan unattended.
● Only fill the pan one third full of oil. Oil is a flammable liquid and can spontaneously ignite if it reaches a temperature of 350°C.
● Dry food on kitchen paper before frying to prevent it spattering oil onto a flame.

PREVENTING OTHER KITCHEN FIRES
● Keep electrical leads clear of the cooker.
● Do not hang tea towels on or over the cooker and avoid putting oven gloves down on the hob.
● Clean toasters regularly and keep them away from curtains.
● Turn off cooking appliances after use.
● Keep pets and small children at least one metre away from the cooker.
● Take particular care if you are wearing loose clothing as it can easily catch fire.

GET HELP Do not hesitate to get out of the house if there is a fire in your kitchen that you cannot put out. Call the Fire and Rescue Service as soon as possible once outside.

WATCHPOINT Gas appliances can be turned off at the control knob and electric at the power point, if it is safe to do so. Or switch off your electricity and gas supply at the mains.

TIME TO ACT Before starting to cook in an unfamiliar kitchen, when self-catering for example, check if the kitchen has a fire blanket. Do not wait until you need it to search for it.

Fire blanket

A fire blanket is a sheet of fire-resistant material used to cover a fire to cut off the supply of oxygen (see left). It is unlikely that you will be able to retrieve the blanket from a fire to use it again, so learn how to use it correctly the first time. You will be able to use the fire blanket more effectively if you have read the instructions or, ideally, been trained in how to use it correctly.

● **MANY USES** It is most useful in a kitchen on small, self-contained fires, especially burning oil. It can also be used on some electrical fires or to wrap around someone whose clothes are on fire.
● **BEST SIZE** Choose a blanket that is at least 1m square, made to British Standard BS EN 1869. Draw tapes will allow you to access the blanket quickly and enable you to hold the blanket safely between you and the fire.
● **CLOSE AT HAND** Keep the blanket accessible in a container on a wall, but not above a cooker or a heater.
● **HOW TO USE** Cover the fire completely. Gaps allow air to get in and feed the flames. Leave the fire covered for at least 30 minutes to make sure it is fully extinguished. Discard the blanket after use and replace with a new one.

GRILL FIRE

■ **GRILL PAN ON COOKER** Keep your grill clean as a build-up of fat and residual food can catch fire spontaneously. Close the door if possible. Turn off the power, if it is safe to do so, but do not lean over the pan to reach the controls. Evacuate the area and call the Fire and Rescue Service immediately.

■ **OUTDOOR CHARCOAL GRILL** Do not use flammable liquids to encourage poorly burning charcoal. If the flames get out of control, close the lid.

■ **OUTDOOR GAS GRILL** If a gas-fired barbecue catches fire, turn off the gas at the main cylinder immediately, if possible. If the gas cylinder is engulfed by flames, evacuate the area and call the Fire and Rescue Service immediately.

MICROWAVE FIRE

1 KEEP THE OVEN DOOR CLOSED Opening the door will allow oxygen inside to feed the fire so keep the door closed. Switch off the power if it is safe to do so.

2 PREVENT FLAMES FROM SPREADING Throw a fire blanket over the microwave to contain and put out the flames.

 TAKE CARE
Most microwave fires are caused through misuse. Never use for drying clothes and do not place any metal objects inside the microwave or use metal containers to heat food.

▶▶See also: **SEVERE BURNS AND SCALDS** p23 • **CAUGHT IN A BLAZING HOUSE** pp122–125

electrical fires

Whenever electricity flows through a wire, the wire heats up: as occurs in an electric radiant heater. Fuses or miniature circuit breakers (MCBs) protect household wiring from overheating and fuses in plugs protect flexes. Misuse of fuses, poor maintenance of appliances and overloading of sockets can all lead to an electrical fire.

action

1 TURN OFF THE ELECTRICITY This needs to be done at the mains supply at the house consumer unit or mains fusebox. Do not touch or remove the plug or appliances until the electricity is turned off to avoid the possibility of an electric shock.

2 EXTINGUISH FIRE Use a fire blanket (see page 217) or a dry powder or carbon dioxide fire extinguisher (see below) on small electrical fires. Never use water as it could cause electrocution.

3 GET HELP If you cannot put out the fire get out of the property and call the emergency services immediately. Wait outside until you are told it is safe to return.

Extinguishers for electrical fire

You will be able to use a fire extinguisher more effectively if you have read the instructions or, ideally, been trained in how to use it correctly.

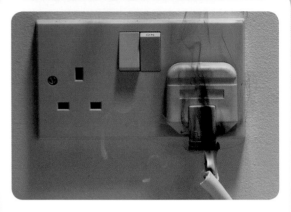

● **DRY POWDER** (blue label) Containing dry powder, these are suitable for electrical fires, on burning solid materials and fires involving flammable liquids. Do not use on cooking oil. A 1kg extinguisher is adequate for home use.
● **CARBON DIOXIDE** (black label) For use on flammable liquids except cooking oil, and for electrical fires. They cause the least damage to electrical equipment, such as computers.

assessment

There are various signs of potential electrical problems. These include fuses that 'blow' frequently, flickering lights and scorch marks on sockets or plugs.

● Many homes have too few sockets, which causes the over-use of adaptors and trailing leads, both of which can result in fire.
● Badly wired plugs with visible loose wires can be a source of sparking.
● Electric flexes running underneath carpets can easily get worn and may overheat.

be aware

● Never overload an adaptor for single appliances or trailing adaptors with several socket outlets.
● Use the correct fuse in a plug – check the appliance manual for information, and use the plug supplied by the manufacturer, replacing the fuse when necessary with one of the same amperage.
● Electrical appliances should be serviced once a year – especially those with heaters and motors.
● Electric blankets should be checked annually and not left on all night unless they are blankets designed for continuous running.

▶▶See also: **ELECTRICAL INJURY** pp110–111

careless fires

Two main types of careless fire occur in the home: more than five fires a day are started by unattended candles, and every three days someone dies in a fire caused by a cigarette. The occurrence of candle fires is rising – between 1995 and 2001 they increased by 47 per cent. Use them to create atmosphere but ensure they are safely housed and tended.

action

CANDLE OR CIGARETTE FIRE

■ **ASSESS THE FIRE** If a cigarette, unextinguished butt or fallen candle causes a fire, ascertain what is on fire in order to take the appropriate action.

■ **BURNING PLASTIC Night-lights and tea-lights can get hot enough to melt plastic which can then ignite.** Use a dry powder fire extinguisher (see box, opposite) to put out fires involving burning plastic.

■ **BURNING CURTAINS** Use water to extinguish burning curtains – throw water onto the fabric from a bucket, or for a smaller fire, pour water from a jug or kettle. Use a water (red label) extinguisher, if available.

■ **SMOULDERING UPHOLSTERY** Use water from a bucket or bowl to douse upholstery. Use a water (red label) extinguisher, if available. If possible, take the furniture outside in case a deep-seated fire continues to smoulder and ignites later.

■ **GET OUT AND STAY OUT** If any fire takes hold and is no longer localised, get everyone out of the house and call the Fire and Rescue Service. Stay out.

If your clothes catch fire

■ **DO NOT RUN** Moving around will fan the flames and make them burn faster.
■ **DROP AND ROLL** Dropping to the ground and rolling around will stop the fire from spreading and engulfing you. As flames will burn upward, lying down will also help to protect your face and head.

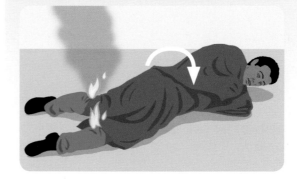

■ **SMOTHER THE FLAMES** To be more effective, wrap yourself in a fire blanket, heavy coat or thick blanket.

be aware

USING CANDLES SAFELY
● Never leave a burning candle unattended.
● Use a snuffer or spoon to put it out. Blowing could spread sparks and hot wax. Do not move it.
● Keep candles out of draughts and away from curtains and other fabrics or furniture.
● Keep clothes and your hair away from the candle's flame.
● Do not drop anything, such as a matchstick, into hot wax, as the candle may flare up.

● Stand candles on a heat-resistant surface in a secure and stable holder so they do not fall over.

SMOKING PRECAUTIONS
● Never leave a burning cigarette unattended.
● Put a cigarette out properly – never discard a lit butt end. Cigarettes burn at 700°C and contain chemicals designed to keep them alight.
● Never smoke in bed or when drowsy.

▶▶See also: SEVERE BURNS AND SCALDS p23

chimney on fire

There are around 10,000 chimney fires a year in the UK. Although a chimney is built to cope with a fire, chimney fires can spread into the loft space or under floors and may cause extensive damage to the fabric of the whole house.

assessment

● One of the first indications of a chimney fire from inside the house is a roaring sound from the chimney. On the outside you will be able to see thick clouds of smoke and there may be flames coming out of the chimney.
● The chimney itself can reach temperatures that are high enough to ignite neighbouring timber in the loft or under floor boards.
● The extreme heat makes the chimney expand, which can cause nearby plaster to crack and cause structural damage.

action

1 **CONTACT THE FIRE AND RESCUE SERVICE** Ring the emergency services immediately.

2 **REDUCE OXYGEN SUPPLY** If you have an enclosed stove, shut all air vents and flue dampers to deprive the fire of oxygen.

3 **MOVE FURNITURE** To avoid further risk, move furniture away from the fireplace and from the chimney breast. This should be done in any room that shares the chimney.

4 **ENSURE FREE ACCESS** Make sure the Fire and Rescue Service has access to the loft space.

5 **HOSE DOWN ROOF** Hose down the roof around the chimney with water, but avoid the chimney itself.

for next time...

● **Chimneys should be swept at least once a year – twice if you are burning wood.** Your insurance company may not pay out for chimney fire damage if this has not been done.
● Use a chimney-cleaning additive or a chimney cleaning log to help dry out the accumulated tar so it flakes off. This should be done a week or so before the chimney is swept.
● Only use well-seasoned wood for burning. Never burn cardboard or Christmas trees. Do not use your fire as a waste paper bin. Use only recommended fuels.
● Have small, frequent 'hot' fires that burn more completely and produce less smoke.
● Burning wood produces a lot of soot and tar, so if you have an enclosed fire, such as a wood-burning stove or kitchen stove, ensure it is connected to a properly insulated chimney liner. It needs a flue pipe connected to a double-skinned stainless steel liner or a lightweight concrete liner. Make sure flues are professionally installed for safety.

danger from lightning

If lightning strikes a house, it can wreck electrical and electronic equipment and start a major fire. The bolt will take the easiest route to earth, through cables, wires or water pipes. The chances of being killed by lightning in the UK are only one in 2 million, but it is a myth that lightning will never strike twice.

action

 WARNING

You are in danger as soon as you hear thunder. Every five seconds that lapse between seeing lightning and hearing thunder represents 1.6km from the centre of a storm. Lightning can strike up to 16km from the centre.

1 UNPLUG APPLIANCES Unplug all non-essential appliances. TV sets and computers are especially at risk as lightning can cause power surges (see box, right). Do not unplug the TV aerial in case lightning strikes at that moment.

2 AVOID USING THE TELEPHONE Only use your landline in an emergency. Use a cordless handset – not the base station – or a mobile phone.

3 STAY AWAY FROM METAL OBJECTS Do not touch metal taps, pipes, radiators or sinks while the storm is in progress as they can conduct electricity.

4 STAY AWAY FROM WINDOWS Resist the temptation to watch a storm from a window in case it shatters.

5 STAY INDOORS Do not go outside until 30 minutes after the last thunder clap, as the greatest risk is to those outside.

Lightning will seek the best conductor – not necessarily the highest building.

Surge protection

One of the effects of a lightning strike can be a sudden increase in voltage – or surge – in your electrical wiring, which can damage appliances. Antisurge adaptors will regulate the voltage. Plug these in between the appliance and the socket to protect vulnerable equipment, such as computers, printers, hi-fi equipment and TV sets. Dishwashers, washing machines and tumble dryers are also at risk.

for next time...

● If your house has been struck by lightning, it may be a good conductor and vulnerable to further strikes. Install a lightning conductor and earth the TV aerial and satellite dish.
● TV aerials can provide a path for lightning. In the USA, where lightning is more common, TV aerials and satellite dishes are earthed.

 TAKE CARE

If someone is struck by lightning, it is safe to administer first aid at once as the casualty will not carry an electrical charge. Check for breathing and give CPR if necessary (see pages 16–17). Treat burns as you would those from any other source (see page 23).

▶▶See also: **ELECTRICAL INJURY** pp110-111 • **CAUGHT IN LIGHTNING** p262 • **POWER SURGE** p330

gas leak

Natural gas leaking from an appliance in your home is rare but dangerous. If a person is trapped in a room with leaking gas, it can result in asphyxiation and, if a leak builds up, the accumulated gas can cause a fire or explosion if set alight.

GET HELP Ring the National Gas Emergency Service on 0800 111 999. This helpline operates 24 hours a day and an engineer will be with you within two hours.

assessment

● You should be able to smell a gas leak as fuel gas is given a very distinctive odour to enable quick detection. Although natural gas detectors are available for the home, they are only necessary if you have no sense of smell.

● A weak smell of gas could be caused by a pilot light going out on a cooker, gas water heater or gas fire, or by a cooker burner flame going out. This is the first thing to check.

● If the smell of gas gets stronger, or persists after you have done these checks, you should take action immediately before the gas has a chance to build up.

action

1 TURN OFF THE GAS
Individual gas appliances have their own gas tap; the mains gas tap is a big lever on the gas pipe next to the gas meter, shown on the right here, in the ON position. Move the lever through 90 degrees to the OFF position and cut the gas supply.

2 AVOID SPARKS AND PUT OUT FLAMES Do not touch any electrical switches as turning them on or off may create a spark and trigger an explosion. Immediately snuff lit candles, turn off gas rings and douse natural flame fires. Lit cigarettes should be extinguished immediately with water.

3 DISPERSE GAS Open all doors and windows to allow any gas to disperse.

4 VACATE AREA Keep everyone away from the affected areas as the fumes could become overwhelming. Tell your nearest neighbours and ask them to pass on the warning.

5 RING THE AUTHORITIES Ring the National Gas Emergency Service on 0800 111 999. They will need to be told your location, name and telephone number, how many people are present, how long the smell has been noticeable and if it is coming from a cellar or basement. Be ready to provide details of any special circumstances or access information.

 TAKE CARE

● Gas appliances should be safety checked every 12 months by a Gas Safe registered engineer. In rented accommodation it is a legal requirement that the landlord maintains the appliances.

● If you live in a block of flats and become aware of a smell of gas, turn off the supply to your flat immediately (see step 1, left). Follow the other steps, alerting people in neighbouring flats, and ring the National Gas Emergency number (see above) explaining your situation; follow their advice.

carbon monoxide build-up

Carbon monoxide (CO) is produced when gas is not properly burnt in a faulty or poorly maintained gas appliance. It has no smell, so you cannot detect it, though you may show signs of a number of physical symptoms if exposed to the gas. If allowed to build up, it can lead to serious poisoning and, ultimately, death.

be aware

● You cannot see, taste or smell carbon monoxide, but it can kill you without warning in a matter of hours.
● **The physical symptoms of CO poisoning include headache, nausea, dizziness, tiredness, stomach pain and confusion,** all of which may be confused with the symptoms of influenza or food poisoning.
● An appliance may produce carbon monoxide if it is poorly installed or maintained, or if there is a lack of fresh air for safe combustion of the gas, or a blocked chimney.
● You are at particular risk if you sleep in a room with a gas appliance such as a gas fire or water heater, which is left on at night and does not have a balanced flue. A balanced flue – a two-part duct leading to the outside – allows the products of combustion of the gas to be taken outside and fresh air for combustion to be drawn in.

action

1 **DISPERSE GAS** Open all doors and windows to allow any gas to disperse.

2 **VACATE AREA** Tell the rest of the family and move them out of harm's way. Notify your neighbours.

3 **SHUT OFF GAS SUPPLY** If possible, turn off the faulty appliance or turn the gas off at the mains gas tap. Ring the National Gas Emergency Service on 0800 111 999 immediately.

■ **SUSPECT SYMPTOMS** If you are suffering from physical symptoms only when at home, visit your GP or local hospital and tell them you suspect carbon monoxide poisoning.

Carbon monoxide detectors

Carbon monoxide detectors warn of a leak. They can be mains or battery-operated, carbon monoxide only or combined CO/smoke detectors. The one shown below is a battery-operated carbon-monoxide-only detector.

● **APPROVED** Make sure your detector has an audible alarm and is approved to the relevant British Standard (BS EN 50291). It must carry a British or European approval mark.
● **INSTALLATION** Battery-operated detectors need little or no installation. Some mains-operated detectors plug into a socket outlet, whereas others are wired into a circuit and need to be installed by an electrician. Refer to the manufacturer's instructions for the optimum location for any detector that you buy.

 WARNING
Make sure that you know the difference between the sound of your CO detector and your smoke alarm.

 **TAKE CARE**
For optimum safety, get your gas appliances checked annually by a qualified person.

central **heating** failure

When the central heating fails, the extent of the emergency will depend on the time of year and whether there are very young or old members of your household. If you have a gas system and have to call a heating engineer, choose someone who is on the **Gas Safe Register**.

assessment

If your electricity supply is working correctly (see pages 138–139) and you have fuel (gas or oil), check your system in the order below. **Call a heating engineer if you are not confident of your ability to make the checks, adjustments or repairs,** or if a component seems to be malfunctioning.

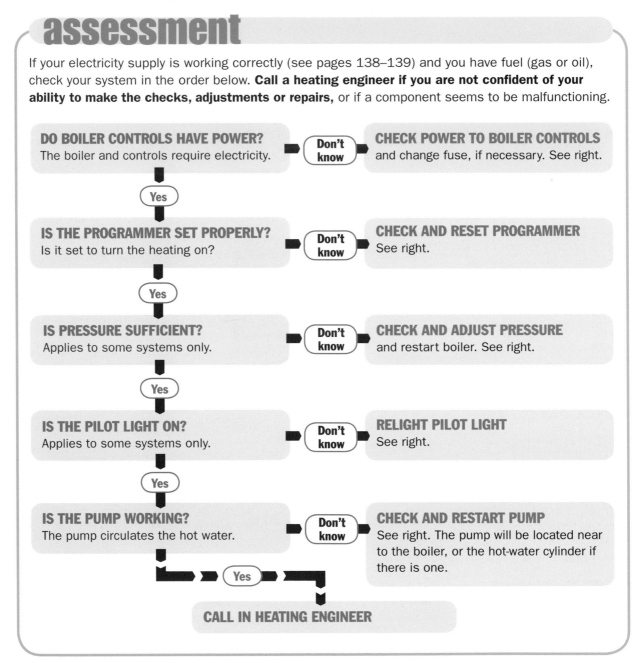

DO BOILER CONTROLS HAVE POWER?
The boiler and controls require electricity.

Don't know → **CHECK POWER TO BOILER CONTROLS** and change fuse, if necessary. See right.

Yes

IS THE PROGRAMMER SET PROPERLY?
Is it set to turn the heating on?

Don't know → **CHECK AND RESET PROGRAMMER** See right.

Yes

IS PRESSURE SUFFICIENT?
Applies to some systems only.

Don't know → **CHECK AND ADJUST PRESSURE** and restart boiler. See right.

Yes

IS THE PILOT LIGHT ON?
Applies to some systems only.

Don't know → **RELIGHT PILOT LIGHT** See right.

Yes

IS THE PUMP WORKING?
The pump circulates the hot water.

Don't know → **CHECK AND RESTART PUMP** See right. The pump will be located near to the boiler, or the hot-water cylinder if there is one.

Yes

CALL IN HEATING ENGINEER

action

NO POWER TO BOILER

1 **CHECK POWER TO BOILER CONTROLS** Check that the boiler is turned on and that it and the controls have an electrical supply. This will usually come from a fused connection unit.

2 **CHANGE FUSE** If there is no power to the boiler and its controls, turn off the power to the connection unit and replace the fuse.

FAULTY PROGRAMMER

■ **CHECK AND RESET PROGRAMMER** Make sure the programmer is set so that the heating is switched on. If it is not working, call in a heating engineer.

INSUFFICIENT PRESSURE

1 **CHECK AND ADJUST PRESSURE** If there is a pressure gauge on your boiler, check the instruction manual to see what the pressure should be. If it is too low, follow the manufacturer's instructions to top it up.

2 **RESTART** After adjusting the pressure, you might have to press a restart button on the boiler, if it has one. If the system keeps on losing pressure, there might be a leak somewhere (see pp146–147).

PILOT LIGHT OUT

■ **RELIGHT PILOT LIGHT** You should be able to see the pilot light through a small window on the front of the boiler. If it has gone out, attempt to relight it by following the manufacturer's instructions. If you cannot access it or light it, call an engineer.

for next time...

Regular servicing of your heating system – on an annual basis – will make it less likely that there will be a sudden failure. Many companies offer a combined emergency call-out service and regular maintenance deal.

PUMP NOT WORKING

1 **ISOLATE PUMP**
A sticking or jammed pump prevents water circulating properly around the system. Some pump types can be freed manually. Switch off the central heating which will turn off the pump. Close the isolating valves above and below the pump with a spanner.

2 **FREE SPINDLE** Be prepared to mop up an inevitable slight spillage of water. Undo and remove the large screw in the centre of the circular cover to reveal the slotted end of the spindle. Insert a smaller screwdriver to turn the spindle to and fro until it feels free. Replace the central screw, restore the water supply and turn the heating back on. If the pump still does not work, call a heating engineer.

Radiator problems

If your boiler and pump are working but some of the radiators are cool or cold, the problem could be in your radiators and pipes.

● **COLD TOPS AND WARM BOTTOMS** This is a sign that air has got into the system. Bleed the radiators with a radiator key to get rid of the air.

● **COLD RADIATORS UPSTAIRS** Bleed the radiators, as right. If this does not work, check the pump.

● **COLD BOTTOMS AND WARM TOPS** This indicates that you have corrosion and sludge is collecting at the bottom of the radiator. A heating engineer will flush out the sludge and add a corrosion inhibitor to the heating system.

▶▶See also: **NO HOT WATER** pp136–137 • **BURST AND LEAKING PIPES** pp146–147

no **hot water**

Life without hot water can be uncomfortable and the problem should be identified and solved as quickly as possible. There are some checks and repairs that you can do yourself but for others you will need to get professional help.

WATCHPOINT With no central heating, an electric shower will still give hot water. Another back-up is an immersion element in an otherwise boiler-heated cylinder.

Follow the flowchart to see what action to take. Call a heating engineer or qualified electrician if you feel unable to make the necessary checks or repairs or if a part seems to be malfunctioning.

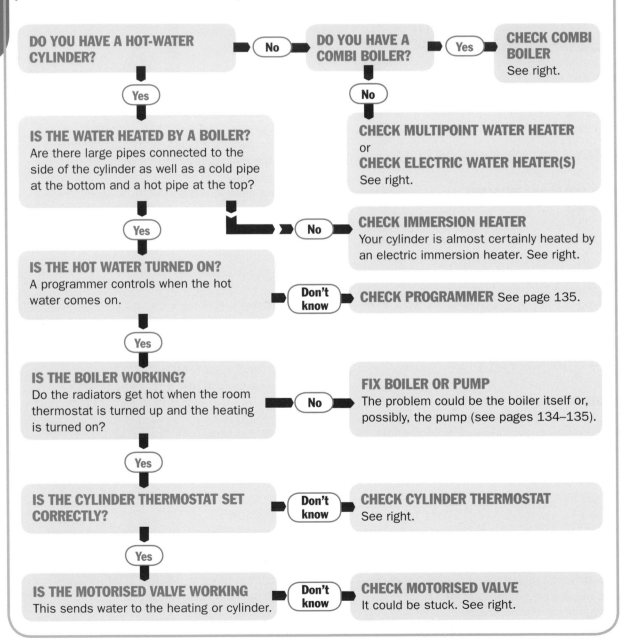

DO YOU HAVE A HOT-WATER CYLINDER?
— No → **DO YOU HAVE A COMBI BOILER?** — Yes → **CHECK COMBI BOILER** See right.

Yes ↓   No ↓

IS THE WATER HEATED BY A BOILER?
Are there large pipes connected to the side of the cylinder as well as a cold pipe at the bottom and a hot pipe at the top?

CHECK MULTIPOINT WATER HEATER
or
CHECK ELECTRIC WATER HEATER(S)
See right.

Yes ↓   — No → **CHECK IMMERSION HEATER**
Your cylinder is almost certainly heated by an electric immersion heater. See right.

IS THE HOT WATER TURNED ON?
A programmer controls when the hot water comes on.
— Don't know → **CHECK PROGRAMMER** See page 135.

Yes ↓

IS THE BOILER WORKING?
Do the radiators get hot when the room thermostat is turned up and the heating is turned on?
— No → **FIX BOILER OR PUMP**
The problem could be the boiler itself or, possibly, the pump (see pages 134–135).

Yes ↓

IS THE CYLINDER THERMOSTAT SET CORRECTLY?
— Don't know → **CHECK CYLINDER THERMOSTAT**
See right.

Yes ↓

IS THE MOTORISED VALVE WORKING
This sends water to the heating or cylinder.
— Don't know → **CHECK MOTORISED VALVE**
It could be stuck. See right.

action

COMBI BOILER OR MULTIPOINT HEATER FAILS

1 CHECK WATER PRESSURE If the hot water from a combi boiler or multipoint heater fails, it could be because of low mains pressure. When this happens, water may not be coming out of a kitchen cold-water tap with its usual force. Contact your water company as you will have to wait for them to address this.

2 CHECK PILOT LIGHT If the pilot light is out (see page 135), relight it, if possible, following the manufacturer's instructions.

3 GET PROFESSIONAL HELP If the pressure and pilot light are working, call in a heating engineer to diagnose and repair the fault. Some boilers have a display that shows error codes to aid fault diagnosis.

ELECTRIC WATER HEATER FAILS

1 CHECK POWER SUPPLY Some homes have hot water supplied by individual electric heaters at sinks, basins or showers. If one is not working, check its power supply. First check the main consumer unit (see page 139) where there will be an MCB or a fuse on the circuit for the heater; reset the MCB or replace the fuse (see page 139).

2 CHECK AND CHANGE FUSE Turn off the power and check the fuse in the connection unit that feeds the heater. Follow the thick flex back from the heater and you will reach the unit. Change the fuse if necessary.

3 GET PROFESSIONAL HELP If steps 1 and 2 do not resolve the problem, call a heating engineer.

IMMERSION HEATER FAILS

1 CHECK IMMERSION HEATER Ensure that the immersion heater is switched on. Check that the timer is working and is set to come on.

2 CHECK POWER SUPPLY Check that the heater is receiving power. First check the main consumer unit

(see page 139) where there will be an MCB or a fuse on the circuit for the immersion heater; reset the MCB or change the fuse.

3 CHECK FUSE Turn off the power and check the fuse in the connection unit – follow the thick flex back from the heater to reach the unit. If the power supply to the heater seems to be working, it means that the immersion heater has burnt out or the immersion heater thermostat has failed. Contact an heating engineer to sort out which and replace.

CYLINDER THERMOSTAT FAILS

■ **CHECK CYLINDER THERMOSTAT** The cylinder thermostat is strapped to the side of the hot-water cylinder and controls the flow of water from the boiler. Turn the dial on the thermostat. You should hear a 'click' as it passes the temperature of the water inside. If you think that the thermostat is not working, ask a heating engineer to replace it.

MOTORISED VALVE STUCK

1 CHECK VALVE Motorised valves control the flow of water from the boiler to the heating or hot-water cylinder. Positioned where the hot water pipe from the boiler divides into two, it feeds the radiators and hot-water cylinder. It may be closer to the hot-water cylinder or the boiler. If there is heating but no hot water, the valve that sends water to the cylinder could be stuck. Some systems have a single three-way valve that sends water to the heating or cylinder; some have two, two-way valves (one for heating, one for hot water).

2 ADJUST LEVER With a three- or two-way valve that sends water to the cylinder, try moving the manual lever. Models vary, but markings usually indicate lever positions. If the lever meets resistance, the valve motor may have burnt out. Call a heating engineer to replace it.

▶▶See also: **CENTRAL HEATING FAILURE** pp134–135

no electricity

We are so reliant on electricity that being without it is extremely problematic. There are a few measures you can take to get the power in your home back on, but before you tackle the problem, it is important to learn how the electricity system works (see box, right).

assessment

Follow this checklist to find out what to do. Call a qualified electrician if you feel unable to make any of the checks, adjustments or repairs, or if a component seems to be malfunctioning.

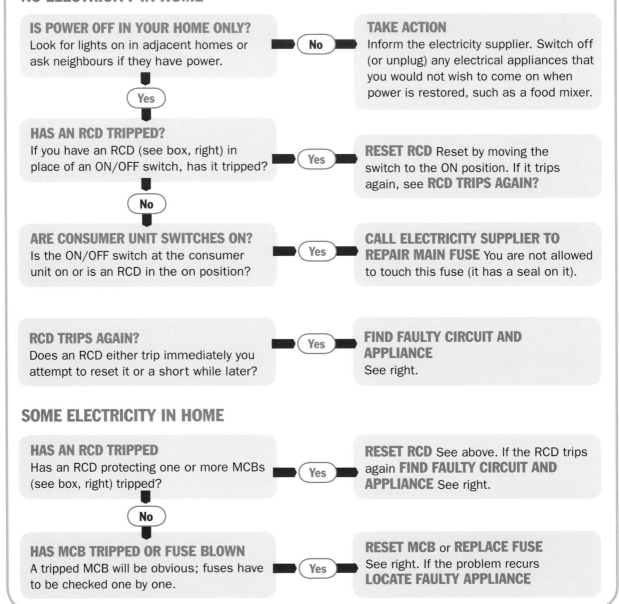

NO ELECTRICITY IN HOME

IS POWER OFF IN YOUR HOME ONLY?
Look for lights on in adjacent homes or ask neighbours if they have power.

No →

TAKE ACTION
Inform the electricity supplier. Switch off (or unplug) any electrical appliances that you would not wish to come on when power is restored, such as a food mixer.

Yes

HAS AN RCD TRIPPED?
If you have an RCD (see box, right) in place of an ON/OFF switch, has it tripped?

Yes →

RESET RCD Reset by moving the switch to the ON position. If it trips again, see **RCD TRIPS AGAIN?**

No

ARE CONSUMER UNIT SWITCHES ON?
Is the ON/OFF switch at the consumer unit on or is an RCD in the on position?

Yes →

CALL ELECTRICITY SUPPLIER TO REPAIR MAIN FUSE You are not allowed to touch this fuse (it has a seal on it).

RCD TRIPS AGAIN?
Does an RCD either trip immediately you attempt to reset it or a short while later?

Yes →

FIND FAULTY CIRCUIT AND APPLIANCE
See right.

SOME ELECTRICITY IN HOME

HAS AN RCD TRIPPED
Has an RCD protecting one or more MCBs (see box, right) tripped?

Yes →

RESET RCD See above. If the RCD trips again **FIND FAULTY CIRCUIT AND APPLIANCE** See right.

No

HAS MCB TRIPPED OR FUSE BLOWN
A tripped MCB will be obvious; fuses have to be checked one by one.

Yes →

RESET MCB or REPLACE FUSE
See right. If the problem recurs **LOCATE FAULTY APPLIANCE**

How electricity is supplied

Electricity reaches your home via a cable or wire that goes to the supplier's fuse (the main fuse). From there it goes to the meter and then to your consumer unit (or fuse box), where there are circuit breakers or, in older systems, fuses.

- **MCB** Circuits run through your home from the consumer unit, each protected by a miniature circuit breaker (called an MCB) or a fuse. If a circuit gets overloaded (which could cause overheating and be a fire risk), an MCB trips or a fuse blows, cutting off the power to that circuit.
- **RCD** On some consumer units a Residual Current Device (RCD) is fitted to protect against

electric shock. Some homes have an RCD in place of a consumer unit's ON/OFF switch and some have an RCD fitted to one or more circuits.

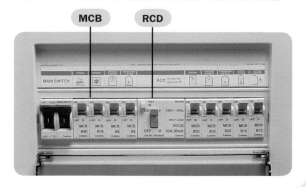

action

RCD KEEPS TRIPPING

1 FIND FAULTY CIRCUIT To work out which circuit is causing the problem, switch off all the MCBs on the circuits protected by the RCD, re-set the RCD and then switch the MCBs back on one by one until the RCD trips again.

2 FIND THE FAULTY APPLIANCE If it is a socket outlet circuit that is causing the problem, switch off at the socket outlet then unplug every item on that circuit. Reset the RCD, then plug in and switch on the power to each appliance in turn until the RCD trips again. The problem is most commonly caused by a power-hungry item such as a kettle, iron, washing machine, tumble dryer or dishwasher. Replace the appliance that caused the trip or have it checked by a qualified electrician.

MCB HAS TRIPPED

■ **LOCATE FAULTY APPLIANCE** When an MCB trips, switch off at the socket outlet then unplug every electrical item on the MCB's circuit. One by one, plug them in and switch on at the socket outlet then turn them on until the MCB trips again. Replace the appliance that caused the trip or have it repaired by a qualified electrician. The process is similar for fuse-based systems.

FUSE HAS BLOWN

■ **REPLACE CARTRIDGE FUSE** Rewirable fuses were succeeded by cartridge fuses, which come in different colours, depending on their current rating. Turn the electricity off at the main ON/OFF switch on the consumer unit. Remove the fuse from the fusebox and replace the cartridge with one of the same rating.

⚠ TAKE CARE

- The contents of a freezer will stay frozen (and so safe to eat) for several hours. To extend the period, do not open it and cover it with blankets.
- A power failure may cause a burglar alarm to go off. If you cannot re-set it yourself, ring the alarm company and ask them to come and do it.

⚠ WARNING

If the power has failed and you are using candles for lighting, never leave them unattended. Be sure to keep children and pets away from naked flames.

▶▶See also: **CENTRAL HEATING FAILURE** pp134–135

tree falls on house

During a hurricane in southern England in October 1987, 15 million trees came down, several landing on roofs. Such a weather event is rare, but tree damage to homes does occasionally happen, so learn how to contain and prevent it.

TIME TO ACT The best time of year to have a tree pruned, pollarded or cut back to make it safe is late autumn when the leaves have fallen; prune broad-leaved evergreens in May.

action

1 GET OUT Use whatever route is safest to leave the property. This may or may not be the same as your fire-escape route (see page 125).

2 CALL THE EMERGENCY SERVICES The Fire Brigade will come and make the house safe.

3 CONTACT INSURERS Get in touch with your insurance company as soon as possible – they will need to agree to cover expensive removal and emergency repair procedures.

4 SECURE YOUR HOME You will need a firm of roofing contractors or builders to make good the roof and any other structural damage. The first priority will be to make it waterproof so that there is no additional damage to your property and possessions.

what next?

● A firm of tree surgeons will be needed to cut up and remove the tree.
● If you are unable to live in the house immediately, ensure it is not a looting target. Secure doors and windows and put valuables in temporary storage.

Trees and the law

● **FELLING** To cut down trees protected by a Tree Preservation Order (TPO) you must apply to the local authority for permission, unless the tree is dying, dead or dangerous, in which case you must give your local authority five days notice of your intention. If there is imminent danger of it falling, you can cut it down without notification, but you may have to provide evidence of the danger.
● **LOPPING** You can cut branches off a neighbour's tree that overhang your property – but the wood and any fruit still legally belong to them, so you should offer them back.
● **ROOT TRIMMING** You are entitled to cut back encroaching tree roots – but it would be wise to take professional advice before doing so.
● **ROOT DAMAGE** If a neighbour has complained to you that your tree roots are damaging his property and you have failed to take action, you could be held responsible for any damage.

 WARNING

A tree that has fallen on a house may not be stable. Stay well away from it and keep children and pets away until it has been made safe.

be aware

● Storm damage to houses by trees (and the cost of removing the tree if it has fallen on the house) is covered by most buildings insurance polices.
● If your tree falls on your neighbours' property, they will need to make a claim on their buildings insurance policy.

● Although unlikely to cause a sudden emergency, tree roots can extend under a property, causing damage to the foundations. The first signs of this might be cracks in the plaster inside the house or cracks in the brickwork on the outside.

chimney collapses

A chimney collapsing is – fortunately – a rare occurrence, but it can cause serious damage to your own and other properties and potentially to people passing nearby. There is nothing you can do if a natural disaster causes the collapse, but you can take steps to ensure that your chimney is not a danger.

be aware

- Chimneys can collapse in a serious storm, such as the one in the UK in October 1987. At least some of those that collapsed would have been weakened beforehand by other causes.
- A chimney fire (see page 130) can weaken chimney stacks because it causes the chimney to expand, which can crack the masonry.
- Cracking can also occur because of failed mortar pointing or failed chimney flashing allowing water to get into the brickwork. If the water freezes, it expands, leading to cracking.
- A satellite dish (or large TV aerial) can cause structural damage to a chimney, especially if it is mounted on a long pole and exposed to strong winds.

 TAKE CARE

One – avoidable – cause of chimney collapse is the illegal removal of chimney breasts where Building Regulations approval has not been obtained. Chimney breasts provide essential support to chimneys – and, in some houses, the whole chimney stack is an essential structural element of the house. Consult an architect or structural engineer before undertaking work on a chimney breast.

action

1 GET HELP Call the emergency services. The Fire Brigade can help to make the property safe and the Ambulance Service will be needed if anyone has been injured.

2 GIVE FIRST AID Do the best you can to help anyone who has been injured. If you are not sure what to do, ask the Emergency Services controller when you ring them.

3 CALL A BUILDER What is left of the chimney will need to be secured and the roof weatherproofed to prevent further damage to your property and to any possessions.

4 CONTACT INSURANCE COMPANY Damage caused by a collapsed chimney should be covered by your buildings insurance policy – the only exception might be if you have caused the collapse yourself by illegally removing the chimney breasts.

 WARNING

Do not go up onto the roof (or even into the loft) to assess or inspect any damage from a collapsed chimney stack. The structure is likely to be unstable and you could cause more damage or injure yourself.

Safe chimneys

- **REGULAR INSPECTION** Inspect your chimney regularly (from the ground with binoculars) looking for cracks, leaning brickwork, loose or missing mortar and damage to flashing (the shaped bits of lead around the chimney stack). If you see any problems, get a builder to make repairs at once.
- **CHIMNEY REMOVAL** Seek professional advice and consult the Building Control Department of your local council if you are thinking of removing a chimney stack.
- **UNSTABLE AERIALS** Be aware of the dangers posed by large TV aerials and satellite dishes on long poles.
- **STRUCTURAL DAMAGE** Have the chimney checked for structural damage after you have had a chimney fire.

broken **windows** and **doors**

Discovering a burglary or break-in at your home is bad enough without the knowledge that your home's security is compromised by damage to windows and doors. There are immediate and effective short-term measures that you can take to secure kicked-in doors and shattered windows, although you will have to have them professionally repaired or replaced later.

assessment

- If you think that your home has been burgled, take care if you suspect that the burglar might still be inside (see pages 164–166).
- If the breakage is the result of a burglary, call the police.
- If a door has been forced to gain entry, it will need to be secured until repaired or replaced. Call a carpenter, especially if you are not confident about making temporary repairs.
- Broken windows can be covered up before the glass is replaced. If you cannot mend a window yourself, call a glazier.

⚠ TAKE CARE

Both broken glass and splintered wood can cause injuries, so always wear thick gloves when handling them – plus eye protectors when removing glass from a window pane.

action

DAMAGED DOOR

1 MEND THE DAMAGE If the door has been forced, it is likely that the door frame will have been damaged so that the lock is useless. Contact a carpenter or builder to replace the frame, and the door, if necessary, so the door can be locked.

2 MAKE TEMPORARY REPAIRS An inward-opening front door with a letter box at about waist height and with a wooden floor on the inside can be temporarily secured with a stout wooden prop (see box, below). An alternative, if the door and frame are of solid wood, is to fit a bolt or two on the inside. This works if the door is inward or outward opening.

Prop a door shut

1 MAKE YOUR PROP You will need around 1.2m of 100mm by 50mm sawn timber or similar for the prop and 300mm for the floor support. This second piece of wood is screwed or nailed to the floor (watch for pipes or cables below).

2 SECURE THE DOOR With one end of the prop held in place by the floor support, jam the other end into the letter box. The prop can be kicked out if you need to open the door in a hurry.

BROKEN WINDOW

1 **MAKE SAFE** Smash out the broken glass from the window with a hammer. **Get a glazier to do this or wear gloves and eye protectors** and spread dust sheets on both sides of the window.

2 **MAKE SECURE** To keep the weather out, tape a sheet of heavy-gauge polythene over a window. If your window has a wooden frame, hold the polythene more securely with wooden battens (see above). A wooden-framed window can be boarded up with plywood or exterior strand board cut to size and screwed or nailed in place.

3 **REPAIR THE WINDOW** Call a glazier or, if you have a traditional wooden-framed window, you may want to replace a single pane of glass yourself. If you have double glazing or if the frame is damaged, get professional help.

what next?

● If the damage was caused by a burglary, you will need a case or crime number from the police for any claim you make from your insurance company. When the police have gone, assess the damage and what you need to do to make your home more secure.
● It is possible that burglars will have found some spare keys to let themselves out of the door so you will need to change the locks.
● Take the opportunity to review your level of security. Perhaps you need more (or better) door locks? Plus some hinge bolts (to prevent the door being levered out)? Think, too, about the type of replacement glass you use for a broken window. For vulnerable windows, toughened or laminated glass offers higher levels of security.

locked out

A door that has slammed shut behind you, locking you out of your home, can be an emergency if there are children or vulnerable people in the house – or if you are cooking.

action

1 **RETRIEVE A SPARE** If you have left a spare with someone, use it to get in. If you have a key that will not work, use the spare to assess whether it is the key or lock that is damaged.

2 **LOOK FOR A WAY IN** Look for a door or window that can be opened so that you can get in without damaging it or injuring yourself.

3 **RING EMERGENCY LOCKSMITH** If you cannot find a spare key or cannot get into your home, call a 24-hour emergency locksmith who will be able to come quickly to your home and either pick the lock or drill it out so you can get in. This can be expensive as you may need to have new locks fitted. In a life-threatening emergency, call the Fire and Rescue Service. Depending on circumstances, there may be a charge for their attendance.

for next time...

● You can save yourself trouble and expense by leaving spare keys with someone you trust. An immediate neighbour or nearby family member are obvious choices.
● You can buy a secure key safe to hold spare keys. This is secured to the wall outside and can only be opened by using a code on the key pad.

 TAKE CARE

● If a key starts becoming hard to use, replace it or the lock before it fails and locks you out.
● You may have to change your locks if you have lost your keys with anything that identifies where you live.

 WARNING

Never leave keys under a flowerpot or stone. Thieves will look there if they want to get in.

▶▶See also: **BREAK-IN AT HOME** pp164–165 • **INTRUDER IN THE HOUSE** p166

water coming through ceiling

When water comes through a ceiling you must act fast to avoid costly structural repairs, as well as serious damage to decorations, furnishings and floor coverings. There can be many causes: the roof may be damaged, a cistern in a loft may have split, a bath may be overflowing or a washing machine in a flat above may be leaking.

assessment

First do the 'Water through ceiling' action steps (see opposite), then identify where the water is coming from. If you cannot perform the procedures yourself, get professional help.

CEILING IS ON TOP FLOOR

IS THE ROOF LEAKING?
Is water dripping from the rafters in a loft or are there no pipes above the ceiling?
— **Yes** →
ARRANGE FOR ROOF REPAIRS
It is unlikely that you will be able to fix a leaking roof, so call a roofing contractor.

No ↓

CHECK PIPES
Can you see or hear water leaking from a pipe or joint above the ceiling?
— **Yes** →
IDENTIFY AND STOP THE LEAK
See Water Through Ceiling, right. Repair a leaking pipe or joint (see pages 146–147).

No ↓

CHECK CISTERN
Is there water on the platform under the cistern? Is the outside of the cistern wet?
— **Yes** →
CISTERN IS LEAKING
Turn off the water supply, and drain cistern (see right).

CEILING IS ON LOWER FLOOR

CHECK BATHROOM OR KITCHEN
Is a bath, shower or sink overflowing on the floor above?
— **Yes** →
EMPTY BATH, BASIN OR SINK
Turn off taps and pull out plug or remove blockage. Contain and mop up any water.

No ↓

IS WATER ON THE FLOOR ABOVE?
Check around radiators, WCs, appliances and pipes (including waste pipes).
— **Yes** →
IDENTIFY AND STOP THE LEAK
See Water Through Ceiling, right. Attempt to contain and mop up the water. Repair a leaking pipe, joint or reconnect waste pipes (see pages 146–147).

No ↓

CHECK UNDER FLOOR OF ROOM ABOVE
If the floor is wooden, lift the floorboards and search for pipe or joint leaks.
— **Yes** →
IDENTIFY AND STOP THE LEAK
See Water Through Ceiling, right. Repair a leaking pipe or joint or reconnect waste pipes (see pages 146–147).

WATER THROUGH CEILING

1 **TURN OFF THE ELECTRICITY** Water can pose a risk of electrocution as well as damaging wiring circuits above the ceiling. **Turn off the electricity using the consumer unit's main ON/OFF switch** (see pages 138–139). Take a torch with you if it is dark.

2 **CATCH THE WATER** Place empty buckets to catch the water so that you can save your flooring. Do not use dustbins to catch the water: you will be unable to lift them when they are full.

3 **TURN OFF THE WATER** If the water is caused by a plumbing problem (see assessment, opposite), turn it off (see right).

CEILING IS BULGING

1 **PREPARE TO CATCH THE WATER** If the ceiling is bulging, you need to take action before it collapses. Start by putting a waterproof covering down, such as a polythene sheet, and then place a large bucket underneath the bulge to catch the water. Have spare buckets or similar-sized containers standing by.

2 **MAKE A DRAINAGE HOLE** Use a pointed stick (or similar) to make a hole in the middle of a large bulge to let the water through.

3 **PROP UP DAMAGED SECTIONS** If it looks as though part of the ceiling is about to come down, make a temporary prop with a length of timber, wedged between two short planks of wood – one on the floor and one on the ceiling – to hold it up.

LEAKY PLUMBING

1 **TURN OFF MAINS WATER** Turn off the water at the mains stop valve (see pages 146–147).

2 **TURN OFF WATER FROM CISTERN** If the leak is in a pipe or appliance fed by a cistern, turn off the flow from the cistern at the red or orange-handled gatevalves (see pages 146–147). Clear any water in cistern-fed pipes or appliances to minimise the amount of water that might leak. Do this by turning on the hot and cold taps, except for the cold tap at the kitchen sink, which is fed direct from the mains, not from the cistern.

CISTERN LEAKING

1 **TURN OFF MAINS WATER** Turn off the water at the mains stop valve (see pages 146–147).

2 **DRAIN CISTERN** Flush the WC and turn on taps supplied by the cistern (see above) to empty it quickly and so minimise the amount of water that can leak from it. Call a plumber to repair or replace the cistern.

APPLIANCE LEAK

■ **SWITCH OFF APPLIANCE** If a washing machine or dishwasher is leaking, switch it off at the plug then turn off its water supply at the red- and blue-handled valves at the end of the machine's inlet hose or hoses. Call a repairman.

what next?

Call in a builder to inspect the ceiling to see if it needs repairing or replacing.

for next time...

If you live in a flat with neighbours above, ask if you can keep a set of their keys. If water comes through your ceiling when they are out, you can get in and take appropriate action. Keep their mobile phone number to let them know of any problem.

▶▶See also: **BURST AND LEAKING PIPES** pp146–147

burst and leaking pipes

Pipes will burst or their joints be forced apart as ice that has frozen inside begins to thaw. You can prevent pipes from freezing in the first place by insulating them effectively, but it is possible to stop a pipe from bursting if you thaw it in the correct way. A leaking pipe or joint may also be the result of other problems, such as damage or corrosion.

assessment

TYPES OF PIPE
● A copper pipe is the most common and is easily split by ice. It can be repaired with a clamp, a 'slip' coupling or a new section of pipe.
● A lead pipe rarely splits but when it does it is difficult to repair. It should be replaced with copper or plastic.
● A plastic pipe is the least likely to split and easiest to repair (with a new section).

BURST AND FROZEN PIPES
● Burst pipes are caused by water freezing in pipes. In the loft and beneath the ground floor are the most likely places for burst pipes.
● In cold weather no water coming from a tap indicates a frozen pipe. This must be dealt with swiftly as the pipe could burst.

LEAKING PIPE OR JOINT
● The first sign of a leaking pipe or pipe joint is likely to be a damp patch on a wall or ceiling. Such a leak may be just a dribble, but must be mended before too much damage is done.
● A separated waste pipe joint can leak out a lot of water and must be reconnected quickly.

Prevent pipes freezing
● INSULATE Cold-water pipes in a loft, under ground floors or outside should be properly insulated. Make sure that there is no loft insulation material under a cold-water cistern, but that the cistern itself is well insulated.
● HEATING Leave the heating on low if you are away in winter; for long absences, turn off the water and drain the system.
● WASTE PIPES To prevent these freezing, mend dripping taps and leave plugs in at night.

action

WATER IS LEAKING

1 TURN OFF THE ELECTRICITY First, turn off the electricity at the main ON/OFF switch on the consumer unit (see pages 138–139). Take a torch if it is dark. Water leaking from pipes or pipe joints can get into electrical fittings (especially ceiling roses and junction boxes), making them unsafe.

2 LOCATE THE LEAK Find the source of the leak as quickly as possible. Do not turn the water off until you have located the problem.

3 TURN OFF THE WATER Turn off the water at the mains stop valve and, if the pipe is fed from the cistern, at the red or orange gatevalve by the cistern as well (see box, opposite). If it is a hot water or central heating pipe that has burst, switch off the boiler and/or immersion heater.

BURST PIPE

■ USE A CLAMP The simplest way to temporarily stop water leaking from a burst or split pipe is to use an emergency pipe repair clamp (see right), screwed in place over the leak.

■ SLIP ON A COUPLING With a burst or split copper pipe, you can use a 'slip' coupling (which has no internal pipe stop and so can be used on pipes in situ). Cut out the affected section and slide on the slip coupling. Call a plumber if you are not confident about doing this yourself.

FROZEN PIPE

1 IDENTIFY THE PIPE If all cold taps (except the kitchen tap) are affected, it is the main pipe leading from the cold-water cistern; just one tap and it is the pipe leading to that tap. For hot taps, it is likely to be the cold feed pipe to the hot-water cylinder.

2 MELT THE ICE Ask a helper to open each affected tap, while you work backwards along the pipe leading to it. Remove any pipe insulation first. If the pipe is made of copper or lead use a hair dryer to heat it until water flows freely from the tap. Treat plastic water pipes in the same way as plastic waste pipes (see below).

3 USE HOT TOWELS If plastic waste pipes are frozen, soak towels in hot water and wrap them round the pipe until the waste water flows away.

LEAKING JOINT

■ **TIGHTEN COMPRESSION JOINT**
If a compression joint is leaking, the leak can normally be stopped by tightening one or both nuts. Always use two spanners, one on the nut and one on the fitting.

■ **REPLACE CAPILLARY JOINT** A leaking soldered capillary joint is difficult to repair. Ask a plumber to drain the pipe, cut out the affected section and replace it with a repair compression coupling.

■ **RE-MAKE PUSH-FIT JOINT** Tighten the plastic cap nut. If this is not possible, drain the pipe and replace the fitting. Call a plumber if you are not confident about doing this.

■ **RE-MAKE WASTE PIPE JOINT** If a 'compression' waste pipe joint (with a knurled ring) has come apart, simply unscrew the knurled ring, push the pipe firmly back into the joint, and retighten the ring.

■ **TIGHTEN RADIATOR NUT** Leaks from radiators can usually be cured by tightening the 'union' nut – the one closest to the radiator at the bottom.

LEAKING PIPE

■ **WRAP IT UP** A temporary fix for a leaking pipe is to wrap self-amalgamating (Alfa) tape tightly over the leaking section (no need to turn the water off first). The layers of tape will merge and create a fully waterproof seal, even on pipes with water at mains pressure.

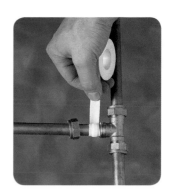

Where to turn off the water

● **MAINS STOP VALVE** This valve controls the flow of water into your home from the water main. It can be found in many different places, including under the kitchen sink, under floorboards or, possibly, outside the house. Turn it clockwise to shut off the water.

● **CISTERN GATEVALVE** A gatevalve (see right) controls the flow from a cold water cistern. Gatevalves often have red or orange handles and are usually found near where a pipe leaves the cistern at its base.

what next?

● If the repairs are temporary, call in a plumber to make permanent repairs.
● Assess the results of the leak or burst and contact your insurance company if ceilings, floor coverings or wallpaper have been damaged.
● Ask an electrician to check the electric wiring before turning the electricity back on.
● Hire a dehumidifier to dry out the property.

▶▶See also: **WATER COMING THROUGH CEILING** pp144–145

flooded **basement**

Water entering a basement or cellar usually has nowhere to go: it just collects and ruins anything you keep down there, and it will probably leave behind an unpleasant smell. There are a number of things you can do to make some types of minor flooding less likely, but tackling a proper flood is a difficult and often dirty job.

action

FLOODING FROM LEAKY PIPE

1 TURN OFF THE WATER If the cause of the cellar flood is a burst or leaking pipe, turn off the water at the appropriate place (see pages 146–147).

2 CATCH THE WATER If possible put a bucket under the leak to catch the water. Have several containers standing by until all the water has drained from the pipe, which might take some time, even after you have turned off the water.

3 PROTECT POSSESSIONS Get anything at risk from damage by the water out of the cellar quickly. Call a plumber to have the pipe repaired.

4 PUMP OUT THE WATER Unless your flood is of fire-brigade proportions (usually when it occurs from an outside source – see below), hire a submersible 'puddle' pump, which will remove all except the last few millimetres of water (the remainder can be sucked up with a wet/dry vacuum cleaner).

FLOODING FROM OUTSIDE

1 USE SANDBAGS If you are threatened by excessive rainfall, overflowing rivers or burst water mains, sandbags (see page 189) will stop water getting in under doors – but not for long.

2 SAVE VALUABLES With localised flooding or a burst water main in the street, you should have sufficient warning to give you time to move at least some of your cherished items out of the basement or cellar.

3 CALL EMERGENCY SERVICES If the basement or cellar is awash, the Fire Brigade will come and pump it out.

be aware

- Serious basement flooding is usually the result of an 'outside agency' – typically excessive rainfall or a nearby burst water main.
- If you are concerned about the possibility of flooding, you can check whether an area is prone to it before buying or renting a house. The Environment Agency has advice about flooding at www.environment-agency.gov.uk/homeandleisure/floods/default.aspx
- Flooding not caused by something like a water-main burst, can be the result of water seeping in through the basement or cellar walls or through the floor. To prevent this, a basement or cellar needs to be 'tanked' – a special waterproof treatment for the walls and floor. This is expensive, but if you use your cellar for storage you may decide it is worthwhile.

running **overflow**

Overflow pipes are deliberately positioned to attract your attention when they start running with water. They are there to warn you that you have a problem with one of your cisterns – either a WC cistern or a cistern in the loft.

TIME TO ACT Turning taps on (but not ones connected to the mains) or flushing WCs will reduce or stop the flow from a loft cistern's overflow while you are turning the water off.

assessment

- Running overflows are invariably caused by a problem with the float-operated valve (ball valve), which lets water into the cistern.
- WC cistern overflows are normally positioned on the outside wall right next to the cistern – though many modern WCs overflow into the WC pan itself rather than through an external wall.

- The overflow pipes for any cisterns in a loft generally come out just under the eaves and often spill onto a paved area so that you can hear the noise of the water.
- Although it is possible to repair faulty ball valves, fitting a new one is a better choice – they are inexpensive to buy and relatively easy to fit.

action

1 TURN OFF THE WATER SUPPLYING A WC Many WCs have a tap-like valve or a small in-line valve (which is closed with a quarter turn using a screwdriver) in the supply pipe nearby. If a WC does not have a valve near it, it is either fed from a cold-water cistern or by water from the mains.

2 TURN OFF WATER TO CISTERN-FED WC If a WC is fed by a cistern, close the red- or orange-handled gatevalve on the pipe leading out of the side of the main cold water cistern low down (see page 147).

3 TURN OFF WATER TO MAINS-FED WC If it is fed from the mains, turn off the mains stop valve (see pages 146–147).

4 TURN OFF THE WATER TO A COLD-WATER CISTERN The supply to a cold-water loft cistern is turned off at the mains stop valve (see page 147).

5 CHECK THE FLOAT HEIGHT It could be that the float height is incorrect so that the ball valve does not stop water entering the cistern until its level is above the overflow pipe outlet.

6 SET THE WATER LEVEL For a cold-water cistern the water level when the valve has closed should be around 25mm below the overflow pipe. **With WCs the correct water height is often marked on the inside of the cistern.** If the level is not correct, adjust the float height using the screw provided (on older ball valves you have to bend the float arm).

7 CHECK THE FLOAT If you have an old type of ball valve and the metal float is punctured, you can make a temporary repair to keep the system running while you buy a new float. Empty as much water out of the old float as possible then wrap a plastic bag around it and secure the bag with an elastic band.

8 REPLACE THE BALL VALVE If you cannot stop the ball valve running, it is faulty and will need to be replaced. If you do not feel capable of doing this yourself, ask a plumber to fit a new (diaphragm-type) ball valve for you.

toilet blocked or will not flush

A WC that will not flush is a problem that needs to be sorted out as soon as possible – especially if there are young children or older people in the home. As an emergency measure you can get the contents of the WC to go away by pouring a bucket of water into the pan. But you need to find out what caused the problem and how to make repairs.

assessment

Follow the chart below to find out what may be preventing the toilet bowl from emptying. Then either unblock it or fix the flush yourself or call out an emergency plumber.

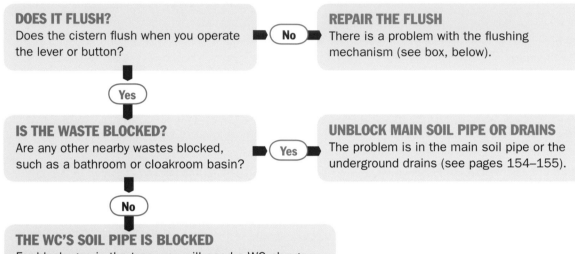

DOES IT FLUSH?
Does the cistern flush when you operate the lever or button?

No →

REPAIR THE FLUSH
There is a problem with the flushing mechanism (see box, below).

Yes

IS THE WASTE BLOCKED?
Are any other nearby wastes blocked, such as a bathroom or cloakroom basin?

Yes →

UNBLOCK MAIN SOIL PIPE OR DRAINS
The problem is in the main soil pipe or the underground drains (see pages 154–155).

No

THE WC'S SOIL PIPE IS BLOCKED
For blockages in the trap, you will need a WC plunger. For blockages further along in the WC's soil pipe, a drain auger may be of more use. If you cannot unblock the WC yourself (see action, right), call a plumber.

How a cistern works

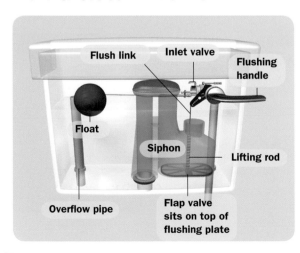

Flush link
Inlet valve
Flushing handle
Float
Siphon
Lifting rod
Overflow pipe
Flap valve sits on top of flushing plate

FLUSH LINK
The flush link is a metal loop that connects the flushing handle to the flushing siphon mechanism.

FLAP VALVE
The flap valve is a sheet of plastic that sits at the bottom of the siphon mechanism and allows water in to fill the cistern but pushes water out when the cistern is flushed. A split flap valve washer can cause the WC to fail to flush, or to fill continuously, as water continues to run into the pan after the WC has been flushed. On a modern cistern continuous filling could also be a sign that the overflow is running (it sends its water into the pan) and there is a problem with the ball valve (see page 149).

GET HELP If you do not feel able to mend a non-flushing cistern or to clear a blockage in the toilet, contact a plumber to do it for you.

WATCHPOINT For all WC repairs, wear protective clothing (heavy-duty waterproof gloves with long cuffs) and cover the floor with old towels. Disinfect equipment after use.

TIME TO ACT If you notice the WC starting to empty more slowly than usual, use a plunger (or an aerosol air blaster) to clear the blockage that is starting to form.

action

BROKEN FLUSH LINK

1 EMPTY THE CISTERN
If the link is broken or has fallen off, it will be easier to replace if the cistern is empty. Turn off the water to the cistern (see page 149). If it is not easy to do this, tie up the inlet valve arm to a piece of wood resting on top of the cistern. Flush the cistern by pulling up the rod sticking out of the top of the siphon mechanism.

2 REPLACE LINK Unscrew the plastic arm from the lever spindle and pull out the link. Buy a new link (and a new arm if needed) from a hardware store or plumbers' merchants, connect them together and hook the metal link onto the end of the siphon rod.

3 SECURE ARM With the lever in its 'rest' (horizontal) position, fit the new plastic arm (with the link connected) to its spindle and tighten the securing screw. Turn on the water or untie the float arm and allow the cistern to fill.

SPLIT FLAP VALVE

1 REMOVE THE SIPHON Modern WCs have the cistern fixed to the back of the pan, and need some complex disassembling – a job best left to a plumber. On older WCs with a separate cistern, turn off the water supply (see left), flush the cistern to empty it and mop out the remaining water. Undo the smaller nut underneath the cistern to disconnect the flush pipe; then undo the larger one to release the siphon mechanism.

2 REPLACE VALVE Remove the lifting rod, take off the failed valve from its base and fit the new one from a hardware store or plumbers' merchants. Cut it to shape if necessary. Re-assemble and test.

BLOCKAGE

1 USE A PLUNGER Plungers for clearing WCs are larger than the ones for basins, sinks or baths, but are used in exactly the same way by pushing and pulling them up and down, using water pressure to clear the blockage. **A household mop, covered with a plastic bag, makes a good alternative.**

2 USE A FLEXIBLE DRAIN AUGER You may be able to wiggle WC blockages out with a straightened-out metal coat hanger. But the correct tool is a drain auger with a turning handle. This needs to be used with a pushing and pulling action as well as a turning one to dislodge the blockage.

 WARNING
Use drain cleaners with care: the chemicals are corrosive. Do not use chemical drain cleaners on fully blocked WCs as the chemical will not drain and will create dangerous fumes indoors.

▶▶See also: **BLOCKED DRAINS** pp154–155

blocked basin, sink or bath

When water will not drain away from a basin, sink or bath, the most likely cause is a blockage in the trap or in the waste pipes under or behind the sink (or basin, bath, shower tray or bidet). If you have the right tools, you can clear the blockage yourself. In winter, the blockage may be due to a frozen waste pipe outside.

action

1 REMOVE VISIBLE OBSTRUCTIONS Use fingers and tweezers (or a straightened-out metal coat hanger) to pull out any bits you can see.

2 USE A PLUNGER Use a wet cloth to block the overflow, fit the rubber cup of a sink plunger over the plughole and pump the handle sharply up and down. Repeat this several times until the waste is clear.

3 BLOW IT OUT If you use an aerosol clearer, which uses a blast of air to shift the blockage, follow the manufacturer's instructions.

4 REMOVE TRAP Place a bucket underneath the trap and unscrew the knurled rings to remove the trap. Clean the trap out in another sink or in a bucket – remember that you cannot use a sink or basin while the trap is in pieces.

5 CLEAR PIPE If the blockage is not in the trap, but is further along the waste pipe, use a sink augur (plumber's snake) to wiggle it out.

Partly blocked waste pipe

● **PROTECT OUTLET** Chemical drain cleaners can be used if waste pipes are slow to clear. To protect the waste pipe outlet from attack by the aggressive chemicals, smear petroleum jelly (Vaseline) over it first.

● **POUR IN CHEMICAL CLEANER** Wearing gloves, pour the chemical cleaner down the plughole, following the instructions. Do not use chemicals to clear a totally blocked waste as these might not run away and so leave a dangerous liquid in your basin sink or bath.

for next time...

● **Avoid putting either grease or fat down the plughole in kitchen sinks** – they solidify and block the waste.

● Similarly, avoid flushing food scraps down the sink and use a plughole strainer. If food does go down the plughole, run the water to rinse it away well.

● In baths, basins and shower trays, human hair is the main problem – pick out loose strands whenever you see them.

● To keep waste pipes clear, pour a cupful of washing soda (bicarbonate of soda) crystals down the plughole once a month (once a week for sinks).

● If the flow from a waste pipe has slowed down, attend to it as soon as you can before it gets fully blocked.

water gushing from gutter

When it rains heavily, water can spill in a splashing torrent out of the gutter, rather than into the downpipes. If left, faulty guttering can cause damp problems, as well as being annoying for you and your neighbours. Grab a brolley and go outside to find out where the water is coming from, then take appropriate action or get professional help.

assessment

- Gushing gutter leaks are most often the result of blockages within the gutter. These are usually caused by leaves and birds' nests and also by moss washed off the roof.
- Similar blockages can happen in the downpipes leading to the drains or soakaway.

- A spilling gutter may not be blocked – it could be that it is sagging (so water runs the wrong way), usually caused by failure of one or more of the gutter brackets.
- The gutter may also be split or leaking at a joint and will need a new joint or some sealant.

action

BLOCKED GUTTER

1 PREPARE YOUR TOOLS Go up the ladder armed with a bucket (plus a hook to secure it to the ladder) and a gutter scoop or garden trowel. Wear gloves.

2 CLEAR DEBRIS Stuff a rag into the top of the downpipe and then work along the gutter from there, scooping the debris out and putting it into the bucket.

3 FLUSH OUT Ask a helper to pass up the garden hose to you. He can then be directed to turn the tap on and off as required so that you can flush the gutter until it is clear. Work from the high end down towards the downpipe.

 **TAKE CARE**
Wait until the rain has stopped before using a ladder to work on gutters and only do so if you feel confident working at a height. The ladder must be properly secured and at the correct angle – one metre out for every four metres up the wall (see page 335).

SAGGING GUTTER

■ **REATTACH BRACKET** Gutters sag when the screw holding a bracket in place has come out. Screw the bracket back into a solid fixing.

BLOCKED DOWNPIPE

1 START AT THE TOP Downpipe blockages usually occur in the 'swan neck' – the double bend at the top. If you can remove this, clean it out under a tap. If not, poke a garden hose into it and flush it out.

2 CLEAR PIPE Use a rag tied securely to a stick to clear out the rest of the pipe, from above and below.

LEAKING GUTTER OR JOINT

1 FIT NEW SEAL With plastic gutters, you should be able to buy a new seal (gasket) for the brackets where lengths of gutter meet. This is simply pressed into place with the gutter removed.

2 USE GUTTER SEALANT On metal gutters (and plastic gutters where no replacement seal is available), you can stop leaks by applying black sticky gutter sealant using a sealant gun, or with self-adhesive gutter repair tape.

blocked drains

The home owner and not the water or sewerage company is responsible for all external pipes and drains up until they join a public sewer. Therefore, it is important to know how to deal with a blocked drain. This can help to avoid emergency call-out charges for problems that you can deal with easily yourself, although if you are not able to do so, contact a professional.

assessment

A blockage can occur in waste pipes, the gully they discharge into or the hopper head where bathroom and basin waste pipes meet; in the soil pipe, which goes straight into the underground drain; or in the underground drain itself (see box, opposite). Look for the following signs:

PROBLEM	WHAT TO DO
OVERFLOWING GULLY An overflowing gully is a sure sign of a blockage.	Clear gully You should be able to clear the blockage yourself (see below).
BLOCKED BASINS AND SINKS If a bath, basin, sink, bidet or shower will not clear (and it is not the trap – see page 152), there is a blockage in an external waste pipe, the main soil pipe or the underground drains.	Clear pipes or drain You might be able to clear a blockage in an external waste pipe (see below) and possibly the soil pipe (see right). Only tackle this if you feel confident that you can (see right). Otherwise, call a professional.
WATER AROUND MANHOLE Filthy water flowing out around manhole covers definitely indicates a blockage in an underground drain.	Clear underground drain Only tackle an underground drain if you feel confident that you can (see right). Otherwise, call a professional.

action

BLOCKED GULLY

1 REMOVE THE GRATING Remove surface debris from the gully grid cover and prise the cover out.

2 USE YOUR HANDS Wearing household rubber gloves, plunge your arm into the gully and scoop out debris. Use a trowel to break up a solid blockage.

3 USE RODS If you have drain rods, use the plunger plus a single drain rod to create sufficient water pressure to force any remaining blockage along the underground drain.

 TAKE CARE
Scrub a gully thoroughly with soapy water when you have cleared a blockage. Disinfect gloves and tools.

BLOCKED HOPPER HEAD

1 INSPECT HOPPER HEAD Where there are separate waste pipes for a bath and basin, blockages are usually near the top, often in the 'hopper head', where the two pipes discharge.

2 REMOVE OBSTRUCTIONS Using a ladder (see page 335), you should be able to remove leaves, bird nests and other debris from this. Use a garden trowel, scraper, or the wormscrew or scraper supplied with a set of drain rods if you have them. **You may find it easier to clear a blockage by hand, wearing household rubber gloves.**

GET HELP If a blockage or leak is persistent, a drain-clearing firm can send tiny cameras along your drains to check for cracks and to find blockages such as tree roots.

TIME TO ACT Drains rarely get blocked suddenly. If they are beginning to slow down, take action to clean them out before they become completely blocked.

BLOCKED SOIL PIPE

1 PREPARE YOURSELF What comes out of a blocked soil pipe is not pleasant, so wear full protective clothing (including goggles) and have large buckets ready to collect it.

2 CLEAR SOIL PIPE A modern plastic soil pipe will have an access point on it (at ground level) with a cover you can unscrew – stand well back! The access point allows you to clear the pipe using drain rods or a large auger (see page 151).

BLOCKED UNDERGROUND DRAIN

1 REMOVE INSPECTION CHAMBER COVERS Each inspection chamber has a cover, sometimes screwed down, which you can lift. Cast iron covers (the most common) are extremely heavy and may need a special, separate handle to lift them. If the built-in handles have broken, a garden spade can be used to lever the cover up.

2 FIND THE BLOCKAGE You may have to lift several inspection chamber covers to find the blockage. Start at the one nearest the house and go on until you find an empty chamber – the blockage is between that chamber and the previous (full) one.

3 USE DRAIN RODS Work from the first empty chamber or the last full one and push a drain rod into the hole at the bottom of the chamber towards the blockage. Drain rods are supplied with various devices: wormscrews and wheels for dislodging blockages, plungers for pushing blockages along the drain and scrapers for pulling them back.

Know your drainage system

- **WASTE PIPE** All homes have pipes leading from basins, baths, sinks, bidets, showers and WCs to take the waste to the drains.
- **OUTSIDE DOWN OR SOIL PIPE(S)** The number of pipes you have depends on the age of your house. Older houses have two: bath, basin, shower and bidet wastes discharge into one down pipe (via a hopper head); the WC discharges into its own down pipe. Modern houses have a single down pipe: all bathroom wastes and the WC discharge into the same down pipe, known as a 'soil pipe'. In some homes, this is actually inside the house.
- **GULLY** The kitchen waste pipe normally discharges into a gully (see right) leading to the underground drain.
- **UNDERGROUND DRAINS** These drains carry waste away from the property to the sewer. They are fitted with inspection chambers (see below) wherever a pipe joins them or wherever they change direction.

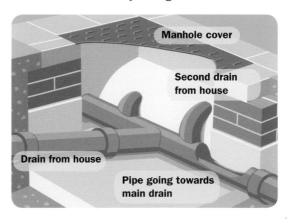

Manhole cover

Second drain from house

Drain from house

Pipe going towards main drain

▶▶See also: **BLOCKED BASIN, SINK OR BATH** p152

vermin infestations

Pests, such as mice and insects, can cause damage to your home and, because many carry germs, may transmit diseases to the occupants. Fortunately, you can turn a siege into a rout if you stand your ground and put up a strong defence.

WATCHPOINT When handling traps, poison or dead vermin, wear rubber gloves to avoid getting poison or germs on your hands. Dispose of the gloves immediately after use.

assessment

● By the time you notice the damage that vermin have caused, their numbers could be in the hundreds if not thousands. Act the minute you discover any signs in your home.

● Serious infestations may require the analysis and advice of a pest-control specialist. Find reputable companies recommended by the local council or on the internet.

SPOTTING SIGNS OF INFESTATION

PEST	WHERE FOUND	SIGNS	
RATS AND MICE	Outhouses, sheds, lofts, cavity wall area and other interior spaces	Rod-shaped black droppings 4–8mm long (mice) or 8–12mm (rats), gnawed holes in packaging and chewed wires and skirting. Both rats and mice give off a distinctive musky smell.	
COCKROACHES	Moist areas such as outside taps and leaking pipes; kitchen areas	Cockroaches are nocturnal so if you see them during the day this could mean you have a serious infestation. In large numbers cockroaches produce an unpleasant almond-like smell.	
CARPET BEETLES	Carpets, fur, leather and wool	Small, round, grey-brown beetles mottled with cream enter houses to lay eggs. The larvae are tiny, hairy grubs, known as 'woolly bears'. Holes appear in carpets and other textiles.	
FLEAS	On pets and their bedding, in carpets and soft furnishings	Your pet is constantly scratching – place it on a white sheet and groom it. If it has fleas, their telltale black comma-shaped droppings will appear underneath. Itchy red bites on humans indicate flea infestation.	
WASPS	Lofts, garage roofs, sheds, the space behind shingles and cavity wall area	Wasps flying in and out of a hole every few seconds is the sign of a nest just a few centimetres inside. Nest building begins in late spring when the fertilised queens wake from hibernation.	
ANTS	Kitchen	Initially single, then streams of, black ants seeking food on floors but also on work surfaces. Winged ants fly into the house (usually in July and August) in an attempt to establish a colony.	

action

RATS AND MICE

1 **CLEAN AREA** Scrupulously clean everywhere, place food in sealed containers and seal waste bins. Make sure there are no food scraps on compost heaps.

2 **SET TRAPS** Use spring mouse traps and rat traps with poisoned bait. Place traps and bait within tamperproof bait stations and cover securely. Set a series of traps and bait with garlic sausage, bacon or offal. Using too few traps or bait stations may prolong the infestation.

3 **PLACE TRAPS** Mice run near walls, so place mouse traps along the perimeter of a room. **Rats will avoid anything new – bait a large number of unset traps for a week before setting them.**

 WARNING

Rats spread disease through their urine, faeces and the fleas they carry. A potentially fatal condition is Weil's disease, also known as leptospirosis. Rats, mice and cockroaches can spread salmonella, causing food poisoning, by contaminating food.

COCKROACHES

1 **BE HYGIENIC** Keep waste bins clean and sealed, do not throw food scraps on compost heaps and sweep up leaves and other organic debris. Ventilate moist areas and check for leaking taps or pipes.

2 **SEAL AND TREAT** Seal all cracks and holes in walls, door frames and where pipes pass through the fabric of the house. Treat with proprietary spray; if this does not clear the infestation, seek professional help.

CARPET BEETLES

1 **REMOVE HEAVILY INFESTED ITEMS** If there is much damage, discard the article along with the carpet moth larvae that have caused the problem.

2 **CLEAN AND TREAT THE AREA** Thoroughly vacuum and clean the affected carpet and furnishings. Dispose of the vacuumed dust and debris. Use a proprietary chemical spray to treat the affected area.

FLEAS

1 **TREAT PET** Consult your vet for the safest and most effective treatment for your pet. Never use a flea treatment intended for dogs on a cat. Once clear, treat your pet with a suitable treatment on a regular basis, on your vet's guidance.

2 **TREAT SURROUNDINGS** Wash bedding using a disinfectant in the water and vacuum thoroughly, discarding the vacuum debris. If your pet is allowed on beds or furniture, wash all bedding and treat mattresses and upholstered furniture with a safe and effective spray, and vacuum as before.

■ **BITES ON HUMANS** If the occupants of the house have bites, it is likely that there is a serious infestation that requires professional treatment.

WASPS

1 **TAKE CARE** Wasps release a pheromone when they sting or are killed that makes other wasps more aggressive. Only treat a small nest – around the size of a tennis ball – yourself and wear a protective veil and gloves – wasp stings can produce an allergic reaction. Use a professional to destroy a larger nest. Nests are vacated in autumn and never reused.

2 **TREAT THE NEST** Spray the whole nest with a proprietary spray if you have access or direct the spray through the nest entrance.

ANTS

1 **DESTROY THE NEST** To eliminate an ant infestation completely, destroy the nest, which will be located outside the home in soft soil or sand, identified by a small hole and ant activity. Apply an ant-specific insecticide according to the instructions. Boiling water poured onto the nest and applied repeatedly, may also be effective in eliminating it.

2 **USE BAIT** If you cannot find the nest, spray the ants, and points of entry to your house, with ant powder, which the ants will take back to their nests or use ant bait stations, which are safe to use if pets and children are in the area.

▶▶See also: **INFECTED WOUND** p66 • **VOMITING** p72 • **DIARRHOEA** p73 • **BITING INSECTS** p317   **157**

trapped bat or bird

Your first instinct will be to get the bat or bird out of the house at all costs. But you can minimise injury to the creature – as well as damage to your home caused by its terrified flutterings – if you keep calm and act slowly and purposefully. If you have a cat, dog or other pet, make sure it is safely out of the way.

action

TRAPPED BAT

1 ENCOURAGE ESCAPE A bat will only fly off at night. Turn off lights and open all windows and external doors. A bat navigates by echolocation (it uses sound waves to locate and avoid objects) so it is unlikely to fly into a closed window and injure itself.

2 REMOVE BAT If it does not fly out, wear gloves, then cover the bat with a shoebox and slide the lid underneath to seal it. Or place a cloth in the box, with a small jar lid filled with water, and gently pick up the bat and put it in the box. Put the lid on. The bat will be able to crawl into the cloth and hide.

3 RELEASE BAT After dusk, place the box outside at least 1.5m above the ground – do not place on the ground as bats need to swoop to become airborne again. Remove the lid and leave the bat to fly off.

PANICKING BIRD

1 PROTECT BIRD Stay at a distance from the bird so you do not frighten it further and make it fly about. Draw the curtains or cover all windows to reduce the risk that the bird will fly into the glass and injure itself.

2 GUIDE BIRD Close internal doors, open wide any external doors and uncover and open the largest window. The bird should then fly towards the light.

3 CATCH BIRD If there is no suitable exit, or the bird does not fly out, darken the room and throw a sheet over the bird. Gently scoop it up and let it go outside.

 TAKE CARE
Do not try to entice a bird with food or water. It will be too frightened to eat or drink. If it is injured, seek advice from a local vet or a wildlife rescue service.

for next time...

BAT IN THE HOUSE
● Young bats learning to fly are most likely to stray inside. Keep large windows and doors closed or partly covered on summer nights.
● Make sure your loft hatch is secure and there are no spaces around pipes, light fittings or between ceiling boards. A young bat residing in the attic can fall through the tiniest of gaps into the room below.

BIRD IN THE HOUSE
● Birds will occasionally fly into a house through open doors. Prevent this with screens, nets or bamboo curtains.
● Most birds are brought in by the family cat. Fitting the cat with a bell or beeper on a quick-release collar, so that the bird is aware of the cat's presence, can reduce the incidence of it bringing in hunting trophies.
● Prevent birds falling down your chimney by installing wire or mesh chimney-pot guards.

pet goes missing

A missing pet usually turns up after a few days – a little bedraggled and hungry, but no worse for wear. If a pet is out for any longer, it may become seriously ill or suffer a road accident. To find your pet promptly, mount a search and enlist help.

WATCHPOINT If your pet is valuable, it may have been stolen. You are reporting a theft, not just a missing pet and quick action may help the investigation.

be aware

● By law, your dog must wear a collar with a tag giving your contact details. To help identify them, cats should be similarly tagged.

● As collars can be removed or lost, it is highly recommended that a pet has a microchip. The microchip is a small radio chip, about the size of a grain of rice, which is harmlessly injected beneath the skin and stays there throughout your pet's life. The pet can then be traced through the national PetLog database.

action

PET HAS DISAPPEARED

1 COMB YOUR HOUSE AND GARDEN Cats and small dogs can get into some unlikely places. Check your property thoroughly, including behind appliances, inside wardrobes, any loft, cellar or shed – even tiny crawl spaces and drains. Do not assume that your pet will respond to your frantic calls.

2 CHECK THE NEIGHBOURHOOD Talk to as many people as possible, including delivery persons and local children. Leave a written description with your neighbours – include your phone number – and ask them to check any outbuildings. Use a powerful torch in your search.

■ **MAKE FAMILIAR NOISES** As you walk around, call your pet's name, rattle a box of treats, squeeze a favourite squeaky toy or use an ultrasonic whistle to get your pet's attention – they work for both cats and dogs. Stop regularly and listen for a response.

■ **ATTRACT WITH SCENT** Animals find their way by smell as well as sound, so place some strongly scented items outside your home – its bedding or a favourite toy, or an unwashed article of your clothing.

■ **MISSING ON WALK** If your dog went missing while off his lead when you were walking him, return to the place where you last saw him. After a reasonable period of time phone home to see if he has returned instinctively. If not, wait for as long as possible before mounting a local search.

PET MISSING FOR LONGER

■ **INFORM THE AUTHORITIES** If a dog is lost, tell the police and dog warden of your loss and obtain a reference number from them. You will need this if you want to claim on your insurance. Contact your veterinary practice to register a dog or cat.

■ **CONTACT ANIMAL ORGANISATIONS** Get in touch with the PetLog register (if your pet is microchipped), and any other relevant national registers of lost pets, such as the RSPCA, Cats Protection, Blue Cross, Dogs Trust and Battersea Dogs Home. Many of these organisations can be found online and there are online organisations where you can register your missing pet (see pages 340–343).

■ **PUT UP A POSTER** Write a full description of your pet, including its colour, size and gender – include as many details as possible – and find a colour photo showing any distinguishing marks. Make up a poster stating when your pet went missing and where it was last seen. Give your contact details and the amount of the reward, if you are offering one. Put up posters around the local area, including lampposts, newsagents and sports facilities (with the permission of the owners).

■ **USE LOCAL MEDIA** To reach as many people as possible in the area, advertise in the local press and on radio stations. To be most effective, do this in the first week after your pet has gone missing.

pet is taken ill

Because of a natural instinct for self-preservation, it is sometimes hard to tell that an animal is unwell until the ailment is fairly well advanced. There are a number of key signs that may signal that a pet is seriously ill. These include behavioural changes, loss of appetite and excessive thirst as well as acute symptoms such as breathing problems.

assessment

Certain signs and symptoms demonstrated by your pet can indicate an acute crisis, which must be treated immediately by your vet. Be especially on the lookout for the following:

DOG OR CAT

SYMPTOM	INDICATION
Breathing difficulties	Can indicate a physical obstruction, heart problem, poisoning or lung disease. See right for emergency action. Consult your vet urgently.
Bloating, vomiting and diarrhoea	Maybe your pet has eaten something that has disagreed with him, perhaps when out. It can indicate something more ominous, such as parvovirus in young dogs. Call your vet and follow his advice.
Loss of appetite	This is very unusual if a pet is healthy and can be a sign of illness or stress. Consult your vet.
Drinking more than usual	May be a sign of serious complaints such as diabetes or kidney problems. Monitor your pet and call your vet to tell him what you have observed. Follow his instructions.
Scratching, shaking head	May be caused by parasites or a foreign body stuck in the animal's ear. If your pet will let you, gently look into the ear, using a torch. Remove any foreign body with tweezers or a cotton bud, being careful not to push it further in. Visit the vet so he can examine your pet whether you have removed a foreign body or not.
Dry skin bald patches	Can be a sign of parasite infection or mange, which if untreated can become a serious condition. See your vet and ask about parasite prevention.

CAT

SYMPTOM	INDICATION
Straining, repeat visits to the litter tray, difficulty urinating and blood in the urine	May be a sign of a blocked bladder, which can be life threatening. Consult your vet immediately.
Membrane over eye	All cats have what is known as the 'third eyelid' – a membrane that covers the eye. This acts to lubricate and is visible in a normal, healthy cat when it wakes or is drowsy. If it is visible at other times, it may indicate an underlying health problem, such as a viral infection. If your cat's third eyelids are visible, consult your vet.

TIME TO ACT An ill or injured cat is likely to hide away until the condition is far advanced. If you do observe any warning signs, act promptly to prevent further deterioration.

WATCHPOINT Do not give your pet anything to eat or drink, unless your vet tells you to do so, as it may need a general anaesthetic later.

GET HELP Always seek veterinary help if possible. An animal in pain may lash out, causing further complications, so be very careful and do not put yourself at risk.

action

 TAKE CARE

● **You have a far better chance of your pet surviving if you can get to a vet's quickly.** Always try to seek advice from a veterinary practice, who may direct you to a local out-of-hours veterinary service.

● If you cannot reach a vet, you may be on a long country walk in the middle of nowhere, for example, the following techniques can be used, but should only be attempted in an absolute emergency. If not carried out properly they could be harmful. Do not attempt these techniques unless your pet's life is in immediate danger. Always put your safety first.

UNCONSCIOUS PET

1 CHECK FOR HEARTBEAT Gently grasp the chest, just behind the elbows, with one hand, whilst supporting the animal with the other hand. If you are sure you can feel no heartbeat, start chest compressions.

2 START COMPRESSIONS Lay your pet on its right side. Place your hands over the ribs just behind the front leg. Compress 2–4cm every second for 5 seconds. Puppies, small dogs, and cats may only need 1–2cm gentle compressions with the fingertips.

3 GIVE RESCUE BREATHS If an animal is not breathing, extend the neck and check and clear the back of the throat. Pinch the mouth shut and make a funnel with your hand around the nose that you can breathe into. Breathe into this funnel, avoiding direct contact with the nose, so that the chest expands. Do this five times, once every five seconds.

4 REPEAT ACTION For a small or medium-sized animal (under 25kg), repeat one breath with three compressions until you can feel a pulse and the pet is breathing. For a larger animal, repeat three breaths with five compressions.

APPARENT CHOKING

1 IS PET CHOKING? In most animals, what appears to be choking is vomiting. Cats rarely choke, and in dogs apparent choking can be a form of reverse sneezing, which, though alarming, is harmless.

2 CHECK FOR AN OBSTRUCTION If possible, get someone to firmly hold the pet's mouth open. Carefully remove any visible blockage – do not push further in. Do not do a blind finger sweep – look into the animal's mouth to avoid injuring your pet. If there is evidence of a needle or fishing hook, do not pull on this, as it can have a thread or line attached.

3 DISLODGE THE OBJECT Lift the animal's back legs; give its body a firm shake to expel the obstruction.

■ **THE HEIMLICH MANOEUVRE** This technique should only be used when all other alternatives have been tried and failed. On a large animal (over 25kg), wrap your arms tightly around its belly just under the rib cage. Give one quick, forceful squeeze, to expel the object. Take the pet to the vet immediately, as the procedure might have caused internal damage.

SUSPECTED POISONING

1 DO NOT INDUCE VOMITING Act quickly if you suspect your pet has ingested poison. Do not attempt to get your pet to vomit as this may cause further damage.

2 REMOVE POISON ON COAT Wash the poison from your pet's coat to prevent more being ingested. Your pet will frantically try to lick it off.

3 CALL THE VET Describe the symptoms. If you know, give details of the poison; keep a sample of it and, if possible, the original container, and take this to the vet if a visit is advised. Follow the vet's advice.

pet is injured

When dealing with pet injuries, a little knowledge of first aid goes a long way. As long as you learn the basics such as how to stop bleeding and what to do if there is a suspected broken limb, you will be equipped to deal with most situations. Be aware that an injured animal is likely to be very distressed.

action

WOUNDS

1 STOP ANY BLEEDING If your pet is bleeding heavily, cover the wound with a clean cloth and apply pressure until the bleeding stops.

2 CLEAN AND DRESS THE WOUND Clean a small wound with a weak salt solution. Dry, and apply a dressing to keep it sterile. **Cat bites, in particular, can form abscesses if not promptly treated.**

3 WATCH FOR INFECTION Always get any wound checked over by a vet. It may need further, professional cleaning and your vet will decide if any other treatment, such as stitches or antibiotics, is required.

BROKEN LIMB

1 KNOW THE SIGNS Your pet may limp or its limb may swell up. It will not necessarily keep still.

2 AVOID BEING BITTEN Your pet may normally be docile and affectionate, but it may bite when in pain. To gently restrain it, use a muzzle or towel if it is safe to do so.

3 CONTACT VET Call your veterinary practice and explain the situation. Follow the advice given.

SHOCK

1 CHECK FOR PULSE AND HEART RATE Shock can result from blood or fluid loss, pain or infection. The animal will have a rapid heart and pulse rate. Check the pulse at the inner thigh or below the ankle.

2 PLACE IN RECOVERY POSITION Lay the animal on its side with its head extended and cover with a blanket to keep warm. Raise the chest and hindquarters above the level of the head by placing a soft support under the animal. Do not give your pet any water.

3 CONTACT VET Call your veterinary practice, explain your pet's symptoms and follow the advice given.

Pet hit by car

Whether it is your pet that is hit, or someone else's, an accident is distressing. Keep calm, clear the road and give the animal first aid.

- **CLEAR THE ROAD** Move the animal away from further harm, making sure you are not bitten.
- **ENSURE AIRWAY IS CLEAR** Check the animal's breathing and pulse.
- **KEEP WARM** Shock can cause a drop in temperature. Cover the animal with a coat or blanket to keep it warm.
- **CONTROL BLEEDING** Hold a clean cloth, such as a handkerchief, firmly over any wound until bleeding slows and stops.
- **MOVE ANIMAL AS LITTLE AS POSSIBLE** After moving the animal away from the road, minimise further movement. Make a rigid stretcher from a car's parcel shelf or similar.
- **GET HELP** Phone a vet or the RSPCA (see pages 339) for advice. Give your location and what injuries you believe the animal to have. If the pet is not yours, check any tags for details, and contact the owner, or ask the vet to check for a microchip.

CRIMINAL
ACTS

break-in at home

Every year, around 300,000 homes in the UK are burgled. Many crimes are opportunistic, with thieves getting in through open doors and windows. Burglary brings a sense of violation and loss – and if you disturb a thief you may be in danger.

 WATCHPOINT Join your local Neighbourhood Watch group or set up a new group, to make the area where you live more secure. For information, visit: www.mynhw.co.uk.

action

BURGLAR MAY BE PRESENT

1 **TRUST YOUR INSTINCTS** If you sense something is wrong as you approach your home, stop and think. What have you noticed that is not quite right? Is the door not shut properly? Did you hear a sound?

2 **LOOK FOR SIGNS OF A BREAK-IN** Has the door been forced or is a window broken? If you find a weapon, or potential weapon, just inside your door, leave at once. **Burglars often place weapons at exits in case they are disturbed.**

3 **RETREAT TO A SAFE PLACE** If anything arouses your suspicion that you have been burgled and that the burglar might still be in your home, go to your nearest neighbour or friend and call the police.

 WARNING

If you walk in on a burglar, try not to appear aggressive and do not challenge him. Either leave quickly yourself or allow him the opportunity to escape. Once you are safe, call the police. Then write down as full a description as you can.

BURGLAR HAS GONE

1 **CONFIRM THAT YOU HAVE BEEN BURGLED** Could there be another explanation for what you have found? Have you definitely been broken into? The burglar may have been disturbed, in which case the theft may not be obvious at first. Do not forget to check the contents of your garage or garden shed, if you have one.

2 **CALL THE POLICE** Phone the local police station (you can get the number from directory enquiries), rather than the emergency services. You may have to wait some time for the police to arrive.

3 **DO NOT TOUCH ANYTHING** Resist the temptation to tidy up or move anything until after the police have been, as you may damage vital evidence. Take photos of everything exactly as you found it.

4 **SECURE YOUR HOME** Once the police have attended (see opposite), take steps to prevent another burglary, such as installing additional or more secure locks. Burglars often come back for valuable items they spotted first time round.

A burglar's-eye view

Your house is likely to become a target if a burglar can spot a weakness in its defences. Learn to look at your property from his point of view.

● **DO YOU HAVE BASIC SECURITY?** Homes without simple security, such as window locks and deadlocks, are 10 times more likely to be burgled. Ensure that all doors and ground-floor windows have locks and bolts, and fit an intruder alarm.
● **IS THERE A DOG?** Dogs are a deterrent. Even if you don't have one, a sign can put off a burglar.

● **HOW GOOD IS THE LIGHTING?** Fit security lighting, with motion or infra-red sensors, around your house. Trim trees or hedges near doors or windows that could provide cover for an intruder.
● **IS ANYTHING VALUABLE ON SHOW?** Keep any valuable items out of view of windows. As soon as it is dark outside, draw the curtains.
● **IS THE HOUSE UNOCCUPIED?** If you go away for a few days, ask a friend or neighbour to pick up your post and open and close curtains in different rooms. Cancel any weekly deliveries.

There can be vital clues at the scene so do not touch or move any items.

REPORTING THE CRIME

1 **GET YOUR THOUGHTS IN ORDER** Think back to the moment that you discovered the burglary. Jot down what time you arrived home and what you first noticed. Start making an inventory of items that have been taken.

2 **GIVE A STATEMENT** When the police arrive they will make a crime report and take a statement from you. This may include questions about how the thief got into your home and what has been stolen. If they anticipate that a crime scene investigator will become involved, they will give you advice on what you can touch or move before his arrival.

3 **SUPPORT THE CRIME SCENE INVESTIGATOR** The crime scene investigator may photograph the signs of break-in, such as tool marks, take fingerprints – including yours for elimination – and search for other evidence, such as footprints or clothing fibres.

4 **KEEP TABS ON THE INVESTIGATION** Once the police have gathered evidence, they will begin their enquiries, starting with your neighbours. You will be given a crime reference number, which you can use to track the progress of the investigation. If a suspect is charged with your burglary, someone from a Witness Care Unit will contact you and advise you on the progress of the case.

for next time...

● Keep cash, jewellery and important papers in a safe bolted to the wall or floor, or hide them somewhere unpredictable, such as in the kitchen. **In around 90 per cent of burglaries, the kitchen was not searched.**
● Mark valuable items such as televisions and computers with your postcode or National Insurance number, using a UV pen.
● Make a list of all your valuable possessions and documents. Take photos of unusual items, such as jewellery or *objets d'art*. Note serial and model numbers and give this list, along with receipts and photographs of the items, to a friend or relative for safe keeping.
● If you don't want to install security systems, opt for a fake alarm box and fake CCTV cameras. These cost very little but can effectively discourage an opportunist burglar.

what next?

● Contact your insurance company at once to report the loss, giving the crime reference number issued by the police. Your insurers may offer an all-hours emergency service to make your home secure.
● Compile a list of all the items stolen or damaged. If possible, locate receipts, photographs or other proofs of purchase. Take your time. You may only notice something is missing when you go to use it.
● If the burglary has left you feeling traumatised, you may wish to contact the charity Victim Support, which offers free counselling for the victims of serious crime. Telephone 0845 30 30 900 (UK) or 0845 603 9213 in Scotland.

TAKE CARE

Close and lock side gates and accessible windows. Store ladders in a garage, if possible, and put away garden tools that can be used to force entry.

▶▶See also: **INTRUDER IN THE HOUSE** p166

intruder in the house

Discovering a stranger in your home can be frightening and disorienting. You will want to do whatever you can to protect yourself, your family and your home. But be careful: the law sets strict limits about the use of force – even against an individual whom you believe may wish you harm – so know your rights before you get involved in a confrontation.

action

1 BE VERY QUIET If you hear a strange noise, keep quiet and listen. Is there really someone in your home? If so, is it one person or more? What are they doing: are they ransacking the place or do they appear to be approaching the room you are in?

2 MAKE YOURSELF SAFE If you are alone, barricade your door or lock yourself in the bathroom. If you can safely access a back door or another way out, leave at once and go to your nearest neighbour for help.

3 GATHER TOGETHER If there are others in the house, take your phone and quickly gather everyone into one room. There is safety in numbers, and it is less likely that you will come to harm if the intruder has to face you all together.

4 CALL THE POLICE Phone the emergency services and tell the police that there is an intruder in your home. Give the police your address and any special directions, tell them where you are located in the house and where you think the intruder might be.

 **TAKE CARE**
If you hear the intruder leave, note down any car registration number but do not pursue him.

What is reasonable force?

While it is not advisable to confront an intruder, you do have a right to defend yourself and your family. But be aware of the legal implications.

● **SELF-DEFENCE** If you are in fear for yourself or others in your own home, you do not need to be attacked before using force.
● **AMOUNT OF FORCE** As long as you only take what action is necessary in the heat of the moment, you are unlikely to be prosecuted – even if this results in injury or death. The more extreme the situation and the greater the fear experienced, the more force would be judged to be lawful.
● **PROSECUTION** Any incidents involving accidents or injury would be investigated, but a prosecution would only be brought for premeditated or malicious violence. A premeditated incident might be if you entrapped and harmed someone who was persistently burgling your property. Malicious violence might be if you continued to hit someone who was defenceless, running away or already unconscious.

for next time...

● Always secure your home before going to bed. Make sure all main entry doors are locked and bolted and all ground-floor, or easily accessible, windows are closed and locked. Remove keys from window locks and keep them in a safe place out of view.
● If you have an alarm, programme it to protect particular zones, such as the ground floor, or entry points, such as doors and windows.

● If you have an alarm monitored by a warden, have a panic button fitted. In the UK, the Redcare alarm system uses a BT line to connect to a central monitoring station of a security company. This station then calls the police. However, if you have two false alarms in a given period, the police may disregard or downgrade your alarm and not respond as quickly as they would under normal circumstances.

stranger at the door

Each year, many people – particularly the elderly – are robbed by tricksters who talk their way in. More than 50 per cent of bogus callers pretend to be employees of the water board; others impersonate builders or handymen who claim that your home needs urgent attention. In some cases, robbery is not the sole motive and the householder can be seriously harmed.

precautions

- Fit a sturdy door chain, or bar, to your front door. This will help you to retain control of who you let in to your house.
- Do not keep large amounts of cash in the house. Make sure your purse or wallet is somewhere safe and out of sight.

action

STRANGER KNOCKS AT DOOR

1 RETAIN THE INITIATIVE Keep the door chain on as you open the door. Do not be badgered by cold callers. Consider the request. If the person is offering something you do not want, refuse politely and close the door. If he has called at an inconvenient time, ask him to come back later.

2 REQUEST PROOF OF IDENTITY If a caller claims to be from the council or a utility company, ask for identification. **But remember ID cards can be forged.** So unless the caller got out of a liveried company van, ask him to wait or call back later so that you can telephone the company he works for. If someone tells you your roof needs fixing or your chimney requires repointing, do not go outside or agree to anything. Instead, take the caller's details and tell him you will look at the problem later.

3 REFUSE ENTRY If you cannot confirm a caller's identity or feel at all uneasy about letting someone in, simply apologise politely and close the door. Alternatively, ask the person to call back later and arrange to have someone with you.

STRANGER COMES IN

1 LEAVE THE FRONT DOOR OPEN If you invite a caller in, show him where to go and walk behind him. Keep the door open so that you will have an escape route should you need it.

2 STAY ALERT If the caller is only going to be in your home for a moment, stay with him. Watch out for attempts to distract you, such as a request for a drink or to fetch something from another room. If he is going to be longer, make sure the room he is in does not contain any valuables. If you let more than one person into your house, try to have someone else with you while they are there.

3 AVOID CASH PAYMENTS If you have to pay a caller, use a card or cheque. Only pay by cash if you trust the caller or are satisfied with the service. Try to have more or less the right money and never take it from your safe or other hiding place in view of the caller. Get a receipt and contact details. If you have any doubts, check the contact details are genuine. If they are not, stop your cheque or card payment.

 WARNING

Some tricksters work in pairs – one knocks on the front door and the accomplice uses the opportunity to enter through the back door.

potential **violence**

Too much alcohol, intense sporting rivalry and groups of people in search of excitement can often be a potent mixture that leads to violence. If you are in the vicinity, you may unwittingly find yourself caught up in an unwelcome and frightening scenario. But you can use prior knowledge to defuse such situations and escape to safety if necessary.

assessment

SIZING UP THE SITUATION

You can easily find yourself in circumstances that bubble over into violence. Be wary of:

- Sporting events, especially where local rivalries increase the risk of violent behaviour.
- Political rallies or protest demonstrations that incite powerful emotions – you might be perceived as 'the enemy'.
- Places where people gather to drink. Alcohol – and drugs – are a major cause of violence.
- Anywhere that is crowded – bumping into someone and infringing personal space can lead to trouble.
- A situation where you are outnumbered by a group or gang who appear threatening.

SPOTTING AN AGGRESSOR

Take note of a person's body language. You can often spot a troublemaker before he has a chance to confront you. Watch for:

- Excessive eye contact and invasion of your personal space.
- Gritted teeth, with head and jaw pushed forward; clenched fists.
- Raised voice and challenging or abusive language.
- Obvious signs of alcohol or drug abuse from the person's appearance or behaviour (see page 56) or the obvious presence of drugs or alcohol.

G20 Protest, in London 2009. Steer clear of demonstrations, even if they appear peaceful.

WATCHPOINT The law allows a pre-emptive strike if it is justified for self defence, but there is a chance you will be charged with assault or affray. If so, get legal advice.

GET HELP If you are injured as a result of violent crime, you may be eligible for Criminal Injuries Compensation. You must report the incident and claim within two years.

action

TENSIONS ESCALATE

1 ASSESS AND APPEASE In any potential conflict you need to make an almost instant risk assessment and act accordingly. If the person you are faced with is armed, very drunk or appears to be on drugs, escape must be your priority (see right). Otherwise, do what you can to calm things down.

2 REMAIN CALM As the adrenaline begins to flow, it is easy to become – and appear – more aggressive, even without realising it. So take a few deep breaths, drop your shoulders and try to stay calm.

3 REGAIN YOUR PERSONAL SPACE When people act in a threatening way, they usually come close to you and invade your personal space. This only heightens the tension, so **try to step back or to the side to increase the space around you**.

4 COMMUNICATE Your voice can be a powerful tool with which to control the temperature of the exchange when tensions escalate. Try to match the person's volume to get your point across but without becoming too agitated yourself.

YOU ARE THREATENED

1 WEIGH UP YOUR OPTIONS As soon as you feel you are in danger, quickly scan your surroundings for escape routes, such as doors, pathways or roads. Are there places of safety nearby, such as public offices, shops or a vehicle, or sources of help, such as the police, security staff or bystanders?

2 LOOK FOR PHYSICAL BARRIERS Anything you can put between you and the person threatening you will make you safer. Inside, this might be a table or chair, or even a lockable door. Outside, it could be a wall or fence, a vehicle or a busy road.

3 SUMMON HELP How you get help will depend on how threatened you feel. Simply walking towards other people might be enough to stop the situation getting out of control. If not, scream and shout as loudly as you can. Only use your mobile phone if you are temporarily secure.

4 COMMIT TO ESCAPING If you must escape, choose your route and run as fast as you can. Do not look behind you, just run until you are somewhere safe. If you can distract the other person, or put a barrier between you before you run, so much the better.

Self-defence

When someone uses threatening behaviour they often want a response that they can use to 'justify' further aggression.

- **APPEAR UNWILLING TO FIGHT** Always try to avoid escalating the conflict. Apologise and appease as appropriate. If there are onlookers, the less 'face' the aggressor loses, the safer you will be. Do not respond to insults or even physical contact. Keep telling the person that you do not want any trouble.
- **KEEP YOUR HANDS UP AND OPEN** If the conflict starts to become physical, hold your hands up, palms out. This looks like a gesture of appeasement or surrender, which is helpful, but it is actually a very good position from which to protect yourself or strike back.
- **HIT AND RUN** Only use force if it becomes absolutely necessary. In such circumstances your best tactic may be to hit and run (see pages 172–175). This is, however, a high-risk strategy (see watchpoint, above) and will only work if you commit to it completely.

encountering a **mugger**

Street robbery, or mugging, is a traumatic experience that can rob you of your self-confidence as well as your possessions. Remember that muggers choose targets whom they believe will be both easy to rob and worth the risk. Find out how to make yourself less appealing on both counts and the best way to respond if you are attacked.

action

YOU ARE MUGGED

1 **GAUGE THE LEVEL OF THREAT** If you are confronted by a mugger who is armed, appears high on drugs or has one or more accomplices, focus on compliance first and then escape.

2 **STAY CALM** Although you may feel frightened, the calmer you appear to be, the more you will reassure the mugger that you are going to comply. He is then less likely to act aggressively or irrationally.

3 **TELL THE MUGGER YOU WILL COMPLY** Once the mugger has made his demands for your money, phone or valuables, verbally confirm that you will comply. This should reassure him that he need not be aggressive. Try to be non-confrontational.

4 **HAND OVER YOUR POSSESSIONS** As you hand over what he wants, try to create some distance so that you can escape: place your wallet on the ground and step back; toss your bag slowly to the mugger so he has to catch it, or hold it at arm's length so that you can step away as he takes it.

5 **FLEE** Unless you are fit and fast, do not simply try to outrun your attacker. Instead, run towards an obvious place of safety that will discourage his pursuit. This might be a shop, pub or office, or simply a more crowded street.

6 **SCREAM OR SHOUT** If you are pursued, scream and shout as loudly as you can and do not stop. Even if no one comes at once, it will unnerve the mugger and he will probably give up the chase.

CAM 1   12:03:22

Do not resist: your safety is more important than your valuables.

12:03:27

WATCHPOINT Avoid alleyways, subways, railway bridges and other isolated routes, even in broad daylight. These offer a mugger the perfect location for an ambush.

TIME TO ACT Tell the police exactly what the mugger took, in case an arrest is made. Advise your bank of stolen credit cards and your insurance company of stolen valuables.

 WARNING

● Never argue or fight with a mugger unless you believe your life to be in danger. If the motive is robbery, giving up your belongings quickly should ensure that you escape unharmed.

● Quickly scan your surroundings to identify your best escape route or nearest source of help. But remember, **complying with the mugger's demands is the safest option in the first instance**.

IF YOU ARE ATTACKED

1 **FIGHT BACK** If the attack continues even after you have given up your belongings, defend yourself (see pages 172–175). The mugger may produce a knife or gun (see pages 178–181).

2 **GET HELP** If you have been injured, seek medical assistance at once. Make a complete record of your injuries as this will help to secure criminal justice. Seek support from friends, family or a trained counsellor if the event leaves you with any lasting feelings of fear, isolation or depression.

be aware

Young men aged 16–24 years old are the most likely to be victims of robbery or violent crime. Weapons are used in a quarter of cases, including hitting implements, knives, bottles and glasses.

Being a good witness

All muggings and robberies should be reported to the police as soon as possible: research shows that the quicker you report an incident, the more likely the offender will be caught.

● **EVIDENCE** Make a note of the time and place of the attack, and write a full description of your attacker and anything he said. The stress of an attack can affect your memory, so the sooner you commit your description to paper, the more accurate it is likely to be.

for next time...

● Try not to flaunt expensive items in high-risk or solitary areas. Carry cameras and laptops in rucksacks or sports bags.

● Do not carry cheques and guarantee cards together or with a record of your PIN. Carry your keys separate from any record of your address.

● Disperse your belongings between your pockets and any bags you may be carrying.

● When travelling in risky areas, consider wearing a cheap watch and taking an old phone with you. Hide cards and cash in a money belt.

● Make a list of everything you have in your wallet, including the numbers you need to call if you lose your cash or credit cards. Keep this safe at home.

PHONE AWARE

● Young people, in particular, are at risk of being mugged for a phone, so children should be taught not to display or 'show off' mobile phones (or other kinds of covetable gadgets) in public. The best advice is to keep a phone hidden when not in use and to only make calls in a public place. When you use your phone, remain alert to your surroundings.

● Make a note of the 15-digit IMEI number, the network contact number, so that you can bar the phone if it is stolen. On most phones you can find the IMEI number by typing in * # 06 #. Call your network provider to bar the phone.

▶▶See also: **PHYSICAL ATTACK** pp172–175

physical attack

Most conflicts can be resolved without resorting to violence, but every year around 3 per cent of adults are the victims of violent crime. If you are attacked, fighting back may be your only option and, whatever your training or physical strength, there are actions you can take to protect yourself and reduce injury.

precautions

- Stay alert and vigilant. When you are in a public place, never switch off. Do not do anything, such as wearing headphones, that cuts you off from your surroundings.
- Be polite but cautious. If you do not wish to engage with a stranger, avoid making eye contact. Keep him in your peripheral vision.
- Manage conflict. If someone steps on your foot, spills your drink or cuts you up when you are driving, take a deep breath and try to defuse the situation. But be alert for the possibility that violence may be the other person's intention.
- Remain sober. Alcohol dulls perception and slows reaction times.

PRACTISING SELF-DEFENCE TECHNIQUES
Help to improve your chances of surviving an attack with minimal injury. Even visualising your response will improve real-life reactions.

- Practise with a partner. A good way to practise palm heel strikes (see opposite) is to get a friend to hold up an old telephone book for you to hit.
- Practise alone. Even when you are alone you can use a mirror to practise strikes (but do not hit the glass). Work on your aim and try not to give away your intentions.
- Go to the gym. Most gyms have a large punchbag or bodybag. This is the ideal target for focusing your aggression and practising elbow strikes, knee strikes and kicks (see pages 174–175).
- Join a self-defence class. Learn how to protect yourself at a self-defence class. Martial arts, such as Karate or Muay Thai boxing, also help to develop physical skills that can help you to defend yourself.

 WARNING

If you enter into a physical conflict, there is a very real risk that you will be injured. But if self-defence is your only option, you must accept this risk and fight on regardless.

Lawful self-defence

In any conflict the law in England and Wales allows for the use of 'reasonable force' to protect yourself or prevent a crime. The use of force is measured against the perceived threat.

- **REASONABLE FORCE** In a situation where an innocent person feels genuinely threatened and responds violently, the actions may *de facto* be considered 'reasonable', simply because they were the actions taken in self defence. Even a pre-emptive action may be considered to be self defence if the person believed that he was at risk of violence by not taking action. Continuing an attack when the other person is unconscious or is fleeing, however, would be considered unreasonable.
- **PERCEIVED THREAT** In a public place, any use of force will be measured against the perceived threat. The greater the perceived threat, the greater the amount of force would be judged to be reasonable, as long as it is used purely in self-defence. But continuing an attack when the other person is unconscious or fleeing is unlikely to be considered reasonable.
- **RETREATING** Failing to retreat when it is possible and safe to do so is not conclusive evidence that a person was not acting in self defence, but is a factor to be taken into account. The defendant does not have to walk away to demonstrate that he does not want to engage in physical violence.

action

APPROACHED WITH MENACE

1 MAINTAIN YOUR PERSONAL SPACE An attacker will intimidate you by invading your personal space. Try to stay calm and retain a safe distance. Your personal space is your safety zone: fists, feet and knives are only effective at close range. Keeping an area around you means your attacker cannot reach you, but you cannot reach him to fight back either. Use your outstretched arms to keep some distance between you and the attacker.

2 HOLD YOUR HANDS UP Keep your hands up, open and in full view. This looks non-threatening, but if violence becomes inevitable you will be ready to either strike first or push and run.

3 REASSURE Let your assailant know that you mean no harm and you do not want a fight. Try to keep your tone of voice calm and reassuring.

4 ASSESS YOUR OPTIONS In most cases of violent assault the conflict lasts less than 30 seconds and the person who is struck first usually suffers most. Quickly make a judgment: if you still feel threatened and cannot flee, you must strike first.

5 BE DETERMINED If you decide you have no option but to strike first, attack with all the aggression you can muster. Aim for your attacker's throat, nose, chin, eyes and groin (see pages 174–175).

ATTACKED FROM THE FRONT

1 BE PREPARED TO ACT Most violent conflicts escalate from a face-to-face argument. To defend yourself against a frontal assault, master your natural instinct to freeze and do nothing. Use surprise, speed and aggression to strike.

2 USE THE HEEL OF YOUR PALM The palm strike is effective only at close range, so you will need to surprise your attacker by moving in quickly. As you do so, fold in your fingers and thumb and flex your wrist back.

3 FOLLOW THROUGH Aim the heel of your palm at your attacker's chin or the base of his nose. Strike using all your bodyweight in an upwards motion to drive your palm full force into your attacker's face. It helps if you are shorter than your attacker; if you are taller, bend your knees.

 TAKE CARE

In a conflict situation the body produces stress hormones, including adrenalin, and the heart rate jumps from 70 to 200 beats per minute. Take deep breaths to help you to control your response.

▶▶See also: **POTENTIAL VIOLENCE** pp168–169 • **ENCOUNTERING A MUGGER** pp170–171 • **RAPE** pp176–177

ATTACKED FROM BEHIND

1 ACT QUICKLY If you are grabbed from behind, either in a surprise attack or when attempting to flee, you need to act quickly. The longer you take to respond, the more time your attacker has to hold you more securely or begin to choke you.

2 USE YOUR BODYWEIGHT Try to unbalance your attacker by rapidly stepping forwards and backwards and by dropping down and then springing up again. Even if these moves do not help you to break free, they will provide you with opportunities to hit out at your attacker.

3 STRIKE BACK The most effective way to break the grip of someone stronger than you is to strike them. If they are holding you from behind, your best options are to use your head, feet and elbows (see right and below).

4 HEAD BUTT Immediately you are grabbed from behind, throw your head backwards into your attacker's face. The back of your head is a lot harder than his nose, teeth or jaw.

5 USE YOUR ELBOW Even a small, light person can generate a huge amount of power with an elbow strike. For maximum impact, throw your elbow back swiftly, with full force, without letting your attacker read your intentions. Keep your hand open and stretched on impact to deliver the most effective strike. Aim directly for the face or the solar plexus, depending on what you can reach.

6 STAMP Use a forceful stamp to the attacker's instep, ankle, knee or shin. Bend your knee and use all your bodyweight and the outside of your heel for maximum force.

PINNED TO A WALL

1 STRUGGLE THEN STRIKE Many attackers use their strength to pin their victim against a wall or restrain them in a grip. The longer you are held, the more vulnerable you become. As soon as you are grabbed, squirm and struggle as violently as you can to make it hard for your attacker to take control. You will then be in a better position to strike.

2 STRIKE QUICKLY Take advantage of any space you have created to knee your attacker in the groin or kick his shins. Punch his throat or gouge his eyes as aggressively as you can (see right). If he is behind you, deliver a forceful elbow strike. Do all you can to stay on your feet.

3 AIM FOR THE HEAD The best targets for an elbow strike are the jaw, neck or temple – but this strike can be so powerful that it will be effective landed anywhere on the head or in the solar plexus. If you can incapacitate your attacker even momentarily, you can make your escape.

⚠ **WARNING**
● Elbow strikes are potentially very dangerous. The elbow bone is hard and sharp, and when the strike is delivered with force to the jaw or temple it can render a person unconscious, fracture his skull or cause brain or nerve injury. Only use an elbow strike when your personal safety is gravely threatened.
● If you strike hard parts of the head, such as the jaw or temple, with your fist, you will very likely damage your knuckles or break bones in your hand or wrist. If you strike your attacker's teeth you could also get badly cut. Always seek medical attention after any sort of attack.

PINNED TO THE FLOOR

■ **STRIKE HOWEVER YOU CAN** In any attack it is crucial that you try to stay on your feet, as once you are knocked down you may be violently kicked or sexually assaulted. Once on the floor, kick your feet aggressively at your attacker in a cycling motion to stop him getting on top of you. Scream and shout to fire yourself up, and fight any way you can.

■ **PUNCH THE THROAT** A single strike to the throat can end a conflict instantly, provided it is carried out swiftly. Try to strike with as much speed and force as you can, without giving away your intention. Use a clenched fist or straight finger strike, with the tips of your fingers aligned and your thumb tucked in.

■ **TARGET THE EYES** When you are being held down, it can be difficult to get sufficient space to put much power behind a strike. In this situation, press your thumbs hard into your attacker's eyes or use your fingernails to claw and attack his face as aggressively as you can.

■ **USE YOUR LEGS** If you are pinned down remember that your legs are powerful weapons. Use them to knee your assailant between his legs and to kick out and unseat your attacker.

Effective techniques

It is vital to keep your actions simple. If you have to fight, use direct strikes with your elbows, hands and feet as soon as you can.

● **EYE ATTACK** An eye attack of any sort – throwing sand, spraying chemicals from a can or even throwing a drink – will make it easier for you to escape, as a blinded attacker cannot follow you. Eye attacks also benefit from the element of surprise, as they are not conventional forms of attack.

● **GROIN ATTACK** A kick to the groin, if on target, can instantly disable a male attacker. But it does require some power and accuracy. If you miss your target or fail to strike hard enough you will simply enrage your attacker. Use a 'snap kick', delivered from a raised, bent  knee, if your attacker is not yet holding you, or your knee if you are already being held.

● **KNEE POWER** Increase the effect of a knee strike by holding onto your attacker and either pulling him onto the strike, or using your bodyweight behind the strike. If you miss his groin you can also aim for his stomach or his solar plexus.

● **CHOOSE THE MOMENT** To strike effectively you have to be at close range and your blow must come as a complete surprise. You may have to step in towards your attacker, suddenly, after seeming to back away.

● **STAY IN CONTROL** There will be lots of adrenaline pumping through your body. Focus on slowing down your breathing to remain calm.

rape and attempted rape

Around 23 per cent of women and 3 per cent of men experience a sexual assault as an adult. Another 5 per cent of women and 0.3 per cent of men are raped, often by people they know and trust. If you find yourself in an uncomfortable or threatening situation that you fear may escalate into a sexual assault, you need to know how to protect yourself from harm.

action

YOU FEEL THREATENED

1 MAKE YOUR WISHES CLEAR If you are in a situation that is moving in a direction you do not wish to go, make it clear that you do not want to have sex and leave, if necessary. If the person you are with is intoxicated, you may need to repeat your wishes or state them more forcefully.

2 CALL FOR HELP If your wishes are ignored, shout or scream for help at once. If you have a personal alarm, use it. The quicker you do this, the more likely it is that you will unnerve your attacker and convince him to leave. Crucially, once you begin screaming or shouting, do not stop until you are sure you are safe.

3 CONSIDER YOUR ESCAPE OPTIONS If you are in a deserted location where calling for help is not an option, you must escape. But before making your move, decide what you are going to do. Given a short head start how far could you get? Is there a nearby room that you could lock yourself in or a vehicle you could get into? Could you rouse a neighbour or reach a public place? Kick off high-heeled shoes so that you can run away faster. These can be a useful weapon in self defence, too.

4 KEEP TALKING Try to control your fear and talk. **Rape is about power and control, so try to stay calm and confident and do not plead or beg.** The longer you can keep talking, the better your chance of being able to escape.

5 FIGHT BACK Deciding whether to fight back has to be a personal decision. There is some evidence that those who resist have better outcomes. But if you do decide to fight, make it count. Look for an element of surprise, strike quickly and hard (see pages 172–175) and then get away as fast as you can.

YOU ARE RAPED

1 SEEK REFUGE Go somewhere you will be safe, such as the home of a good friend or family member.

2 TALK TO SOMEONE Think about whether or not you want to report the rape to the police: the sooner you report it, the more evidence there will be to support your case. Confide in a friend, whatever you decide, or phone a Rape helpline (see Get Help, opposite).

3 PRESERVE EVIDENCE Do not shower or bathe, clean your teeth or discard clothing until you have spoken to the police. Do not smoke – the smoke or the saliva that smoking generates can make it less easy to identify any residual saliva or semen that the rapist has left.

4 VISIT A SEXUAL ASSAULT REFERRAL CENTRE (SARC) If you do not want to go directly to the police, call a helpline (see Get Help, opposite) and ask a friend to accompany you to a Sexual Assault Referral Centre. Here you can have a forensic and medical examination, and have any evidence stored.

5 GET MEDICAL HELP You may need to get medical treatment, emergency contraception or tests for sexually transmitted diseases. Visit an A&E department, Family Planning clinic or your GP.

Personal alarms

If you travel alone, a personal alarm that emits an ear-piercing shriek can be reassuring. Personal alarms can be gas or battery powered, and the loudest are capable of volumes up to 140dB. Such an alarm can unnerve an attacker, giving you time to escape, or help attract the attention of anyone nearby.

WATCHPOINT More than 80 per cent of rapes are committed by friends, relatives or acquaintances of the victim, which can make the decision to report the rape more difficult.

GET HELP For immediate help and advice, contact the Rape & Sexual Abuse Support Centre helpline on 0808 802 9999, Victim Support on 0845 30 30 900 or www.rapecrisis.org.uk.

be aware

- If you are alone, stick to well-lit public areas. Avoid going to an isolated area or getting into a car with someone you do not know.
- Use a licensed taxi or a mini-cab from a firm you know.
- Try to sit with other people or near the driver when you travel on public transport.
- Walk facing the traffic. If a car stops and you carry on walking, it has to reverse or turn around to follow you. If a motorist asks for directions, stand well away from the vehicle as you give them so that you are out of reach.
- If you are leaving your car in daylight when you know you will return after dark, park under a light or in a public place. Think ahead. When you return to your car at night, have your keys in your hand and lock the door once inside.

- Do not accept drinks from strangers and ask your friends to watch over your drink if you leave it at a party or bar so that it cannot be tampered with. Keep your hand resting over the top of your glass or bottle.
- Drinking alcohol can make you more vulnerable. Book a cab to take you home well in advance and stay with your friends at all times.

Seek counselling

Rape is considered to be a very violent crime and is frequently followed by feelings of fear, isolation, guilt and depression. The sooner you have professional counselling, the better your recovery is likely to be.

- **CONTACT A SUPPORT SERVICE** Rape Crisis and Victim Support are both national bodies with advisers and counsellors in local centres around the UK (see Get Help, above).
- **JOIN A SUPPORT GROUP** Gain strength and come to terms with what has happened by talking with other victims of rape, either online or in person, www.aest.org.uk/helplines/uk_survivor.htm lists local groups.

what next?

- If you decide to report an incident, contact your local police station. A specially trained Sexual Offences Liaisons Officer (SOLO) will chaperone you through the whole reporting process.
- You will be examined and asked to provide some 'early evidence' samples, such as urine samples and mouth swabs, for forensic evidence. Clothes or bedding may be collected.
- You will be asked for a full account of what occurred and this will form the basis of your statement. This may be given to your SOLO chaperone or be recorded on video. At this time you may like to make your own detailed notes about what took place, as the case may not come to court for a long time.

▶▶See also: **PHYSICAL ATTACK** pp172–175

knife attack

In 2007–8 there were 277 deaths by stabbing reported in England and Wales. A number of high-profile murders of young people in larger cities during this period highlighted the prevalence of teenagers carrying knives. While most victims of random knife crime are from these groups, it is worth knowing how to defend yourself against a knife attack.

action

THREATENED WITH A KNIFE

1 **TAKE THE ATTACKER SERIOUSLY** If someone pulls a knife on you, assume that he intends to use it and immediately go on the defensive. No amount of self-defence training can guarantee your safety.

2 **KEEP TALKING** Stay calm and try to persuade the attacker that you do not want a fight. If he wants your possessions, give them to him. Talking also gives you time to weigh up your options, including calling for help or trying to escape.

3 **KEEP YOUR DISTANCE** While you are talking, do anything you can to increase the distance between the knife and your body. Try to stay balanced so that you can move quickly.

be aware

● In any dispute – even when you know you are in the right – try to keep calm and avoid being drawn into a physical encounter. **Many stabbings occur when an argument escalates into a fight.**
● If you are unavoidably drawn into a conflict, such as with an aggressive drunk or road rage driver, always assume that the person could be armed with a knife and act defensively.
● Being aware of what is going on around you is your best defence. Many knife attacks occur suddenly, with the victim unaware that he has been stabbed until he sees the blood.
● Avoid dangerous flashpoints at home and abroad. These include places where rival fans are likely to come together at international or local derby football matches and parts of cities that have a reputation for violence.

Knives are often carried concealed or held low; be wary if you cannot see someone's hand.

ATTACKED WITH A KNIFE

1 **ESCAPE IF YOU CAN** If someone comes at you with a knife, you need to escape, but if you turn your back on the attacker there is a risk you will be stabbed in the back. Try to distract your attacker first, by throwing your bag or wallet at him or pulling something, such as a table or chair, between you. Then run as fast as you can without looking back.

2 **DEFEND YOURSELF** If you cannot run, try to block the knife with anything you can grab, such as a chair, a book or a coat. If there is nothing to hand, turn your body sideways to present a smaller target.

3 **FIGHT BACK** In a serious attack, fighting back may be your only option and you must commit to fighting for your life. Use anything you can as a weapon; otherwise, attack using your hands, feet, elbows and knees (see pages 172–175). Try to keep the palms of your hands away from the attacker to prevent serious injuries to your tendons. Scream and shout at your attacker as you fight and try to trap the arm holding the knife and make him drop it.

4 **DISENGAGE** Once your attacker flinches or doubles up, disengage immediately and escape to a safer place, putting as many obstacles between you and him as possible.

SOMEONE IS STABBED

1 **ASSESS THE SITUATION** Whether you have been stabbed or you have witnessed a stabbing, once there is no threat of further violence, try to assess the injuries. All puncture wounds require urgent treatment. If you can, ask someone to call the emergency services while you staunch any bleeding.

2 **APPLY FIRST AID** If possible, elevate the injury to reduce blood flow and then apply pressure directly to the wound to stop the bleeding (see page 99), using a towel or a clean piece of clothing if you can. Never remove a knife that is still embedded as its presence may be helping to limit the bleeding.

3 **PROTECT AGAINST SHOCK** If you are helping an injured person, make him lie down and loosen any tight clothing. Reassure him that help is on its way and try to keep him calm.

 WARNING

● Always do your best to help someone who is being attacked or who has been stabbed, but do not put yourself at risk. Call the police as soon as you can and find other bystanders who can help.
● If you see someone brandishing a knife or witness a knife crime, call the emergency services at once.

Areas of greatest risk

Any penetrating injury, whatever the depth, that perforates a major organ or arteries in the neck or thigh can be fatal.

● **CHEST** A stab wound just 4cm deep can penetrate the heart. Stab wounds just 3cm deep can puncture a lung.
● **ABDOMEN** Wounds to the liver, spleen, bowel or kidneys can lead to major haemorrhaging.
● **HEAD AND NECK** A head wound can cause a brain haemorrhage; a wound to the neck may cause paralysis or sever an artery, resulting in rapid blood loss, unconsciousness and death.

▶▶See also: **UNCONSCIOUS ADULT/CHILD/BABY** pp14–19 • **SEVERE BLEEDING** p22 • **STAB WOUND** p99

gun attack

In the USA around 30 people are killed in gun incidents every day and 240 shot and injured. Although only 1 per cent of violent crimes in the UK involves firearms, there are still 28 gun crimes every day and the problem is growing. Even if you are faced with this situation it is possible to minimise your risk of injury and to help a casualty of a gun attack effectively.

action

YOU HEAR GUNFIRE

1 STOP AND LISTEN If you hear a sound that you think might be gunfire, stop and listen. Do not move towards the sound, as you could be heading for danger. As you listen, scan your surroundings for possible escape routes and places to shelter.

2 TAKE COVER If you recognise the sound as gunfire, take cover at once. Try to identify the direction of the sound and get to the far side of a barrier that will protect you, such as a wall, a tree or a vehicle.

The shopkeeper let the armed robbers take the money and was unharmed.

22:15:43

3 GET DOWN If there is no cover in your immediate vicinity, get down on the ground and keep as low as possible. Lie motionless, as if dead, while you decide on your next move.

4 ESCAPE FROM THE AREA Can you pinpoint the gunman's location? Is he firing in your direction? If he is, the best tactic is to play dead until the shooting stops and you believe he has gone. Otherwise, make a run for cover or escape the area.

YOU ARE FIRED AT

1 SEEK SHELTER Put barriers between yourself and the gunman. Even though some of these may not be bullet proof, if they obscure you from view the gunman may choose an easier target.

2 RUN FOR COVER If you decide to run, try to run at a 90-degree angle to the gunman's line of fire. Do not stop, even if bullets hit the ground near you, and do not waste time zig-zagging. A fast-moving target across the line of fire is the hardest to hit.

3 KEEP RUNNING If you are hit by a bullet, keep running. Unless it is a serious wound and you drop automatically, you should not stop, as this will make you an easier target.

Identify the weapon

● Automatic weapons pose the greatest danger as they can spray a wide area with bullets. You will hear the rapid gunfire immediately.
● Rifles are deadly at several hundred metres.
● If you are more than 50m from a handgun or shotgun, you are likely to be beyond effective range.

SOMEONE IS SHOT

1 **GIVE EMERGENCY FIRST AID** Gunshot wounds should be treated in the same way as any other wound. Staunch the bleeding with a pad of clean material, torn from clothing if necessary, applied firmly to the wound (see page 98).

2 **CONTACT THE EMERGENCY SERVICES** Call, signal or send someone for help as soon as you can. But recognise that you may have to wait a considerable time, as medical personnel will not be allowed to enter the area until it is considered safe.

3 **REASSURE THE VICTIM** Try to keep the victim as calm as possible and watch for symptoms of shock (see pages 38–39). Reassure him with the statistic that 90 per cent of people who are shot survive and that you will do all you can to help.

4 **MAKE A MOVE** If you fear for the life of a gunshot victim and help is not at hand, you must balance the risks of staying where you are with making a move to get help. Remember to put your own safety first.

5 **IMPROVISE TRANSPORT** If the person is badly injured or unconscious, the safest way to move him is on a stretcher made from a door, desktop or ladder. If you are on your own and he is too heavy to carry, wrap him in a coat, blanket or rug and drag him behind you as gently as you can.

be aware

- If you know someone who is seriously disaffected with society in general or has been the victim of a conflict, take any threat he makes very seriously – especially if you know he has access to firearms. Raise your concerns with his family and your local police.
- Some public shootings have followed video warnings broadcast on the internet. If you discover a blog or website containing such threats, pass the details to the police at once.
- If you are travelling to a country with a reputation for gun crime, be especially vigilant. Avoid areas that are known to be hotspots.

 TAKE CARE

- Whenever you are passing banks, jewellers or security vans, be vigilant for anything suspicious. Pay particular attention to anyone who appears to be loitering nearby or for people sitting in cars waiting. If you are seriously concerned, leave the area and call the police or alert a member of staff.
- If you own or have access to firearms, you are legally required to keep them in a locked cabinet and to keep ammunition separately. It is also wise to store weapons partially dismantled, with key components kept elsewhere.

Armed robbery

If you are caught up in an armed robbery, you will be at great risk. Instead of facing a lone gunman, firing randomly – as is often the case in a gun attack – this violent crime is likely to involve several highly motivated, ruthless criminals who use the threat of firearms to guarantee that their demands are met.

1 **KEEP CALM** Faced with an armed gang at close quarters, there is little chance of escape. Keep a low profile and do not challenge them.

2 **DO AS YOU ARE TOLD** Follow the robbers' instructions obediently and do not make any sudden movements. If you need to move or reach for something, ask permission first, in case your movements are misconstrued.

3 **DO NOT BE A HERO** While no one is being harmed, do not resist in any way or hinder the robbers. Let them steal what they want and make their getaway.

4 **BE A GOOD WITNESS** While sitting or lying still, try to memorise the robbers' appearance and actions, without staring at them too obviously. After they have left, try to get a description of their vehicle and note their direction of travel.

5 **CALL THE POLICE** Once the robbers have left, call the police immediately, even if an alarm has been activated. If you are in a shop or bank, close the doors and wait for the police to arrive. All witnesses to the robbery should remain at the scene, ready to provide statements.

▶▶See also: **SEVERE BLEEDING** p22 • **SHOCK** pp38–39 • **GUNSHOT WOUND** p98

stolen car

Discovering that your car has been stolen can become a serious emergency if you find yourself isolated, especially at night or in an unfamiliar place, without any transport. But there are a few simple precautions that can help to reduce the chances of you becoming a victim of car crime and increase the chances of your vehicle being found.

action

YOUR CAR IS MISSING

1 CONFIRM THE THEFT If you find that your car is missing, first consider whether your partner or another keyholder may have taken the car.

2 CONTACT THE POLICE Call your local police station and give the make, model and registration number of the car and details of anything valuable or potentially dangerous that it contained. The police will give you a crime reference number. Do not call 999.

3 CONTACT YOUR INSURERS Report the theft to your insurance company so that you can make a claim.

A CAR IS BEING STOLEN

1 RAISE THE ALARM If you see someone attempting to steal a car, call the police.

2 STAY SAFE Do not confront the thief or get too close to the front or rear of the car if it is about to be driven away. No vehicle is worth a serious injury.

3 MAKE NOTES Jot down as much detail as you can, including a description of the thief, how he stole the car, the direction he took and the time it occurred.

Tracking devices

A tracking device fitted covertly to your car will allow it to be tracked using GPS in the event of theft. For a monthly fee or annual contract, your car's location is monitored constantly. Some systems allow you to see where your car is on your own PC; others allow the police to track and locate your vehicle.

YOU FIND YOUR STOLEN CAR

1 DO NOT TOUCH IT If you find your car through your own endeavours – cars are often abandoned in car parks or streets nearby – contact the police before you touch it. They may want to examine it for clues.

2 RECORD ITS CONDITION Photograph the car exactly as you found it. This will support any insurance claim you make for damage.

3 MAKE A SAFETY CHECK Before you drive your car away, consider having it checked over by a mechanic to ensure that it has not been damaged by the thief.

precautions

- Always lock your car and ensure it is alarmed. Consider fitting a steering wheel immobiliser or a wheel clamp if it is often parked for a long period of time.
- Keep your car keys safe at all times. Do not leave your keys in a hallway where they can be stolen through a letterbox or by someone entering your house temporarily.
- Keep the purchase receipts for your car and any extras fitted. Take photographs of your car.
- Never leave valuables on display. Remove or hide CD or DVD player fascias and satellite navigation devices when you leave the car.
- Keep your car garaged, if possible. Otherwise park in well-lit, public places.
- Have your car's vehicle identification number (VIN) engraved on the windows and other parts. Some councils provide this service for free. You can also buy DIY kits and engrave the number yourself. Register the VIN on a database that buyers can check to find out if a car is stolen.

identity theft

Your name, date of birth and address are often all that an identity thief requires to impersonate you. If your identity is stolen, it can be fraudulently used to obtain credit, open bank accounts or acquire official documents.

> **TIME TO ACT** If you have been a victim of identity theft, request a copy of your credit report from a credit reference agency. Ask them to correct any inaccuracies.

How can you tell?

- **CREDIT REFUSAL** You are refused a loan or new credit card despite a good credit history.
- **UNEXPECTED BILLS** You receive demands for payment for goods or services that you did not order or request.
- **STATEMENT ERRORS** Unauthorised items appear on your bank or credit card accounts.
- **MISSED POST** Important post from your bank or financial company fails to arrive.
- **BENEFIT DENIAL** You apply for a state benefit and are told that you are already claiming.

action

YOU DISCOVER A THEFT

■ **INFORM YOUR CARD PROVIDERS** If you suspect the fraudulent use of your bank account or credit cards, contact the service provider at once. They will have a specialised department that investigates criminal activity. You will usually get your money back, but the responsibility is on you to check your statement. The card company may be less willing to help if you have given your card details to someone, especially if the transaction was on the internet and used the extra level of security attached to most cards.

■ **REPORT MISSING OR STOLEN DOCUMENTS** If you discover that important documents, such as your passport or driving licence, have gone missing, inform the police. You will be required to fill in a number of forms in order to obtain replacements.

■ **CONTACT THE MAIL SERVICE** If you believe that your mail has been or is being stolen, contact the Royal Mail Customer Enquiry Line on 08457 740740. They can also tell you if a mail redirection service has been set up falsely in your name and stop it at once.

YOUR IDENTITY IS STOLEN

■ **CLOSE ALL FRAUDULENT ACCOUNTS** Contact all the companies that have been used by your impersonator and close all fraudulent accounts.

■ **MAKE NEW MAIL ARRANGEMENTS** If you cannot guarantee the security of your mail, arrange to have your mail delivered to a trusted friend or relative.

■ **TAKE OUT CIFAS PROTECTIVE REGISTRATION** Register with the Credit Industry Fraud Avoidance System (www.cifas.org.uk) to alert potential lenders that you have been a victim of identity fraud. Additional security measures will be put in place to ensure that any future applications are genuine.

for next time...

- Dispose of documents that contain personal information with care. Shred sensitive material, such as bank or credit card statements.
- Never give personal information to cold callers. If someone asks you for sensitive information, request proof of their identity. **You would never be asked for a PIN number over the phone,** even by your bank.
- Only give personal information to trusted sites when you use the internet, and only when on a secure page (see page 185).
- Protect your mail. Fit a lockable mailbox if you live in shared accommodation. Ask your bank to arrange for you to collect debit and credit cards from the branch. If you move, set up a mail redirection service from the previous address.

▶▶See also: **CASH/CREDIT CARD CRIME** pp184–185

cash/credit card crime

Cash and credit card crime is on the increase. An apparently ordinary cashpoint can conceal a trap set up by criminals to snare your card and your PIN number. And the online world can be full of potential traps and loopholes in which you can unwittingly lose cash. So when you visit a cashpoint, buy goods online or check your emails, take some prudent precautions.

action

LOST OR STOLEN CARD

1 CANCEL YOUR CARD Call the card company immediately – the number is on your bill but it is worth storing in your phone. Note the time of the call and who you speak to. You will need your account number, details of when you noticed the loss and, ideally, the last legitimate transaction you made. Follow up the call with a letter.

2 CONTACT THE POLICE If you believe that your card was stolen, provide a full account to the police of where and how you believe it was taken.

TROUBLE AT A CASHPOINT

■ **CHECK THE ATM** If anything about the machine looks at all suspicious, do not use it. Check that there is no exterior fitting on the slot where you enter your card and run your finger along it to check for the edges of a plastic sleeve (see right). Report any suspicions to the bank or machine owner.

■ **ENTER YOUR PIN ONLY ONCE** If you forget your number, cancel the transaction and contact your bank to avoid losing your card. If a machine does not return your card, contact your bank immediately. If possible, stay at the machine to make the call to prevent criminals gaining access to it.

■ **CHECK FOR LOITERERS** Be suspicious of helpful strangers, who could be trying to observe your PIN number or who may try to distract you by saying you have dropped something while you are at the ATM. It has been known for criminals to sit in a parked car and use binoculars to watch the machine. So be aware of lines of sight and keep the keypad shielded with your hand, purse or wallet as you enter your PIN.

CLONED CARD

1 STUDY YOUR STATEMENTS Although chip and PIN cards are almost impossible to clone, there are ways that they can be used fraudulently if criminals gain access to some of your details. Check your bank and credit card statements carefully to ensure that all the transactions are genuine.

2 REPORT UNAUTHORISED TRANSACTIONS If you find any transactions on your bill that appear suspicious, contact your card company immediately. They will investigate for you (see page 183).

Look for a miniature camera fitted anywhere around the machine. This is used to record your PIN as you tap it in.

FREE CASH WITHDRAWALS
IMPORTANT

The Lebanese Loop is a simple plastic sleeve that fits inside the card slot. It prevents your card being read so you have to re-enter you PIN, which gives the criminal more chance of recording it. The card gets stuck and the criminal retrieves it once you have left.

WATCHPOINT Always keep your PIN secure. UK banks will not reimburse 'phantom' cash withdrawals from a chip and PIN card not reported lost: they say these cards cannot be cloned.

GET HELP If your credit card is refused, contact your card company immediately. They may have observed an unusual pattern of spending and suspect fraudulent use.

TIME TO ACT Before you buy from an unfamiliar or dubious website, check the contact details and try to phone them. If you are unsuccessful, do not make a purchase.

SENT AN E-MAIL SCAM

■ **IGNORE 'PHISHING' EMAILS Beware email requests for personal information** (known as 'phishing'). The request may come disguised as a communication from your bank or an online company such as PayPal, and claim to be updating your security information. Such requests are always fraudulent.

■ **DELETE UNSOLICITED PROPOSITIONS** Many email scams involve offers of well-paid work, unclaimed competition winnings or romantic liaisons. Many feature long, persuasive storylines intended to get you hooked. Inevitably what follows is some plausible request for 'expenses'. Delete on receipt.

■ **NEVER CLICK A LINK** Links in emails are often not what they seem and may take you to a fraudulent site. If you hover your cursor over a suspicious link or right click on it and choose 'Properties', you will see its true address (see box, right). If in doubt, type out web addresses directly into your browser.

CAUGHT IN A WEB SCAM

■ **AVOID SPOOF SITES** Spoof sites are built to look like genuine ones and tempt the unwary to enter their credit card details. If your browser warns you that a site is suspicious, or if it does not open a secure page (see box right) when it requests personal information – leave at once.

■ **SHOP WITH CAUTION** When you shop online, apply the same caution that you would in a market. Does the site look genuine? Does it have real-world contact details? Are the prices what you might expect or are they suspiciously cheap?

■ **BEWARE ONE-PRODUCT SITES** A typical scam is to set up a site that advertises a popular Christmas item, such as a games console, at a very competitive price. In a week or two the site will be shut, your money will be lost and the thieves long gone.

On-line safety

Internet fraud is growing faster than any other sector. Be cautious when providing your details.

● **PERSONAL INFORMATION** Only ever enter personal information, such as credit card details, on a web page that is secure. You can tell when a page is secure by the appearance of a locked padlock icon in your browser window. If you click on the padlock you will be able to see more information about the site and its security rating. On a secure page the prefix to the web address will also change from 'http' to 'https'.

● **UNWARY PAYMENTS** If you ever fall for a scam and send a payment to a fake website, contact your bank or credit card provider at once and cancel the card. Depending on the precise circumstances, you may be liable for some or all of the money lost.

for next time...

● Keep your browser software up to date. The latest versions will be the most secure and so protect you more effectively.
● Consider installing security software that checks that websites are genuine and that any security certificates they may have are up to date.
● Keep a separate credit card for your online transactions and use a separate email address for online subscriptions that you can cancel if you need to.
● Use the internet to research online scams. Sites such as www.crimestoppers-uk.org, www.onlinescamsexposed.com and www.fraudwatchers.org keep you up to date with the latest online frauds.

threatening **calls**

Receiving an abusive or intimidating call can be particularly frightening if you live alone. But there are effective ways to deal with and stop these calls, and you can prevent further intrusion with the help of the latest technology.

GET HELP Do not hesitate to report abusive calls. In the UK, making malicious or abusive telephone calls is a criminal offence under the 1984 Telecommunications Act.

action

1 DENY THE CALLER SATISFACTION If you pick up a call that is abusive or threatening, put the receiver down immediately and leave the phone off the hook until the caller hangs up. **Do not respond in any way – this may just encourage the abuser.** Repeat this response each time you receive this type of call. Disconnect your landline and turn your mobile off at night so you are not disturbed.

2 KEEP A RECORD Note the date and time of the calls and write down what the caller says. Alternatively, record the call; some answering machines have the capacity to record calls or you can buy a recorder that makes it easy to record the phone calls for the police to hear. This fits between your phone and the phone socket. A cheaper version has a lead that you plug into your own recorder.

3 REPORT ABUSIVE CALLS Tell your phone provider. They may monitor your line or block a particular number. Call your local police station if you feel threatened by calls.

4 BLOCK CALLS With many modern phones you can not only see the caller's number, so you can choose to not answer calls from certain numbers, but can also automate the process and simply bar them. You can also choose to bar all calls from numbers that are withheld.

5 CHANGE YOUR NUMBER If the problem persists, ask your phone provider to change your number and ask to be ex-directory. Although this service usually incurs a fee, if your provider has been monitoring your case, or the police have been involved, they may offer this without charge.

 WARNING

If the caller makes any kind of threat against you or your family, contact the police at once.

Mobile phones

Abusive calls – and texts – to mobile phones can be extremely invasive as many people carry their mobile with them at all times. Young people, in particular, are often victims of this form of abuse.

- **SCREEN CALLS** All mobile phones feature caller ID, and if you add all your contacts to your address book you will see the name of the caller, if it is someone you know. If you do not recognise the number, or it indicates 'number withheld', you can choose to ignore it or let the call go to voicemail.
- **BAR CALLS** Many mobile phone handsets also feature call barring and text barring. Add the nuisance number to a 'blocked list' so that when the phone receives a call from that number it disconnects immediately.

for next time...

- Remember that you have the option of keeping your number private whenever you have a new phone line installed or take over an old one. Simply request to be ex-directory.
- Use a phone with a 'caller ID' feature, so that you can see who is phoning before you answer a call.
- Use the prerecorded message on your answerphone rather than your own voice. It is preferable for a male member of the household to be the voice on the answerphone. Avoid saying 'I am not here at the moment' as this makes it clear that you live alone.

PUBLIC EMERGENCIES

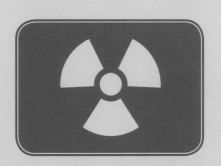

flood

Flooding is one of the most widely occurring natural disasters. Short periods of intense rainfall may produce flash floods, prolonged heavy rain can cause rivers to break their banks and tidal surges give rise to widespread coastal flooding. The severity of a flood can be unpredictable, so it is advisable to err on the side of caution and prepare for the worst.

be aware

THE POWER OF WATER

- 15cm of fast-moving water can knock a person off his feet and will reach the bottom of a car. It may cause a driver to lose control or stall the car.
- 30cm of water is enough to float many family cars.
- 60cm of fast-moving water will float and sweep away larger SUVs (sports utility vehicles) and vans.

HELP AND INFORMATION

- If heavy rain and flooding is forecast, check online at www.environment-agency.gov.uk/homeandleisure/floods/default.aspx to find out if your area is at risk.
- Listen to local radio and television for Flood Warnings or phone the Environment Agency Floodline: 0845 988 1188. Act as soon as a warning is given for your area.
- Call the Environment Agency on 0845 988 1188 to find out if you are eligible for the 24-hour Floodline Warnings Direct service, given by phone, text, email or pager.

Flood warnings

Government flood warnings, which are given by the Environment Agency and the Met Office, advise you on what action to take.

- **FLOOD WATCH** Warns of the risk to low-lying ground that is prone to flooding, and cautions people in these areas to remain alert.
- **FLOOD WARNING** Warns of flooding to vulnerable properties and recommends that defensive action, such as sandbagging (see box, opposite) be taken at once.
- **SEVERE FLOOD WARNING** Warns of serious widespread flooding with additional risk to life. Prompt action and evacuation is required by all those in affected areas.
- **ALL CLEAR** Warnings no longer apply.

Tewkesbury, July 22, 2007. 4,000 homes in Gloucestershire were flooded after torrential rain.

TIME TO ACT Make an emergency plan that includes provision for your family and pets, so that you are ready if a warning is issued. Buy sandbags (see below) in advance.

WATCHPOINT Fill jugs and saucepans with drinking water before floodwater enters your home or keep bottled water with you. Water supplies may become contaminated.

action

HOME IN DANGER

1 FIT PROTECTIVE BARRIERS Board up windows and doors and cover air bricks and low-level ventilators. Use proprietary products designed for this purpose, marine plywood, or chipboard and PVC sheeting. Put plugs in sinks and baths and weight down.

2 CUT OFF UTILITIES Turn off gas, electricity and water supplies before floodwater enters your home.

3 MOVE UPSTAIRS If you live in a two-storey house, move as many possessions upstairs as you can. Begin with important documents, personal treasures and expensive electronics. Then consider furniture, carpets and curtains.

4 RAISE ITEMS ON BLOCKS Items that cannot be carried upstairs should be raised off the ground. Move or protect the contents of your garage or shed.

YOU ARE IN DANGER

■ **IF YOU HAVE TO DRIVE THROUGH FLOODWATER Keep your speed down, stay in a low gear and keep the engine revs high to avoid stalling.** If you can feel water coming in beneath your feet, stop and get out at once. You will be safer on foot than in an uncontrollable vehicle floated by the floodwater.

■ **IF YOU ARE SWEPT AWAY** Try to lie on your back with your feet out in front of you. Watch out for obstacles or debris in the water that might injure you. Look around for something you can grab or climb onto and pull yourself to a place where the force of the water is not as strong.

■ **IF YOU ARE STRANDED** Whether at home, in your car or on isolated high ground, if you are in immediate danger from rising floodwater, phone the emergency services.

Building a sandbag wall

Sandbags are a very effective way of keeping water out of your property, especially when used with PVC sheeting. How high you build the wall depends on the severity of the expected flood. As a guide, you will need 80 sandbags to build a 60cm wall.

1 LAY DOWN SHEETING Clear debris and lay PVC sheeting on the ground, preferably on a firm, level site. One edge will be held in place by the sandbag wall and the surplus sheeting should face towards the flood.

2 TO BUILD A SINGLE THICKNESS WALL Lay sandbags lengthways and build up the wall in layers. Use half-filled sandbags to stagger the joints. Draw up the PVC sheeting so that it is taut and secure it under the top row of sandbags.

3 TO BUILD A DOUBLE THICKNESS WALL Lay two rows of sandbags lengthways, side by side. Place the next layer of sandbags across the first layer, with bag mouths facing inwards (see right). Pull up the sheeting.

blizzard conditions

Heavy snowfall, combined with high winds and poor visibility, causes major disruption, both for travellers and those at home, especially in more isolated areas, as power lines come down and water supplies freeze. Even a prolonged cold snap has its dangers, especially for the elderly. Prepare yourself so that you can keep warm and safe, whatever the conditions.

precautions

- Make sure that you have torches and spare batteries, candles, gas or oil lamps and matches handy in case of a power cut.
- Insulate all your pipes to reduce the risk of them freezing.
- Where the risk of power failure is high, consider installing gas appliances or purchase a portable gas or coal-fired stove and heater.
- Keep a well-stocked first-aid kit (see page 334) and make sure you always have at least a week's supply of any prescription medicines.
- Use the internet or a mobile phone to get accurate weather forecasts for your location.
- Conserve supplies (see below).

Care of the elderly

- **SPECIAL CARE** If you have elderly friends or relatives, consider inviting them to stay until the weather improves. Alternatively, visit them regularly to make sure that they are well and have everything they need.
- **IF YOU ARE ELDERLY** Stay indoors and keep warm (see right). Eat at least one hot meal a day and sip hot drinks regularly all day long. Take a flask containing a hot drink to bed with you in case you wake up feeling cold. Remain as active as you can, doing light chores in between periods of rest. Arrange to phone a friend or relative first thing in the morning and last thing at night.

action

HEAVY SNOWFALL PREDICTED

1 SAVE WATER If there is a chance that your pipes may freeze, fill the bath and every spare container you have with water. To make a leaky bath plug more watertight, first dry the plug and the plug hole and then coat them thickly with petroleum jelly. **If you allow water to drip from the cold tap, the constant slight movement in the pipes may help to prevent them from freezing.**

2 BUY FOOD PROVISIONS If you live in, or are visiting, an area prone to heavy snow and low temperatures, always keep a week's supply of food, using frozen or canned goods to supplement fresh fruit and vegetables. Be aware that people may start panic buying as soon as heavy snow is forecast.

3 CHARGE YOUR BATTERIES Make sure that your mobile phone and laptop, as well as any spare batteries you may have for them, are fully charged while you still have electricity.

SNOWED IN

1 BE EFFICIENT To clear snow, sweep it forward and then to the side – this is less tiring than shovelling compacted snow. Take care not to overdo snow-clearing if you are not used to doing vigorous exercise. Work slowly and rest as often as you need to. Share the task with neighbours if possible.

2 TAKE PREVENTIVE MEASURES Salt essential paths and driveways with rock salt (used by many councils on the roads) or table salt. These both lower the melting point of snow and ice and help to prevent water refreezing. Alternatively, scatter sand, grit or a gritty substance such as fresh cat litter.

TIME TO ACT If a cold spell is forecast, make sure that you are up to date with all your utility bills. This is not the time to have your gas or electricity supply cut off.

WATCHPOINT Moderate snowfall can escalate to blizzard conditions in a short space of time. Avoid travel on high or exposed routes where you are particularly vulnerable.

GET HELP If you are in an emergency situation, dial 999. Similarly, if an elderly relative is not answering the door or responding to phone calls, alert the emergency services.

LOSS OF HEATING/POWER

1 DRESS IN LAYERS You will be much warmer if you wear several thin layers of clothing rather than just one or two thick items.

2 WEAR A HAT Although your head may not feel cold, a hat will help you to conserve body heat.

3 CONSUME HOT FOOD AND DRINKS While there is still power and sufficient food, have plenty of hot food and warm drinks. If you are relying on an emergency supply of gas, oil or solid fuel, use it to heat food or water, rather than heating the house.

4 HEAT ONE ROOM If you have lost power to your home, or have a limited source of heat, insulate and warm a single room as effectively as you can. Use this room day and night.

5 EXCLUDE DRAUGHTS Heat escapes through any opening. Draught-proof windows with cling film. Stretched taut over the window frame and taped down, cling film still lets the light in but traps another layer of air between it and the glass. Draw heavy curtains. Put draught-excluders, or wedge old clothes or tea towels, around doors. Block up disused chimneys with cushions, blankets or boards held tightly in place by furniture.

6 BURN GAS If your cooker is on mains gas, use it to warm your kitchen. It is safer to use the oven than the hob, but the burner may not ignite without electricity. If you use the oven, do not leave the door open while it is on or you may melt the control knobs. A gas barbecue can provide a useful emergency source of hot food and warmth, but make sure that you use it in a well-ventilated area (see Warning, right).

When all else fails

If you are in a completely isolated area, with no heat source, you may have to generate your own. Do so with extreme care.

● **CONTAIN AN OPEN FIRE** Use house bricks to contain your fire and its ashes. Stacked bricks will allow pans and kettles to be heated and will retain heat after the flames have died down.
● **MAKE A CANDLE HEATER** Stand a candle in a candle holder and put it on a heat-resistant surface. Place an upturned terracotta pot over the top, supporting the edges on bricks. Not only will you gain some light, but the pot will retain most of the candle's heat.

 WARNING

● If you use an open fire, gas heater or the cooker for warmth, it is vital that the room has adequate ventilation. When fuels, such as gas, oil, wood and coal, do not burn fully, carbon monoxide is produced, which can be fatal.
● Never leave an open fire or candles burning unattended. Extinguish them before you go to bed.
● Be aware that an elderly person could suffer from hypothermia (see page 46) if she is without warmth for some time. How long this might take depends on the temperature, how healthy and active she is, and the availability of warm clothing, hot food and drink. A frail person could succumb in just a few hours.

 TAKE CARE

Avoid all unnecessary travel. If you have to travel by car, wait until the roads have been gritted and take warm clothes, boots, water, food, a torch and spade. Let someone know your route and when you expect to arrive. Drive slowly – it can take 10 times longer to stop in snow and ice – and use the highest gear possible. If you get stuck, stay with your car.

▶▶See also: INHALING FUMES pp44–45 • HYPOTHERMIA p46

avalanche

Each winter, huge amounts of snow and ice build up on steep mountainsides in an unstable union of friction and gravity. If you are caught in an avalanche, swift and appropriate action can be the difference between life and death.

GET HELP Programme the number of the local emergency services or Mountain Rescue Service into your mobile phone so you can call quickly if you have a signal and need help.

be aware

- Avalanches are a product of the interaction between the terrain, the snow and the weather conditions. Heavy snowfall on a steep rock face, high winds or overnight temperatures that stay above freezing all increase the risk.
- Always check the local International Scale of Avalanche Hazard Rating before you ski or snowboard off piste. Ask the local ski resort for information. Ski with a qualified Rep or Ski Guide and take safety equipment (see right).
- Be wary of areas of deep snow for three days after a snowfall. Avoid pockets of deep snow on the north or lee side of mountains.

Safety equipment

If you are planning to ski or snowboard off piste, three pieces of equipment are essential.

- **AVALANCHE TRANSCEIVER** This radio device transmits a signal that can be tracked if you are buried in an avalanche.
- **AVALANCHE PROBE** Use a probe to find a person's exact location beneath the snow. It saves unnecessary digging and precious time.
- **AVALANCHE SHOVEL** Speed is essential to survival. Using a lightweight, collapsible shovel is far more efficient than using your hands.

action

CAUGHT IN AN AVALANCHE

1 **SCREAM AND SHOUT** Warn your companions to make sure that they have seen the avalanche – and you. If they know where you are, they will have a better chance of rescuing you. As soon as you sense an avalanche, look up to see if you are in its path and get out of its way as quickly as you can.

2 **DISCARD HEAVY ITEMS** Get rid of bags, clothing and anything that will drag you down deeper into the snow. Discard your ski poles.

3 **'SWIM' THROUGH THE SNOW** If you get caught up in the avalanche, try to 'swim' to keep yourself at the top of the snow. Grab hold of anything, such as a tree, bush or rock: the more snow that passes you by, the less there will be to bury you.

4 **PUT UP A HAND** Try to keep one hand raised to help mark your position and the other in front of your face. As the avalanche slows, try to maintain a pocket of air in front of your nose and mouth.

As the snow settles around you, try to keep moving. Rock your head and wiggle your body. The more space you can create around yourself, the better.

5 **REMAIN STILL** Once you are buried you may not be able to move, so try to control your breathing and stay calm. Snow is a good insulator, so do not waste oxygen shouting. If you feel faint, allow yourself to black out. You will use less oxygen if unconscious.

An avalanche is most likely on sheltered slopes of 28 to 45 degrees.

SOMEONE IS BURIED

1 GET HELP Shout a warning to those around you, then watch closely. Try to pinpoint the last spot that you saw the person before he was buried.

2 ASSESS THE RISK Ascertain whether another avalanche is likely and plan your escape options. Then mark the point where the victim was last seen with a ski pole.

3 ALERT MOUNTAIN RESCUE Use a phone or radio to request assistance, but only send someone for help if you can spare him. He will be more valuable helping to dig: **if you can find the victim in 15 minutes, he has a 90 per cent chance of survival;** after 35 minutes, this drops to 30 per cent.

4 SEARCH If you have an avalanche transceiver, set it to 'receive' to locate the buried skier. Otherwise, look quickly for clues, such as ski poles or clothing. These may give you a trajectory you can follow to focus the search area. Look for signs in the snow that someone might be buried underneath.

5 DIG Use shovels or your hands to dig down to where you think the victim might be. Clearly mark the places that you have already searched.

6 MAKE AN AIRWAY As soon as you locate the person, reach in with your hands to create an airway to his face. Dig him out as quickly as you can.

7 BEGIN CPR If he is not breathing, begin resuscitation at once (see pages 16–17).

8 AWAIT RESCUE Keep him warm, but do not move him if he is unconscious in case there are unseen injuries. If he is conscious and moving him causes no pain, transfer him onto a dry surface and keep him comfortable until medical help arrives.

⚠ TAKE CARE

● Whether you are going for a walk or skiing off piste, always let someone know your planned route.
● If you are skiing or snowboarding off piste, go in a small group with a minimum of three people.
● Never enter or traverse a slope above other people as you could trigger an avalanche. About 85 per cent of avalanches are caused by people moving.
● Take note of avalanche hazard warnings and flags: yellow indicates low risk; yellow and black check, considerable to high risk and black, very high risk. Never cross an avalanche warning fence.

▶▶See also: **UNCONSCIOUS ADULT/CHILD/BABY** pp14–19

earthquake

About half of the world's largest cities are situated in regions where there is a possibility of a serious earthquake. Although tremors often strike without warning, there are precautions that you can take if you are in a high-risk area.

WATCHPOINT In coastal areas a tsunami (see pages 200–201) may follow an earthquake. Stay away from the beach, listen for warnings and be prepared to move inland.

precautions

- If you plan to travel in a high-risk zone, check with your tour operator that your accommodation meets local 'earthquake-proof' building standards.
- When you arrive at your accommodation, identify places of safety, indoors and out, and make sure your travelling companions are aware of them too.
- Agree with your companions what you will do if an earthquake strikes, including how you will make contact with each other if you are apart. Choose a relative or friend who lives a long distance away as a contact point – long distance calls are often easier to make as local networks will be overloaded.
- Take a survival kit (see pages 334–337) and keep it handy. Keep your mobile phone fully charged.

High-risk areas

- Minor earthquakes can occur almost anywhere, but earthquakes are most frequent, and most frequently severe, at places where the Earth's tectonic plates meet.
- Where these locations coincide with high human population density, the potential exists for a major disaster. Such areas include large parts of the northern and north-eastern Mediterranean and the so-called Ring of Fire, which circles the Pacific Ocean and includes the Philippines, Indonesia, Japan, and the west coast of the United States.
- Over the past 20 years, the most deadly earthquakes have occurred in Haiti, Indonesia, China, Pakistan, Iran, India, Turkey, Japan, Afghanistan, Mexico and Colombia.

L'Aquila, central Italy, in April 2009, after it was rocked by an earthquake with a magnitude of 6.3. 250 people died.

action

INSIDE A BUILDING

1 **STOP WHAT YOU ARE DOING** Even if you feel a very slight tremor, prioritise your safety until the all-clear is given. You may simply have felt a foreshock that precedes a much more powerful earthquake.

2 **DROP TO THE GROUND** If the shock is more severe, get down. This will lower your centre of gravity and reduce the chance of being hit by debris.

3 **TAKE COVER** Get under a sturdy table or other piece of furniture for protection and hold onto it. If there is nothing suitable nearby, **crouch down in a corner where two interior walls meet**, well away from windows or other glass. Cover your head and face with your arms. Do not shelter in a doorway – if it doesn't have a load-bearing structure, it may collapse.

4 **STAY WHERE YOU ARE** Do not move until the shaking stops, even if the lights go out or automatic sprinklers come on. Most people who are injured are those who move about during an earthquake.

OUTSIDE A BUILDING

■ **RUN TO AN OPEN SPACE** Quickly move away from buildings, trees, overhead wires or anything else that might fall on you. The larger the open space you can find, the safer you will be. People are rarely injured during an earthquake simply by the ground moving.

■ **DRIVE TOWARDS AN OPEN SPACE** If you are in a car, find an open space, such as a large car park, and stop the car. Do not stop on a bridge, beneath an overpass or beside tall buildings or trees. Stay in the car until the shaking stops.

TRAPPED UNDER DEBRIS

1 **COVER YOUR NOSE AND MOUTH** Avoid inhaling potentially harmful dust. Try to get your bearings and check yourself for injuries.

2 **GET HELP** Listen for sounds of rescue and try to tap on something to alert rescuers. If you can get to it, use your mobile phone to call someone or to generate intermittent music, beeps or other sound. Only shout as a last resort, as it is tiring and can result in you inhaling more dust.

 WARNING

If you find yourself trapped, do not strike a match for light. Dust-filled air can be explosive and gas may have escaped from broken pipes.

what next?

● If you are inside, do not go out until you are certain that it is safe. Be alert for broken glass, loose slates or tiles or damaged masonry. Beware of the risk of fire.

● If you are outside, do not approach a building that looks unsafe. If in doubt, do not enter. Seek advice from the authorities or wait for the all-clear.

● If you are in a car, drive cautiously and slowly. Watch for large cracks or potholes. If possible, avoid driving over bridges and through underpasses.

● Do not smoke as there may be leaking gas pipes.

● Try to obtain up-to-date information from the emergency services, internet, radio, television or by telephoning someone outside the area.

Aftershocks

An earthquake is usually followed by a series of aftershocks. Their size and frequency is unpredictable, although generally, the bigger the main earthquake, the greater the size and number of aftershocks. Aftershocks are especially dangerous because they cause further collapse to already damaged buildings and infrastructure. Treat them seriously and act as you would for an earthquake.

▶▶See also: **CRUSH INJURY** p102 • **EMERGENCY PREPARATION** pp334–337

volcanic eruption

Between 50 and 60 volcanoes erupt every year: 20 to 30 produce sometimes deadly lava flows and the same number are more violently explosive, creating clouds of suffocating ash. There is also the possibility of mudflows and flooding.

TIME TO ACT Volcanologists are increasingly skilled at predicting when a volcano is likely to erupt, but evacuation warnings may be given just hours beforehand.

action

ERUPTION PREDICTED

1 KEEP INFORMED Listen to the radio, watch television or use the internet to keep up to date with events. The website www.noaawatch.gov/themes/volcanoes.php gives hourly volcano reports.

2 HEED OFFICIAL WARNINGS Be ready for evacuation. Plan what to take, where you are going and the safest routes to get there. Follow any evacuation order issued by the authorities immediately. If you are not required to evacuate, make sure you have supplies of water, food and batteries.

3 PREPARE A SURVIVAL KIT You should include goggles and disposable breathing masks for each person as well as standard items (see page 333).

 WARNING

The danger area around a volcano is usually a radius of about 30km, but be aware that ash can spread to cover up to five times this distance, depending on the nature of the eruption and weather conditions. Stay upwind of an eruption if at all possible.

 TAKE CARE

● Keep pets indoors until the all-clear is given.
● Turn off electricity and gas at the mains.
● Agree how to reunite your family. Ask a relative or friend who lives a good distance away to act as a contact point and make sure that everyone has their phone number and address. Keep your mobile phone fully charged.
● Erupted volcanic material ranges from ash-sized particles to larger volcanic 'bombs' as big as a fridge. Be aware of what is likely in your area.

Heimaey, Iceland, 1973. Around 25 million cubic metres of lava and ash destroyed over 350 homes.

FALLING ASH

1 **PROTECT YOURSELF** If you are outside when ash starts to fall, use clothing to cover yourself as far as you can and put up an umbrella, if you have one, to protect yourself from sharp particles of rock. Wear goggles and a mask, if possible. If you do not have a mask, tie a scarf or handkerchief soaked in water over your mouth and nose. Wear spectacles instead of contact lenses.

2 **FIND SHELTER** If you can, take shelter inside a building or a car. If you are in your holiday accommodation when the ash begins to fall, stay inside – unless there is a risk that the roof will collapse – and keep all windows tightly closed. Seal off other vents and chimneys with cardboard and duct tape.

3 **PREVENT STRUCTURAL DAMAGE** If you are sheltering in holiday accommodation with a flat or low-pitched roof, periodically clear the ash from the roof to prevent it collapsing under the weight. Once mixed with water, ash becomes even heavier and may solidify like cement.

4 **AVOID TRAVEL** Do not drive unless essential or you are told to evacuate. If driving, do so slowly to avoid kicking up ash that could affect the engine. Use your headlights and ensure washer fluid is fully topped up. Use lots of water to keep the windscreen clear.

⚠️ **WARNING**
Volcanic ash is gritty and acidic, and can cause lung damage, such as silicosis. The young and old, and those with respiratory illnesses, are most at risk.

Mudflows

Volcanic mudflows, known as lahars, are a potentially deadly combination of water and volcanic ash. They are often produced when lava melts snow or ice during an eruption, or as a result of the breach of a crater lake. But mudflows can also be triggered long after the eruption by heavy rain. Mudflows can travel at 80km/h and are capable of sweeping away houses, roads and bridges, and burying everything in their path beneath tonnes of mud that rapidly sets like concrete.

LAVA FLOWS

1 **EXERCISE CAUTION** Although lava flows are the least hazardous aspect of a volcanic eruption, travelling at speeds of just a few metres to a few hundred metres per hour, **they are extremely hot – temperatures reaching 700–1,400°C**. Do not approach them or you risk burns. Beware of walking on lava, even once it appears solid and cold.

2 **FORMULATE AN ESCAPE ROUTE** The direction of a lava flow can generally be predicted and monitored. If you find yourself in its path, you will have time to plan your escape. The best tactic may be to dodge it by moving uphill or to one side.

PYROCLASTIC FLOWS

■ **MOVE QUICKLY** Made up of hot clouds of gas, dry rock fragments and dust, pyroclastic flows can move far faster than you can run or drive in a car. Your best hope of escape is to evacuate, avoiding the stream channels, depressions and valleys that a pyroclastic flow usually follows. Make for high ground as fast as you can.

what next?

● If you are evacuated, do not return to your accommodation unless you are advised that it is safe to do so. If you are staying in a holiday home that has been damaged in any way, have it inspected to confirm that it is structurally safe.
● Ash can damage car engines. Do not start your car unnecessarily during or shortly after an ash fall. Before you use it again, flush out any ash from the engine compartment with a garden hose and have the car serviced as soon as possible.

▶▶See also: **INHALED FUMES** pp44–45 • **BURNS AND SCALDS** p23 • **EMERGENCY PREPARATION** pp334–337

hurricane and typhoon

Hurricane, typhoon and cyclone are all names for large tropical storms characterised by swirling winds of 250km/h and more. Although the destruction they cause to property can seldom be avoided, there is usually sufficient warning to guarantee your personal safety. Follow advice from the authorities on whether to take shelter or evacuate.

be aware

If you are travelling to an area where hurricanes may occur, find out when they are most likely so that you can avoid them. The main hurricane regions and their seasons are given below.

● Caribbean Sea and Gulf of Mexico, including Central America, Mexico and US Gulf States: June to October. Worst months: August to September.
● East North Pacific (eastern seaboard of the USA): June to October. Worst months: August to September.
● West North Pacific, South China Sea, including Japan: June to November. Worst months: August to September.
● North Indian Ocean, Bay of Bengal, Arabian Sea: May to November. Worst months: July to September.
● South Indian Ocean: December to April.
● Australia – north, north-west and west coasts: January to March.
● South Pacific, including Fiji, Samoa and New Zealand: December to March.

PLAN AHEAD
● Make sure that your car has a full tank of fuel and you have packed everything you need, including a survival kit (see pages 334–337).

HURRICANE CLASSIFICATION

Hurricanes are categorised from 1 to 5, based on their windspeed, pressure and destructive potential. Take local advice on when to stay in your accommodation and when to evacuate.

CATEGORY	WIND SPEED	DAMAGE
1	120–150km/h	Minimal: signs, vegetation, unanchored mobile homes. Storm surges up to 1.5m.
2	151–175km/h	Moderate: mobile homes, roofs, small craft, electricity. Storm surges 1.8–2.5m.
3	176–210km/h	Extensive: small buildings, low roads cut off, electricity. Storm surges 2.6–3.9m.
4	211–250km/h	Extreme: roofs destroyed, trees down, roads cut off, mobile homes destroyed, beach homes flooded, electricity. Storm surge 4–5.5m.
5	251km/h +	Catastrophic: most buildings destroyed, vegetation destroyed, major roads cut off, homes flooded, electricity. Storm surge of more than 5.5m.

action

HURRICANE PREDICTED

1 STAY INFORMED Check the radio, television or internet (www.nhc.noaa.gov) for up-to-date information. It is worth using a portable radio in case of electrical failure. If you are staying in a hotel, check in the foyer for information.

2 CHECK YOUR HOTEL'S SAFETY PROCEDURES These should give details of safe areas within the hotel, including the location of the hurricane shelter (see box, below) if there is one, or procedures for evacuation to nearby national shelters.

3 PREPARE FOR EVACUATION Put together essential items to take to the shelter (see box, below) or pack in readiness for evacuation. Holiday representatives may be able to organise transport and flights home, if these are available.

Hurricane shelter

As soon as you are advised to, or the hurricane hits, go to a hurricane shelter. If you are not staying in a hotel, find the location of your nearest shelter by searching on the internet or by contacting the local Red Cross or public services, such as local libraries, councils and the police.

- **WHAT TO TAKE** Many national shelters recommend that you come equipped with certain items, including water (1–2 litres per person per day), canned foods, milk and beverages, medicine, toilet paper, sanitary towels, nappies, baby food and baby supplies, battery operated radio, torch, eating utensils, blankets or sleeping bags, passport and valuable papers, cards, games and books.

 WARNING
The term Hurricane Watch means that a hurricane may threaten within 36 hours. Hurricane Warning indicates that winds of 120km/h or more will affect an area within the next 24 hours.

tornado

Tornadoes are the most violent – and unpredictable – of all storms. With winds of up to 500km/h, they can cut a destructive swathe 2km wide and over 100km long.

be aware

- Find out whether the region you plan to visit is prone to tornadoes. Although these storms can occur almost anywhere, and at any time, they are more common in some areas. In the USA they are more frequent in spring and early summer and between the hours of 3pm and 9pm.
- Tornadoes generally form from the trailing edge of a thunderstorm. So whenever the weather turns stormy, be alert and listen to government weather bulletins for tornado warnings.

action

■ **MOVE TO SAFETY** Try to move to the centre of the building you are in and hide beneath something strong to protect yourself from falling debris. Move to a shelter if possible (see left).

■ **ESCAPE** Tornadoes typically move at 50km/h, with winds 10 times this speed, but can travel twice as fast. So **if a storm is about a kilometre away, you have a minute or so to find shelter** or move out of its path. If you are in a car on the open road, you should drive away from the storm.

■ **GET OUT** If you are in a stationary vehicle, caravan or mobile home, get out at once and seek shelter in a building or storm shelter. Failing that, you will be safer sheltering in a ditch or on open ground away from trees and fences: vehicles are often tossed around in the violent winds.

tsunami

A tsunami is a series of huge waves created by an underwater disturbance, such as an earthquake or rockslide. To survive, you need to act quickly: tsunamis can reach more than 30m and travel at 500–1,000km/h, inundating whole islands.

WATCHPOINT There may be time for a warning if the earthquake is distant, but if the quake is closer to the shore you may only have minutes before the tsunami hits.

be aware

REGIONS AT RISK OF TSUNAMI

● In the USA, the coastlines of California, Oregon, Washington and Alaska are most at risk because of their position near tectonic plate boundaries in the Pacific. Coastal landslides can trigger tsunamis in Hawaii.
● Countries in and bordering the North and South Pacific Oceans along the so-called Ring of Fire are particularly prone to tsunamis, including Japan. The Maldives, Indonesia, Thailand, Sri Lanka and India may be affected by the Indian plate moving.
● You could be at risk if you are on the coast and at low altitude. Land less than 8m above sea level and within 2km of the shore is vulnerable.

MAKE AN EVACUATION PLAN

● If you are in an area at risk, prepare an emergency three-day pack for each person (see page 334–337) and a family evacuation plan.
● Consider where you will go and how to contact each other. Keep your mobile phone fully charged.
● Choose a relative or friend at home as a back-up contact point. Make sure that everyone knows their phone number.

UNDERSTAND THE WARNINGS

● If an earthquake has occurred in the Pacific basin and may generate a tsunami, an advisory warning is issued. Tsunami Warning Centres in Hawaii will issue hourly bulletins for the USA and countries of the Pacific basin. For details of warnings see http://prh.noaa.gov/ptwc/.
● 'Watch' status is given if a tsunami may have been generated but is at least two hours away.
● A 'Warning' is given if a tsunami has been generated that could cause damage.

Spotting the signs

● **RUMBLINGS OF AN EARTHQUAKE** If you hear or feel rumblings offshore, it could be an underwater earthquake. If it is near enough to hear, a tsunami could be upon you in minutes.
● **CHANGING SEA LEVELS** A rapid change in the level of coastal waters – either rising or falling – means a tsunami is imminent.
● **TIDE IN REVERSE** If the tide goes out suddenly, it is being sucked into the wave and will return as a wall of water that sweeps all before it, travelling as far as 2.5km inland.

 WARNING

● Everything that is in the water will be swept back to sea with the tsunami or dumped on the way – most tsunami-related deaths are caused by drowning and injury from floating debris. If you can climb aboard something that floats, it will help you to conserve energy and protect you from collisions with other flotsam.
● If you know that the building you are in is secure, it may be safer to stay inside and move to as high a floor as possible, above water level. Do not stay on the ground floor.

The first of six tsunami roll towards a beach in Thailand on 26 December, 2004. Around 230,000 people died in countries from Indonesia to Africa.

action

WARNING OF TSUNAMI

1 LEAVE AT ONCE Put your evacuation plan into effect immediately a tsunami warning is issued, or if you have reason to believe a tsunami may be imminent (see box, left). Major cities often issue warnings just a couple of hours before the wave hits.

2 RUN TO SOMEWHERE HIGH If you notice **the sea rapidly receding, leaving a large area of the shore uncovered, you may have only minutes before a tsunami hits**. Run for higher ground or the upper floors of a sturdy building. Climb a tree only as a last resort: unless the tree is strong and tall, it may be knocked over or submerged by the tsunami.

3 KEEP MOVING INLAND Tsunami come in waves, so the flooding may continue to get worse. Distance is important, and you should try to move at least 2.5km inland, but so too is altitude. If a wave hits the coast, the waters will rush inland along channels and other low-lying land, so avoid valleys and rivers.

4 STAY PUT If you have reached somewhere safe, stay there for at least a day. Waves can keep coming for up to an hour and even when they have stopped, the affected area may be extremely dangerous. Flooding may take a while to recede, roads may be damaged and utilities may be suspended. Check with the emergency services before returning.

SEPARATED FROM FAMILY

1 PHONE YOUR AGREED CONTACT NUMBER If you set up a contact point as part of your emergency plan, phone to find out whether other family members or travelling companions have phoned in.

2 SEARCH LOCALLY If there has been no contact, find out if there is a Survivor Reception Centre or a Humanitarian Assistance Centre where you can register your details and those of anyone who is missing. Take photos if you have them. The British Red Cross (www.redcross.org.uk) and Disaster Action (www.disasteraction.org.uk) also help to trace missing persons.

wildfires

A threat to life in any large area of forest, scrub or grassland, wildfires can move at speed, sometimes burning at 60km/h or more, jump rivers and roads and change direction as quickly as the wind. Often, evacuation is the only safe option.

GET HELP If you see a fire – or a situation you consider to be a fire risk in dry weather – dial 999 in the UK, 112 in Europe and 911 in the USA to alert the emergency services.

be aware

- Whether you are staying in a villa in Greece, taking a walking holiday in the south of France or camping in the USA, if you are holidaying in an area that is surrounded by woodland, scrub or grass, you need to be alert to the possibility of fire. The risk is especially high during a prolonged period of dry weather.
- Listen to weather reports on local and national radio and television. High winds and low relative humidity increase the risk during times of drought and wildfire danger ratings are often given with the general forecast.
- Check danger ratings for your particular area and the progress of current wildfires on the appropriate National Park or Forest Services website on the internet.
- If wildfire threatens, keep up to date with reports and evacuation information. Follow the advice that is given by the local authorities.

action

IN A BUILDING

1 **TAKE PREVENTATIVE ACTION** Do what you can to reduce the fire risk for the property you are staying in. Move combustible materials, such as garden furniture, barbecue grills and gas bottles away from the building and turn off gas supplies at the mains. Douse buildings with water (see box, right).

2 **PREPARE TO LEAVE** Plan several different escape routes in case one is blocked. Pack your belongings in the car, together with plenty of drinking water. Park the car facing outwards with the keys in the ignition and all the windows and air vents closed.

3 **EVACUATE** If the authorities advise evacuation, follow their advice. Before you leave, put on all interior and exterior lights to make your accommodation visible to firefighters.

Bushfires in Canberra, Australia's capital, in 2003 claimed 500 homes and four lives.

IN A CAR

1 **STAY IN THE VEHICLE** If you are cut off by a wildfire in your car, **do not get out and try to flee on foot.** Close all the windows and air vents to prevent smoke from getting into the vehicle.

2 **STOP SAFELY** Do not drive in thick smoke, but if you can get the vehicle away from any large trees or thick bush, then do so. Then stop, turn on your lights to make the car visible, and turn the ignition off. Get onto the floor of the vehicle and cover yourself with coats or blankets.

3 **MAKE A SMOKE MASK** Moisten a scarf or a piece of cloth with a little water and hold it over your nose and mouth to help you to breathe.

4 **BE PATIENT** Stay in the vehicle until the main fire passes. It may get hot and smoky and the vehicle may start to rock, but do not panic. The tyres may burst but petrol tanks rarely explode.

IN THE OPEN

■ **CLOTHES CATCH FIRE** If your clothes catch alight, quickly drop to the ground. Flames, and their heat, rise up, so by lying on the ground you are more likely to prevent them from reaching your face and hair. Roll around vigorously to extinguish them.

■ **CUT OFF BY FIRE** Try to find a ditch or other depression in the ground that will afford you shelter. If there is time, quickly remove as much wood, brush or other flammable material from the immediate area as you can. Lie down and cover yourself with a coat or blanket and wait until the fire has passed.

⚠ **TAKE CARE**
● If you are camping in a National Park or forest area, check the local wildfire danger rating. Respect any temporary restrictions placed on access to high-risk areas and bans on campfires.
● Site a campfire at least 3m from trees, bushes or buildings and contain it in a fire pit or with a ring of stones. A fire pit should fully contain the hot embers: dig it to about a third of the width in depth. Keep a bucket of water nearby to extinguish the fire. Ensure that all the embers are cold to the touch before you go to bed or leave the area.

Protecting property

If you are staying in holiday accommodation, you can take action to reduce its flammability while it is still safe. But always put your own safety first.

1 **USE HOSES AND SPRINKLERS** Use the firefighting technique of soaking house walls, roofs, fences and other nearby structures with water. Put a lawn sprinkler on flat roofs. Douse surrounding trees and grass.

2 **LET TRAINED FIREFIGHTERS FIGHT THE FIRE** Do not stay to fight the blaze. Leave before you and your escape routes are overtaken by fire.

what next?

● Wait for the fire service to give the all-clear before returning to an area affected by wildfires. Fires can reignite from hidden hotspots many days after all visible flames have died down.
● Watch out for damaged power lines and keep a safe distance. Report any damaged pylons or poles to the local authorities.
● Be aware that charred trees or buildings may be unstable. Use caution and good judgment when re-entering any building affected by fire.
● Avoid falling into ash pits. These are holes full of ash that are created when trees burn right down to their roots. Mark any that you find to warn others.

⚠ **WARNING**
If you are found to be responsible for causing a wildfire, you may be liable for the cost of fighting it, as well as other damages.

▶▶See also: **BURNS AND SCALDS** pp112–113 • **CAUGHT IN A BLAZING HOUSE** pp122–125

heat wave

A prolonged period of hot weather can be more than simply uncomfortable. Dehydration and heatstroke can affect anyone and the death rate – among the elderly, in particular – can rise sharply, so make sure you know how to stay well.

TIME TO ACT Do not wait until you are thirsty to drink: you will already be dehydrated. In hot weather, a sedentary adult needs to drink at least 2–3 litres of water a day.

precautions

- Stock up on bottled water, fruit juice and other cold drinks before the weather turns hot.
- Plan for power cuts, which are common in hot weather when the national grid is overloaded. Keep a torch and candles to hand and your freezer fully stocked: food stays colder for longer in a power cut when the freezer – or fridge – is full.
- Make lots of ice, and ice lollies for children. These can also help to fill your freezer.
- Buy fans or air conditioners, if possible, to help keep you cool.

Who is vulnerable?

The elderly and the very young are most susceptible to heat-related illness, including dehydration, heat exhaustion and heatstroke. Pay particular attention to:

- **SPECIAL HEALTH NEEDS** If someone's heart condition or breathing problem becomes worse in hot weather, seek medical advice.
- **KEEPING COOL** If you cannot cool a house adequately, find out if there is a local air-conditioned community centre or library that the person could visit.

action

KEEP YOUR HOUSE COOL

■ **USE SUN SHADES** Keep all windows that are in direct sunlight closed and covered. Use awnings, shutters, garden umbrellas or gazebos to block out the sun.

■ **VENTILATE** While the air temperature outside is lower than that inside your home, open windows that are in the shade. Open doors and windows early and late, but close them during the heat of the day.

■ **SWITCH OFF** Avoid unnecessary use of electrical appliances and lights, especially halogens. Low energy bulbs and fluorescent lights run coolest.

■ **MICROWAVE FOOD** If you want to eat hot food, use a microwave – it produces less collateral heat than the oven or hob.

■ **COOL THE AIR** Fans help you to stay cool by moving the air and improving your body's ability to sweat. Make your own air cooler by placing a fan behind a shallow bowl filled with ice and water.

STAY COOL

■ **DRESS APPROPRIATELY** Wear light, loose clothing made from natural fibres or from technical sports synthetics designed to wick away perspiration.

■ **CHOOSE COLD DRINKS** Chilled water or fruit juice will rehydrate and cool you. Tea or coffee may quench your thirst, but will raise your temperature. Avoid drinking alcohol as it increases dehydration.

■ **EAT COLD MEALS** Eat light, low protein, uncooked meals such as salads. These can meet your energy needs without firing up your metabolic rate; they also have a high water content.

■ **SHOWER OR BATH** Have a cool shower or bath. A wet towel draped over your head or shoulders can also be very cooling.

■ **REST BY DAY** Carry out any strenuous activities, such as housework, very early in the morning or at night. Try to exert yourself as little as possible during the hottest part of the day (11am to 3pm).

 See also: **HEAT-RELATED ILLNESS** pp48–49 • **DEHYDRATION** pp50–51

pandemic influenza

A pandemic is an epidemic that becomes very widespread, affecting a whole region, a continent or the world. Sometimes it is caused by the mutation of an animal virus into one that affects humans. The virus may also change as it spreads, becoming more dangerous and resistant to drugs. Because it is new, or has not been active for long, no-one is immune.

assessment

The World Health Organisation alerts the world to a new pandemic, classifying it into six phases.

Phases 1–3: The virus has been observed predominantly in animals – in phase 1, there is no human infection; by phase 3 there may be sporadic cases of human infection.

Phase 4: Human-to-human transmission occurs in significant numbers in a community.

Phases 5: There is widespread human infection in at least two countries in one WHO region – it usually signifies an imminent pandemic.

Phase 6: A new outbreak in a different region or continent to phase 5 signals a pandemic.

SYMPTOMS OF INFLUENZA
- Sudden high fever of 38°C (100.4°F) or more
- Headache and aching muscles
- Dry cough/shortness of breath
- Runny nose/sore throat
- Diarrhoea or vomiting

 WARNING

Anyone with the above symptoms who is aged over 65, is pregnant, has a pre-existing medical condition or is less than five years old should seek immediate medical advice.

action

IF FLU IS ABOUT

1 PRACTISE GOOD HYGIENE To prevent the spread of germs, cough or sneeze into a tissue and put it in a bin. **Wash your hands frequently, and always after you have caught a sneeze or cough in your hand or a tissue;** clean surfaces regularly.

2 DO NOT RELY ON A MASK Most masks that are generally available do not filter out virus particles, which are particularly small. The moist conditions these masks create may even increase the chances of catching the virus. Only masks that conform to European standard FFP3 (or US standard N95) are effective and these require training in how to wear them and how often to change them.

3 CONSIDER A VACCINE If you have a serious chronic underlying illness, such as heart or respiratory disease, a compromised immune system, are pregnant or usually receive a vaccination against seasonal flu, ask your GP if you should have a vaccination to protect against pandemic flu.

IF YOU HAVE FLU

1 STAY AT HOME Drink plenty of fluids and take paracetamol-based cold remedies to bring down a fever and relieve symptoms.

2 CONTACT YOUR GP OR FLU HELPLINE If you fall into one of the high-risk categories (see above), seek medical advice immediately by phoning your GP or the National Pandemic Flu Service on 0800 1 513 100 (www.direct.gov.uk/pandemicflu). You may be offered anti-viral drugs to prevent complications.

3 GET A FLU BUDDY Ask a friend or relative to collect prescriptions and medicines for you, and to prepare meals. If you keep your distance and practise good hygiene, your friend should not become infected.

4 SEEK MEDICAL ADVICE If you suddenly get much worse, or if your condition is still deteriorating after seven days (five days for a child), phone your GP or the Pandemic Flu Service on 0800 1 513 100.

contaminated water

With well over half the human body comprised of water, this precious liquid is also our most vital requirement. If your water supply becomes contaminated with harmful bacteria or dangerous chemicals, it is possible to stop it affecting you.

GET HELP If someone is ill after drinking contaminated water in the UK, call NHS Direct on 0845 4647 or NHS24 in Scotland on 08454 242424.

be aware

- Take heed of any local authority or water company warnings concerning water quality and stock up on bottled water in case your supply is compromised.
- Be particularly vigilant during and after flooding, as water supplies frequently become polluted at such times.
- If you receive a warning of a possible threat to your water supply, store as much water as you can in containers and the bath.

⚠ WARNING

- Only give cooled boiled water to bottle-fed babies, as some bottled waters contain a dangerously high concentration of mineral salts.
- **Wash dishes using boiled water and disinfectant, not the dishwasher.** The water temperature in a normal dishwasher cycle is unlikely to be high enough to kill all bacteria.
- When travelling in developing countries, avoid having ice cubes in drinks, or eating ice cream, salad and fruit, unless you wash and peel it yourself. Drink bottled water that you can verify has a proper seal and use bottled or boiled water to clean your teeth.

Water treatment

Contaminated water can be treated using either filters or chemicals. Both are available from outdoor shops and on-line.

- **CHEMICAL TREATMENTS** These use iodine or other chemicals to remove bacterial, viral and parasitic contamination.
- **FILTER SYSTEMS** Filters that use active carbon, and membrane filters, remove bacteria, chemicals, pesticides and heavy metal pollution.

action

SUSPECTED CONTAMINATION

■ **CHEMICAL CONTAMINATION** Examine your water. Fill a large glass and allow the water to stand for five minutes. If it remains cloudy, has an oily surface or smells strange, you should treat it as contaminated. Drink bottled water until the situation is resolved or use specialist filters or chemical treatments (see box, below left).

■ **BACTERIAL CONTAMINATION** Bacterial, parasitic and viral contamination can be neutralised by boiling the water for at least three minutes. Remember to boil the water you use to wash your food in and the water you use to brush your teeth. Store boiled water in containers cleaned with a mild disinfectant or a weak solution of bleach.

SYMPTOMS OF ILLNESS

1 WATCH FOR SYMPTOMS Diarrhoea, vomiting and fever are common symptoms of bacterial infection such as *E. coli* or viral infections such as rotavirus. Symptoms of chemical poisoning can be similar but also include headache, dizziness, change in skin colour, throat pain, blistering of the mouth, respiratory problems and abdominal pain.

2 SEEK HELP Contact your water company for information and seek expert medical advice. Avoid further consumption of the contaminated water. Drink plenty of clean, fresh water, eat normally and rest. Avoid alcohol.

WARNING

Babies and young children with diarrhoea are at much greater risk of dehydration. Seek medical help at once if they develop additional symptoms.

radiation incident

Radiological accidents are extremely rare and stringent measures are in place to prevent them. If you are located near to a nuclear reactor, radioactive waste processing plant or where radioactive materials are transported, you should know the official emergency plan to minimise the effects in the unlikely event of exposure.

be aware

- Radioactive materials are routinely safely transported by road, rail, sea and air. Both their packaging and transport are bound by strict regulations laid down by the International Atomic Energy Agency to minimise the risk to the public.
- There is an authorised Emergency Plan for an at-risk area in case of a radiological accident in the UK. You may be notified of an incident by siren or the emergency services. For example, for residents in a 2km radius of Plymouth's nuclear dockyards, the 'Informer' system sends out text and phone messages. The utility company that operates the power plant is legally required to have plans in place for contacting people in the community during an emergency and must inform the community each year of its evacuation plans and routes.
- Make sure that you have at least one battery-powered radio so that you can listen to news bulletins even if there is a power cut.

action

- **FOLLOW THE ADVICE GIVEN** Listen to the radio, television or check the internet and follow the instructions given by the authorities. Do not evacuate until you are advised to as you must ensure you know which way the radioactive plume is travelling and how to avoid it.

- **STAYING SAFE INDOORS** There are some important safety measures that you must follow if you are told to stay indoors: close all doors and windows and turn off any fans and air conditioners, and any heating units that bring in air from the outside. Take shelter in the centre of a room that has the least number of windows.

- **IN CASE OF EVACUATION** Follow the instructions given to you by offical sources on how to travel to an evacuation shelter. Ideally, before you leave, close all doors and windows of your home or accommodation, if travelling, and turn off any heating and ventilation systems. In your car, keep the windows closed and turn the ventilation off.

THE EFFECTS OF EXPOSURE

Gy units measure the absorbed dose of radiation.

MILD EXPOSURE	MILD TO MODERATE EXPOSURE	MODERATE EXPOSURE	SEVERE EXPOSURE	EXTREME EXPOSURE
0.5–1.0 Gy	1.0–2.0 Gy	2.0–3.5 Gy	3.5–10 Gy	10–20 Gy
Mild radiation sickness, headaches and nausea. Seek medical advice. Almost certain survival.	Medical treatment required; bone marrow damage likely. Survival rate of around 90 per cent.	Medical assistance urgently required. Survival likely.	Medical treatment essential. At lower levels survival rate around 50 per cent; at higher levels death probable within 1–3 weeks.	Death certain within 2–5 days.

▶▶See also: BURNS AND SCALDS pp112–113

chemical release

Chemical weapons are usually hard to detect as they often take the form of gases or innocuous-looking liquids. They have been used in a number of terrorist attacks, including the sarin gas attack on the Japanese subway in 1995, when 12 people died.

TIME TO ACT The chemical agent released may only be known once you exhibit symptoms. Do not wait at the scene of exposure; flee quickly, covering your nose and mouth.

be aware

● Chemical agents can be deployed as a liquid or a gas. Many gases are colourless and odourless and the first sign of a release may be the reaction of people around you.
● How and where a chemical weapon is deployed will affect how you should respond. Chemical agents can be spread using an explosive device, some form of aerosol spray or even a crop-dusting aeroplane.
● Similar poisoning can occur from exposure to organophosphates and carbamate insecticides. Organophosphorus insecticides are related to nerve agents such as sarin, tabun and soman.

action

SUSPECTED CONTAMINATION

1 BE OBSERVANT A sudden strange smell, people choking or dizziness are all signs of a chemical release. Move away at once, as you will not be able to help if you become affected.

2 GET AWAY Hold your breath and move as quickly as you can to an exit. If you are in any kind of confined space, move to a larger space if possible. The greater the air volume, the more dilute the chemical agent will be. Get outside the building.

3 CLIMB HIGHER Most chemical agents are heavier than air, so as you make your escape try to move upwards. Take the stairs, stand on chairs, climb on a wall; do whatever you have to do to get higher.

Japanese security forces practise an anti-terrorism drill to deal with the aftermath of a sarin nerve gas attack.

4 SHUT YOURSELF IN If escape is impossible, find somewhere that you can shut yourself in, such as a nearby room, compartment or cupboard. Once inside, try to seal it as effectively as you can. Stuff clothing or paper into every crack and block vents and keyholes. Phone someone to tell them where you are and wait for rescue.

5 PROTECT YOURSELF Cover as much of your skin as possible, using a scarf, handkerchief or even your shirt as a makeshift mask to protect your eyes, nose and mouth. Depending on the kind of chemical agent that has been released, this could prove to be an invaluable precaution.

6 DECONTAMINATE YOURSELF As soon as you are somewhere safe, decontaminate yourself by removing your clothes, which will eliminate up to 90 per cent of contamination. Seek urgent medical advice.

7 SEEK MEDICAL ADVICE If you suffer any symptoms following a chemical release, such as a persistent headache, diarrhoea or a rash, you should seek medical advice. Some symptoms are delayed for a number of hours.

Chemical agents

There are four basic categories of chemical weapon that may be used in a chemical attack.
● **NERVE AGENTS OR NEUROTOXINS** These act on the nervous system and can kill in 1–10 minutes. They include sarin, a colourless liquid or gas with a faintly fruity odour.
● **BLISTER OR VESICANT AGENTS** Mustard gas is the most well known. These agents burn and blister the skin and damage the eyes and lungs. They can incapacitate or kill.
● **CHOKING AGENTS** These attack the lungs and can cause death within 48 hours. One example is phosgene, a colourless gas that smells like new-mown hay.
● **CYANIDE COMPOUNDS** The most common are hydrogen cyanide (hydrocyanic acid) and cyanogen chloride. Cyanides inhibit metabolism, resulting in asphyxiation.

biological release

The deliberate release of germs or other biological substances can cause mass sickness and terror. It may be aimed at a population centre or at the food supply.

be aware

● Smallpox, plague and anthrax are the three biological agents most commonly feared in terrorist attack. Smallpox and plague are the most dangerous as they spread rapidly in large populations.
● It may not be immediately obvious that a biological attack has taken place. Health workers may report a pattern of symptoms and alert the authorities.

action

1 ISOLATE YOURSELF If you suspect or anticipate a biological release, your best chance of survival is isolation. Either quarantine yourself in your home or escape to as isolated a location as possible.

2 STAY INFORMED Public announcements will be made on television and by radio. Listen for information on symptoms and medical advice.

3 MAXIMISE HYGIENE Act as you would to prevent the spread of any infection: wash your hands frequently, avoid touching your eyes, avoid contact with infected people, wash surfaces and clothing.

4 WATCH FOR SYMPTOMS It may be impossible to know whether you have been affected by a biological agent, so stay alert for symptoms. Many illnesses begin with flu-like symptoms. Skin rashes or boils are also common.

5 SEEK MEDICAL HELP If you believe you have become ill as a result of a biological attack, phone the medical services. In England and Wales call NHS Direct on 0845 4647; in Scotland, NHS 24 on 08454 242424. Do not go to hospital or visit your local GP as you may be contagious.

▶▶See also: **CHEMICAL ON THE SKIN** pp116–117

caught in a **riot**

A large angry crowd can be as unpredictable and dangerous as any natural disaster. If you find yourself caught up in any kind of demonstration, try to keep to the periphery and stay alert. That way you can escape if it turns into a riot.

TIME TO ACT Demonstrators often have a destination in mind, such as a large square or political building. This is where the riot is likely to be most dangerous, so leave the area.

precautions

- Unless you feel compelled to take part in a demonstration, avoid any location where a large rally or protest is being held.
- Keep up to date with news bulletins, even when you are travelling. Riots do not usually happen spontaneously: most large demonstrations require considerable planning and preparation, and there is a legal requirement to alert the authorities.
- When visiting an unfamiliar city or town, carry a map so you can plan an alternative route in order to avoid a demonstration – or an escape route if you find yourself an unwilling part of one.
- Arrange a meeting place if you are travelling with friends or family, in case you get separated.
- Stay back from the front of the crowd. If the police decide to move forward, use batons, rubber bullets or a riot control agent (RCA), such as tear gas, you need to be as far away as possible.

- Watch out for a police signal to use an RCA or for police pulling on gas masks. Some tear gas grenades explode in the air, delivering a hot metal canister that can cause serious injury if it hits you. Exposure to RCAs is painful and debilitating: eyes burn and stream and breathing can be difficult. If you have any respiratory disorders, RCAs can have an even more serious effect.

⚠️ WARNING

- Once you become swept up in a riot, you will appear to be part of it – whether or not you are present intentionally.
- Do not approach police lines, make eye contact or call out to the police while you are part of the crowd. In the heat of a demonstration the police will regard you as a threat and react defensively.

action

CAUGHT IN A CROWD

1 **ACT AT ONCE** When a demonstration starts to become violent, you need to get away as quickly as possible. Do not wait to see if the situation calms down – it usually only gets worse.

2 **GET INSIDE** Most of the conflict and violence is likely to be outside. If you can shelter inside any kind of building, you will be safer. Once inside, stay away from windows, especially if missiles are being thrown. Try to find a back way out and stay alert for any signs of fire.

3 **MOVE SLOWLY** If you cannot get out of the crowd, move as slowly and casually as you can, even if things turn violent. Running will draw attention to you – and can make it look as though you are guilty of wrongdoing. Only begin to move away when you can see an escape route. Until then, stay with the crowd.

4 **GO WITH THE FLOW** People in a crowd move like water, with the centre often moving faster than the sides. Never try to move against the crowd. Flow with it, but as you are pushed forward a few steps try to take one step to the side. Be patient.

5 **WATCH YOUR FOOTING** Try to create some space around you so you can stay balanced. If the crowd surges, move with it. Take small steps and if you stumble, grab the person next to you. If you do fall, curl up in a ball and protect your head. If others fall on top of you, stay calm; the crowd is more likely to avoid a number of fallen people than just one.

RIOT CONTROL AGENT USED

1 **FLEE THE AREA** As soon as an RCA, such as tear gas, is fired, get away as quickly as possible. **Move to higher ground or climb a wall or fire escape, as most RCAs are heavier than air.** Run into the wind if you can.

2 **COVER YOUR FACE** Use a scarf or piece of cloth soaked in water if you have some, as long as you are sure it has not been contaminated by the RCA.

3 **DO NOT RUB YOUR EYES** If you have been exposed to an RCA, flush your eyes with cold water repeatedly until the pain subsides.

4 **REMOVE CONTAMINATED CLOTHES** Wash clothes that have been exposed to RCAs. If a T-shirt or jumper has been severely contaminated, consider cutting it off, rather than pulling it over your head.

5 **WASH YOUR SKIN** Shower with cool water only for about 10 minutes – hot water will open the pores of your skin. Then shower normally.

6 **SEEK MEDICAL ATTENTION** If symptoms, such as blurred vision or chest pain, persist, get help.

 TAKE CARE
Remove contact lenses after exposure to an RCA. Do not put them back in your eyes. Seek advice from your optician about cleaning and reusing hard or gas permeable lenses.

Crowd control formations

You may be able to predict the police control tactics by the crowd control formation they adopt.

● **LINE FORMATION** Used to block access to a building or area and to drive crowds back or to pen them into a street or square for containment (a tactic known as corralling or kettling).

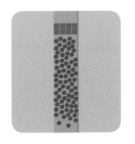

● **WEDGE FORMATION** Used to split and weaken a crowd by separating it into sections.

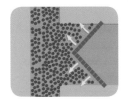

● **ECHELON FORMATION** Used to divert crowds or turn them in a particular direction.

 **KEY** ■■■ POLICE ●●● CROWD

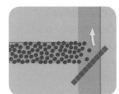

fire in a public place

Even in recent years, fires in shopping centres, hotels and railway stations have claimed hundreds of lives around the world. A fire in a public building can be terrifying, and it is likely to cause panic as large numbers of people may be involved, the majority of whom will be unfamiliar with possible escape routes and safety procedures.

be aware

- Make sure that you know all the escape routes in public places that you use regularly. If any of these is a high-rise building, find out which floors link one exit stairwell with another.
- Make sure that your employer has regular fire drills and attend them.
- In unfamiliar buildings, **make a point of establishing two possible escape routes as soon as you arrive.**
- Never ignore a fire alarm.
- A fire escape may be outside (see right). Make sure you know how to access it.

action

■ **ACT QUICKLY** Leave at the first sign of fire – a burning smell, smoke or the sound of a fire alarm or shouting. Do not wait until you know that it is definitely a fire and do not stop to collect belongings.

■ **THINK FOR YOURSELF** Do not assume that someone in authority will tell you what to do. Head for the nearest fire exit. Be forceful and determined to get out of the building. Jump over or knock over obstructions if you need to.

■ **MAKE CONTINUAL ASSESSMENTS** If you need to go through a door, feel the door first. If it is hot, do not open it: go to another exit. If it is cool, open it cautiously and check for fire and smoke before going on. Close doors behind you.

■ **AVOID SMOKE** If you encounter thick smoke, turn back and use another emergency exit route, if possible, or drop to the floor where the air is clearer and crawl to the exit. Smoke, heat and noxious gases all rise. If you have a bottle of water, it can be used to dampen clothing to improvise a mask.

■ **USE THE STAIRS** Never use the lift: the electricity supply often gets cut off during a fire.

■ **DO NOT GET SWAMPED BY THE CROWD** If you find yourself in a crowd of people all trying to get out, stick to the periphery so you do not get trampled.

■ **RAISE THE ALARM OR USE YOUR MOBILE PHONE** Only do this once you are safely outside, or nearly outside, the building.

■ **IF YOU ARE CUT OFF BY SMOKE** Take refuge in a room, seal the door with tape or clothing, open a window and lean out. Call for help or attract attention by waving a sheet, curtains or clothing.

 WARNING
Do not attempt to put out a fire unless it is contained (in a waste bin, for example) and is small enough to be put out with a portable fire extinguisher.

lift gets stuck

Although being stuck in a lift for an uncertain length of time is stressful and uncomfortable, it is rarely hazardous. Most lifts are extremely safe; even if one does stop, it is unlikely to stay there for long or to drop suddenly down the lift shaft.

TIME TO ACT Lift safety depends on the owner acting on safety checks which should be carried out every six months. If you experience a malfunction, always report it.

be aware

- Lift accidents are infrequent and rarely fatal. Most injuries involve bruising or broken limbs after a lurch or short fall.
- You are more likely to experience dehydration when stuck in a lift than physical harm. Try always to carry a bottle of water with you when you go shopping or travelling.

action

STUCK AT A FLOOR

1 PRESS DOOR OPEN BUTTON If this does not work initially, try again. Then try all the floor buttons, one at a time, starting with the floor you are on.

2 USE THE EMERGENCY PHONE Report your plight to the lift caretaker or maintenance operative using the emergency phone or intercom. Failing this, press the alarm button or phone the emergency services directly if you can get a signal inside the lift.

3 ATTRACT ATTENTION Bang on the lift door to attract the attention of people outside. Use a shoe or other hard object so you do not hurt yourself.

4 SHOUT LOUDLY If there are other people in the lift, take it in turns to shout loudly. Stop after shouting and listen to see if anyone is responding on the other side of the door. Ask them to press the door open button on the outside of the lift.

 WARNING
If the lift starts to fall, position yourself with your back straight against one of the lift walls and your knees bent to help to absorb the impact. Hold on to a handle, if there is one, to keep yourself upright. Jumping up and down will not help.

STUCK BETWEEN FLOORS

1 DO NOT PANIC Try to stay calm: you are in no immediate danger. If there is a power failure, emergency lighting will come on.

2 USE THE EMERGENCY TELEPHONE Look for the emergency telephone or intercom inside the lift. Try to make verbal contact with the lift caretaker or maintenance operative and let them know where you think you are stuck.

3 PRESS THE ALARM BELL If you cannot reach someone using the telephone or intercom, press the alarm bell. Hold it down or push two or three times in quick succession to get attention. Wait for a minute, then try again.

 WARNING
Do not try to open the lift doors between floors or the maintenance hatch in the ceiling. If the power comes back, you could be crushed between the doors or stranded on top of the lift.

Claustrophobia

Anyone with claustrophobia has a fear of enclosed spaces and crowded situations. Being trapped in a lift might trigger a first panic attack. Symptoms include:

- Sweating
- Accelerated heartbeat
- Accelerated breathing
- Nausea
- Light-headedness or fainting
- Shaking

In the case of an attack, help the sufferer to sit down and take slow, deep breaths.

▶▶See also: **PANIC ATTACK** p75

plane hijack

A hijack is arguably every air passenger's worst nightmare. At 10,000m, with no escape possible, it is easy to become paralysed by fear. For the best chance of survival, you need to assess the hijacker's motives and then respond appropriately.

WATCHPOINT Once on the plane, pay attention to the safety briefing. Count the seat rows to the exits both in front and behind you and memorise the number to help you escape.

precautions

- Fly from a secure air hub. The better the airport security, the safer you will be in the air.
- Check whether there are any government warnings about travelling to your destination. If there are, consider postponing your trip.
- For long flights, try to choose an airline from a country with no political enemies.
- Choose economy class and dress anonymously. If hostages are going to be shot, they are more likely to be chosen from first-class or those wearing military or religious insignia or clothing.
- Watch your bags prior to check in to make sure no one interferes with them.
- Never accept a request to carry something on to a plane from anyone you do not know.

assessment

To decide how to act, try to make a rapid assessment of the hijackers' motives.

- Do they want the plane and its passengers as a bargaining chip? Or do they want to use it as a missile and kill everyone on board?
- The way the hijackers announce themselves and the weapons they have or deploy can tell you a lot about their motives. Note their nationality, any religious or political insignia. Are they simply threatening violence or have they already hurt anyone?
- Keep a close watch on developments. The changing situation will affect the hijackers' mood and their methods. Re-evaluate the situation constantly.

action

YOU ARE HELD HOSTAGE

1 STAY CALM The hijackers will be extremely tense and may behave unpredictably. They will also be looking for ways to exert their control. So in the first few moments you need to stay calm but alert, so you can decide on the best response.

2 CO-OPERATE Release your seat belt and breathe slowly. Keep a low profile. Avoid eye contact. Comply with instructions and do not complain. Answer questions but do not volunteer information. Make requests for water or food respectfully and in a reasonable manner. Ask for what is possible.

3 BUILD RAPPORT The longer you are in contact with the hijackers, the more important it is for you to build some sort of rapport with them. Look for points of personal contact, such as family life, that avoid political or other potentially confrontational topics.

4 STAY POSITIVE Do what you can to stay in the best physical and mental shape. This will help you to be ready should the opportunity arise to escape or challenge the hijackers.

Stockholm syndrome

If the hijackers gain permission to land the plane, negotiations may begin and you may be held captive on the tarmac for several days. In these circumstances, it is common for hostages to come to feel sympathy towards their captors. What begins as a survival mechanism borne out of fear of violence, when any small act of kindness is seized on and given undue importance, can end in perverse feelings of loyalty to the hostage takers.

Elite French troops storm an Airbus on December 26, 1994. Fundamentalist Algerian hijackers had seized it two days earlier and killed three hostages.

ASSESSING DANGER

■ **POISON GAS If the hijackers are wearing gas masks, you must assume that they may be about to gas the whole plane**. In such circumstances an immediate response may be your only option.

■ **VIOLENT INTENT** If the hijackers begin killing passengers or make it obvious that they intend to crash the plane, you need to fight back at once. The longer you delay, the more control they will have and the more disastrous the consequences.

YOU HAVE TO FIGHT BACK

1 CO-ORDINATE AN ATTACK You are more likely to be successful if you can co-ordinate an attack with other passengers. In this case, you have two possible options: a simultaneous strike by several parties, or a distraction by one group of passengers, followed by an attack by others.

2 USE WHAT WEAPONS YOU HAVE It is unlikely that you will be able to reach the overhead lockers, so attack with what you have to hand. Scalding hot drinks, pens or pencils make useful weapons. Cushions, blankets and ripped-out seats can be used to defend against knives or daggers.

3 SCREAM AND SHOUT Use your voice as a weapon as you attack. If you are going it alone, shout commands to other passengers. A spirited attack will encourage others to join in.

4 IGNORE INJURY Injuries are inevitable. Use your adrenaline to continue your attack even if you become injured. Tell yourself that the consequences of failure will be worse.

5 DIRECT YOUR ATTACK Use your hands, elbows or weapons to attack the hijacker's eyes and throat, particularly the Adam's apple if the hijacker is male (see page 176). Once incapacitated, disarm the hijacker and get other passengers to secure him while you deal with any others.

▶▶See also: **PHYSICAL ATTACK** pp172–175

bomb attack

Until 2001, most bomb attacks in Europe and Western nations were triggered remotely. But that year's attack on the World Trade Center and, in 2005, on the London transport network, brought the terrifying techniques of the suicide bomber to the USA and Europe. But for most people, the chances of being caught up in a terrorist attack remain very low.

be aware

- Keep up to date with the news. If you know where the hot spots are, you can avoid them. Heed government warnings about the danger of travelling to certain countries.
- When you use public transport, always sit or stand in the emptiest carriage of the train or at the back of a bus.
- When you enter an unfamiliar building, such as a hotel, restaurant, cinema or nightclub, always familiarise yourself with the emergency exits and plan at least two escape routes.
- Take note of the people around you. If you feel something is not right, move away or leave a building. Trust your instincts.

In recent suicide bomb attacks, the explosives were carried in a rucksack.

 WARNING

If you find a package tucked under a seat, hidden in a waste bin or that is in any way suspicious, do not touch it. Move away from it at once and warn others.

action

SUSPECT PACKAGE OR BAG

1 ASK AROUND If you see an unattended bag, first look around for its owner. Ask people nearby if it belongs to them or if they saw it being left.

2 ALERT SOMEONE IN AUTHORITY How suspiciously you should treat an unattended bag will depend on where and when it has been left. Ask yourself if the location is a likely target and if there is a high perceived threat of terrorist attack. If you are on a bus, inform the driver at once. If you are on a train, pull the emergency handle only once you have stopped at a station. Then get off the train and tell the driver or guard about the parcel or bag.

3 MOVE AWAY Put as much distance between yourself and the suspect package as possible and let the professionals decide how to deal with it.

SUSPECTED SUICIDE BOMBER

1 SUSPICIOUS BEHAVIOUR If you see someone acting suspiciously or in an excessively anxious manner, look closer. Is he perspiring freely or looking around furtively? He may be constantly thrusting his hands in his pockets or nervously fiddling with belongings.

2 SUSPICIOUS CLOTHING A suicide bomber may be wearing bulky clothing that seems inappropriate for the weather conditions or his apparent body size.

3 INFORM THE POLICE Leave immediately and inform the police of your suspicions.

BOMB EXPLODES

1 MOVE AWAY If you hear an explosion, do not move towards it. Terrorists frequently plant several bombs and trigger subsequent explosions to target security forces and other first responders.

2 AVOID GLASS If you are in a building, move away from the windows in case a second blast shatters them, to avoid being hit by flying glass.

3 GET OUTSIDE If you are in any kind of enclosed space, try to get outside. The pressure of an explosion will dissipate more rapidly outside, so you will be safer should another bomb go off.

4 DO NOT PANIC The panic caused by a bomb blast often causes further injuries. Try to stay calm, look around you and think logically about the safest way you can move to safety.

YOU ARE UNDERGROUND

1 DROP TO THE FLOOR If a bomb goes off underground, there will be a lot of smoke and dust. The air may be clearer lower down. Cover your face with a handkerchief or scarf.

2 ORIENTATE YOURSELF If you find yourself in total darkness, try to orientate yourself. **Use your mobile phone for light.** Keep out of passageways to avoid blocking the emergency services.

3 OFFER FIRST AID If you are uninjured, offer first aid to others who are hurt. Try to reassure them that help is on its way and that you will help them.

4 IDENTIFY THE QUICKEST ROUTE TO SAFETY Find the nearest way out. If you have to evacuate a train when it is between stations, try to remember whether you are likely to be closer to one station than the other and then walk in that direction.

YOU ARE TRAPPED

■ **SIGNAL TO RESCUERS** Use the torch, music or an alarm on your phone to signal. If underground, tap on a pipe or wall, or whistle. Only shout as a last resort, as you will inhale dust.

⚠ WARNING
Underground trains frequently draw their power from an electrified third rail and if you touch it and another rail or the ground, you will be electrocuted. However, if all the lights are out it is likely that the fail-safe system has activated and the power is off.

what next?

● Shock often prevents you from feeling pain, so examine yourself for signs of injury. Remain calm and try to apply some first aid to yourself, such as using pressure on a wound to stop bleeding or lying down and raising your legs if you feel faint.
● Move if you can. Emergency services may take time to reach you, especially if they are unsure whether the area is safe. So if you can move, with or without the help of others, try to get away from the site of the explosion.
● Help others. If you are uninjured and you feel that it is safe to do so, you may be able to offer help or first aid to others (see below).

Helping the injured

In the aftermath of a bomb blast, there will be multiple casualties with injuries of varying severity. Make sure that there is no immediate danger from building collapse or fire before offering help.

● **PRIORITISE CASUALTIES** Stay calm and look around you for those most urgently in need of help. Check quiet casualties first: they may be unconscious or in shock. Then help those with severe bleeding.
● **GIVE FIRST AID** If a casualty is unconscious, clear the airway (see pages 14–15) and apply CPR if necessary (see pages 16–17). Staunch bleeding by applying pressure to the wound, avoiding any objects, such as glass, embedded in it (see page 22). Those who are in shock, with no apparent injuries, may have internal bleeding (see pages 38–39).
● **BE AWARE** Many casualties will be unable to hear you because of perforated eardrums. Stay calm and use reassuring body language.

suspect post

Improvised Explosive Devices (IEDs) sent through the post present a danger not only to the intended victim, but to anyone who might inadvertently touch the package. These devices can be hidden in anything from a thick letter to a small parcel. If you handle a lot of post, watch out for the tell-tale signs that suggest you should treat an item with suspicion.

assessment

How to recognise a suspect package:

GREASE MARKS – are there any grease marks or areas of transparency on the packaging?

METHOD OF ADDRESSING – is there anything strange about the method of addressing? Is it in handwriting you don't recognise?

OTHER SIGNS
● Is there anything odd about the packaging that makes you suspicious?
● Is the package perforated anywhere or are there any signs of wires either under the packaging or protruding slightly?
● Is the package unusually heavy or lop-sided in shape or weight? An effective letter IED typically weighs between 50g and 100g, making it a little heavier than the average letter.
● Has dry transfer lettering been used, such as Letraset or Uno Stencil?

POINT OF ORIGIN – look at the postmark or name of sender. Is it from an unusual point of origin or a sender you do not recognise?

SMELL – does the package have an unusual smell, such as that of almonds or marzipan?

action

1 PUT IT DOWN Immediately you identify a letter or parcel as suspicious, place it gently on a firm, horizontal surface. Try to shield your face and body as you put the parcel down.

2 LEAVE THE ROOM Keep everyone away from the package until you have ascertained whether it is safe. Leave the room and shut the door. Lock the door, if possible, and pass the key to the police.

3 CONTACT THE POLICE If you cannot confirm that the item is genuine, contact the police and keep everyone at a safe distance until after they have dealt with it.

 TAKE CARE

If in doubt, contact the sender. If the package is marked with the sender's details, contact them to confirm that the item is genuine.

 WARNING

Letter bombs can maim and kill. Along with the explosive there may be nails or glass, designed to maximise injury. **Do not flex or bend an envelope in an attempt to work out what is inside: you do not need to open it to set off the bomb.**

DRIVING EMERGENCIES

witness to a **road accident**

The actions you take at the scene of a road-traffic accident can have important consequences for the casualties involved and other road users. Even if you do not have medical training, there are many ways in which you can help the injured. Stay calm, warn other traffic, and call the emergency services.

assessment

Calmly assess the scene. Give the emergency services as many details as possible:

● How many casualties are there and do they include babies and children?
● Is there an immediate danger of fire and/or are there hazardous chemicals involved (see Warning, below right)?
● If there are multiple casualties, give first aid in the following order:
– To those who are unconscious and not breathing (see pages 12–19)
– To those who are bleeding severely (see page 22)
– To those who are unconscious but breathing (see pages 12–19)
– To those who are injured and conscious (see pages 28–30)

Motorway crash

● **DO NOT ALWAYS STOP TO HELP** Stopping to help can cause delays for the rescue services. But if someone is lying injured in the road or a vehicle is on fire it is advisable to stop on the hard shoulder or drive to the next exit to call the emergency services.
● **EXIT CAR FROM NON-TRAFFIC SIDE** Always get out of the car on the non-traffic side and ensure any victims do the same. You must leave any animals in the vehicle or, in an emergency, keep them under tight control on the verge.
● **WALK TO AN EMERGENCY PHONE** Use the arrows on your side of the carriageway to direct you to the nearest emergency phone (see page 233). These are preferred to mobile phones because they give an exact location. If you do use a mobile phone, refer to the motorway marker posts to give your location.

action

INVOLVED IN A CRASH

1 **PARK WELL BEHIND THE ACCIDENT** Use your hazard warning lights to alert other traffic. At night, shine your headlights onto the crashed cars.

2 **SAFEGUARD THE SCENE** Except for a motorway crash (see page 233), place a red warning triangle at least 45 metres behind the crashed cars in order to prevent another collision. Ideally there should be a second triangle at the front of the cars. If possible, ask someone else to stop the traffic.

3 **MAKE THE VEHICLE SAFE** Switch off the ignition of the crashed vehicles to reduce the risk of fire, but do not remove the key as this may lock the steering. Check that the handbrake is on. If it is not, put it on.

 WARNING

● If there are any early signs of fire, such as smoke coming from the bonnet, get everyone out of the car and well away. Call the emergency services if the car is on fire; do not try to tackle it yourself.
● **Do not get close to any spillage.** Trucks that carry hazardous materials are marked with codes showing the type of load. Make a note of these symbols and tell the emergency services immediately.

WATCHPOINT Make sure j22 that nobody is smoking near the accident scene. There could be petrol either in the gutter or leaking across the road if a fuel tank is ruptured.

TIME TO ACT If possible, send someone to slow down the traffic. Ensure that they keep to the side of the road. At night use a torch to signal to other drivers to slow down.

GETTING HELP

1 CALL EMERGENCY SERVICES Tell the controller how many vehicles are involved, how many casualties there are and whether anyone is trapped. Describe the location as accurately as possible.

2 OFFER TO BE A WITNESS Do not leave the scene of the accident without leaving your contact details. If the police are not involved, offer to act as a witness for the drivers involved.

PEOPLE ARE INJURED

1 DO NOT MOVE CASUALTIES Doing so risks making any injuries worse, especially neck injuries where there is a danger of long-term damage to the spine. The only exception is if the injured person is in immediate danger, such as a car being at risk from catching fire (see pages 236–237).

2 CHECK FOR BREATHING Casualties who are quiet are probably the most seriously injured. Ensure they can breathe freely. Carefully loosen any tight clothing around the neck. If they are not breathing, it may be necessary to give CPR (see pages 16–17).

3 CHECK FOR BLEEDING Firm pressure on a wound with a clean cloth will stem bleeding (see pages 96–97). For head wounds, use light pressure as the casualty could have a fractured skull.

4 KEEP THE CASUALTY WARM Cover the casualty with a blanket or rug to keep him warm and prevent shock. But do not give him anything to eat or drink as he may later need an anaesthetic.

5 PROVIDE REASSURANCE Be encouraging and tell the casualty that help is on its way. Keep him calm by talking to him.

Your rights as a witness

One of the most valuable ways in which you can help at an accident scene is to offer your services as a witness. Legally you do not have to give your name and address if you witness an accident, but if you do, be aware that:

● **THE POLICE MAY BE INVOLVED** The police may ask you to provide a statement if you witness a road traffic accident. If interviewed by the police, you must answer all questions truthfully. Frequently drivers disagree about the cause of

a crash so the whole case can hang on your testimony. Your witness statement may also be used by the insurance company to decide a settlement so it can be crucial in deciding who is held responsible.
● **A COURT CASE CAN FOLLOW** If the case goes to court, you may be summoned to give evidence. You must attend the court. If you fail to attend after receiving a summons, you may be found in contempt of court.

involved in a **road accident**

Collisions are rarely complete accidents. Two-thirds of them are due to driver error and many others are caused by poor road or driving conditions, or vehicle defects. If you are involved in a road-traffic incident, try to stay calm enough to help others who may be injured and make careful notes of all the information that you may later need to rely on.

action

COLLISION WITH CAR

1 **STOP IMMEDIATELY** It is an offence not to stop after an accident. You must also stop if you are involved but your car is not damaged.

2 **GET HELP** Call the emergency services if someone is injured or the road is blocked. Ask for the fire brigade if there is a risk of fire (see pages 236–237). If someone tries to leave the scene without exchanging details take down their car registration number.

3 **WARN OTHER TRAFFIC** Use any means necessary to alert other road users. Turn on your hazard lights, place warning triangles in the road and try to enlist the help of others to alert oncoming traffic about the collision. It is best not to move any vehicles involved in a collision before the police arrive, even if the accident is minor. In the meantime, note down the vehicles' positions (see step 5).

4 **EXCHANGE DETAILS** Give your name, address and car registration number to the other motorists or to anyone whose property is damaged. If the vehicle you are driving is not yours, you must give the owner's name. Avoid any arguments and **do not admit liability at the scene of an accident**.

 TAKE CARE
Ensure that the ignition has been turned off in all the vehicles involved in the crash.

5 **SKETCH THE SCENE** Draw the road layout, pictured from above, showing the cars' positions. Show the direction in which the cars were travelling, the collision points and the road names. Put an X where any witness was present. Compass points are useful as they are often referred to in police reports. You can find the compass points from a map, or print out a map from the internet later, enlarge it and draw on the position of the cars.

6 **TAKE PHOTOGRAPHS** If you have a camera or a mobile phone with a camera, take photographs of the scene and any damage caused. Take photographs from a variety of different angles.

7 **SEEK WITNESSES** Write down the names and addresses of any witnesses who would be willing to make a statement either to the police or your insurance company.

WATCHPOINT Accidents are most likely to occur after driving for five or six hours (even with breaks), at times when you would normally be asleep, and an hour after meals.

TIME TO ACT Be prepared. In the glove compartment, keep your insurance information, a pen and a notepad. A small camera or a mobile phone with its own camera is also useful.

COLLISION WITH MOTORBIKE

1 GET MEDICAL HELP Motorcyclists are far more likely to sustain a serious injury than car drivers because of the lack of protection. Quick action is vital with life-threatening injuries. Call the emergency services as soon as possible.

2 DO NOT REMOVE HELMET Ignore your instincts and leave the helmet on as taking it off can aggravate any head, neck or spine injuries. The only exception is if the motorcyclist has stopped breathing and you need to resuscitate him (see box below).

 TAKE CARE

● As a road user, look out for motorcyclists, especially when you are turning into a major road. The most common accidents occur at T-junctions where the motorist fails to see a motorbike.
● Bends are a danger area for motorcycles – 15 per cent of accidents occur on a curve or corner.
● As a motorcyclist, you can reduce accident rates by wearing fluorescent clothing and a brightly coloured helmet to make yourself as visible as possible. Dipped headlights in the daytime also aid visibility.

COLLISION WITH PEDESTRIAN

1 STOP IMMEDIATELY Legally you have to stop if someone is injured and give details of the accident. Protect the scene with warning triangles and redirect traffic around the injured pedestrian.

2 CALL EMERGENCY SERVICES The pedestrian is the first priority. Call the emergency services and inform them that someone is injured. Do not move the casualty, but reassure him that help is on its way. To prevent him going into shock (see pages 38–39), keep him warm by covering him with a rug or coat.

3 GET WITNESSES Try to find witnesses who are willing to testify on your behalf. This is especially important in cases where a personal injury claim is possible. Write down all names and addresses at the scene as it is easy to lose contact with witnesses in the confusion following a collision.

 WARNING

If you hit a pedestrian at 20mph they have a 97 per cent chance of survival, at 30mph an 80 per cent chance, and at 40mph only a 10 per chance.

If you need to resuscitate

If the casualty is talking, it means he is breathing, so do not remove his helmet. The only circumstances in which you should remove a motorcyclist's helmet is if he is not breathing and you need to resuscitate him (see pages 12–17). To remove the helmet carefully you will need help. One person should support the casualty's head and neck, while the other carefully undoes the strap.

1 SUPPORT NECK AND JAW Place your fingers, spread wide, under the base of the helmet to support the casualty's neck and hold his jaw firmly.

2 CAREFULLY REMOVE HELMET Get your helper to tilt the helmet clear of the chin, then clear of the base of the skull. He should then lift the helmet off slowly while you continue to support the neck and jaw.

after the accident

Sorting out the paperwork following an accident can be time-consuming but it is worth doing immediately. Fill in the accident report supplied by your insurance company as soon as you can so that you do not forget key pieces of information. Do not admit liability, even if the accident appears to be your fault. The issue of blame is best left to the insurers – and the courts – to sort out.

REPORTING THE ACCIDENT

1 INFORM THE POLICE If you do not do so at the time of the accident, **you must report the incident to the police within 24 hours** if it has caused injury, or damaged a car or property. You are legally obliged to produce your insurance certificate for the police within seven days.

2 DO NOT ADMIT LIABILITY Never admit liability even if you think you are in the wrong. If you admit liability, you are prejudging the issue and this may affect any insurance claim.

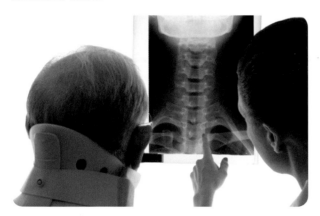

3 SEEK MEDICAL HELP Following the forceful jerk of a collision, you could suffer whiplash or other injuries. Do not ignore even minor aches and pains as these can turn into chronic complaints in the weeks ahead. Remember that doctors' records are extremely important in any compensation claim.

4 GET A REPAIR ESTIMATE Get at least two estimates for repairs. But do not have any repairs done if you intend to get the insurance company to pay for them. The insurers may want to assess the damage themselves.

5 DRIVE AGAIN Many people do not want to get back behind the wheel after having a road accident. The only way to conquer your fear is to drive again. Ask someone to be a passenger if you lack confidence.

SETTLING YOUR CLAIM

1 CONTACT YOUR INSURER Inform your insurer within 24 hours of the accident. Ask them to send you an accident and claim report. Check your entitlement: you may be allowed a replacement car for the time it takes to repair yours or have personal injury cover.

2 DECIDE WHETHER TO CLAIM Telling the insurer does not mean that you have to claim. That will depend on the costs of the repair and the effect on your no-claims bonus. The insurer will explain how much of your no-claims bonus you will lose if you make a claim. Check your excess as well as this will affect how much you have to pay.

3 RECORD YOUR EXPENSES Keep a careful record of all extra spending, including taxi receipts, transport costs and prescription charges, as these can often be reclaimed on your insurance policy.

How to make a claim

● **ACCIDENT REPORT** Fill in and return the accident report from your insurance company.
● **GATHER EVIDENCE** Note down anything else you think is relevant. A sketch of the accident scene and/or photographs (see page 222) are good evidence to support a claim.
● **DO NOT CORRESPOND WITH OTHER DRIVER** Pass on any letters straight to your insurer. Do not correspond with the other driver's insurer.
● **POLICE PROSECUTION** Let your insurer know if you receive a police prosecution notice.
● **CAR VALUATION** The insurance company will pay 'market value' for any written-off car, but it is likely to be less than the replacement cost. Talk to your motoring organisation if you are unhappy with the valuation – the insurers may improve the offer if you dispute it.

unable to stop

Although it rarely happens with modern cars, it is possible for an accelerator to jam and for the brakes to fail. There are specific driving skills that can help to prevent serious accidents and possible injury in this emergency situation.

TIME TO ACT Alert other drivers by sounding your horn and flashing your lights. In extreme emergencies, phone the police who may be able to clear the road ahead.

action

ACCELERATOR GETS STUCK

1 TAP THE PEDAL Depress the pedal slightly – it may come unjammed. If that does not work, hook your toes under the pedal and try to lift it up. Ask a passenger to see if anything is stuck under the pedal or, if travelling alone, try to see yourself. The floor mat may be caught under the accelerator. In this case, try to move it.

2 BRAKE HARD If the accelerator is still jammed, shift down through the gears as you brake.

3 DO NOT TURN OFF IGNITION Turning off the engine could disable the power steering, making the car extremely difficult to manoeuvre. Some older or diesel-powered cars may not respond to this. If it is imperative, turn the key one notch to kill the engine and allow the car to decelerate. Do not turn the key so far as to engage any steering lock.

4 SHIFT TO NEUTRAL This action should be a last resort as it can cause the car to over-rev, which can destroy the engine, but it should slow the car down.

BRAKES FAIL

1 PUMP THE BRAKES Press down the brake pedal, ift your foot and press it down again. Keep pumping. You cannot usually pump anti-lock brakes, but it may sometimes work in the case of brake failure.

2 SHIFT TO LOWER GEAR Change down to a lower gear – second or third – bringing the clutch up slowly and smoothly. This will slow the vehicle down and allow you to use the handbrake to slow down. In cars with an automatic gearbox, select L or 2.

3 APPLY HANDBRAKE As the car slows, use your handbrake to help stop the car. Keep a firm grip on the steering wheel as the use of the handbrake may cause the rear wheels to lock and the car to skid.

4 DO NOT TURN OFF IGNITION As tempting as it may be, this will only make matters worse because you will not be able to use the engine to slow down the car as you shift to a lower gear. The steering could also lock if you switch off the ignition.

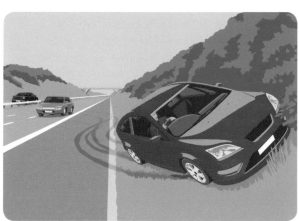

5 SEARCH OUT SAFETY If all other action fails, the only option is to use a slope or a bank to help stop the car. Drive gradually up at an angle to prevent rolling the car. Scraping along a hedge or a fence may also slow you down.

 WARNING

● **Never ignore a warning light on the dashboard.** If the brake system alert comes on when you are driving, get the brakes and fluid levels checked as soon as possible.

● The moment you start to slow down, signal left and show that you intend to move over as the car could decelerate rapidly once you take action.

▶▶See also: **CAR BREAKDOWN** pp232–233

car jacking

If someone tries to steal your car by force, or the threat of force, it is not only your car that is at risk – your personal safety could be threatened. Faced with such an attack, you should always put your own safety first.

WATCHPOINT Even if you are getting out for just a moment, lock your car and take the keys with you. Most insurance companies refuse to pay if the keys were left in the car.

be aware

- Be extra alert at 'ambush sites' or places where you have to slow down, such as junctions that are controlled by traffic lights or pelican crossings.
- Car jackers may loiter near cash machines, roadside shops, petrol-station forecourts and car-wash facilities as many motorists leave the keys in their cars when at these sites.
- When returning to your car, stay alert. Walk confidently, key in hand, get in quickly, lock the doors and drive off as soon as possible.
- Never leave children or pets alone in your car, even when loading or unloading.
- When selling a car think twice before offering a test drive. Take someone else with you and do not leave the keys in the ignition when changing seats, or let them out of your sight at any time in case they are copied or switched.

precautions

- When driving, always keep the doors locked and the windows never more than partially open, especially when driving through urban areas. Make sure that your boot is also locked.
- Anticipate traffic conditions that might force you to stop. Move to a middle lane if there is one, and brake early, so you can keep rolling for as long as possible. If you have to stop, leave sufficient space for you to manoeuvre around the car in front, should you need to drive away.
- If a stranger asks for directions or help, talk to him through a partially open window and keep your doors locked. If he has broken down, say you will phone for help but stay in your car.
- A car jacker may bump a vehicle gently from behind. When the driver gets out, the thieves strike. **If you are suspicious about a low-speed collision, drive to somewhere public, such as a garage forecourt, before getting out.** Or drive to a police station to report the incident.

action

ATTACKED BY CAR JACKER

1 DRIVE AWAY If a thief starts hammering on your window, or even smashes it, drive away quickly – in whatever direction you can.

2 MAKE A NOISE Sound your horn to attract the maximum amount of attention. Then report the attack as soon as possible to the police.

CAR JACKER GETS IN

1 GET OUT AND AWAY If you are alone, and a car jacker gets into your car or orders you out with a weapon, get out or away at once. Do nothing to stop him taking the car. Focus solely on your own safety.

2 FIGHT FOR TIME If you have a child with you, tell the carjacker. Make it clear that you only care about your child, not about the car. If you get no response, grab the ignition keys and throw them away. Flip the bonnet- or boot-release levers or open the doors – anything that will give you enough time to free your child.

3 ATTEMPT ESCAPE If a car jacker tries to abduct you, fight back in any way you can. If he is driving, keep talking to distract him, then grab the steering wheel or handbrake. While he attempts to regain control, jump out of the car.

4 CRASH THE CAR If you are driving, slow down and consider crashing the car into a wall or parked car. The sooner you do this the better.

road-rage attack

Once behind the wheel of their cars, many people behave with uncharacteristic aggression. If you find yourself in a threatening encounter with another road user, it is always best to take defensive action and prioritise your safety.

 WATCHPOINT If you are being followed or feel threatened, call the police on a hands-free mobile or from a safe public place. Give your location and direction of travel.

action

FOLLOWED BY ANGRY DRIVER

1 DRIVE NORMALLY Do not let the other driver's actions make you lose concentration. Focus on driving safely. **Avoid making eye contact with the other driver** as this only personalises the conflict.

2 TAKE A DETOUR If another driver persists in following you, try to deter them by taking a small detour. But stick to busy areas (see box, below).

3 DRIVE TO A PLACE OF SAFETY If the other driver continues to intimidate you, drive to a police station. Or drive to a place of safety and then use your mobile phone, or a landline, to call for assistance.

Escape manoeuvres

If another driver is angry enough to try to force you to stop or to drive you off the road, your priority should be to get to somewhere safe. Stick to main roads that are likely to have plenty of witnesses and CCTV cameras. Heavy traffic will provide witnesses and will allow you to put cars between you and the other driver.

CAR HIT BY ANGRY DRIVER

■ **DRIVE AWAY** Although by law you must report all accidents, if you suspect you were hit deliberately, or fear for your safety, do not stop or get out. Keep your doors locked and drive to the nearest police station or place of safety.

■ **STAY IN YOUR CAR** If your car is undriveable or you are boxed in and the other driver gets out of his car, stay in yours. Depending on how threatening the behaviour is, try to appease the angry driver through a partially opened window. Alternatively, sound your horn and activate your hazard warning lights to attract attention, and phone the police immediately for assistance.

■ **MAKE A STATEMENT** Report a road-rage incident to the police and give them as much information as you can about the offender and/or vehicle.

 WARNING

If someone is following you and behaving in an aggressive manner, do not drive to your home. You do not want them to know where you live.

for next time...

● Some drivers seem to enjoy provoking conflict. Be alert for signs of erratic or aggressive driving and make an effort to keep out of the way, even if it delays your journey by a few minutes.
● Keep your own emotions under control. If you react aggressively with an offensive gesture or a long blast of the horn, you may provoke a violent response.
● If you make a driving error, raise a hand to acknowledge it and apologise.

▶▶See also: **KIDNAPPED ABROAD** pp294–295

tyre emergencies

Punctures and blowouts are less common in modern tyres but flat or damaged tyres are still the second most common reason for calling out a breakdown patrol. Check all your tyres regularly for signs of wear and tear and know what to do if a tyre bursts while you are driving or you need to change one in an emergency.

precautions

- Regularly inspect your tyres for cuts, cracks and bulges. These can all cause blowouts.
- Check for any nails, stones or anything else piercing the tyre casing. Change the wheel and repair any tyre damage.
- Check for even tread wear on all four tyres. Uneven tyre wear could be a sign of faults in the braking or suspension systems, or that the wheels are not properly aligned.
- Always ensure that your spare wheel is adequately inflated. Make sure that the jack and wheel brace are in good condition.
- Fit reinforced 'run-flat' tyres. Many cars now have these as standard. While more expensive to replace, these should allow you to continue driving for up to 50 miles if you have a puncture.

- Always keep tyres at the pressure recommended by the manufacturer. Check them when the tyres are cold before you set off, as **warm or hot tyres can give a misleading reading**.

- Cars must have a minimum tread depth of 1.6mm across the main treads. Use a tread gauge (above), available for less than £15, to measure this.
- Check the pressure and tread every two weeks, and always before a long journey.

action

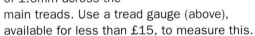

FRONT TYRE BURSTS

1 AVOID BRAKING If a front tyre bursts, the car will pull heavily to the side on which the tyre has burst. Put your hazard warning lights on and do not change gear, unless your car is rear-wheel drive, when engine compression will help lower speed. If possible, try to avoid braking. The aim is to let the car lose speed naturally.

2 COUNTER THE PULL To slow down, take your foot off the accelerator and clutch and turn the steering wheel smoothly to counter the pull. If you do use your brake, apply it very gently.

3 PULL OVER When you have slowed sufficiently, signal left and steer the car to the side of the road to pull up. Try to stop on hard ground rather than soft as you need a firm base to change the wheel.

BACK TYRE BURSTS

1 BRAKE GENTLY If a back tyre bursts, the back of the car may slide to one side. The car will have a tendency to weave, especially at speeds over 50mph. Brake gently; if you brake hard, you may lose control of the car. Changing to a lower gear will help in a front-wheel drive car provided you can control the steering with one hand.

2 MAINTAIN FIRM GRIP Keep looking ahead and keep a firm grip on the steering wheel to maintain a straight course. If you do have to brake quickly, be prepared to counter a slide at the back.

3 SLOW SMOOTHLY The aim is to slow as smoothly as you can, pulling up as soon as it is safe to do so. Make sure that the car is parked well off the road if you intend to change the wheel yourself.

EMERGENCY TYRE CHANGE

1 **SWITCH OFF ENGINE** Put the handbrake on, put the car in first gear or park for an automatic. Remove any heavy luggage and the spare wheel.

2 **LOOSEN WHEEL NUTS** Remove the hubcap, if necessary, and loosen the wheel nuts by half a turn before attempting to use the jack.

3 **DEACTIVATE AIR SUSPENSION** If your car has air suspension, check the manual for how to deactivate it before jacking up the car, or you will not be able to raise the car high enough to remove the wheel.

4 **JACK UP CAR** Check the owner's manual to locate the wheel bolts and to see the correct place to put the jack. Use the jacking point nearest the wheel you want to change. This is usually just behind the front wheel or just in front of the rear wheel. Once the jack is in place, wind or pump up the jack.

Using a jack safely

Jacking up a car is the single most risky part of the whole operation. For your own safety:

● **ENSURE SURFACE IS LEVEL** Only ever use a jack on a firm, level surface.
● **POSITION SECURELY** Make sure that the jack is securely positioned before raising the car.
● **EMERGENCY USE** The jacks supplied with most cars are for emergency use only and not designed for working underneath a car. Never get under a car that is supported only by a jack.

5 **REMOVE WHEEL** Remove the nuts completely, taking the top one off last and ensure they do not roll away. Remove the wheel with the deflated tyre.

6 **REPLACE WHEEL** Fit the spare wheel. Replace the nuts, tightening them up by hand. Work on opposite pairs at the same time so that the wheel goes on evenly. Tighten the nuts clockwise with the wheel brace. Lower the car with the jack and tighten the nuts completely. Place the hubcap back on, if you have one. Check that the nuts are at the correct torque at a garage as soon as possible.

⚠ TAKE CARE

● In very hot weather, as the temperature outside rises, air pressure in the tyres increases. Over-inflation can lead to loss of grip so check your tyres are correctly inflated.
● If you are not confident about changing a tyre, call your breakdown service. They will have no objection to carrying out this procedure.

►►See also: **CONTROLLING A SKID** pp230–231 • **CAR BREAKDOWN** pp232–233

controlling a **skid**

Loss of control from skidding usually results from driving too fast for the road conditions. The tyres lose grip, leaving the vehicle in a seemingly uncontrollable slide. How you react depends on which wheels are causing the skid. Keep a cool head because a violent or sudden reaction can be extremely dangerous.

action

FRONT-WHEEL SKID

In a front-wheel skid, the car keeps going straight on even though you have turned the wheel to navigate a bend.

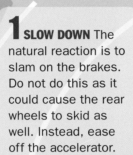

1 SLOW DOWN The natural reaction is to slam on the brakes. Do not do this as it could cause the rear wheels to skid as well. Instead, ease off the accelerator.

2 STRAIGHTEN THE WHEELS Reduce the amount that you have turned the car to help you regain grip on the front wheels. It will feel as if you are running wide of the corner.

3 REGAIN CONTROL Once you have regained grip, you can steer gently in the direction that you originally intended. Do not oversteer or you risk losing control of the car again.

REAR-WHEEL SKID

In a rear-wheel skid, the back of the car feels as if it is breaking away and could even spin round.

1 STEER INTO THE SKID As the rear tyres lose grip on the road, the back starts to swing out. Turn the steering wheel in the direction that the rear wheels are sliding. So, if the back is sliding to the left, you should steer to the left.

2 DO NOT OVER REACT Do not turn the wheel too far. If you steer too hard into a skid you could easily set off a secondary skid in the opposite direction, causing complete loss of control.

3 BRING THE STEERING BACK A you regain contro you will feel the wheels gain tract and you can bring them back smoot towards the cent

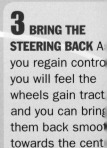

⚠️ TAKE CARE

Front, rear and four-wheel drive vehicles behave slightly differently in a skid, but the basic principles of controlling the skid are the same. Familiarise yourself with the way your vehicle handles and read the owner's manual for further information.

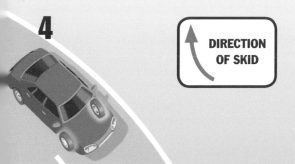

DIRECTION OF SKID

4 DRIVE ON As the car moves back on course, accelerate gently. Maintain reduced speed until you have complete control and drive according to the conditions.

4 ACCELERATE GENTLY When all four wheels are in line, gradually increase speed again. Keep your speed down until you have full control of the car.

precautions

● Recognise the danger signs. Pay particular attention to the weather conditions and road surface: ice, snow or standing water are all especially dangerous. Black ice (see page 245) is a major risk because it is so difficult to spot.

● **Take special care when rain falls after a long dry period**. **Oil and dust mix with the water to create a lethal slippery surface**.

● Heavy acceleration, sudden braking and sharp changes of direction all cause the tyres to lose grip. Smooth, calm, steady driving is he best way to avoid skidding in the first place.

● Look after your car carefully. Worn tyres, badly maintained brakes or poorly aligned steering can cause, or aggravate, a skid.

● Many drivers react too slowly because they fail to recognise the signs of a skid until it is too late. If you are concerned or frequently drive long distances, consider taking an advanced driving course at a driving school.

Four-wheel skid

Harsh braking can cause all four wheels to lock, leaving the car to slide forward at speed. The only way to regain control is to release the brakes then reapply them more gently.

● **STOP BRAKING** Release the brakes until the tyres start to roll again and re-establish their grip on the road. Do not push down the clutch.

● **PRESS SMOOTHLY** Most vehicles are now fitted with anti-lock braking systems (ABS), which ensure that the wheels will not lock when you reapply the brakes. Instead, ABS automatically 'pumps' the brakes to guard against wheel lock. If you have ABS, simply press down on the brake pedal in a smooth motion and keep the pedal depressed until the skid is under control.

● **BRAKE GENTLY** If you do not have ABS, re-apply the brakes with a pumping action, repeatedly pushing them on and off in order to avoid locking the wheels again. This is known as 'cadence' braking.

● **STRAIGHTEN THE WHEELS** When you regain control over steering, straighten up the wheels. This should allow you to get back on course.

▶▶See also: **DRIVING IN SNOW AND ICE** pp244–245   **231**

car **breakdown**

The UK's breakdown services are called out to around 20,000 stranded drivers everyday. A breakdown can be an emergency, especially if you are alone or in an exposed or dangerous position close to fast or heavy traffic. Your first priority should always be your own – and your passengers' – safety, then you can move on to dealing with the problem with your car.

be aware

● Know your car. Keep your owner's manual in your car. It will tell you everything from the jacking points for fixing a puncture to what the warning lights mean. A basic car maintenance manual is also handy for routine checks.

● Keep a set of jump leads. A flat battery is a very common cause of callouts for breakdown patrols.

● At each service, check that the battery terminals have been cleaned and protected from corrosion.

● Around 40 per cent of breakdowns happen at home so when buying a breakdown policy consider one that has 'homestart' cover.

● Free transport to your local garage is also a useful part of your rescue cover as around 10 per cent of problems cannot be repaired by the breakdown patrol at the roadside.

● Motoring organisations say that 90 per cent of callouts are due to inadequate servicing, so regular checks are advisable. Ensure that your car is serviced annually, or according to the mileage or at the frequency stated in your driver's handbook, in addition to the required MOT check.

action

BREAKDOWN ON MAIN ROAD

1 **STOP AT FIRST HINT OF TROUBLE** Look for a safe place to stop the moment a dashboard warning light flashes or odd noises start coming from the engine. Get your car off the road and into a lay-by or garage forecourt if possible. Finding a safe place to stop is far better than having to stop on the carriageway.

2 **GET OUT OF DANGER** Get everyone out of the car first, by the non-traffic side where possible. Warn other traffic by using your hazard lights and place a warning triangle (if it is safe to do so) at least 45 metres behind your vehicle. **Never stand between your vehicle and oncoming traffic.** At night, turn on the sidelights and wear a reflective jacket if you have one.

3 **LOCATE THE FAULT** If it is something simple, like running out of petrol or a puncture, you may be able to get back on the road without help. But never attempt to fix a puncture on the driver's side when you are parked by the side of the road.

4 **CALL A BREAKDOWN SERVICE** If you cannot fix the fault yourself, call a breakdown service or a local garage. Even if you are not a member of a motoring organisation, most will allow you to join on the spot – though you may have to pay a supplement.

 TAKE CARE

● Carry a light-coloured waterproof coat in the car and a high-visibility jacket in case you break down at night or in bad weather and have to go for help. A torch is also an essential part of any emergency kit (see box, opposite).

● If you are driving in bad weather and are likely to encounter snow and ice, assemble a winter survival kit (see page 244).

GET HELP Rescue services give highest priority to female or other vulnerable drivers. Tell the controller if you are travelling alone, especially if you feel at risk or in danger.

WATCHPOINT Rejoin the road by building up speed on the hard shoulder, being aware of any other stationary cars. Watch for a safe gap before rejoining the carriageway.

BREAKDOWN ON MOTORWAY

1 PULL OVER Leave the motorway at the next exit or pull into a service station if you can. If forced to use the hard shoulder, pull over as far to the left as you can and near an emergency phone if possible.

2 LEAVE FROM THE LEFT Turn on your hazard warning lights and sidelights and leave the vehicle by the non-traffic door. Make sure your passengers do the same. If you have a reflective jacket, put it on. Note that it is illegal, for safety reasons, to use warning triangles on a UK motorway.

3 KEEP ANIMALS IN THE CAR Any animals should be left in the car, but leave a window slightly ajar. If it is essential to let them out of the car, keep them under tight control on the verge.

4 PHONE FOR HELP Locate the nearest emergency phone using the arrows on the posts by the hard shoulder. On motorways, they are spaced at intervals of a mile. Use these phones to report your breakdown rather than a mobile phone as they contact the police or the Highway Agency directly and give an exact indication of your location.

5 DO NOT ATTEMPT ANY REPAIRS Return to your car and wait near your vehicle well away from the carriageway and the hard shoulder. Up on the bank, or behind the barrier is the safest option, in case other traffic crashes into your immobile vehicle.

Emergency kit

Having the right equipment can make all the difference between being stuck beside the road for hours and getting to your destination quickly. Here are some items:

Essential:
- Torch
- Basic tool kit
- Jack and wheelbrace
- Jump leads
- Duplicate ignition key
- Warning triangle
- Reflective clothing
- First-aid kit

Useful:
- Owner's manual
- Tow rope
- Duct (gaffer) tape
- Water-repellent lubricant
- Fire extinguisher
- Blanket
- 5l petrol can
- Spare bulbs
- Spare fuses

If you do not have the right equipment, here are some good ways to improvise:

- **DUCT (GAFFER) TAPE** Temporarily stops leaks in cars and is ideal for patching up holes in radiator hoses while you drive to a garage.
- **WIRE** Carry a small coil of thin insulated wire for electrical repairs or for tying up loose parts, such as trailing wires.
- **BATTERY CONNECTIONS** If the battery connections are corroded, clean them inside and out with glass or paper.

 WARNING

If you feel at risk from another person, even if they appear to be trying to help, return to your car by the non-traffic side, fasten your seatbelt and lock all doors. Do not try even the simplest repairs. Wait for professional help to arrive. If you feel threatened, use your mobile phone to call the police.

▶▶See also: **DRIVING IN ADVERSE WEATHER** pp240–242 • **DRIVING ABROAD** pp286–289

shattered **windscreen**

Almost all modern cars are now fitted with laminated glass that will crack or chip rather than shatter completely. But even a cracked or chipped windscreen requires prompt repair as it can obscure your vision and cause an accident. It may also be illegal to carry on driving depending on the size or position of the chip (see below).

precautions

- Fit laminated glass on an older car. This multiple layered windscreen has a plastic film sandwiched in between the glass to prevent the screen from shattering. No matter how hard they are hit, these kinds of screens should only crack or chip and not shatter.
- Drive slowly on a newly surfaced road to prevent loose chips hitting the windscreen. Maintain a good distance from the car in front.

- Do not ignore a chip because it can weaken the glass and allow water to seep between the layers, causing long-term damage to the windscreen.
- A chip can also cause a car to fail its MOT (see box, below).
- Check your insurance policy to see whether it covers windscreen repair. Many insurers will cover the cost of repairing chipped glass (or shattered windscreens) with no risk to your no-claims bonus.

action

WINDSCREEN SHATTERS

1 **PULL UP** The first priority is to stop safely at the side of the road. **Avoid the temptation to punch out the glass as by doing this you risk cutting your hand.** Instead slow down and lean forward to get as good a view of your surroundings as you can and then find a safe place to stop.

2 **CLEAR THE GLASS** Stuff rags or newspapers down the heater and demister vents to prevent shards of glass getting into the heating system. Spread newspaper or a blanket on the bonnet. Protect your hand with gloves or rags and push the glass out onto the bonnet. Alternatively, gently tap the glass out with a spanner or jack handle.

3 **GET A NEW WINDSCREEN** Drive slowly to the nearest garage. If you do drive on, make sure that all the glass fragments have been removed from the windscreen surround as these can get blown into your face. Or call a specialist to fit an emergency windscreen at the roadside, although this can be expensive at night or at weekends. Check your breakdown service as it may offer a discount.

Repairing a chip

Chips can be repaired but get professional advice first as many windscreen repairs are covered by car insurance.
- **DIY REPAIR** Kits that pump resin into the chips are available from car repair shops.
- **SIZE OF CHIP** A chip larger than a £2 coin is likely to be too big for repair.

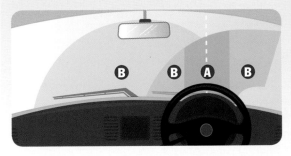

A car with a chipped windscreen will fail its MOT depending on the position and size of the chip:
ZONE A A chip larger than 10mm will result in a fail if it is in the driver's line of vision.
ZONE B A chip larger than 40mm will result in a fail if it is in the rest of the area swept by the windscreen wipers.

locked out of car

The cost of replacing lost car keys rises sharply each year as car-entry and anti-theft systems become more sophisticated. Always keep a spare set of keys and choose a breakdown recovery service with lockout cover.

WATCHPOINT Opt for a breakdown or car insurance policy that has a 'keycare' option. This covers you against locksmith charges and the cost of replacing a lost key.

precautions

- Make sure that you know the whereabouts of your spare key. Sixteen per cent of people have lost car keys at least once and calling out a locksmith can be very expensive.
- If you do not have a spare set, get one cut. One in 10 people do not have a spare set. Copies of modern keys that have transponder chips to operate alarm and immobiliser system cost up to £350.
- Conceal your keys in a safe place at home as burglars may take them and also steal your car.
- Keep a copy of your keycode as this will save time and money if you need a replacement. Technology is developing all the time for car keys. Modern anti-theft systems have rolling keycodes that switch each time you use them. Older cars, with remote-entry systems, tend to have fixed keycodes.
- Check your breakdown policy carefully. Some will tow you to the nearest garage while others will refuse to do anything other than call a locksmith for you.

 TAKE CARE

If you are buying a secondhand car, make sure that it already has a spare key.

 WARNING

Replacing the master set of keys for a modern car, with a sophisticated alarm and immobiliser system, can entail reprogramming – or even refitting – the car's computer system. This can be time-consuming and cost £1,000 or more.

action

LOST KEY

■ **CALL YOUR BREAKDOWN SERVICE** Phone your breakdown service in case they can help. They may be able to tow you to the nearest garage, which could have tools for getting into locked cars.

■ **PHONE A LOCKSMITH** Get quotes from three locksmiths as prices vary greatly, especially at night and weekends. They will need to know the model number and the registration date to give you a quote. Some are able to cut keys at the roadside.

■ **CONSIDER BREAKING IN** If you are forced to break a window – because a child or animal is trapped in the car, for example – make sure it is a side one, as these are cheaper to replace. Check if your insurance covers you for such an action.

FROZEN LOCK

■ **USE A HAIR DRYER** If you are at home, a hair dryer is probably the most effective way to defrost a frozen lock, providing you can get an extension cord to the car. Or you could heat the end of the key with a match or a lighter before inserting it into the lock.

■ **LUBRICATE** Squirt a few drops of lubricant into the door. Anti-freeze or lighter fuel may also work. Once open, to prevent the lock from re-freezing, squirt a drop or two of oil on the key and turn it in the lock a few times to coat the interior.

 WARNING

Most side windows are still made of toughened glass. As an anti-theft measure in new cars, motoring organisations recommend replacing this with laminated glass as it is more difficult to break.

car fire

Every year there are thousands of vehicle fires in Britain, mainly as a result of mechanical and electrical faults. In a worst case scenario, where the fire spreads to the fuel tank, the whole car may explode. Motorhomes are particularly vulnerable to electrical fires and – as with all vehicles – regular maintenance is the key to spotting potential problems.

precautions

- As well as regular maintenance and replacing faulty parts, check your vehicle for worn fuel pipes. Fuel leaks in the vehicle's engine are a common cause of fire. All fuel lines should be inspected regularly.
- Take particular care where you park. **Many fires occur when a vehicle is parked in long grass**. The catalytic converter on the underside of a car gets extremely hot and can cause grass or piles of dry leaves to ignite.
- Carry spare fuel only in an approved metal container. Secure it in an upright position to prevent it sliding around in the boot.
- Do not use heat, exposed flames or welding tools near the fuel tank or feed pipes.

Fire extinguishers

- Carry a fire extinguisher. Fire experts recommend a dry-powder extinguisher with a capacity of at least 1.5kg. A bigger, bulkier fire extinguisher can also make a useful escape tool as it can be used to smash a window.
- Make sure that the fire extinguisher is stored securely in an easily accessible place, such as under the dashboard or fixed under the driver's seat. Never keep extinguishers in the boot.
- Be wary of smaller car fire extinguishers. Some last for just eight seconds, which is probably not enough time to put out a fire.
- Most extinguishers require an annual inspection by the manufacturer to ensure that they are functioning properly.

action

CAR ON FIRE

1 SWITCH OFF IGNITION If you are driving pull up by the side of the road at the first sign of fire. Turn off the ignition to shut down the fuel pump. Do not remove the key or you could lock the steering.

2 KEEP THE BONNET CLOSED Do not be tempted to open the bonnet as this will cause the flames to flare up. But do pull the bonnet release catch to enable the fire brigade to access any fire.

3 GET PASSENGERS TO SAFETY Get everyone out of the car and well away from the vehicle. If you have stopped at the roadside, their exit should be from the non-traffic side of the vehicle. Take particular care with petrol-fuelled vehicles as they are more explosive than cars fuelled by diesel, which is more difficult to ignite.

4 GET HELP Call the fire brigade and ask passengers to flag down any passing vehicles – especially lorries – as they may have a fire extinguisher. Even if you already have one, two extinguishers are better than one.

5 TACKLE ONLY SMALL FIRES Only tackle a fire in its very early stages and if you believe it is safe to do so. A small fire, such as smouldering upholstery or wiring, can be tackled with a fire extinguisher or smothered with a fire blanket before the flames take a significant hold. If the fire is under the bonnet, aim the extinguisher through the radiator grille or under the edge of the bonnet. If the fire is under the chassis and threatens to reach the fuel tank, abandon any attempt to fight the fire and get well clear of the vehicle.

6 CHECK THE DAMAGE Do not drive the car again until it has had a full safety check by an auto electrician or a qualified mechanic.

GET HELP The fire brigade offers safety advice to prevent car fires occurring. Call them for advice on which type of fire extinguisher is suitable for your vehicle.

TIME TO ACT Take particular care in the danger zone behind the fuel tank (usually at the rear, but do not assume that). If the tank explodes, the blast may reach up to 30 metres.

WATCHPOINT Unattended cooking is the main cause of fires in caravans and motorhomes. Never leave a cooking appliance unattended while it is in use.

USE A FIRE EXTINGUISHER

1 PREPARE THE EXTINGUISHER Ideally, you should have checked how to use the extinguisher when you first installed it. Prepare the extinguisher carefully, following the instructions. Make sure that the extinguisher is always maintained in line with the manufacturer's instructions.

2 AIM AT THE BASE OF THE FIRE Direct the extinguisher at the base of the fire. Be methodical. Start at the edge of the fire closest to you and sweep the extinguisher back and forth until the fire is out. Do not spray aimlessly at the flames as this will waste the contents.

3 WATCH FOR FLARE-UPS Remember that fires can often flare up after they seem to have been put out. A common mistake is to use the entire contents of the extinguisher in one frantic first effort to put out the flames. Try to save some of the contents to tackle flare-ups.

4 CHECK THE VEHICLE Even if you think you have put the fire out, call the fire brigade to check over the vehicle and ensure that the fire is fully extinguished.

Motorhomes

The presence of propane gas for cookers makes motorhomes especially prone to fire incidents. There is also a greater risk of electrical fires in motorhomes because of their complex wiring systems.

- Make sure that you have smoke and gas detectors fitted.
- Ensure that all the equipment is installed and inspected by a qualified technician.
- Be careful about what you cook. Chip-pan fires are a major risk in caravans and motorhomes due to low ceilings.
- Purchase a large-capacity fire extinguisher as flames can take hold quickly in the confined space. Know where it is kept and how to use it, especially if you are renting the vehicle.
- Only keep the gas cylinders that you need rather than storing several in the motorhome.
- Never smoke or use candles in a motorhome because of the heightened risk of fire.

sinking car

If your car plunges into water, you must escape quickly. You have between 30 seconds and two minutes before the car sinks. Once it is submerged, you can survive for only three to five minutes without oxygen so you must act fast.

TIME TO ACT Cars usually sink engine-end first, leaving an air pocket at the other end of the car. If the car sinks, put your head in the air pocket while you try to escape.

be aware

- Most instances of cars sinking occur in lakes. Driving in low-lying countryside where there are roadside dykes or fens is another danger.
- Speeding or unsafe driving is another factor in most water fatalities so keep your speed down near lakes or rivers.
- Listen carefully to weather warnings, especially when driving at night in flood-hit areas or places prone to flash floods.

action

1 DO NOT WASTE TIME Do not phone for help – rescuers are unlikely to be able to reach you in time. Wait until you are back on dry land before phoning the emergency services.

2 TURN ON LIGHTS Unbuckle the seat belts and turn on the interior and exterior lights. Do not turn off the engine. Car electrical systems are built to withstand water so should keep working. Lights will help rescuers find the car and prevent the occupants from panicking.

3 TRY TO OPEN A WINDOW Tests show that windows represent your best chance of escape, as water pressure holds the doors shut. Even if you did manage to open a door, the rush of water into the car would cause the car to sink very quickly. Open the window as soon as possible. Keeping your engine running means that electric windows should continue to work, even when the car is sinking.

4 WAIT FOR PRESSURE TO EQUALISE Wait until the car fills with water and the water pressure equalises between the inside and the outside. Try not to panic and keep calm as the car fills. Hold onto the open window edge, or the door handle so you do not get disorientated if the car sinks at an angle.

5 SMASH A SIDE WINDOW If the window jams, kick it as hard as you can to smash the glass. Side windows are usually weakest; try the corners first where the glass is easiest to break. If you have a centre punch or wheel nut lock these may also be effective to break the glass. Expect a rush of water when you open the window.

6 LEAVE THE CAR Take a deep breath just before the water rises almost to the roof, then you may be able to open a door or window. Expect some resistance as you push a door against the water outside. Push off from the car and swim to the surface.

■ **IF THERE ARE CHILDREN IN THE CAR** Get any children out of their car seat or seat belt and into the seat next to you. Once you have the window open and the pressure has equalised, push them out of the escape window first before following them to the surface.

 WARNING
Prepare and discuss an escape plan with your family. If everyone in a car keeps calm and follows an agreed plan, escape and survival from a sinking car is possible.

stuck on a **level crossing**

More people die on level crossings each year than in rail crashes or derailments. Car driver error causes the majority of accidents. Never rush to beat the lights or take risks for the sake of gaining a few minutes. Take extra care on unmanned or open crossings. If you are unlucky enough to stall or break down on a level crossing, save yourself rather than the car.

be aware

- Level crossings are considered the biggest safety risk on the rail network. Around 20 vehicles a year are hit on level crossings, with many more near misses. The chances of a motorist surviving such a crash are minimal.
- Approach all level crossings with care at a moderate speed. Only drive onto a level crossing if you can see that the exit ahead is clear.
- Do not park on the approach to a level crossing.
- Never overtake on a level crossing.
- Never think about jumping the

barriers. There can be as little as 27 seconds between the lights starting to flash and the train crossing.
- Know your barriers. Most have traffic-light signals with a steady amber light, twin flashing red stop lights, and a sound alarm to warn pedestrians of approaching trains.
- Some level crossings have full barriers; some half barriers (barriers that extend over one lane on each side). Open level crossings with no barriers, gates, light or attendant are by far the most dangerous.

action

BREAKDOWN ON CROSSING

1 GET AWAY FROM THE CAR Get everybody out of the car and away from the level crossing as quickly as possible. Make sure that you are all a safe distance from the crossing.

2 USE THE EMERGENCY PHONE Use the phone by the barriers to tell the signalman that there is a car on the line. Only use your mobile phone to call the police if there is no phone at the barriers. Never try to move your car before phoning the signalman.

BARRIERS COME DOWN

1 ABANDON THE CAR The moment the lights start flashing and the barriers come down, the first priority is to abandon the car. With modern crossings there is only a matter of seconds before the train arrives with potentially devastating consequences when it hits the car.

2 GET AWAY FROM THE TRACKS Stand well clear of the tracks. If you are too close, you could be in danger of being injured by the car wreckage.

MOVING CAR OFF CROSSING

1 PUSH THE CAR FREE If there is no train approaching, you may be advised by the signalman to try to move the car off the tracks. If the engine will not start, take off the handbrake, put the car n neutral and push it out of the way.

2 USE THE STARTER MOTOR In a manual car, try using the starter motor to move the car. Put the car in first gear, take your foot off the clutch and turn the ignition on. Keep your right hand on the ignition as you steer with the left. The car should lurch forward.

3 INFORM THE SIGNALMAN Let the signalman know that the obstruction has been cleared the moment you succeed in moving the car.

driving in adverse weather

Heavy rain and strong wind, especially when combined, can cause hazardous driving conditions and floodwater adds significantly to the risk. Do not travel in adverse weather unless your journey is essential. If you do have to drive, go equipped for the worst of the elements and adapt your driving techniques to the conditions.

be aware

- Keep abreast of weather changes. Internet access on some mobile phones provides up-to-date satellite images and local radio can help. If you find yourself on the road in storms or floods, it is vital to keep a close eye on the weather.
- Do not continue if you are uncertain about the depth of water on the carriageway. Any water level above 30cm could damage the engine. Look for the kerb, if it cannot be seen the water is at least 15cm deep and caution is required.
- Drive with extreme caution. Motoring organisations say that drivers tend to underestimate the dangers of wet weather.
- Stopping distances are substantially longer in wet weather (see page 246). Keep at least a two-second gap between you and the nearest vehicle under normal conditions. In the wet, this

should be at least doubled and increased further under icy conditions.
- Always use dipped lights, even in daytime, as these allow others to see you more clearly.
- Flooding is most likely in low-lying areas by rivers and lakes, in dips and under bridges. Take particular care when driving in these areas or where there are signs warning of flooding.
- Do not drive at night during flood alerts as it is nearly impossible to judge the depth of water.

 WARNING

Never try to drive through fast-moving water. Cars are surprisingly buoyant and can be swept away all too easily. A car can float in as little as 60cm of water.

action

STORMY CONDITIONS

1 TURN WIPERS ON FULL Turn your wipers on to the fastest speed. Dip the headlights to lessen the glare and turn on the demister to combat condensation.

2 TURN BACK IF NECESSARY Stop if you are unsure and turn back along familiar roads if the weather worsens. Turning off a main road into a minor road to escape a storm can expose you to danger as secondary roads are more prone to flooding.

3 HEAD FOR SHELTER If driving conditions worsen, you have no option but to seek shelter. Service stations or multistorey car parks are ideal shelters for a car if you can reach one. In really treacherous conditions, you should abandon the car and seek shelter for yourself in a near-by building.

BLIZZARD CONDITIONS

1 SWITCH ON THE WIPERS The easiest test of whether there is any point in continuing the journey is to switch on the windscreen wipers. If they cannot push aside the snow accumulating on the glass, then you have no option but to seek shelter.

2 PREPARE A RETREAT At the first sign that you cannot continue, find a safe place to turn and head back. Retreating may allow you to outrun the storm. Look for potential shelter, such as a service station or restaurant.

3 ACT NOW Do not push ahead in the hope that you will find somewhere. Blizzards can close roads in a matter of minutes. If you have to shelter in your car by the side of the road, do not risk venturing out as you may become stranded (see page 245).

TIME TO ACT Watch the cars in front to see how they cope with the driving conditions. They can give you a good indication of what lies ahead.

WATCHPOINT Rain is most dangerous after a dry spell. The roads will have accumulated deposits of oil and rubber in the cracks. These mix with water to produce a slippery surface.

WINDY CONDITIONS

1 STEER FIRMLY Keep both hands on the wheel at all times particularly on exposed stretches of the road and on bridges, or when overtaking.

2 MIND THE GAP Other vehicles may be blown off course. Keep at least a two-second gap from other vehicles, taking particular care near caravans, cyclists, motorcyclists and horse riders.

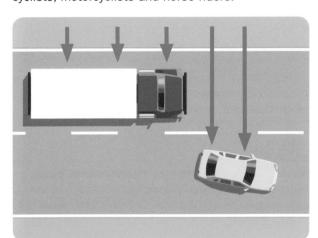

3 EXPECT SUDDEN GUSTS Be prepared for unpredictable gusts of wind on open stretches of road, when passing vehicles or gaps in hedges, or when overtaking high-sided vehicles. If you are caught in a gust, hold the wheel tightly to maintain control. The car may be rocked by the wind, but winds seldom have the strength to blow the car off the road.

4 WATCH FOR DEBRIS Drive carefully on country roads, especially at night or in the early hours of the morning when you are most likely to encounter branches or trees on the road. Watch out for twigs and small branches – these could indicate larger branches around the next corner.

TORRENTIAL RAIN

1 SLOW DOWN In wet weather drivers tend to underestimate the dangers caused by rain and drive at their normal speed. In reality, the combination of poor visibility and slippery, rain-sodden roads can make torrential rain one of the most risky driving situations. Keep your speed down and double your stopping distance (see page 246).

2 TEST YOUR BRAKES One of the main dangers of heavy rain is wet brakes, which can dramatically increase the car's stopping distance. To keep them dry, occasionally press lightly on the brake pedal. The heat from the friction should help to remove any moisture.

3 GET A GRIP If the steering becomes unresponsive, then it probably means that water is preventing the tyres from gripping the roads. This can cause aquaplaning (see below). If you lose grip, ease off the accelerator and slow down gradually.

CAR STARTS TO AQUAPLANE

1 REDUCE SPEED Aquaplaning is caused by the rain being so heavy that the tyres lose all grip and you lose steering control. It can also be the result of inadequate tyre tread. Braking will have little or no effect. The only answer is to take your foot off the accelerator and slow gradually.

2 STEER STRAIGHT Hold the steering wheel firmly, anticipating the moment that the tyres regain their grip. The car may swerve when this happens so maintain a firm hold on the wheel to enable you to steer out of trouble.

▶▶See also: **DRIVING IN A FLOOD** p242

driving in a flood

Flooding is often localised, and as flash floods can occur in an instant, they can be difficult to anticipate. Never take the risk of driving through any water if you are unsure of how deep it is.

A depth of as little as 60cm of water can cause a car to float away. Beware, too, of the risk of stalling in floodwater as it can cause irreparable damage to the engine of your vehicle.

action

FLOOD CONDITIONS

1 DRIVE SLOWLY Driving through flood water, even at slow speeds, creates a wave of water called a bow wave at the front of the car. Keep your speed down to limit the size of the wave, which can obscure your vision and swamp your engine. In a car with a manual gearbox, drive in first or second gear; in an automatic, opt for L or 1. Drive slowly but keep the revs high. The flow of exhaust gases will help to stop water entering the exhaust and the engine stalling.

2 KEEP THE ENGINE REVVING To avoid stalling, maintain steady pressure on the accelerator while slipping the clutch by pushing the clutch pedal down a little. All cars are susceptible but turbo-charged and diesel engines are the most vulnerable.

3 STAY IN THE SAME GEAR Do not change gear as any change in engine speed runs the risk of sucking in water and damaging the engine.

4 TEST YOUR BRAKES As soon as you leave the floodwater, test your brakes. Lightly press down on the brake pedal several times to check the brakes are pulling evenly on all the wheels. To dry them out, drive slowly pressing lightly on the brake pedal.

■ **IF THE CAR STALLS IN STANDING WATER** You have no option but to get out and push the car clear. Do not try to restart the car – you will just compound the damage to the engine. Be careful as there is a further risk that the airbag may be accidentally deployed due to water in the electrical system.

■ **IF THE CAR IS FLOODED OUT** Bail out the water with a bucket. Dry out the car as best you can, mopping up any water with rags or towels. Take out damp carpets and underlay. A professional dehumidifier and air blower can speed up the drying process. Get a garage to check over your car thoroughly before driving it again.

WARNING

Keep your speed down even in shallow water as there might still be a bow wave. The surge of water may swamp the engine compartment and cause the engine to stall.

stuck in mud

In this situation, do not try to power your way out by revving the engine. Patience and perseverance are required. Utilise something, be it carpets or tree branches, to provide traction. Be prepared to rock or push your way back onto the road.

WATCHPOINT Stand well clear if the car is being pulled out using tow ropes. If they become loose, there is a risk of the tow hooks flying off the car and hitting someone.

precautions

● In muddy conditions, drive in as high a gear as possible while keeping your speed low. This will reduce torque on the wheels and will decrease the risk of wheel spin.

● Keep your speed down on country lanes and other roads with ditches. Cars that end up mired in mud or stuck in ditches are usually going too fast for the road conditions.

● If you are renting a car for a holiday in a remote area with rough terrain, opt for a four-wheel drive vehicle with high ground clearance.

● The best protection from getting stuck is to travel in pairs of cars if you know you will be driving through muddy terrain. That way one can pull the other if you do get trapped.

action

1 GET A GRIP Straighten your wheels and pack something under the driving wheels to provide grip. Sand, gravel, sacking, old carpets, even tree branches can work. On a front-wheel drive, the grip is needed on the front wheels so add the material here; on a rear-wheel drive on the rear wheels; on a four-wheel drive do the front wheels first, then the back wheels if you have sufficient material.

2 ACCELERATE GENTLY Push the accelerator gently, starting in second gear to reduce wheel spin. Try to move the car gently forwards, using the clutch as necessary to keep the engine going; do not rev too hard. Enlist the passengers to help push the car.

3 ROCK THE CAR If the car is stuck in a rut or a ditch, try rocking it out. Move forwards a few inches in first gear, then while it is as far forward as it will go, quickly switch to reverse so that it moves slowly backwards. Repeat the movements in a gentle rhythm that will, hopefully, rock the car out of its rut.

4 USE TOW ROPES Towing the car out is the last resort. Check the position of the chassis to ensure that you will not damage the underside of the car. Phone for a professional tow truck if you have any

doubts. **Make sure that you attach the tow ropes to the frame of the two vehicles – the bumper is not strong enough** – and ensure that you have the right straps. You need recovery straps (see right) rather than towing straps as they stretch when pulled and are less likely to snap.

⚠ TAKE CARE
Once you have released your vehicle, drive slowly to a firm surface. Do not stop to let passengers back into the vehicle until you can feel sufficient grip.

driving in snow and ice

Only make a journey in heavy snow if it is absolutely vital, but if you do have to travel, make sure that you have appropriate survival equipment and supplies in case you have a breakdown or get stuck. With frostbite and hypothermia being a real danger in extremely cold weather, it is important to stay warm and keep fully awake.

precautions

- Keep an eye on weather forecasts for warnings of snow. Do not drive if there are warnings unless your journey is essential.
- Do not attempt to drive in a blizzard. Driving is impossible if the snow is more than 30cm deep.
- Ensure that the car battery is working well as flat batteries are a leading cause of winter breakdowns. A load test by a mechanic will tell you if the battery is sufficiently charged.
- Do not forget blankets. Cars can provide shelter but only limited warmth.
- Make sure that you have warm clothing, blankets, warm drinks and emergency food rations with you (see box, right).
- Carry snow chains or consider fitting 'winter' tyres, which provide better traction in snow and ice.

⚠ TAKE CARE

Check that your tyres are properly inflated as under-inflated tyres can seriously impair steering. **Tyres lose pressure in freezing conditions – around 1psi of pressure for each 6-degree centigrade fall in temperature.**

Winter survival kit

- Scraper and de-icer
- Fully charged mobile phone
- Shovel and long-handled brush
- High-energy food and drinks
- A vacuum flask with a hot drink
- Warm clothing and blankets
- Torch and spare batteries
- Sacking to provide tyre grip in icy conditions
- Jump leads for the car

For more extreme conditions:
- Snow chains
- Can of spare fuel
- Tow rope

action

DRIVING IN SNOW

1 CHOOSE YOUR ROUTE CAREFULLY Stick to major roads, which are likely to be gritted during winter weather. If you can, avoid minor country roads and steep hills, which are particularly treacherous. Take care when overtaking gritting vehicles, especially if you are riding a motorcycle.

2 ACCELERATE GENTLY Avoid harsh acceleration that can cause the wheels to spin and get the car bogged down in the snow. If it does get stuck, do not accelerate hard to pull away. Instead, pack something under the wheels to provide grip and accelerate gently, using the same techniques as when a car is stuck in mud (see page 243).

WATCHPOINT Keep a careful eye on the car exhaust. Ensure that the area round the exhaust pipe is kept clear so that the poisonous fumes can escape when you use the heater.

TIME TO ACT Slow down and take particular care when the ice starts to melt, as a thin layer of water forms on the road, which can make it even more slippery.

DRIVING ON ICE

1 **SLOW DOWN** Steer gently and avoid all sharp turns, braking or acceleration. Stopping times are 10 times longer in icy weather so leave a 10-second gap between your car and the next vehicle.

2 **USE A HIGH GEAR** Motoring experts recommend pulling away in second gear to avoid wheel spin. Drive in as high a gear as possible to limit wheel spin and prevent skidding. Make sure that this does not result in your speed creeping up.

3 **BRAKE GENTLY** When braking you should get into a low gear earlier than usual as this will allow the speed of the car to fall. If you do not have an anti-lock braking system (ABS), gently apply pumping pressure to the brakes to slow down.

4 **CORNER CAREFULLY** When cornering, allow the speed to fall well before the bend by easing off the accelerator gradually.

5 **WATCH THE GRADIENT** Do not try to power up hills. Use a low gear and try to get a bit of momentum before reaching the hill and let this carry you up. Reduce speed once you reach the top of the hill and drive down in a low gear as slowly as possible.

TRAPPED IN SNOW

1 **SHELTER IN THE CAR** The main priority is to stay warm and keep awake to protect against frostbite and hypothermia. Use the car for shelter. Do not risk going for help as there is a serious risk of exposure.

2 **CONSERVE YOUR FUEL** Running the engine all night to power the heater can empty the tank. To conserve fuel, only turn on the engine and the heater for 15 minutes an hour. Leave a window open a crack to let fumes escape.

3 **KEEP WARM** Use blankets, rugs and coats for warmth. Newspapers can also conserve body heat if wrapped around limbs or stuffed down clothes. Wear a hat, scarf and gloves as well.

4 **STAY AWAKE** Try to stay awake. If there is a group of snowbound vehicles, join forces with other motorists. Teaming up in one vehicle saves fuel, provides warmth and will boost morale.

5 **AWAIT RESCUERS** If the car becomes completely buried, open a window and poke an air hole through the snow with an umbrella or torch. To move the car out of deep snow, provide traction with carpets and rock the car free (see page 243).

Black ice

Dark patches caused by water freezing on the roads are notoriously difficult to spot and pose one of the biggest dangers in icy weather. One sign is frozen puddles by the side of the road; another is a feeling of light steering or a lack of noise coming from the tyres on the roads. To reduce skidding, drive more slowly in lower gears and ease off the accelerator when you want to reduce speed, rather than hitting the brakes.

driving in **fog**

As well as reducing visibility, fog causes drivers to lose the sensation of speed by muffling sounds and blotting out familiar landmarks. Use your lights to make sure that you are seen by other drivers and leave plenty of time and space for braking.

WATCHPOINT Fog lights dramatically enhance visibility in foggy conditions, but they must be switched off if conditions improve to avoid dazzling other drivers.

precautions

- Know how to switch your fog lights on and off and when to use them.
- Drive with your window partly open to help you to listen out for traffic, especially at junctions.
- Fog makes the roads more slippery so increase your stopping distance (see below).
- Follow the kerbside or near-side verge as a guide to your road position.
- Switch on your windscreen wipers and demisters to improve your vision.

⚠️ **WARNING**

- Fog is patchy and often comes in pockets so keep driving carefully even if you think you have hit clearer weather.
- Low-lying areas, valleys and wooded areas on cool autumn and winter mornings are most susceptible to foggy conditions.
- If you have to pull over, try to ensure that you park off the road.

action

1 DIP YOUR LIGHTS Drive with dipped headlights during the day or night. Sidelights are not bright enough and full-beam headlights dazzle because they reflect off the fog particles. Turn on your fog lights when visibility is seriously threatened.

2 SLOW DOWN Reduce your speed so that you can stop within the distance that you can see ahead. Do not accelerate if the car behind is too close. You could easily end up too close to the car in front.

3 KEEP YOUR DISTANCE Maintain at least a two-second gap with the car in front; three seconds in heavy fog. It is a mistake to get too close to the car in front in order to stay in sight of its tail lights; this is a major cause of multiple pile-ups.

4 TURN RIGHT WITH CARE Signal in good time, wind down the window completely and listen for traffic before crossing the other lane to turn right or at major junctions.

Stopping distances

In wet and foggy conditions, allow extra space between cars for braking.

Thinking distance
Braking distance

STOPPING DISTANCE IN DRY CONDITIONS AT 40MPH

12m   24m

= 36 METRES
9 CAR LENGTHS

STOPPING DISTANCE IN WET CONDITIONS AT 40MPH

12m   33m

= 45 METRES
11 CAR LENGTHS

driving in a remote area

Driving in remote areas exposes you to more risk and requires preparation. Before you leave, make sure that your vehicle is in a sound condition and appropriate for the terrain you will encounter. Check that you have the correct equipment and supplies in case of a breakdown and be sure to inform someone of your plans, including timings.

precautions

- Study the owner's manual before going off-road, especially if your vehicle is rented.
- Be aware of changing weather conditions and be especially cautious of fast-running water when crossing rivers or streams.
- Make sure that you have all the right equipment for emergencies (see page 233).
- Ensure that your vehicle is up to the task. A four-wheel drive vehicle is recommended for difficult terrain.
- Check the tyres, water level (in radiator), oil level and battery condition before you leave.
- For remote, off-road trips, travelling in two or more vehicles is a good idea as there will be someone to tow you or to go for help if there is a problem.

action

FUEL RUNS LOW

1 DRIVE AT A STEADY PACE Keep to a speed of around 25–30mph in top gear in order to conserve fuel for longer. Avoid unnecessary stops and starts. If possible, turn off the air-conditioning.

2 ACCELERATE GENTLY When approaching hills, build up speed first, then change down so that you can keep going without having to press hard on the accelerator.

YOU BREAK DOWN

1 STAY WITH YOUR CAR Do not risk getting lost or injured by setting off on a fruitless hike for help. The only exception is if you know that there is definitely somewhere within walking distance.

2 RAISE YOUR BONNET This instantly signals to other road users that you have broken down and hopefully encourages them to stop.

3 CONSERVE SUPPLIES Take extra food and water if travelling in a remote location. Provisions for at least 14 days and at least 4–5 litres of water per person per day are recommended if driving in hot, remote places. Carefully ration supplies if you are stranded.

 TAKE CARE

If you must leave the vehicle, attach a note to the steering wheel showing your proposed route. If you are in a hot area, move at night when it is cool and mark your route so that you can be followed.

 WARNING

- Tell someone your route and expected return time. Arrange a call-in time when you are due back so the alarm can be raised if necessary.
- Make sure that your mobile phone is charged although there is no guarantee of getting a reception in a very remote area.

hitting an **animal**

More than a million animals die and hundreds of motorists are injured yearly in animal collisions in the UK alone. Take care on rural roads, especially at night, and know the correct procedure if you should hit an animal, especially a large one.

WATCHPOINT Take care at twilight. Many animals, including deer and rabbits, are crepuscular. This means they are most active at twilight and likely to stray onto the roads.

be aware

- Take special care at night when the majority of collisions occur. Animals get mesmerised by the glare of headlights and tend to freeze in the middle of the road.
- Remember that animal warning signs on roads are there for a reason. Even if you cannot see any animals, they may well be lurking around the bend or over the brow of the hill.
- When you see one animal, expect others. Animals rarely travel alone.

- In areas where wildlife tends to stray onto the roads – where woods border the roads, for example, or where signs warn of animals – alternate your headlights between dipped and full beam to scare animals out of the way.
- If you are travelling in an area that is prone to deer on the road, attach a deer whistle or siren to the grille of your car. These can be heard by the animal but not by the human ear.

action

1 DO NOT SWERVE Instinctively, you will want to swerve or slam on the brakes, but sudden manoeuvres increase the risk of an accident because you could hit a tree or another vehicle. Generally, it is safer to slow down and continue on your normal track when an animal strays into your path as it may well move out of your way.

2 PULL OVER Stop as soon as you can after an impact. Check to see if the animal is dead or injured.

3 APPROACH WITH CARE An injured animal is likely to be in a distressed state. Approach slowly, talking soothingly. Be especially wary of wild animals. Do not try to handle an injured deer, fox or badger as it could inflict a serious injury.

4 MOVE IT If the animal is small, try to move it to the side of the road to reduce the danger for other drivers. A blanket makes a good improvised stretcher for smaller animals.

5 HELP THE ANIMAL If the animal is injured, the best organisation to contact is the RSPCA. Call them and they will give you advice and details of any local animal organisations that can help.

6 CALL THE POLICE Although it is not always a legal necessity, it is worth calling the police as they may help either to move the body or to find treatment for an injured animal.

Should you report it?

Surprisingly, you do not always have to report a collision with an animal to the police:

- **SPECIFIC ANIMALS** The Road Traffic Act requires you to tell the police only if you injure the following animals: dog, horse, cow, sheep, pig, goat, bull, ass or mule.
- **GIVE DETAILS** If you hit any of the specified animals, you must give your name, address and registration number to anyone else involved. If it is a stray animal tell the police within 24 hours.
- **UNSPECIFIED ANIMALS** If you hit any other animal, even a cat or a protected species such as an otter, you are not obliged to report it to the police or RSPCA, although it is advisable to do so.

OUTDOOR INCIDENTS

drowning

Every year tens of thousands of people get into difficulties in water and in the UK as many as 600 people drown – most of them in inland waters. This tragic statistic includes those who drown attempting to rescue someone else. Follow these rules to keep yourself safe in water, and if you do see someone who may be drowning know how to help them safely.

be aware

KEEP YOURSELF SAFE IN WATER

- Always swim with others and ideally where there is a lifeguard.
- Do not dive into water unless you know the depth and what lies below the surface.
- Do not swim out of your depth unless you are a confident swimmer.
- Pay attention to tides and water currents that may carry you into deep water.
- Take care not to exhaust yourself in open water, where it is easy to misjudge distance.
- Do not float on lilos or large inflatable rings when the tide is going out or there is a strong offshore wind.
- Always wear a personal flotation device when participating in any kind of water sport.
- Never let children swim unattended. Fence or cover unattended pools, spas and ponds.
- Ensure that your children learn how to swim and lifesave.

RECOGNISE WHEN TO RESCUE

- Look for the signs that someone is drowning, rather than fooling around. Typically, his head is back, his mouth open, his arms waving frantically but he is making no sound. He is vertical in the water with his head submerging periodically.
- **Always attempt a rescue from land first** to avoid putting yourself at unnecessary risk. Remember the mnemonic: 'reach or throw before you go'.

 **TAKE CARE**

If you are reaching out to pull someone in from the side of a swimming pool, lie down on the edge, otherwise you may end up in the water yourself. Encourage them to climb out unassisted if they are able to.

Surviving in water

Known as 'drownproofing', this technique enables you to float in open water when you have no life jacket. In water temperatures of 15°C or more, you may have 1–2 hours before hypothermia sets in; in colder water, much less.

1 HANG IN THE WATER Use your body's natural buoyancy to float just below the surface of the water. Extend your arms in front of you and put your face in the water to hang in a relaxed position and conserve energy.

2 LIFT YOUR HEAD OUT OF THE WATER When you need to take a breath, raise yourself up by pushing your arms down and kicking your legs. Exhale completely as your head breaks the surface, then take a deep breath in.

3 RETURN TO THE REST POSITION With your lungs full of air, close your mouth and return to the rest position (see step 1, above). If you stay relaxed and get into a rhythm of rising, breathing and resting, you can stay afloat indefinitely without getting tired.

action

RESCUE FROM LAND

1 **SHOUT AND SIGNAL FOR HELP** Call out to the person and encourage him not to panic and swim if he can.

2 **THROW A BUOYANCY AID** This could be anything that floats – such as a life jacket or ball.

3 **PULL TO SAFETY** Throw him a line to grab hold of, tying a loop in it first if you can. A line with a lifebuoy is the best option. An electrical extension lead or a tow rope could be used or something rigid enough to pull him to safety, such as an oar, fishing rod or branch.

4 **WADE OUT** As a last resort, wade out, staying within your depth, with a life belt that you can throw to the person. Two buoyancy aids would be even better. If the person is too far out, consider entering the water with a flotation device that the person can hold on to while you tow him to safety.

⚠ TAKE CARE

A drowning person may grab hold of you in panic and pull you under the water. To escape his grip, actively swim down deeper; he should then release you.

⚠ WARNING

● When back on shore, if the victim is not breathing, perform CPR at once (see pages 16–17).
● If the water is cold, remove the person's clothing and wrap him in blankets. Give a conscious casualty a warm, but not very hot, drink.
● In every case of near drowning, seek medical advice urgently as lung complications are common.

Life-saving skills

Those who have a life-saving qualification could attempt the following techniques to rescue a drowning person from the water.

1 **TOW WITH AN EXTENDED ARM** If you do not have a flotation device and the person is cooperative or unconscious, cup his chin to raise his head out of the water and then swim back.

2 **USE A CROSS-CHEST TOW** To keep the victim's face higher out of the water in a rough sea or choppy conditions on a lake or river, reach over his shoulder and hold him into your side, gripping his belt or a belt loop so you have a firm hold. Use side stroke to bring him to safety.

▶▶See also: **ATTENDING TO A CASUALTY** pp12–13 • **CPR** pp16–19 • **HYPOTHERMIA** pp46–47

falling into a river

The power of a fast-flowing river is frequently underestimated. Even a small stream in full flood can knock an adult off his feet. Whether you are attempting a crossing or strolling along the bank, a few straightforward guidelines will keep you safe.

WATCHPOINT Rivers can be unpredictable and water levels can rise dramatically. Heavy rain or snow melt in distant mountains may result in a rapid rise in water levels downstream.

precautions

- If you plan to walk near a river or need to cross one, consider the depth and speed of the water, the risk of collision with rocks and the temperature of the water. Always try to find a bridge to cross before resorting to wading through the water.
- Watch out for warning signs that a river is in flood. These include discoloration of the water, the sound of small rocks and boulders being rolled along the river bed and large branches or other debris floating quickly past.
- Do not walk too near the water's edge, especially on the outside banks of bends. These are often undercut by the river, which flows most quickly here, and are prone to collapse.
- Use a map to decide where a river can be safely crossed. Identify the location of hazards such as weirs, waterfalls or dams.
- Insist that children wear a life jacket and wear one yourself if you plan to spend time on or near a major river.

action

YOU SEE SOMEONE FALL IN

■ **STAY ON LAND You are more likely to be of help if you stay on the bank** and attempt a rescue from there. If the person is moving rapidly downstream, try to run ahead of him along the bank. Shout and signal for help as you do so.

■ **THROW SOMETHING BOUYANT** So that he can stay afloat, throw him something buoyant (see box, right) that he can cling to until he can be rescued.

■ **THROW A LINE** Keep a look out for a point where you may be able to reach him with a line or a long branch and pull him to safety.

■ **ROW OUT** If you are confident of handling a rowing boat or canoe, row or paddle out. Do not try to haul him on board unless you are rescuing a child or you have someone else to balance the rowing boat. Instead, throw him something buoyant or get him to hold on to the side and tow him to safety.

Emergency river crossing

Before fording a river that is knee high or deeper, spend some time looking for the best place to cross. Try to get above the river so you can look down and take note of deep channels or hazardous rocks. Do not cross near rapids or waterfalls.

■ **IF YOU ARE CROSSING ALONE** Improvise support. Find a stout stick about 2m long and hold it diagonally across the front of your body. Push the stick into the river bed about a metre upstream from your feet, then lean on the pole as you step forward. Once you have a secure footing, reposition the pole and repeat the process.

1 TO CROSS AS A GROUP Line up along the bank so you have the strongest individuals at the upstream and downstream ends and the rest of the group in between. Rope yourselves together, interlock your arms or grasp each other's pack straps so that if one person stumbles, the others can offer support.

2 ENTER THE WATER TOGETHER Step off the bank and into the river simultaneously. Walk slowly across the river, crossing in a line parallel to the bank and making sure that you stay in line with the current at all times.

YOU FALL IN

■ **CALL FOR HELP** If there are people nearby, call out as loudly as you can to attract their attention. Remove a heavy pack or any equipment or heavy boots that may drag you under the water.

■ **TRY TO REACH A SAFE PLACE** If you can touch the river bed easily, try to use it to push yourself – in a series of small jumps – towards the safety of the bank or a large rock that you can climb onto. If the current is strong and the water is above your thighs, work with the flow of the water, not against it, even if this carries you downstream. It is safer to swim or crawl than try to stand, as you may get a foot trapped on the riverbed.

■ **PROTECT YOURSELF** If you are out of your depth and find yourself being swept along by the flow, lean back and float feet first. Keep your knees slightly bent and be ready to use your feet to push yourself away from rocks or any other hazards. Try to steer using your hands and arms as paddles.

■ **WATCH OUT FOR RIVER DEBRIS** A floating log might provide a useful lifesaver, but a submerged tree or large branch might cause you injury. If you spot a potential hazard in the water, try to swim round it or, if you have to, over it.

■ **PROTECT YOUR HEAD** If you find yourself heading towards a waterfall or weir, try to roll into a ball and use your hands and arms to protect your head.

■ **SWIM TO SAFETY** As soon as you encounter slower-moving water, flip onto your front and swim front crawl as strongly as you can. Swim diagonally across the current towards the bank. Get out of the centre of the river as soon as you can and avoid the outside of bends, as this is where rivers flow fastest.

DOG FALLS IN

■ **STAY ON THE BANK** Dogs are good swimmers and are unlikely to come to any harm. Try to follow the dog from the bank and encourage it to come out of the water. If possible, get ahead and drag the dog to safety with a branch or an oar.

■ **USE A BOAT** If there is a boat you can use, row out to the dog and either haul it in, kneeling in the boat to avoid capsizing, or tow it by the collar.

 WARNING

Do not swim out to rescue a dog. It may panic and resist rescue, putting you in danger of drowning.

Makeshift lifesavers

In an emergency, many everyday items can be used to make an improvised lifesaver.

● **PLASTIC-COVERED CUSHIONS** While not very buoyant, foam cushions may float for long enough to win you sufficient extra time to effect a rescue.
● **FOOTBALL** Although not easy to hold on to, plastic footballs float well and can be thrown or kicked a long way.

● **EMPTY PLASTIC PETROL CAN** Many people keep plastic petrol cans in their cars. When empty, they make good buoyancy aids.
● **LARGE PLASTIC BOTTLES** Empty 5 litre containers with screw tops provide an ideal impromptu lifesaver. If possible, tie a line to the handle and pull the person to safety. Throwing a container to the person to hold against his chest may help him to float.

▶▶See also: **ATTENTING TO A CASUALTY** pp12–13 • **CPR** pp16–19 • **HYPOTHERMIA** pp46–47

caught in a rip current

Getting caught in a rip current, also known – less accurately – as an undertow or rip tide, can be a frightening and occasionally life-threatening experience. It can usually be avoided if you learn to identify the warning signs, both out at sea and on the beach. If you find yourself in one of these currents, escape is possible, provided you use your strength effectively.

action

1 TRY TO GET OUT OF THE WATER If a strong current knocks you off your feet, try to stand up and get out of the water as quickly as you can.

2 DO NOT FIGHT THE CURRENT If you find yourself out of your depth, do not fight the current as you will only become exhausted. If you cannot swim well, try to signal for help at once. Wave both your arms and shout as loudly as you can.

3 SWIM IF YOU CAN Try to see which way the current is pulling you and swim at right angles to this. Rip currents are seldom more than 30m wide, so even if you are carried a little further out to sea, it should not take too long to swim clear of the current.

4 REST If you get tired, float on your back and continue to shout and signal for help.

5 SWIM BACK TO SHORE Rip currents usually weaken 100–150m from the shore. Once you are out of the rip current, make for the shore, swimming diagonally away from the current to avoid re-entering it.

be aware

● Rip currents can occur wherever there is surf. **Look for a tell-tale 'dead spot' in a line of otherwise white breakers.** The water in a rip current may be slightly discoloured due to the sand or silt it is carrying.
● Remember, the bigger the surf, the stronger the potential rip current will be.
● Look out for warning signs on beaches that are known to be prone to rip currents (below).
● Test the water. If, when you walk into the surf, you can feel a powerful current pulling you away from the shore, walk along the beach to find a safer spot to enter the water.
● Avoid swimming within 30m of piers or jetties, as permanent rip currents often form near such structures.
● Try to swim where there are lifeguards. Where there are no lifeguards, seek out local knowledge about the safety of a beach.

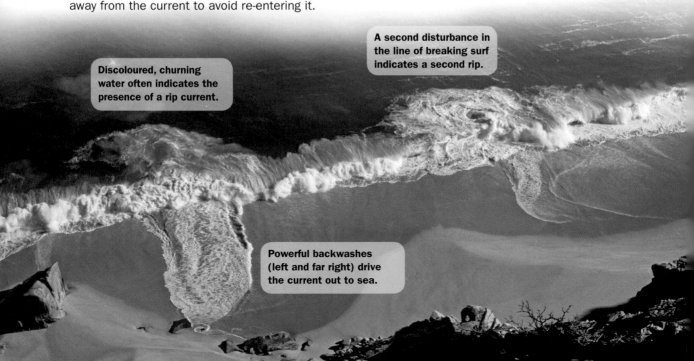

A second disturbance in the line of breaking surf indicates a second rip.

Discoloured, churning water often indicates the presence of a rip current.

Powerful backwashes (left and far right) drive the current out to sea.

cut off by the tide

You need to take particular care if you are following a path along the shore. High cliffs and high tides can prove a dangerous combination for the unwary walker or for anyone on a day out on a beach.

GET HELP If you have a phone, call the emergency services immediately and ask for the coastguard. Give them your position and the number of people in your party.

precautions

- Check your route on a map before setting out if you intend to follow a coastal footpath for any distance. Where the sea meets high cliffs there is often a severe wave action against the cliffs, so avoid this part of the beach at all costs.
- Try to estimate the time it will take to complete each leg of your route and plot a timeline of the walk. Most people can manage about 5km/h on all but the roughest terrain. Check the local tide tables to see what time the tides are at their height and compare these with your timeline.
- When taking an unplanned stroll along a beach, pay attention to warning signs, such as visible evidence of high tide lines, and note whether the sea is receding or approaching.
- Allow plenty of leeway in your timing. Leave potentially dangerous bays or headlands before low tide – do not wait for the tide to turn.
- Be especially cautious when exploring rocky coastlines and caves. Always plan an escape route in case you find yourself cut off.
- Listen to local advice about coastal dangers.

action

1 HEAD FOR SAFETY If you are a long way from the shore, you are unlikely to be able to outrun the tide. Do everything you can to get off the beach or, as a last resort, look for rocks, or sand or shingle banks that are higher, to give you more time to be rescued.

2 RAISE THE ALARM If you can, phone for help. Alternatively, attract the attention of anyone nearby in a boat or on the cliff top. Shout or give six long blasts on a whistle or six long flashes with a torch, repeating the sequence at intervals of one minute. This is an internationally recognised distress signal to which you may receive three long whistle blasts or flashes of light in response.

3 LOOK FOR USEFUL ITEMS As you make your way to your chosen point of safety, pick up anything you can find that floats, such as large pieces of wood, polystyrene packaging or large plastic bottles.

4 REMOVE HEAVY CLOTHING Before the sea catches up with you, remove any clothing that is likely to hinder swimming. Once the sea comes above your knees, continue swimming as calmly as you can towards your destination.

■ THE HELP POSITION
If you find yourself in open water with a makeshift lifesaver and little hope of reaching the shore or a place of safety, relax in the water and adopt the HELP position (Heat Escape Lessening Posture) – keep your arms crossed, hugging yourself. Hold any buoyant object you have close to your body.

 WARNING
Large flat bays and beaches can be especially dangerous because the tide can come in extremely quickly. Within seconds you can find yourself in deep, turbulent water, a long way from the shore.

▶▶See also: HYPOTHERMIA pp46–47

sailing boat/canoe capsizes

If you go sailing or canoeing, sooner or later you will almost certainly experience a capsize. How serious this is will depend on how you capsized and the depth, temperature and roughness of the water you find yourself in. Controlled capsize practice in a dinghy or canoe will give you the confidence to deal with the real situation and help to keep you safe in the water.

precautions

- Do not sail in conditions beyond your ability, such as in high winds or heavy seas.
- Never sail or canoe alone.
- Always canoe in waters that are within your ability. If white-water canoeing, check the difficulty of a particular river before entering it.
- **Make sure you have practised a capsize drill repeatedly** under controlled conditions before taking on more challenging waters.
- Always wear a life jacket or buoyancy aid when sailing or canoeing.

Keep children in view on the water.

action

BOAT CAPSIZES

■ **STAY WITH THE BOAT** When you capsize any kind of boat – dinghy, rowing boat or inflatable – your first priority should be to stay with the boat. If your attempts at righting it are unsuccessful and you need to be rescued, the boat is bigger and easier to spot than a swimmer in the water. The boat will float, so if you can, climb onto the hull and signal for assistance from other boat users.

RIGHTING A DINGHY

1 **CHECK THE BOAT** Uncleat and loosen any sheets (the ropes attached to the sails) so that the boat does not start sailing by itself once righted. Check for any tangled lines and make sure that the centreboard, if retractable, is fully down.

2 **GET IN POSITION** If there are two of you, the strongest or heaviest person should swim to the hull, holding the end of the main sheet as a safety line. The second crew member should hold onto a seat or crossbeam inside the boat so that he is lifted into the boat as it is righted.

3 **USE YOUR WEIGHT** Once in place, the heavier crew member should drop the main sheet, pull on the upper jib sheet and lean, then stand on the centreboard to bring the boat up. (Lean, rather than stand, on a wood centreboard or it may snap.) The crew member inside the boat kneels and helps the person in the water back into the boat by pulling on the shoulders of his life jacket.

■ **SAILING SOLO** The process is similar if you are alone. To get on board, swim to the widest part of the boat, pull down on the side and 'swim' into the boat. Sort out the sheets and tiller before sailing.

WATCHPOINT UK water temperatures are cold, so make sure that you wear appropriate clothing: normally a drysuit in winter and a wetsuit at other times of the year.

 TIME TO ACT Multiple capsizes will be physically tiring. Take note of your physical condition and come off the water before you become exhausted or cold.

 GET HELP If someone is injured or a dinghy is disabled, signal for help. Attract attention by raising and lowering your arms over your head or by setting off a distress flare.

CANOE CAPSIZES

1 KEEP HOLD OF YOUR PADDLE Try to hold on to your paddle as you capsize so that you can paddle once you retrieve your canoe.

2 PROTECT YOURSELF If you are in fast-flowing, dangerous waters, focus first on self-protection. In water deeper than knee high, float on your back and travel downstream feet first (see page 253).

3 QUICKLY ASSESS THE SITUATION If the water is dangerous or if there is a weir ahead, your priority must be to reach safety first and retrieve your canoe second.

4 RECOVER YOUR CANOE If the water is quite calm, try to recover your canoe. If it is within reach, grab it from the upstream end.

5 GET BACK IN In a river it is usually easier to swim the canoe to the bank and get back in. In the sea or a lake, if you are a long way from shore, you should right the canoe (see right) and try to get back in.

What to do in a kayak

● **ENLIST HELP** If you capsize in a kayak, call for help from another kayaker. He can paddle his kayak so he is perpendicular to the bow of yours – making a T-shape – then haul your kayak up and across the bow of his kayak to drain it. Once emptied, it can be flipped back over and pulled alongside the other kayak.
● **GET BACK IN** As you pull yourself back in, the other kayaker can keep the craft balanced by putting as much weight as possible onto the nearside of the cockpit.
● **DO NOT KAYAK ALONE** If you get thrown out of your kayak when it turns over, it is difficult to drain the boat and get back in alone. Do not venture out alone unless you are experienced.

RIGHTING A CANOE

1 GET UNDER THE CANOE First lift one edge out of the water to ensure that there is air under the canoe. Then swim under the canoe.

2 LIFT THE HULL Once you have got your breath back, hold firmly on to the hull, lift it clear of the water and flip it away from you to one side. If there are two or more of you, make sure that everyone pushes towards the same side at the same time.

3 PULL YOURSELF IN Once the canoe is righted, grasp a far edge and pull yourself diagonally into the boat. Try to get as much weight across the canoe as quickly as possible to prevent a further capsize. If there are two of you in the water, one person should hang on to the opposite side of the canoe as you climb in, to keep it level on the water.

boat emergencies

Running aground remains a common sailing hazard and a serious leak can quickly become an emergency. A fire on a boat must be dealt with urgently due the flammable nature of the craft. Make sure the crew are drilled in safety procedures.

GET HELP Seek immediate assistance. Send a distress signal (see page 259) on a DSC (digital) radio, followed by a Mayday message on Channel 16 (DSC and VHF).

precautions

- **Always be aware of your position, especially when you are in unfamiliar waters.**
- Make sure you have up-to-date charts, a good compass or a GPS. If you are at all unsure of your position, slow down – if you do hit an obstacle, the results will be less severe.
- When in tidal waters, make sure that you know the tide times and the tidal range.
- Consider joining a towing organisation and keep their details in a safe place on the boat.
- Prepare a 'grab bag' of essential items you need in a life raft. Include a first-aid kit, handheld VHF and GPS, torch, water and food.
- Ventilate the cabin, engine compartment and bilges regularly to prevent a build-up of gas.
- Turn off the gas bottle when not in use.

action

BOAT RUNS AGROUND

1 ASSESS THE SITUATION First find out whether anyone is hurt, whether the hull has been damaged and what kind of obstacle you have hit. What did the collision sound like?

2 CHECK YOUR CHARTS If you are in tidal waters, check where you are in the tide cycle. Are you likely to float off on a rising tide? Locate the closest deep water. Although you may know that deeper water lies behind you, there could be a channel even closer, right in front of you.

⚠️ WARNING

Stow belongings carefully below deck before setting sail. When the boat goes aground, injuries are just as likely to be caused by objects flying across the cabin, as by the jar of the impact.

3 USE AN ANCHOR If there is any chance that the wind, waves or current will drive your boat further aground, set a kedge (auxiliary) anchor behind you in deep water. Set it as far from the boat as possible, using a tender (small boat) if you have one.

4 BACK OFF If you have run aground on a soft spot, try backing off slowly. It may help if someone goes over the side and rocks the boat as you do this.

5 GET A TOW If you can not back off, enlist help from another boat. You may need a combination of reverse engines, a rising tide and the tug of another boat or winching against the anchor to pull you free.

Heeling the boat over

Only attempt to heel the boat over if you have been trained to do so. This technique will help to reduce the boat's draught (its depth below the water line) and may help free it. Use the weight of the crew on one side or  drop the mainsail on a sailing boat and weight the boom with a crew member – wearing a life jacket and safety harness – on one side.

Fuels and flammable solvents set ablaze by a spark are a frequent cause of on-board fires.

BOAT SPRINGS A LEAK

1 TURN ON THE PUMPS If you discover water in the bilges, turn on the pumps immediately.

2 FIND THE LEAK It could be a failed seal, a split seam, a leaking stern gland on the propellor shaft or a puncture through the hull. If the pumps are not coping with the influx of water, start bailing as fast as you can.

3 BLOCK A HOLE Use cushions or towels wedged in place with lengths of timber. Small holes can be sealed with bungs or filled with marine epoxy.

4 SEAL OFF THE AFFECTED AREA Consider whether the leak can be isolated. Is there a way to seal off the affected area to limit the spread of water?

5 USE YOUR RADIO Make sure the rising water is not about to compromise your boat's batteries. Send an emergency message while your radio is still working.

6 PREPARE TO ABANDON SHIP Put on life jackets, get your grab bag with emergency supplies (see precautions, opposite) and make sure the life raft is accessible. Only abandon ship if you are sure that it is about to sink.

FIRE ON BOARD BOAT

1 GET TO SAFETY Get everyone as far away from the fire as possible. If you are in a smoke-filled cabin, drop to the floor where the air is cleaner. If you can not exit through the hatches, smash a window, covering it first with a blanket to minimise injury.

2 PREPARE TO ABANDON SHIP Ensure everyone is wearing a life jacket, that the life raft is accessible and you have your grab bag (see precautions, opposite). Send a distress call (see box, below).

3 FIGHT THE FIRE Without compromising your safety, aim fire extinguishers at the base of the flames. Seal all hatches and vents to starve it of oxygen.

Sending a distress call

● **USE A DSC RADIO** If you have a DSC (digital selective calling) radio, press the red button to send an automatic distress signal to the coastguard and commercial ships in the area. Follow the distress alert with a Mayday call.
● **SEND A MAYDAY MESSAGE** Make sure that all crew members know how to send a Mayday message on Channel 16 (DSC and VHF). Give the boat name, your position, the nature of the emergency and number of people on board.

▶▶See also: **BURNS AND SCALDS** p23 • **INHALING FUMES** p44–45

storm at sea

A storm at sea in a small boat can be dangerous, even for an experienced sailor. In the UK in 2008, nearly 8,000 people had to be rescued by the Royal National Lifeboat Institution (RNLI). Keep your boat in good order and prepare for all situations.

GET HELP Seek immediate assistance. Send a distress signal (see page 259) on a DSC (digital) radio, followed by a Mayday message on Channel 16 (DSC and VHF).

be aware

- Monitor the weather constantly. If a storm is forecast, stay in port or alter your course to avoid it, if possible.
- Ensure your boat is absolutely seaworthy. Any small failing, such as an ill-fitting hatch or an unreliable engine, could be disastrous in storm conditions.
- Make sure that the crew have practised a 'storm drill' and are confident that they can handle a boat in storm conditions.
- Ride out the storm in deep water if you are at sea when the storm hits. It is far safer than trying to enter port in bad weather.

Lightning precautions

Lightning can strike nearly 10km from a storm, so if you see a flash and can count to less than 30 before you hear the thunder, you are in range. Most sea-going boats have some form of lightning protection device, but if you are unsure, move to the centre of the boat, crouch down as low as possible and avoid touching anything that conducts electricity.

⚠ TAKE CARE

Ensure everyone is wearing foul-weather clothing and life jackets. Crew above deck need harnesses.

action

1 KEEP WATER OUT Seal and fasten all hatches, close ventilators and turn off the seacocks (valves) to sinks and the toilet to make the boat watertight.

2 PUMP THE BILGES DRY This empties the bilges of water and ensures the pump will work in the storm. Clear cockpit drains so water can drain out quickly.

3 PROTECT GEAR Make sure all equipment is stored securely where it will not be damaged or be a danger to the crew. Tie down anything loose on deck, such as the tender. Fasten cockpit lockers. Check emergency equipment, such as first-aid equipment, radio, flares and torches.

4 DELEGATE Give each crew member a specific job or responsibility for the duration of the storm.

5 DEPLOY A SEA ANCHOR Use this or a drogue (a conical-shaped device that is dragged behind a boat to reduce speed) to help stabilise the boat and keep the bow into the wind. Turn on your navigation lights.

6 SLOW YOUR SPEED Reduce your sail in good time before the storm hits. Slow your speed and head the boat into the wind, turning the boat at an angle, approaching 45 degrees, as you take each wave to reduce the chance of crashing down from the top. Take the same approach if motoring.

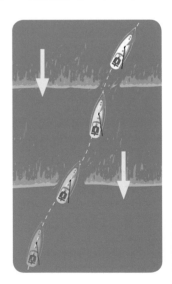

7 USE THE PUMPS Keep the bilges as dry as possible by pumping them out regularly throughout the storm. Extra weight here will increase the vessel's tendency to roll.

person overboard

A person can fall overboard at any time and in any conditions but it is a particularly serious emergency if the water is cold as hypothermia can swiftly set in. Whatever craft you are sailing, take precautions and practise a 'man overboard' routine regularly so that your response is automatic whether it is you that falls in, or you need to rescue someone else.

action

SOMEONE FALLS OVERBOARD

1 SHOUT 'MAN OVERBOARD' Select a crew member to keep the person in the water in view and point at him throughout the rescue.

2 REDUCE POWER Cut the engine or reduce the sail, maintaining enough speed to manoeuvre.

3 MARK THE POSITION If possible, throw the person a life buoy and line. Use an underarm throw for greater distance and accuracy. Fenders or cushions can also be used. If the boat has satellite navigation with a 'Man Over Board' (MOB) function, use it to mark the position of the accident.

4 USE FLARES At night set off flares as necessary to locate the person in the water.

5 RAISE THE ALARM Even if you make a recovery, the person may need medical help.

6 APPROACH THE PERSON Turn the boat around so the course is 180 degrees from the original course.

7 HELP THE PERSON OUT OF THE WATER If you have a boarding ladder, help the person up the steps. Otherwise, attach a halyard (a rope that hoists the sails) to his life jacket or harness, or throw him a line with a loop in the end to secure under his arms, then pull him back on to the boat.

 WARNING

● Send out a distress signal as soon as someone falls overboard in case you lose sight of the person in the water or are unable to make a rescue.
● Do not attempt to recover a person overboard using a stern ladder in rough seas, because of the danger posed by the engine's propeller. Recover them from the side of the boat using a halyard.

YOU FALL OVERBOARD

1 STAY CALM If the water is cold you will initially go into cold shock and your breathing will speed up. Tread water and try to get your breathing under control. Turn your back to the waves and tighten any wrist or ankle closures on your clothing to reduce heat loss.

2 SHOUT AND WAVE Attract the attention of the crew on the boat with your whistle and light, if you have one, so they can get a clear fix on your position.

3 HOLD YOUR POSITION Do not try to swim after the boat. Save your strength, look for a life buoy that may be thrown and let the boat come back to you.

 TAKE CARE

If you are motoring towards someone in the water, approach slowly, bow or side on: never back towards him. When close by, put the engine into neutral.

Safety on a boat

● Always wear a buoyancy aid or life jacket.
● Never overload a boat or carry more people than its safe capacity.
● Take care when moving about in a small boat, as changes to the weight distribution can easily make the boat tip.
● Wear life jackets and harnesses in rough water and at night. Carry a whistle and light.
● Ensure all guard rails are sturdy and in good order. Treat slippery surfaces with non-skid paint or grip strips.

caught in lightning

Lightning is one of Nature's more dramatic special effects. But if you are out in the open, it can pose a real hazard; 30–60 people are struck by lightning in Britain each year. Taking the right action can reduce your chances of a strike.

WATCHPOINT If you are part of a group, spread out so that you are at least 6m apart. This means that if anyone is struck there should still be someone to offer first aid or call for help.

be aware

• Check the weather forecast before setting out on a hike. Thunderstorms tend to be more common in summer than winter and occur more frequently in the afternoon.
• Seek shelter in a safe place, such as a building or vehicle, as soon as you hear thunder. Lightning can strike as far as 16km away from a thunderstorm and can literally come out of a clear blue sky.
• Obey the 30–30 rule. If thunder follows lightning within 30 seconds, the storm is less than 10km away and you need to get inside urgently. Do not go out again until 30 minutes after the last thunder clap.

Person struck by lightning

Anyone struck by lightning will need urgent first aid. There is no risk to you from touching the casualty so check that he is breathing and give CPR if necessary (see pages 16–17). Keep him warm. Treat burns as you would those from any other source (see page 23).

⚠ TAKE CARE

• Once inside a building, stay away from the plumbing, electrical appliances and the telephone.
• Avoid smaller structures with no plumbing or wiring to direct lightning to earth as they may draw a strike without affording you sufficient protection.
• Vehicles can offer protection, but once inside, take care not to touch any metal parts.
• If sheltering in a tent, stay as far as possible from metal poles. Choose a campsite where tents are not erected on the highest land.
• Motorbikes and bicycles also attract lightning. Get off and shelter until the storm is over.

action

■ **IF YOU ARE IN, ON OR NEAR WATER** Get out and move away from the water at once. Swimmers are at extreme risk from lightning as even if they are not struck directly, water is such a good conductor that they risk electrocution if lightning strikes nearby.

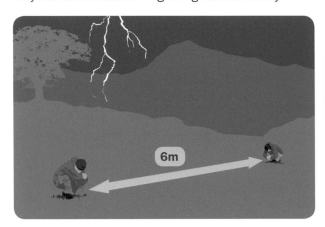

■ **IF YOU ARE NEAR A TALL OBJECT** Lightning will generally hit the highest good conductor. Make sure that it is not you: crouch, or lie, down and move well away from tall trees, rock spires or metal fences. Once lightning has hit something, the bolt of electricity can either jump sideways or run along the ground so **leave at least six metres between you and another person, or any higher object**.

■ **IF YOU ARE PLAYING GOLF** Golfers are frequently struck by lightning as they are often out in the open with metal clubs and umbrellas, which turn them into excellent conductors. Stop playing at once. If you can not make it to the club house, abandon your clubs and crouch down in a bunker with your head tucked in.

■ **IF YOU ARE RIDGE WALKING OR RUNNING** Immediately move to lower, less open ground. Although single tall trees should be avoided, sheltering among a plantation of more or less equal height trees is safer than remaining out in the open.

falling from a **cliff**

Towering cliffs are often prone to collapse, making them hazardous to climb and unsafe to walk along. When someone falls from a cliff, knowing how to respond will be critical and will ensure you do not become a casualty too.

GET HELP Call the emergency services immediately if someone has fallen down a cliff or mountain. They will coordinate the rescue, including a helicopter, if necessary.

action

YOU FALL OFF A CLIFF

■ **IF YOU LOSE YOUR FOOTING** Try to twist your body so that it faces the cliff and reach for anything solid that you can hold on to on the cliff top. Call for help.

■ **IF YOU ARE FALLING** Try to keep your limbs as loose as possible to reduce injury. If you have any control over your movement, try to slow your fall by grabbing at anything you can, such as any bushes or roots that might protrude from the cliff.

■ **REACHING THE BOTTOM** Try to roll and tumble. Although this will not protect you from injury, it may reduce the severity of a hard impact. Protect your head with your arms and hands.

■ **MAKE YOUR POSITION SECURE** Once you have stopped moving, try to make your position safe by finding more secure finger and foot holds. If the cliff face is soft, try to excavate these holds by gouging or kicking the cliff face. If you have a pocket knife, use it to make deeper, more effective hand holds.

■ **STAY CALM** Once you are secure, try to relax and decide on your next action. If you are uninjured and fit, your best option may be to climb up or climb down. If you are injured or are not a competent climber, stay put and await rescue.

SOMEONE ELSE FALLS OFF

1 DO NOT RUSH TO THE EDGE If possible, lie down some way back and ask someone to hold your ankles as you crawl towards the edge.

2 TRY TO LOCATE THE PERSON Shout out to him if possible, to see if he is conscious.

3 TRY TO PULL HIM UP If he is stuck just below the edge, try to hold out something you can pull him up with, such as a branch, a dog lead, wire fencing or an item of clothing. But make sure that someone else is holding you or that you are tied to something secure – a tree or telegraph pole, for example. If the person is too far down, try to find out if he is injured and tell him that you will get help.

4 CALL THE EMERGENCY SERVICES If you cannot pull him up or he has fallen to the base of the cliff, call 999. Tell the emergency services exactly where the accident has occurred.

5 THROW A LIFE LINE If you can find some rope or wire, make a large loop in the end and lower it down to him. Get him to put his arms through the loop and tighten it. Even if you cannot pull him up, by tying the rope to something secure, you can help ensure that he remains safe until rescued.

precautions

● Follow basic outdoor safety rules: dress appropriately, tell someone where you are going and when you expect to be back, carry a whistle and a mobile phone.
● Do not follow cliff-top paths blindly. If the path wanders too close to the edge or the ground appears at all unstable, move inland at once.

● Keep dogs on a lead when walking on cliffs and do not walk near the edge.
● Stay alert for crumbling or slumping cliffs. High tides and storms both weaken cliff faces.
● Only climb a cliff if you are competent, have the proper safety equipment and know that the cliff is made of a stable rock.

stranded on a mountain

Every year rescue teams attend to hundreds of people who get into difficulties while climbing a mountain. Even the best equipped walkers and climbers can suffer an injury or become separated from their party. To prevent a mishap – whether a twisted ankle or a sudden change in the weather – from becoming a life-threatening emergency, plan and prepare thoroughly.

precautions

● Gather and study every piece of information you can about your proposed route, from maps, photographs, accounts from other walkers and climbers, and the internet.

● Get the most accurate weather forecast you can and check with other climbers on unusual local conditions you might expect.

● Never rely on a GPS device alone. Always take a map and compass.

● Do not hike or climb in the mountains alone. Make sure that you tell others where you are going and when they can expect you back.

● Carry a full pack with emergency equipment and supplies (see right).

● Always be ready to change your plans. Do not 'carry on regardless' to the summit or next waymark, if it would be dangerous to do so. Safety must always be your first priority.

● Ensure your mobile phone is charged in case you are in an area where you can get a signal.

WHAT TO TAKE

● Sufficient food and water for approximately twice as long as you expect the hike to take. The colder the conditions, the more food you should take.
● Iodine water-purifying tablets or water filter
● First-aid kit
● Head torch and spare batteries
● Spare clothes, waterproofs, warm hat, gloves
● Emergency shelter and sleeping bag
● Fire-lighting equipment
● Knife, rope and mobile phone

 WARNING

Weather in the mountains can change dramatically from one hour to the next and even one hill to the next. In the UK, the Met Office gives Mountain Area Forecasts twice daily for each major mountain area of the UK. These include risk levels for snow, wind, chill effect, rain and thunderstorms.

GET HELP Call the emergency services and ask for the police and then mountain rescue. Try to give details of your location (including grid reference if possible) and details of injuries.

TIME TO ACT Keep an eye on the time and the light. Night can fall fast in the mountains and it may become bitterly cold very quickly.

WATCHPOINT Make sure that you allow time to make your way down from anywhere that is high or dangerous before the light goes. Walking in the dark can be extremely hazardous.

CANNOT DESCEND MOUNTAIN

1 MAKE A DECISION The most important action is to accept when it is safer to remain on the mountain than to continue walking in the dark, through very bad weather or with an injury.

2 KEEP WARM Depending on your location and the time of year, keeping warm is likely to be your top priority (see box, below). Be aware of signs of hypothermia (see page 46), which include shivering, feeling cold and confusion.

3 DESCEND IF POSSIBLE If conditions permit, descend as far as you can before darkness falls or the weather closes in. It will be warmer lower down. As you walk, look for a sheltered site for your camp.

4 CONSERVE ENERGY Walk as steadily as you can to conserve energy and avoid perspiring too much. When resting, do not sit directly on snow or ice.

5 DRINK WATER Drink from a stream in preference to eating snow if you are thirsty. Snow will make you feel colder and will not provide as much liquid.

Keeping warm

- **COVER YOUR HEAD** Wearing a hat is essential as you can lose more than 50 per cent of your body heat from your head.
- **FIND SHELTER** Get out of the wind to reduce wind chill or erect an emergency shelter (see page 267).
- **LIGHT A STOVE** A stove will warm a small shelter quickly. Heat water to make a warm drink, which will raise your core temperature.
- **REASSESS YOUR CLOTHING** If you have a damp layer next to your skin, consider replacing it with dry clothing which will make you feel warmer.

PERSON WITH HYPOTHERMIA

1 STOP AND FIND SHELTER Protect the casualty from the cold and wind, ideally inside a shelter or a tent. Replace wet clothing with dry if you have any. Do not give him your clothes as you need to stay warm.

2 PROTECT THE CASUALTY FROM THE GROUND If you cannot find shelter, lay the casualty on a layer of dry material, such as leaves, to insulate him from the ground. Wrap him in a sleeping bag and/or blanket to keep his head and body warm. Hug him gently using your body heat to prevent further heat loss.

3 WARM UP GRADUALLY If there is no danger of the casualty getting cold again, warm him up gradually. Give him a warm (not hot) drink or energy-giving carbohydrates, such as chocolate, to eat.

4 GET EMERGENCY HELP The casualty will need to be taken to hospital by stretcher. If you are in a remote place and cannot call the rescue services using a mobile phone, someone may need to go for help. If possible, one person should stay with the casualty and two should go together for help. If there are just two people in the party, make the casualty as comfortable as possible, make a note of his location (see page 268) and go for help.

surviving a **night outside**

When conditions force you to spend an unplanned night outdoors, finding shelter will rapidly become a top priority. If you have a tent, bivouac or tarpaulin with you, you will have a head start. If not, then you must look to your environment to furnish you with adequate protection from the elements.

precautions

- Make sure that your kit contains a knife, some fire-lighting equipment and a torch, as well as a first-aid kit, whenever you undertake an outdoor activity in the open countryside.
- Include a survival bag. This lightweight sack is waterproof and has some thermal insulation. It can be used as a groundsheet or as an improvised tent and can help to prevent (or treat) hypothermia (see page 46).

assessment

- Assess the climate. What poses the biggest threat: cold, rain, wind or all three? Work out the wind direction so that you can build your shelter in the lee of a slope or rockface.
- Assess your environment. Check for dangers, such as rockfalls and dead trees, and for animal hazards, such as ticks, ants, hornets – or scorpions or snakes.
- Use the lie of the land to make a shelter. Look for a natural shelter, such as a safe cave or crevice. Add rocks or snow (and your backpack) to raise the height of a small ridge or bank. Avoid valley bottoms and deep hollows, which are colder and liable to frost and mist, and dry riverbeds, which may be prone to flash floods.

 WARNING

If there are large predators, such as bears, in the area and you have food with you, put the food in a bag – preferably sealed – and hang it from a high branch well away from your camp.

action

NIGHT IN THE WOODS

1 **CHOOSE YOUR SITE** Choose a dry, sheltered site that is not in an area that is boggy. Align your shelter so that its back faces the prevailing wind.

2 **MAKE AN A-FRAME** Find a long, sturdy branch for a ridgepole and two shorter branches to push into the ground to form an 'A'. Push one end of the ridgepole into the ground and tie the other on top of the 'A'.

3 **CREATE WALLS** Fix more branches to the ridgepole at intervals along each side then weave long flexible twigs and branches between them. Fill in the gaps with a thatch of leafy evergreen branches, heather or dried bracken or grass. Cover the floor with ferns or conifer branches for warmth.

TIME TO ACT Allow yourself time to find or make a shelter while it is still light. In most situations, shelter and warmth are the two most important factors for survival.

WATCHPOINT If two of you are digging a snow cave, one should remain outside in case of collapse. Always keep your shovel with you inside the cave so you can dig yourself out.

GET HELP If you experience hypothermia or frostbite, call 999 in the UK, 112 in Europe or 911 in the USA. Give your location, the nature of the problem and phone number.

NIGHT IN THE SNOW

1 FIND A SITE FOR A SNOW CAVE Look for an established snow drift with a firm crust near a ridge or trees. The drift needs to be at least 1.2–1.5m deep. Avoid freshly fallen or powdery snow.

2 DIG AN ENTRANCE TUNNEL Use a shovel, snow shoe or your hands to dig a 1m tunnel into the snow drift on the leeward (sheltered) side of the drift.

3 EXCAVATE A SMALL CAVE Make a lower entrance, where cold air can collect, and a higher ledge that is large enough for you to sit on. Keep the walls at least 45cm thick and create a smooth, domed roof for strength and to prevent meltwater dripping.

4 MAKE AN AIR HOLE Use a stick or ski pole to make a vent in the roof at least 5cm in diameter. Line the floor of the ledge with conifer boughs for warmth and mark your snow cave with branches, skis or clothes placed outside to make you visible. Block the entrance with your backpack.

 TAKE CARE

When you build a snow cave, always consider the avalanche risk (see pages 192–193). Do not shelter on, or near the base of, a slope of 30–50 degrees, especially in moderate to high winds after a snow fall, in rain or when overnight temperatures rise above freezing.

MAKING A FIRE

■ **OUTDOOR FIRE** Locate your fire close to your shelter where it is not a fire risk to your shelter or trees. Build up the fire in the shape of a tepee with dry grass, wood shavings or pine needles as tinder, then small twigs as kindling. Set light to the tinder and, once the fire is going, add fuel that burns more slowly, such as dry logs or dried animal dung.

■ **USING A STOVE** A stove will quickly warm a snow cave. Place at the lower level (see left), but make sure that your ventilation hole stays open and never go to sleep with the stove still lit.

Makeshift shelters

● **A-SHAPED TENT** A rectangular tarpaulin, emergency blanket or poncho take up little space in a pack and can quickly be transformed into a shelter. Simply lay a tarpaulin or blanket over a line tied between two trees and peg out the lower edges to create a simple tent (above). Most tarpaulins have eyelets for this purpose. Use a Mylar sheet as a groundsheet for warmth.
● **USE A SURVIVAL BAG** Find somewhere sheltered, then put the survival bag over your head, cut small air holes at head height so you can breathe and sit upright inside it. Sit on your backpack to insulate your body from the ground.

▶▶See also: **HYPOTHERMIA** pp46–47 • **FROSTBITE** p47 • **ENCOUNTERING A BEAR** pp310–311

lost in a wild area

Walkers and hikers are drawn to isolated woodlands, mountains and outback areas to test their mental and physical strength, but losing your way a hundred kilometres from the nearest settlement can have disastrous consequences. Survival in this situation comes down to making a few simple decisions correctly.

precautions

- Planning, preparation and practice are all crucial to your safety. If you are new to wilderness walking, take as much expert advice as you can. Plan and check your routes, research the weather conditions, make sure that you have all the equipment and clothing you will need – and ideally rehearse all your skills, from map reading to fire lighting, in a safe location.
- Make sure key pieces of equipment – such as maps, compasses and GPS devices – are at least duplicated within the party. Never keep them together in the same bag or tent.

- **Do not travel alone and make sure someone knows where you are going** and when you expect to arrive so that they can raise the alarm if you fail to arrive within a given period.
- Keep a note of the time and distance you have walked, and check your position frequently.
- Turn around every so often to get a feel for how the path looks from the other direction. Take photographs with your mobile phone or with a digital camera of the path and waymarks of interest that you pass in case you have to find your way back along the route.

action

LOST YOUR WAY

1 STOP As soon as you realise that you may have gone the wrong way, stop. The next decision you make may well be the most important. So take your time. Stop for a drink, a rest or a meal or even camp for the night. Consider your position carefully.

2 LOOK FOR LANDMARKS
If you still have your map and compass, look around and try to identify two or, ideally, three landmarks, such as mountain peaks, that you can find on your map. Circle them with a pencil. If you are travelling in a group, make sure that everyone agrees that you have correctly identified the features on the map.

3 TRIANGULATE YOUR POSITION Align your map and compass to north, and then turn the base of your compass so its direction of travel arrow points to your first landmark. Now draw a line on your map from the landmark at this angle. Repeat the process for the other landmarks. The triangle where the lines cross shows your position.

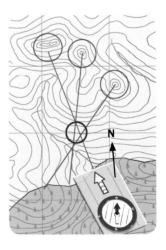

4 GUESS INTELLIGENTLY If you cannot triangulate your position, think back to when you were last certain of where you were. Average walking speed is 4.5km/h, so draw a circle around your last position with a radius that is the number of kilometres you could have travelled from that point. Try to locate a linear landform on the map, such as a river or ridge that you can see, and walk towards it.

GET HELP A mobile phone is unlikely to work in remote areas. If you plan to spend time in this kind of place, consider renting a satellite phone, which works almost anywhere.

TIME TO ACT In wilderness areas, night can fall very quickly. It is better to make camp early rather than risk getting lost or injured by carrying on in poor light.

NO COMPASS

1 USE YOUR WATCH AND THE SUN Where the sun is visible, set a watch that has a face and hands (rather than a digital watch) to true local time, taking daylight savings into account. If you have a digital watch, make a drawing of the time showing a traditional watch face and hands.

2 FIND DUE SOUTH In the northern hemisphere, point the hour hand at the sun. Due south is found mid-way between the hour hand and the numeral 12. In the southern hemisphere, point the numeral 12 at the sun. Due north is found mid-way between 12 and the hour hand.

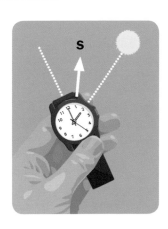

USE SHADOWS TO NAVIGATE

1 USE A LONG STICK AND THE SUN Find a long stick and push it into the ground. Ideally, it should be at least 1m long and upright. Mark the end of the stick's shadow with a stone. Wait for three hours and mark the end of the new shadow with a stone.

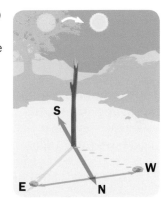

2 DRAW YOUR COMPASS POINTS Draw a line between the two stones to give you an east–west line. To find north–south, mark a line at 90 degrees to the east–west line, taking it through the centre of the line and the middle of the stick.

Emergency signals and codes

If injury or other circumstances make it impossible for you to carry on, one option is to stay put and signal for help. This strategy makes most sense when you have informed someone of your journey, who will raise the alarm when you do not arrive. Most search and rescue missions in remote areas are done from the air. There are several actions you can take to help the search.

● **MAKE YOURSELF VISIBLE** Select a location where you will be seen, such as a rocky outcrop or open hill top.
● **BUILD A SIGNAL FIRE** By day, throw damp vegetation onto the fire to produce smoke. At night, use drier wood that will burn brightly.
● **USE A MIRROR** Signal to passing aircraft using a mirror to reflect sunlight.
● **USE FLARES** Set off smoke flares to identify your location to passing aircraft.
● **LAY OUT LARGE MESSAGES** Use whatever contrasting materials are to hand to lay out signals on the ground. SOS is the universal distress signal but where space or materials are limited, a simple I means someone is injured, while an X means you are stranded and unable to move; F means you need food and water. A triangle is also recognised as a distress symbol.

TAKE CARE

If you are travelling in remote areas abroad, consider taking a Personal Locator Beacon (PLB). This is a small, phone-sized transmitter that can send out a distress signal and identify your location, via satellite, to the rescue services. Although in the UK you can only legally use a PLB at sea, in many countries their use is permitted on land and water.

▶▶See also: **HEAT-RELATED ILLNESS** pp48–49 ● **DEHYDRATION** pp50–51

poisonous plants

One of the most common causes of accidental poisoning is the consumption – usually by children – of poisonous plants. A surprising number of familiar plants contain dangerous poisons. It is worth learning to recognise the common culprits, including deadly nightshade and mistletoe, and the symptoms they produce.

precautions

- When out and about try to keep children well away from potentially poisonous plants. This is particularly important if the plant produces attractive fruits.
- Teach children not to eat anything that is not a recognised food.
- Never pick or eat wild mushrooms. It is difficult to identify mushrooms accurately and some cause death very quickly and have no known antidote.
- Cover up when working near plants known to be a skin irritant. Wear long-sleeved tops, trousers and gloves.
- Familiarise yourself with the symptoms of plant poisoning (see chart, opposite) so that you can seek medical advice promptly.

Poison ivy

Widespread in North America, poison ivy and the shrubs poison oak and sumac all produce a resin called urushiol that causes severe burning, itching and blistering on contact with skin. The more quickly you treat it, the less severe the rash will be.

1 CLEANSE If possible, cleanse the affected areas with surgical spirit within 10 minutes of exposure. Then wash in plain water.

2 TAKE A SHOWER As soon as you can, take a warm shower, using soap to wash thoroughly. Then put on gloves and wipe all clothing and other items you had with you with surgical spirit.

3 TAKE ANTIHISTAMINES If the rash develops, take antihistamines. In severe cases, seek medical help: oral steroids may be prescribed.

action

POISONED BY A PLANT

1 ASSESS THE SITUATION If an adult or child appears to have eaten a possibly poisonous plant, make sure that any remaining plant material is removed from his mouth. **Keep whatever you extract or get him to quickly identify the plant he has eaten.** Before going to hospital, collect a sample in a container to help medical staff diagnose the problem. It is also helpful to take any prescribed medication that the casualty is taking.

2 MAKE SURE THE PERSON IS SAFE If he is conscious and breathing normally, sit him down with a receptacle in case of vomiting and call your local Accident and Emergency Department, NHS Direct (England and Wales) or NHS24 (Scotland) for advice. These are all supported by the National Poisons Information Service and will be able to give medical advice.

3 CALL THE EMERGENCY SERVICES If the person is drowsy or unconscious, put him in the recovery position (see page 15) and call the emergency services immediately. You should also call the emergency services if he has swelling of the mouth, face or tongue.

4 PROVIDE INFORMATION If possible, tell the emergency services the name of the plant eaten, when it was ingested and how much was eaten, and whether the person is conscious. Take their advice and while you wait for help, monitor the casualty's condition.

■ **IN CASES OF SEVERE SKIN IRRITATION** Go to your GP or local Accident and Emergency Department with a sample of the plant or plants you suspect may have caused the reaction.

RECOGNISING POISONOUS PLANTS

Many plants contain poisons, which cause symptoms from contact dermatitis to vomiting, diarrhoea, heart or respiratory problems, headache, hallucinations, coma and death. These are some of the most common.

PLANT NAME	DESCRIPTION
Castor oil plant *Ricinus communis*	A woody garden shrub with glossy, star-shaped green/bronze leaves. Its bean-like fruits, produced in clusters at the top of the plant, contain the poison ricin. A few seeds can be fatal.
Daphne *Daphne sub-species*	A genus of deciduous and evergreen garden shrubs notable for their fragrant flowers and poisonous berries.
Deadly nightshade *Atropa belladona*	A branching perennial wild plant with purplish stems, large leaves and dull purple flowers followed by black berries. All parts are poisonous. One leaf or 2–5 berries can be fatal for a child.
Foxglove *Digitalis purpurea*	Found wild and in gardens. Spikes of colourful tubular flowers 30cm to 2m tall. The leaves can cause irregular heartbeat and digestive upset.
Hemlock *Conium maculatum*	1.5–2m tall wild plant with green stem, lacy leaves and umbels of small white flowers. Can be mistaken for parsley, fennel or wild carrot. All parts are poisonous, causing muscle paralysis.
Common thorn apple *Datura stramonium*	1m tall garden plant with long, violet or white trumpet-shaped flowers. The chambered seed pods are round and spiny. All parts of the plant are poisonous but especially the roots and seeds.
Mistletoe *Viscus album*	This parasitic plant grows high up in the branches of trees such as apple. Its berries can be extremely poisonous, causing intestinal pain, diarrhoea and even death to both children and adults.
Oleander *Nerium oleander*	A garden shrub or small tree with straight, dark green leaves and red, pink, white or yellow flowers. Produces brown seedpods. All parts contain a heart stimulant similar to digitalis.
Rhubarb *Rheum rhaponticum*	Red-stemmed perennial grown for its edible stems. The large green leaves contain oxalic acid and can cause convulsions and coma.
Wisteria *Wisteria sub-species*	A woody garden climber with pendulous purple or white racemes. Its seeds are produced in pods and are capable of causing severe digestive upset.
Death camas *Zigadenus sub-species*	Standing up to 70cm tall, the long grass-like leaves and cream and white flowers grow from a bulb that resembles an onion but does not smell like one. All parts of this garden plant contain highly poisonous alkaloids.

DAPHNE

DEADLY NIGHTSHADE

COMMON THORN APPLE

OLEANDER

WISTERIA

DEATH CAMAS

▶▶See also: **UNCONSCIOUS ADULT/CHILD/BABY** pp14–19 • **ACCIDENTAL POISONING** pp114–115

breakdown in the desert

The desert landscape is a hostile environment for people. There is very little water, temperatures can be extreme – both hot and cold – and settlements are few and far between. So if you're taking a trip that involves driving through a desert, you need to take every precaution to avoid breaking down – and know how to cope if you do.

precautions

● Make sure that your vehicle is thoroughly serviced. Ensure that the tyres, including the spare, are in good condition and inflated to the recommended pressure for desert driving (usually slightly lower than normal driving).

● Take tools and a spares kit, including a powerful torch, fan belt, radiator hoses, a second spare tyre. Carry a shovel in case blown sand blocks the road.

● Pack extra food and water – ideally twice as much as you expect to need for the trip. In desert conditions you should allow 5 litres of water per person per day.

● Pack a large sheet of thin polythene and a 2m length of tubing in case you need to build a solar still (see box, right). A sheet measuring 2 x 4m is enough for two stills.

● Take a first-aid kit with extra sun block and Mylar emergency blankets, which have a reflective surface that will help to keep you cool.

● Ensure everyone has sunglasses and hats as well as clothing appropriate for the conditions.

● Make sure that your phones are fully charged (carry a car or solar charger for back up) and ideally, check that you have network coverage across the area where you plan to travel.

● Tell someone when and where you are going and agree an estimated arrival time when you will call them again. Then if you do not call, they can alert the emergency services.

action

VEHICLE BREAKS DOWN

1 **STAY WITH YOUR VEHICLE** You are more likely to be rescued if you stay put. Drive or push your car to a place of safety beside the road.

2 **PUT THE BONNET UP** This is a clear sign that you have broken down. At night, if you have sufficient battery power, keep the hazard flashers on.

3 **CREATE AS MUCH SHADE AS POSSIBLE** Wedge towels, sheets or your emergency blankets along the top of the doors and then stake out the lower edges or secure them with rocks to create shelter.

4 **USE A MYLAR BLANKET** If your car is a dark colour, securing a silver Mylar blanket on the roof will help keep it cooler by reflecting the sunlight and it will make it easier to spot. Drape a brightly coloured garment over the boot or bonnet to make your vehicle more conspicuous.

STRANDED IN THE DESERT

■ **FIND SHADE** Your overriding priority is to stay cool and help your body to conserve water. Stay in the shade, limit physical activity until after dark, wear long-sleeved clothing and a head scarf to absorb sweat and cool your skin, and sit on a cushion or improvised seat instead of the hot ground.

■ **STAY HYDRATED** Although you may need to ration your water, you do need to drink regularly to avoid dehydration. **Sip water at regular intervals; do not wait until you are thirsty as you will already be dehydrated**. Your body needs about a litre of water an hour in temperatures above 38°C (100.4°F). Build a solar still to provide drinking water (see box, right).

■ **CONSERVE WATER** If water is in short supply, eat less food to limit the amount of water you need for digestion and moisten your lips and mouth before swallowing. To conserve as much bodily moisture as possible, keep your clothes on, move about as little as possible during the day, eat less and do not smoke or drink alcohol.

■ **LOOK OUT FOR SANDSTORMS** Keep your nose and mouth covered and wear goggles if you have them. Stay in your shelter and wait for it to pass.

 WARNING

Do not be tempted to drink the water from your car's cooling system unless you know that it only contains water. The cooling systems of most modern cars are filled with a mixture of water and antifreeze all year round – and antifreeze, despite being sweet tasting, is highly poisonous.

 **TAKE CARE**

● If you do not drink enough water you are likely to get heat exhaustion (see pages 48-49), heat cramps and heat stroke, which can be fatal.
● Monitor your urine colour: if it is light, you are drinking enough fluid; it if is dark, you need to increase the amount of water you are drinking.
● Recycle your urine in a solar still to produce more drinking water.

Building a solar still

A solar still will generate valuable drinking water. Make sure that you carry the equipment needed (see precautions, left).

1 **SELECT A SPOT IN DIRECT SUN** Look for a dry riverbed (wadi), sandy wash or depression where water might collect and dig a few sample holes. Check for moisture in the subsoil.

2 **DIG A HOLE** Once the sun goes down, extend the hole to 1m across by 1m deep, with gently sloping sides. Lay any vegetation on the sides, urinate in the hole and add dirty water: the still will only capture pure, evaporated water.

3 **INSERT A CONTAINER** Fix a cup or bowl in the centre of the hole. Run a length of tubing from the container out of the hole to allow you to drink without dismantling the still.

4 **COVER THE HOLE** Stretch polythene over the top and secure the edges with sand to make the still airtight. Put a small, smooth stone in the middle so that it dips down to a point just above – but not touching – your container.

5 **WAIT FOR THE SUN** The sun will evaporate the moisture in the hole so it condenses on the plastic sheet and drips into the container. Once the hole has become dry, repeat steps 1 to 5.

▶▶See also: **HEAT-RELATED ILLNESS** pp48–49 ● **DEHYDRATION** pp50–51 ● **SEVERE SUNBURN** pp52–53

falling through **thin ice**

Entering onto frozen bodies of water is extremely hazardous and should be avoided at all times. Over the last 10 years, 20 people have drowned after falling through ice in the UK and many more have been rescued. Children are particularly at risk. Much of the danger comes from the water's freezing temperature, which can swiftly lead to hypothermia.

precautions

- Never venture onto the ice in the UK. It is thin and can rarely support the weight of a person.
- Educate children about the dangers of ice.
- Ice over salt water is always potentially weaker than ice over fresh water.
- Be aware that ice under snow is potentially weakened.
- If you are travelling in a region such as Canada with the express intention of ice-skating dress appropriately, wearing layers of clothing for maximum warmth. Make sure that you take spare clothes, an emergency blanket, a vacuum flask with a hot drink and the means to light a fire.

 **WARNING**

The more pressure you put on the ice, the more likely it is to crack. Pressure is the effect of weight divided by area: if you stand on one leg, you double the pressure on the ice. **If you feel the ice beneath you cracking, lie down immediately and roll back the way you came.**

**TAKE CARE**

In the UK, half the fatalities caused by falling through thin ice occurred when someone was attempting to rescue another person or a dog. Never follow a dog onto ice as they are often able to scramble out on their own. Avoid throwing sticks or balls to dogs near frozen water.

Where walking on ice is traditional, always check with locals for safe areas.

action

YOU FALL IN

1 TRY NOT TO PANIC On contact with the icy water your body will go into cold shock and you will begin hyperventilating. Try to stay calm. Do not immediately try to get out. Tread water and lean back. Concentrate on keeping your head above the water and getting your breathing under control. You have plenty of time.

2 DITCH HEAVY ITEMS Remove a backpack, if you are carrying one, or anything else that is likely to pull you down. Do not remove clothing.

3 TURN Once your breathing has begun to normalise, turn to face the way you came, towards the ice that originally supported your weight.

4 TRY TO PULL YOURSELF OUT Lift your arms onto the ice and try to pull yourself as far out of the hole as you can. If you do not have enough strength to get all the way out, rest on your elbows and let some of the water drain off you as this will make you lighter. If you still cannot lift yourself out, try to swim out by kicking hard with your legs both to raise your body to the horizontal and provide extra propulsion. If possible, use a makeshift 'ice pick', such as car keys, a knife, a pen, or any other object on your person that would help you to grip the ice.

5 ROLL AWAY FROM THE HOLE Once out of the water, do not immediately try to stand up. Instead, roll on your side away from where the ice has cracked. The further away you roll, the safer you should be.

⚠️ TAKE CARE

● If you cannot get out of the water, lift as much of your body out as possible. You will lose less heat to the air than the water. If you hold your arms in one position on the ice, they should freeze in place and hold you up. Although you may lose consciousness, if you can avoid drowning you can survive for up to an hour – increasing the chance of rescue.

● When off the ice, return to a shelter or vehicle at once. Try to keep warm and phone for help.

SOMEONE ELSE FALLS IN

1 STOP If you follow someone who has fallen in, you may end up in the water with him. Shout and signal for help and try to get him to pull himself out (see left). If you have a phone, call the emergency services (see above).

2 FIND A RESCUE PROP If the person is having difficulty getting out of the water, try to find a way of pulling him out. If there is a house nearby, try to find a ladder, a rope or a long electrical extension lead. A long branch may also suffice.

⚠️ WARNING

A human chain, where a group of people lie down on the ice and inch forward carefully with each person holding the ankles of the one in front, should only be attempted on ice that is known to be thick and able to withstand the weight. Ice in the UK would not be thick enough for this. If a chain is attempted, the strongest, heaviest members of the group should remain furthest from the hole so they can pull everyone back should the ice begin to crack.

stuck in quicksand

The thought of being slowly sucked down into a bottomless pit of quicksand is, for many, the ultimate nightmare scenario. Fortunately, this fate is largely a figment of the imagination. Quicksand is real enough and it can exert a powerful pull, but it is seldom more than waist deep. So even when it cannot be avoided, escape is possible as long as you know how.

precautions

- Check your map for indications of boggy or waterlogged ground when you are planning a walk through an unfamiliar area. Organise your route to avoid these areas.
- If you are walking near water where there might be quicksand and carrying a pack, undo the waist or chest straps so you can slip out of it quickly should you need to.
- Avoid walking unfamiliar trails when you are alone.

- Carry a long stick so that you can check how firm the ground is in front of you.
- Ensure you always have a means of calling for help, such as a whistle, which you can wear around your neck so it is easily to hand.
- For quicksand to form, sand or similarly granular soil must become waterlogged. Keep a lookout for quicksand when you are walking near riverbanks, lake shores, beaches, marshes, springs and streams.

WARNING
Soft Sand & Mud

action

YOU GET STUCK

1 SIT DOWN If you take a step onto ground that instantly swallows up your boots, you may be able to save yourself if you immediately sit down or fall backwards. With your upper body still on dry land and less weight on your feet, it should then be easy for you to slowly pull your legs free.

2 DO NOT PANIC Even if you find yourself sinking deeper into the quicksand, try not to panic. The more you thrash about, the deeper you will sink and the more tired you will become. If you are wearing a backpack, try to remove it.

3 MOVE SLOWLY Your body is less dense than the quicksand. Try to stay relaxed and move slowly, as if you were swimming. If you lean back and slowly paddle your legs, you should find that you can push yourself gradually backwards.

4 DO NOT STAND UP Once you have released yourself, monkey crawl – army-style on your stomach, using your forearms and knees to propel you along – until you are on firm ground.

SOMEONE ELSE IS STUCK

1 TRY TO STOP THE PERSON PANICKING If he is carrying anything heavy, tell him to discard it.

2 REACH OUT Lie down at the edge of the firm ground and extend your arm or a branch for the person to hold on to. Get him to lean forwards on the surface of the quicksand and ease himself gradually out as you pull him slowly with a long, steady pull.

⚠ TAKE CARE

Quicksand forms where water saturates a sandy soil to the extent that the particles of sand are forced apart. This reduces the friction between the particles to the point where the sand behaves like a thick liquid. If you try to move quickly, you will find yourself fighting both the weight of the liquid sand and the suction effect caused by its viscosity. **Long, slow movements are always the most effective way to release yourself from its grip.**

TRAVEL EMERGENCIES

airport crises

A delayed or cancelled flight is stressful and can play havoc with your travel plans, while missing a flight or losing your luggage can ruin the start of your holiday. But it is possible to reduce the impact of these events, or even to avoid them.

WATCHPOINT Try not to book the last flight of the day because if it is cancelled there are fewer alternative flights. Early flights also tend to have fewer delays than later ones.

action

DELAYED FOR HOURS

1 TIME THE DELAY EU regulations require airlines to help passengers during delays. For short-haul flights, you are entitled to meals, refreshments and phone calls for delays of more than two hours; on long-haul flights, entitlements begin after four hours.

2 INSIST ON YOUR RIGHTS If a delay extends beyond five hours, passengers can choose not to travel and demand a refund. Airlines sometimes try to avoid paying, citing 'extraordinary circumstances' such as weather or 'safety reasons'. If necessary, consider pursuing the airline through the small claims court.

3 AVOID A MISSED CONNECTION Make sure that the airline knows that you have a connecting flight. Insist that it arranges another connecting flight before you accept any change to your travel plans.

4 CARE FOR CHILDREN There are no special conditions for children who are victims of delays. If you have children flying with you, make airline staff aware of this and tell them about any requirements the children might have, such as special foods.

Making complaints

Complaints are best resolved at the airport where staff can offer upgrades or give vouchers for meals or accommodation. If this fails:

- **WRITE TO THE AIRLINE** Include all flight details and copies – never the originals – of tickets, receipts and documents to back up your claim.
- **CONTACT THE INDUSTRY WATCHDOG** If you are still unhappy, complain to the Air Transport Users Council (AUC), the consumer watchdog for the aviation industry, at www.auc.org.uk.

CANCELLED FLIGHT

1 KNOW THE LAW EU regulations protect the passenger if a flight is cancelled less than 14 days before the scheduled departure, or if a flight has been overbooked and you cannot board.

2 SEEK AN ALTERNATIVE FLIGHT First ask the airline for a suitable alternative flight. If the flight is cancelled less than seven days before take off, the airline is duty bound to find you a replacement flight that arrives within two hours of the original flight. If it does not, you can still take the replacement flight and could be entitled to compensation of up to 600 euros. If your flight is cancelled between 7 and 17 days before you were due to fly, the flight must arrive no more than four hours later than the original flight.

3 IGNORE THE EXCUSES Do not accept excuses such as maintenance problems or crew shortages. Stand your ground. If a suitable replacement flight is not provided, ask to transfer to a different airline.

4 MAKE A CLAIM If you are unhappy with your treatment, make a claim against the airline citing EU regulation 261/2004. Before you do so, refer to the Air Transport Users Council website at www.auc.org.uk for full details of the regulations.

5 CONSIDER COURT ACTION If a claim cannot be settled amicably, you can consider going to a small claims court for compensation. Do check your travel insurance to see whether you are covered for flight delays or cancellations.

 TAKE CARE

Before you travel, ensure the name on your ticket matches the name on your passport. Arrive in good time to check in; late check-ins are more likely to result in mislaid baggage, or being denied boarding.

In the EU you are entitled to hotel accommodation if your flight is delayed overnight.

FLIGHT OVERBOOKED

1 CONSIDER OFFERS Airlines routinely offer free flights, upgrades or mileage bonuses to those who agree to a later flight so consider accepting an offer.

2 INSIST ON BOARDING It is your right to fly and if there are not enough volunteers, airlines can deny boarding to other ticket holders. EU passengers denied boarding are entitled to compensation of up to 600 euros in cash plus another flight.

MISSED FLIGHT

■ **NEGOTIATE WITH STAFF** It is up to you to get to check-in on time. You have no rights if you are late. Try to get on the next flight. Airlines often allow even passengers with cheaper, restricted tickets to switch flights. If later ones are fully booked, ask to fly to an alternative airport. Most airlines charge a flat 'rescue' fee for switching a flight plus the difference in fares. These fees are negotiable, so try to persuade check-in staff to waive the fee if you have a valid reason (see below) for missing your flight.

■ **CHECK YOUR POLICY** Make sure you read the small print, as insurers may only pay out if you have missed the flight in particular circumstances, such as a public transport failure or car accident.

LOST LUGGAGE

1 SEE IF BAGGAGE TURNS UP Airlines have effective systems for tracking luggage – around 98 per cent of misplaced bags are returned to users within hours.

2 REPORT THE LOSS Do this at the airport. Fill out a form even if the airline says the bag will be on the next flight. Make sure the airline agrees to deliver the bags to your address free of charge.

3 CLAIM FOR EXPENSES Most airlines will pay any reasonable expenses you incur while you wait for missing bags. Negotiate what these are in advance as you can only make this claim at the airport.

4 FILE A CLAIM If your luggage is not recovered within 21 days, it is deemed officially lost and you have to fill out a more detailed claim. The Montreal Convention lays down maximum compensation levels for lost baggage of around £970 per passenger, but payouts vary between airlines. It is worth checking the policy of your particular airline. If you are not happy with the settlement, complain in writing.

 WARNING

Bags are most likely to be lost on a transfer between connecting flights so fly direct if you can. Fix address and flight details inside and outside the bag.

▶▶See also: **HOLIDAY DISASTERS** pp280–281

holiday **disasters**

What are your rights if your holiday firm or airline goes bust? Or if your hotel is not as advertised, or disclaims all knowledge of your booking? In the past, industry-backed schemes provided protection. With internet booking, there is no guarantee of getting a refund, but you can reduce the risk by checking the firm you use has known guarantees and cover advertised.

precautions

- Book a package holiday. If the airline goes bust or the hotel closes, your tour operator is obliged to find an alternative or give you a refund (see box, below).
- **Travel bookings should always be made by credit card:** for purchases over £100 you have the right to claim a refund from your card provider if the service is not provided.

HOTEL BOOKINGS

- Pay with a credit card.
- Confirm the hotel booking in writing.
- If booking online, use companies that are accredited (see box, below).
- Find out what to expect. Read internet reviews or, even better, get advice from people you know who have been to that destination.

FLIGHT BOOKINGS

- Take out comprehensive travel insurance. Good policies include airline failure coverage.

Travel guarantees

These logos in holiday brochures and travel agents are a sign of security.

- **ABTA** Protection is provided if a member of ABTA (formerly Association of British Travel Agents) goes out of business but some exclusions can apply.

ABTA
The Travel Association

- **ATOL** (Air Travel Organisers' Licensing.) The Civil Aviation Authority will fly you home or refund your fare if the company fails as long as the firm has an ATOL licence.

ATOL PROTECTED

action

AIRLINE GOES BUST

■ **PACKAGE DEALS** If you bought a package holiday, your tour operator will protect you by providing an alternative flight or a refund, as applicable.

■ **OWN FLIGHT BOOKING** If you bought the tickets direct from the airline, you have no protection apart from a possible credit card or insurance claim.

■ **CLAIM ON YOUR CARD** Provided you bought the ticket on your credit card and it cost more than £100 you should be covered. If you purchased the ticket using a debit card, then the Consumer Credit Act does not apply. You may simply have to join the list of creditors, which will make it much more difficult to retrieve your money.

■ **CHECK YOUR INSURANCE** Some travel insurance policies include cover for scheduled airline failure (chartered flights are usually covered by an ATOL agent). If you have this in your policy, you should be able to claim a refund. Travel agents can offer you the ABTA Protection Plan, an insurance to protect against travel provider failure.

HOLIDAY FIRM GOES BUST

■ **HOLIDAY WITH FLIGHTS** If you bought a package holiday with flights from an ATOL holder then you are covered. ATOL will arrange to get you home or refund your money if the holiday company goes bust.

■ **HOLIDAY WITHOUT FLIGHTS** If you booked a package holiday that does not include flights you will be covered, most likely through ABTA. If you have booked through a travel agent and the company goes bust, you have more protection if you bought the holiday through an ABTA member. ABTA will ensure that the tour operator provides you with the holiday.

TIME TO ACT Call to confirm your hotel booking the day before you arrive. Like airlines, hotels tend to overbook assuming that someone will not show up at the last minute.

WATCHPOINT It is especially important to use a credit card when booking online. The card company is jointly liable if the supplier fails to provide the services you paid for.

UNACCEPTABLE HOTEL

1 BE CALM AND POLITE Report problems at once. Explain the problem clearly and concisely to the front desk staff. Do not exaggerate. Just be straightforward about how you want the fault rectified. A smile and a clearly stated solution will get the best results.

2 TALK TO SOMEONE IN AUTHORITY Determine whether the person you are talking to can resolve the problem. If not, ask to speak to the manager (at a hotel) or get in touch with the most senior tour rep (if you are on a package holiday). Most hotels will readily arrange a room swap if they have space. Tour reps may be able to transfer you to a different hotel.

Substandard facilities and noisy building work can be grounds for complaint.

3 GATHER EVIDENCE Keep a photo diary and send it to the tour company when you return with details of your complaint. ABTA members have 28 days to respond. Any compensation you get will depend on the extent to which your enjoyment of the holiday was spoiled by the problems you have recorded.

NO RESERVATION AT HOTEL

■ **CHECK YOUR BOOKING** Make sure that it is not a simple mistake such as a name misspelled in the register. It is essential to carry and show written confirmation of your booking.

■ **DEMAND A ROOM** Do not leave the front desk. Politely but firmly ask a manager for a room. Find out what alternative options are on offer.

■ **ASK FOR AN UPGRADE** Ask if there are any other types of rooms, such as suites, available, but do not pay more than your original guaranteed room rate even if you are given a better room.

■ **MOVE HOTEL** If the hotel wants to accommodate you at a nearby hotel, make sure it is not simply providing you with a cheaper alternative. It should agree to pay the cost of transferring to the hotel and any difference between room rates at the two hotels. It should reimburse you if the hotel you are moved to is a cheaper one.

■ **COMPLAIN IN WRITING** Write to the hotel management or booking agent upon your return setting out your full case together with all the evidence, including booking details. State that you intend to write about your experiences on travel review sites such as www.tripadvisor.com. Make sure that what you say on such a site is true, and you can back it up with evidence. If what you say is false and damaging, then you might be successfully prosecuted for libel.

 WARNING

You have far less financial protection if you book your own flights and hotels online, especially if you use companies that are not members of ABTA or ATOL. In this case, you will have to look to your insurer or credit-card provider if things go wrong.

▶▶See also: **AIRPORT CRISES** pp278–279

lost ticket or passport

If you do not have a ticket to fly, you may be turned away at the airport, while a lost passport will mean that you cannot book into many hotels, change money or even travel home. With careful planning you can minimise the impact of such losses, while ever-improving communications usually allow tickets and passports to be quickly replaced.

action

LOST PAPER TICKET

■ **PLEAD YOUR CASE** Test the goodwill of the check-in desk by arguing your case. **They might allow you to travel without a ticket if you can prove your identity and address, especially if you have a photocopy of the original ticket**. If they follow the rules, though, you will have to buy a new ticket.

■ **BUY A NEW TICKET** This may cost more than your lost ticket if you buy it just before you fly. You should be able to claim a refund for a higher-priced ticket when you file a lost ticket claim with the airline.

■ **SEEK A REFUND** Fill in a lost ticket application with the airline. Refunds can take anywhere between 30 days and as much as a year to come through.

■ **NEGOTIATE OVER FEES** Airlines vary in their policies but there is usually a processing charge of £30 or more. This may be worth challenging, especially if there are mitigating circumstances, such as the ticket being lost in the post.

■ **CONTACT YOUR INSURER** Depending on your travel insurance policy, your insurer may pay for any loss.

LOST OR STOLEN PASSPORT

1 GO TO THE POLICE Report the loss at once to the police. Make sure you get a police report.

2 GATHER YOUR ID Before you can get a passport from a British consul (see box, below), the consul will need verification of your identity and to be satisfied you are a British national. Take along as much identification as you can, but expect the consul to make further checks. This can delay travel plans. A photocopy of your passport can speed up the process, as can a photocard driving licence.

■ **EMERGENCY PASSPORT** To obtain an emergency passport, valid for one journey, call the nearest consulate and take the police report plus two passport-size photos and identification. Consulates may offer out-of-hours services to provide an emergency passport but this will involve an extra fee. Reclaim replacement costs on your insurance.

■ **PERMANENT PASSPORT** A consulate should be able to replace a permanent passport relatively quickly if you have sufficient identification.

precautions

TICKETS
● Buy an electronically issued e-ticket. You just need to prove your identity at check-in. Keep your confirmation number for a fast check-in.
● Photocopy all tickets. If it is an e-ticket, keep a paper receipt.

PASSPORTS
● Keep a photocopy of your passport. It will speed up the process of getting a replacement.

The British consul

A British consul can help British subjects abroad. Services include replacement of lost passports and help for Britons who have been detained or imprisoned, fallen ill or been the victim of a crime. A consul might be in the embassy (High Commission in Commonwealth countries) in a nation's capital or a consulate elsewhere. Look up contact details of the nearest consular service on the Foreign and Commonwealth Office website: www.fco.gov.uk/en/travel-and-living-abroad/find-an-embassy/

money problems abroad

If you are suddenly deprived of funds when cash is lost or stolen, or the bank blocks a credit card, it can ruin your holiday and leave you surprisingly vulnerable as you will not even be able to pay for essentials. But it is now very straightforward to get money transferred in an emergency – and there are a number of ways to safeguard your cash.

action

LOST OR STOLEN WALLET

1 RETRACE YOUR STEPS Once you report a missing credit card, the process cannot be reversed, so first check that the card really is lost. Do not delay. Quickly look over places that you have been and thoroughly search through all your belongings.

2 CALL YOUR INSURER OR BANK Most good insurers accept reverse-charge calls and will – while you are on the phone – cancel your cards and have new ones issued. If they are unable to do that, or you do not have the right travel insurance, phone your bank or credit-card company to cancel cards. Most have toll-free numbers. If you do not have the numbers use the internet or call the local directory enquiries.

3 FILE A POLICE REPORT Go to the nearest police station and file a police report. Make sure you get a copy – the insurance company will require one.

4 WIRE FUNDS If your insurer, bank or credit card company cannot provide emergency cash, you can get money wired from your bank through transfer companies such as www.westernunion.co.uk. The service is not cheap, but it can be set up in minutes.

CREDIT CARD REFUSED

1 FIND OUT WHY Call the card company (carry the number with you when you travel) to find out why the card has been blocked. Be aware that some cards are refused even when users have phoned to say they are going abroad (see For next time, right).

2 GET THE CARD UNBLOCKED Insist that the card is unblocked immediately. Much depends on the bank and the attitude of call-centre staff. Talk to a supervisor if you do not get results. Try to call on a toll-free number as phone charges can mount up.

Emergency money

Most consulates (see box, opposite) can give you advice on how to get funds transferred from home, but will not make cash payments unless it is an extreme emergency.

 TAKE CARE

Keep your money safe when you are out and about. For daily use, a money belt under the waistline of your trousers is the safest option. Do not carry all your money and cards in one place, such as in a handbag where it can be easily stolen, but spread them across several pockets, all with zips or Velcro.

for next time...

- Let the card company know you are going abroad. This may stop the card being blocked due to 'unusual' overseas transactions.
- Before you go on holiday, if you have access to webmail, email yourself your insurance policy number and all the credit card contact telephone numbers and account numbers. You can access the webmail at an internet cafe if you have lost all your papers.
- Do not keep all your cash in the same place. Keep an emergency supply of cash or travellers' cheques in the hotel safe.
- Make sure the bank has your up-to-date contact details, including mobile phone number. Banks are supposed to call before blocking.
- Take spare cash and credit card, travellers' cheques or a prepaid 'travel money card' from the Post Office as a back-up and leave them somewhere safe when you are out.

medical help abroad

Getting medical help overseas can be traumatic. Language problems, difficulties finding an English-speaking doctor, paying for treatment and worries about getting home, all add to the stress. Even if you have comprehensive health insurance there are steps you can take to improve the situation. If you are not covered by insurance, you still have options, albeit limited.

action

GETTING A DOCTOR

1 CALL THE EMERGENCY SERVICES For a serious injury or health problem get medical help at once by calling the emergency services. In all EU countries the number to call is 112; in the USA and Canada it is 911. Get to a hospital as fast as you can. If you are in a remote area, get to a major city, where you may find better health care, as soon as possible.

2 CONTACT YOUR REP OR TOUR GUIDE If your condition is not serious, but you still need help, contact your tour guide or holiday rep if you are on a package holiday. If you arranged the holiday yourself, talk to the hotel front desk or call the consular service (see page 282). All of these should have contact lists of doctors or other medical services.

3 FIND AN EXPERT The consular service can provide a contact list of English-speaking doctors, clinics and hospitals and their areas of expertise. Another useful source of information is the International Association for Medical Assistance to Travelers (IAMAT) www.iamat.org. This maintains a worldwide network of doctors who speak English.

4 GET IT IN WRITING Get written details of any treatment you have and any test results so you can show these to your GP at home.

Make sure your travel insurance covers you for sports such as skiing.

TIME TO ACT When travelling at high altitudes, you may get altitude sickness. If symptoms such as a headache, tiredness, dizziness and vomiting occur, it may be best to descend.

WATCHPOINT Time differences may require an adjustment in your medication schedule, especially with drugs, such as insulin. Ask your GP for advice before you travel.

PAYING FOR TREATMENT

■ **CONTACT YOUR INSURER** Call your insurer before going for treatment if possible. Do not assume you will be covered in private clinics. Depending on your policy, there may also be an excess to pay.

■ **CARRY YOUR POLICY DOCUMENTS** If using travel insurance, give your policy details to the hospital. Some doctors will charge you upfront and ask you to reclaim fees; others will recover costs themselves.

■ **USE YOUR EHIC** Access health care in Europe with a European Health Insurance Card (EHIC). Not all care is free – you may have to pay a share of the costs (see box, right).

■ **GET RECEIPTS** Use these for insurance claims.

GETTING HOME

1 ASK FOR HELP If you are on a package holiday, contact the tour rep, if not, call the airline direct, who may agree to waive the fees for switching flights to return home early on compassionate grounds.

2 CONTACT THE CONSULAR SERVICE In serious cases, the consular service (see page 282) can contact your friends or family in the UK, and will visit you in hospital and help to arrange your repatriation.

3 CALL YOUR INSURER Liaise with your insurer on anything that is likely to result in a claim, especially extra payments for getting you home early.

what next?

● Show all your medical notes to your doctor when you return home.
● If travelling abroad again soon afterwards, declare the medical incident on any travel policies you take out as failure to do so could invalidate the policy.

 TAKE CARE

Ask your GP for extra supplies of any prescribed drugs. These should be carried in your hand luggage. If you forget or lose your medicines, contact the consular service (see page 282). Note the generic name of any drug, as some brand-name drugs are not available abroad. Take the phone number of your GP and pharmacist in case you need to call them.

Medical cover

● Get a European Health Insurance Card (EHIC). This gives you the same state-provided health care as nationals for most European countries. Apply online at www.ehic.org.
● Take out comprehensive travel insurance. The EHIC card does not cover all treatments nor necessarily the full cost of all care. A good insurance policy will also cover the cost of relatives flying out and back in the case of emergency, as well as their hotel costs.

for next time...

● Consider having both a dental and a health check-up before you go, especially if you are going on a long trip.
● Get vaccinated. Find out what vaccinations are required at www.cdc.gov/travel. Your GP will advise on vaccination schedules.
● Take a letter from your GP about any pre-existing medical conditions. Get this translated or find someone to act as a translator if you cannot find an English-speaking doctor.
● Drinking contaminated tap water can cause sickness. If the water cannot be trusted and bottled water is unavailable, a battery-operated handheld water purifier, which uses ultraviolet light to kill bacteria, is a useful gadget.

car accidents abroad

Driving abroad really is more dangerous. You are twice as likely to die in a road accident in France; three times more likely in Portugal. In addition, you may be driving in a strange car on the wrong side of unfamiliar roads. Ensure that your insurance policy covers you for every eventuality and familiarise yourself with national conventions before travelling.

precautions

- Take frequent breaks when driving long distances. Stop the moment you feel sleepy.
- Watch your speed, especially in countries where speed limits are higher than in the UK. Do not be forced by other traffic to drive at speeds where you do not feel in control.
- Drive within the regulations and conventions of the country you are visiting (see page 288). Your chances of a fatal accident are far higher overseas. Many countries have much higher rates of fatal accidents than the UK.
- Talk through your insurance policy with your car insurer before you leave so you know exactly what is covered. You may be able to take out additional cover. Ensure you have adequate breakdown cover to provide roadside assistance and rescue and to deal with emergency repairs when overseas.

action

AVOIDING CRASHES

■ **DRIVING ON WRONG SIDE OF ROAD** If you are driving on the opposite side of the road, take extra care when you resume driving after a break. To avoid pulling off on the wrong side, stick a note somewhere where you cannot avoid seeing it, such as on the steering wheel, stating clearly which side of the road you should be driving on.

■ **WHEN OVERTAKING** Take extreme care when overtaking, especially in a right-hand-drive car in a country where they drive on the right as your ability to see oncoming traffic will be impaired.

■ **AT ROUNDABOUTS** At a roundabout, the driver inexperienced at motoring abroad may find the flow of traffic confusing and go the wrong way round. When driving on the right, go right at roundabouts.

When you are driving on the opposite side of the road to normal, take special care at roundabouts. Follow the directional arrows.

GET HELP Immediately call the emergency services – 112 in the EU; 911 in the USA and Canada – if anyone involved in an accident has been injured, no matter how slightly.

WATCHPOINT If you do not speak the language, insist on an interpreter in police interviews. If arrested, you are entitled to seek help from the British consul (see page 282).

AFTER A CRASH

1 STOP AT THE SCENE Get the other driver's full details, and names and contact details of witnesses. Photograph damage for use in any insurance claim.

2 CALL POLICE In most countries, police have to attend accidents involving foreign vehicles. You may be asked to sign a European Accident Statement, which is designed to help drivers exchange facts. Do not sign if you are not happy with the statement: it can be legally binding; ask your insurer if unsure.

3 REPLACE YOUR CAR Minor cosmetic repairs can usually wait until you return to the UK. If you cannot drive the car, the insurer can sort out repairs. Many comprehensive policies provide immediate car hire and will pay for the car to be shipped back to the UK or expenses to collect the repaired car overseas.

■ **HIRE CAR DRIVERS** Report the accident. Tell the police, your rental car firm and your own insurer. If the accident was not your fault, make sure this is clearly stated in the accident reports.

 WARNING

Before you hire a car, find out what the insurance covers. The basic package is usually only the legal minimum and may leave you liable for injury claims. Even extra insurance from the hire firm can still leave you liable for some damage to the car. It can be cheaper to take out separate hire car cover before you go – speak to your insurer.

YOU HIT A PEDESTRIAN

1 CALL EMERGENCY SERVICES The first priority is to help the victim, so call the emergency services (see Get Help, above). Protect the scene with warning triangles and get someone to redirect traffic around the injured pedestrian. Do not move the victim, but give reassurance that help is coming.

2 STAY AT THE SCENE You must stop at the scene of the accident and give your details if asked to do so.

3 GET WITNESSES Try to find people who saw what happened and are willing to testify on your behalf. Write down all names and addresses at the scene so that you can contact the witnesses later.

4 FIND A TRANSLATOR Ensure a translator is present at all police interviews. The consular service (see page 282) will have a list of English-speaking lawyers. Make sure they are used to dealing with road accident and personal injury claims.

Take your documents

Make sure you pack all the documents required for driving overseas, but do not leave them in your car in case it is stolen.

● **FULL UK DRIVING LICENCE** Provisional licences are not valid abroad. Take the paper counterpart as well if you have a photocard licence.
● **VEHICLE REGISTRATION DOCUMENT** Required in some countries if you are taking your own car.
● **MOTOR INSURANCE CERTIFICATE** Make sure that it covers where you are driving.
● **BREAKDOWN COVER DOCUMENTS** Take these with you in case you have to call for roadside help or help with repairs.
● **INTERNATIONAL DRIVING PERMIT** Required for hiring cars in some African and Asian countries.

▶▶See also: **MOTORING PROBLEMS ABROAD** p289

car accidents abroad

As if the trauma of an accident is not bad enough, there can be the added complication of dealing with an uninsured driver. Find out what you can do to get recompense in such a situation.

As insurance is a legal requirement almost everywhere you drive, you do have the law on your side, but there is specific action that you must take at the roadside.

action

HIT BY UNINSURED DRIVER

1 GET THE DRIVER'S DETAILS Write down the vehicle's registration number, make, model and colour. Ask for the driver's name and address, although these often prove to be fake for uninsured drivers.

2 GATHER EVIDENCE Take as many pictures of the damage and the scene as you can, including one with the other driver if possible. Note down anything the other driver said, what the conditions were and any details about the accident that might be useful, such as whether the other vehicle had its lights on if the visibility was poor.

3 INVOLVE THE POLICE Notify the police. Their report will form a vital part of your insurance claim.

■ **CALL YOUR INSURER** With a comprehensive policy, you will get your car repaired minus any excess. With a third party only policy, your insurer will not pay for your repairs and as the other driver is uninsured, there will be nothing to claim from his insurance.

■ **RECOVER YOUR MONEY** Never travel with just third party insurance. You will not get anything from the other driver unless you can trace him and succeed in a court action. Contact the Motor Insurers Bureau (www.mib.org.uk), a fund set up by the insurance industry to deal with cases involving uninsured drivers. You may have to pay an excess in any claim.

⚠ TAKE CARE

● Stop well off the road. If this is not possible, station someone to redirect traffic around you.
● If it is necessary to help someone or carry out repairs at the side of the road, do not turn your back to oncoming traffic.
● Put out warning triangles and wear a reflective jacket (see box, right).

Be prepared abroad

Motoring organisations have web pages that give advice for motorists driving abroad (see page 340). Be aware of the following before you drive abroad:

● **SERVICE SAFETY** Service your vehicle before leaving home. Check it complies with all the requirements of the countries you are visiting.
● **HEADLIGHTS** When driving on the opposite side of the road to the UK, headlights need to be adjusted so that the dipped beam will not dazzle motorists. Converter kits are available but a dealer may need to make the adjustment.
● **SAFETY EQUIPMENT** Warning triangles are compulsory in almost all European countries. Some countries insist that you have two, especially if towing a caravan. Reflective jackets must be worn in many countries if a car breaks down. A fire extinguisher is required in Greece and recommended elsewhere. In Spain you have to carry a spare set of bulbs and the tools to change them, as well as spare spectacles or contact lenses.
● **SPEEDING** Obey the limits and remember the speed-limit signs are usually in km/h not mph. Radar detectors are banned in most countries.
● **DRINK LIMITS** In Spain and France, the limit is 0.05 per cent of alcohol in the blood compared with 0.08 in the UK. In Sweden, it is just 0.02.
● **WINTER DRIVING** Winter tyres are either recommended or compulsory in many countries including Austria, Finland, Germany and Sweden. Chains are also advisable when driving in snowy conditions.

motoring problems abroad

The AA estimates that at least 150,000 drivers put the wrong fuel in their car every year – one every three-and-a-half minutes. It is bad enough at home as you can ruin the engine if you drive off, but is far more serious abroad. And globally, nearly 5 million cars are stolen annually, some belonging to unfortunate tourists who have taken their vehicle abroad.

action

FILLED UP WITH WRONG FUEL

1 **DO NOT START THE CAR If you realise you have filled up with the wrong fuel, avoid starting the engine. You could cause major damage.** Contact your breakdown recovery service (see Precautions, page 286) at once. If you have started the car, pull up and call your breakdown recovery service.

2 **WATCH FOR OVERCHARGING** You will need to have the fuel tank drained. Motoring organisations say the cost of draining a tank should be as little as £150. If the car has been started and driven, the cost will probably be much more and will depend on the make and model of the vehicle and the damage done. If a garage wants to charge you more, check with your insurer or motoring organisation before they start.

 WARNING
Diesel vehicles can take both the wider diesel and the narrower petrol nozzles, so they are more often filled with the wrong fuel than petrol vehicles.

 TAKE CARE
New unleaded fuels that are mixed with ethanol can damage vehicles registered before 2000.

YOUR CAR IS STOLEN

1 **CONTACT POLICE** Call the police immediately. Give them your name, address, the car's make, colour and registration and ideally the chassis and engine numbers too (on Registration Certificate V5C).

2 **EXPECT THE WORST** Only around a quarter of stolen cars are recovered so be aware that the chances of getting your car back are slim.

3 **GET A REPLACEMENT** Phone your insurer to find out exactly what you are entitled to in terms of a replacement car. Most policies will provide a hire car while the police investigate.

■ **CLAIM FOR ANY DAMAGE** If the car is found, you are entitled to claim for any damage just as you would after a car accident. Ensure you get a garage to check any damage and give a full report of what needs doing. If the car is drivable, most insurers will be happy to leave this until you return to the UK.

for next time...

WRONG FUEL
● If you are a diesel driver, consider buying insurance to cover filling up with the wrong fuel.
● Diesel owners might want to buy a 'smart' fuel cap that distinguishes between nozzles and prevents use of a narrower petrol nozzle.

CAR THEFT
● To prevent theft, invest in an electronic engine immobiliser if your car does not already have one fitted.
● Ensure that all doors are locked when you are driving and never open them to anyone unless it is an emergency.

▶▶See also: **CAR ACCIDENTS ABROAD** pp286–288

robbed abroad

If your appearance makes it clear that you are a tourist, you may be more of a target for thieves. Keep valuable items well hidden in your room or a hotel safe, and money and expensive items out of view when you are out and about.

TIME TO ACT Contact the police at once. There is a chance they might be able to catch the thief and you will need a police report for any insurance claim.

action

PICKPOCKETS

■ **DO NOT GET DISTRACTED Watch for distractions, such as young children who stop you to ask for help.** While you are giving assistance, a pickpocket sneaks up and steals from you.

■ **DO NOT GET JOSTLED** Beware the 'sandwich' technique where one person stops suddenly so you collide with her, while her accomplice then bumps into you from behind and steals your wallet.

BAG SNATCHED

1 DO NOT RESIST Let the bag go. It is not worth the risk of getting attacked to keep your possessions. If you do get involved in a struggle, scream at the top of your voice. It will attract the attention of bystanders and may force the robber to flee.

2 GET A GOOD LOOK Try to notice details of the thief's build and appearance and tell police immediately. Write down details of any witnesses and make sure you get a police report.

ROBBERY FROM HOTEL

1 INFORM THE HOTEL If you have anything stolen, tell the front desk at once. If you know when it was stolen, ask the hotel to examine any CCTV footage – most hallways and lobbies have security cameras.

2 TELL THE POLICE Do not leave it to the hotel to sort things out. Make your own statement to police. If it is a big hotel chain, make sure you also file a complaint on your return. At the very least, it will force the hotel to fully investigate the theft.

for next time...

● Do not carry money or valuables in a pack on your back. Carry a backpack on your front in busy areas or use a shoulder bag kept under your arm or across your front.
● Choose a bag that has a zip or Velcro fastening as these are much more difficult for a thief to open without you noticing.
● Always keep enough cash on you for a short taxi ride if you need to get out of a neighbourhood where you feel threatened.

● Do not keep all your money in one place. Divide it between different bags and various pockets.
● Never keep valuables in your back pocket. Front pockets are safer, but a money belt underneath your clothes is the safest option.
● Never keep any valuables unsecured in your hotel room; use the room safe or, if the room does not have one, put them in the hotel safe.
● In hotels, leave the TV on just loud enough to be heard through the door to deter thieves.

ripped off abroad

Con artists have tried-and-tested ways to rip off tourists. Many of their methods rely on targets with a gullible nature and willingness to believe anything if it seems like a bargain. Here are seven of the most common scams and how to avoid them.

WATCHPOINT Keep up your guard, but do not mistrust everyone. The vast majority of people you meet have no intention of ripping you off. Rely on your instincts.

SCAMS YOU CAN AVOID

Generally speaking, your common sense should keep you safe, but there are some confidence tricks and scams that can catch out even the most wary traveller.

SCAM

METAL DETECTOR SCAM – You put a laptop onto an airport security scanner conveyor while a couple of people wait for the metal detector. One passes through, but the next triggers the alarm and slowly empties his pockets. When you get through, your laptop has gone.

THE UNLICENSED TAXI CON – A 'taxi driver' comes into the airport and offers a cheap rate to your hotel. Unsure of your new surroundings, you accept only to find that by the time you reach your destination the fare has tripled. There is, of course, no meter in the cab.

FAKE RECEPTIONIST – You get a call to your room late at night saying that the front desk wants to confirm your credit-card details. On your return home you find your credit card has been used for thousands of pounds worth of purchases and that the caller was a crook.

TOO GOOD TO BE TRUE – A gem dealer offers you a great deal on uncut gems that he says are worth several times what you will pay for them. He offers to mail them back to the UK. The ones that arrive turn out to be nothing more than cut glass.

GREAT EXCHANGE RATE – You are offered a great rate of exchange from an unlicensed dealer. He counts out the cash, but on returning to your hotel you find that he miscounted and gave you far less than he promised or fake notes. The dealer cannot, of course, be found.

BOGUS POLICE – Beware of fake police. There are numerous reports of people being asked for identification details by people who claim to be 'plain clothes police' and who subsequently steal their passports or wallets.

CREDIT-CARD CON – A store or restaurant worker takes your credit card to a back room and copies your details using a skimming device. The card details are then used to make purchases. The first you learn of it is when you return home to find a huge credit-card bill.

SOLUTION

Check conveyor is clear – At airports, never put anything onto the conveyor belt until the metal detector is clear. When you do put something on the conveyor, keep an eye on your possessions at all times to ensure that no one makes off with them.

Take only licensed cabs – Never get into a cab that does not have a meter and never take a ride in a taxi that does not have a licence. The risks of being ripped off are simply too high. Even licensed drivers sometimes take a long way round to get extra money.

Only give out card details in person – Only ever give out credit-card or passport details in person – to the hotel front desk or to anyone else. Never give them out over the phone.

Beware of cheap deals – Never accept a deal that sounds too good to be true. It probably is. In the case of gems, there are genuine bargains to be found in parts of Asia, but only buy from a licensed dealer. If in doubt, ask for a second opinion.

Only use official money changers – Never be tempted by good rates from unlicensed dealers. The only way to ensure a fair deal is to choose a reputable bank or recognised money changer.

Uniforms only – If you are ever approached by someone claiming to be a non-uniformed policeman, ask to speak to a uniformed colleague and request to be taken to a police station. At the very least ask to see his identification.

Never let your credit card out of your sight – All cards should be processed in front of you. Keep all receipts so that you can identify the fraudster to the credit-card company when you return home.

child goes missing abroad

A child going missing abroad, whether disappearing from a park, beach or street, is a nightmare scenario, made even more difficult by communication problems and being in a strange place. Make sure that your child knows how to contact you and what to do if she becomes separated. Contact the police immediately if you fear she has been abducted.

precautions

- Write your mobile phone number on a wristband to be worn by your child.
- Give an older child a mobile phone. Even if she does have her own phone, it is a good idea to lend a spare handset to a child when she is in an unfamiliar place.
- Introduce a child to receptionists or tour reps and tell her to go to them if she gets lost.
- Teach children that it is OK to speak to certain kinds of 'safe' strangers, such as police officers or store workers, if they get lost.
- Teach a child phrases in the language to use if she gets lost. Make sure she can say the name of your accommodation.
- Pick a rendezvous point and say clearly that this is the place to meet if anyone gets lost.

When you are relaxed on holiday, you may be less vigilant and not notice that a toddler or young child has wandered off.

 WARNING

Notify police immediately if you believe the disappearance is suspicious. The first few hours are crucial in establishing a child's whereabouts.

action

MISSING IN A PUBLIC PLACE

■ **SEARCH METHODICALLY** Ask someone to wait at the meeting point (see above) while you quickly search the area where the child was last seen. Find someone who knows the language to help you and give them as much information as possible that they can pass on.

■ **NOTIFY POLICE** After a quick search, **immediately call the police. Impress on them the urgency of the situation: time is critical in missing children cases.**

■ **MAKE AN ANNOUNCEMENT** If there is a public address system – for example in a store or at a station – get an announcement made.

■ **LOOK IN FAVOURITE PLACES** Think about places that have particularly attracted your child, such as an arcade or a playground.

MISSING AT HOTEL

1 INFORM HOTEL STAFF Tell the hotel front desk at once and ask them to circulate a description of the child throughout the hotel. Post someone to monitor entrances and exits, while staff assist in the search.

2 SEARCH ALL PUBLIC AREAS Include potential hazards, such as swimming pools, in your search. Ask other hotel guests to help. Think about where the child may have gone – perhaps to a play area.

3 CALL POLICE If the missing child is not found within 10 minutes, phone the police. Insist that they come immediately.

4 LOOK FOR CLUES Ask the police to organise a search of the area around the hotel. Together with the police, examine the area where the child went missing for any clues.

Reporting a missing child

When reporting someone missing, as well as giving details such as name and age, it is vital to provide the police with all the detail necessary for a successful search.

- **HAVE A GOOD-QUALITY PHOTO** Make sure it is as recent as possible showing the same hairstyle and, ideally, similar clothes to when the child disappeared. To be sure you have one, take a picture on every birthday and store it on your phone or keep a print in your wallet.
- **DESCRIBE HIM ACCURATELY** Give his height, weight and build. Carefully describe anything he had with him when he went missing.
- **NOTE ANY DISTINCTIVE FEATURES** Mention any birthmarks, scars, or mannerisms that make your child easily identifiable.
- **DESCRIBE CLOTHING** Be as specific as you can about clothing, accessories, shoes and hats – anything that would aid recognition.
- **GIVE ALL THE FACTS** Think carefully about what might help explain the disappearance.
- **LOOK THROUGH POSSESSIONS** Search through an older child's belongings for notes or clues as to why he has gone missing.

MISSING OLDER CHILD

■ **AGREE A RETURN TIME** Before an older child or teenager goes out, check that she has her mobile phone and jointly set a time that she is expected back. Text her if she is not back by the agreed time.

■ **LIAISE WITH PARENTS AND FRIENDS** If you have got to know any other parents on holiday, find out who saw the missing children last, when and where. Try to recall if your child has made any friends. Where were they planning to go? Who did they go with? Compile a list of all the likely places and look there.

■ **CHECK HER HAUNTS** If your child has mentioned any places she has been and liked on the holiday, such as clubs, cafes or bars, go there to look.

■ **CONTACT THE POLICE** If the children have not turned up within four hours and you have not heard from them, report them missing to the police.

lost abroad

Try not to panic if you lose your bearings while exploring an unfamiliar place. There are a number of practical steps that you can take to get safely back to your accommodation.

action

■ **ASK FOR DIRECTIONS** Speak slowly and calmly. Say that you are lost and ask clearly for directions. Ask if you can walk to where you want to get to or if you need to call a taxi or use public transport.

■ **PUT IT IN WRITING** If you do not speak the language, point at a map. Use your hotel's card or if you do not have one, write down the name or address of your destination in your language.

■ **LOOK FOR LANDMARKS** You will almost certainly not be far away from a known location. Look for traffic signs or signposts.

■ **RETRACE YOUR STEPS** Attempt to go back over the route you have taken until you find your way again.

 TAKE CARE
Be cautious of anyone you ask for directions. Nothing can be certain about the intentions of anyone you approach; police and uniformed officials are the safest choice. Otherwise, ask someone only when there are plenty of other people around. Before you ask, put any valuables out of sight.

for next time...

- Mark your hotel on a map the moment you arrive and scan the map for nearby landmarks.
- Use a guidebook that has detailed maps.
- Never leave the hotel without its business card and detailed instructions on public transport links.
- Always carry a small amount of cash so that you can pay for a cab if you do get lost.
- Note the position of your hotel in relation to major landmarks and places of interest. Ask the front desk to tell you the local landmarks a taxi driver would know. Take a walk around the hotel to ensure you know how to get to your lodgings from these places.

kidnapped abroad

In some parts of the world, kidnapping is an endemic problem for locals and even holidaymakers are at risk. You may also be a target in volatile political situations. If an attempt is made to kidnap you, you should try to escape at the earliest opportunity. If you cannot get away, developing a relationship with your captors may help speed your release.

be aware

- Kidnapping hot spots include Colombia, Mexico, Brazil and the Philippines. Be extra vigilant in these countries.
- Take self-defence classes (see pages 172–175). If you are going to areas renowned for street abduction, lessons in how to resist attackers might prove invaluable.
- Avoid becoming a target for kidnappers by trying not to show your passport in public.

action

YOU ARE ABDUCTED

1 CREATE A BARRIER Put something between you and the attacker. Whether it is a car or a group of people, an object between you may be enough to delay him.

2 MAKE A SCENE Exactly how you react depends upon the situation. Are the kidnappers armed? Have they restrained you? Security experts all agree that your chances of escape are far higher in the first few moments of capture. Try to distract your abductors. Make a scene. Yell, scream. Shout out exactly what is happening: 'A man is kidnapping me.' It might just be enough to persuade your kidnappers to flee.

3 GIVE IN TO THE CAPTORS If fleeing is unrealistic and the captors are violent or armed, be co-operative.

4 WATCH YOUR CAPTORS Observe and remember as much as you can. Try to track your travel time, so you have some idea of how far you have been taken. How many captors are there? Are they well prepared? Where are you being held? What are the opportunities for escape? Listen for sounds around you, as these can give clues to your location.

If your child is kidnapped

- **CONTACT THE POLICE** Ignore the demands of kidnappers and call the police right away. Give them a recent photo (see box, page 293). They will tell you exactly what to do. You will need a translator if you do not speak the language. Take a look around for anything that might help them. Collect used clothes to give police for a DNA sample or for dogs to use for the scent.
- **GIVE ALL THE DETAILS** Police will want to know details of your child's friends, including any new ones made on holiday, and of any suspicious incidents before the event.
- **STAY BY THE PHONE** Ensure that someone stays by the phone, whether abroad or at home, at all times in case the kidnappers call.
- **SEEK SUPPORT** Enlist friends to help you. Ask for someone to come out to help you and ask people at home to set up a support system so they can give help from a distance.

Do not give up; most kidnappings are resolved without loss of life.

GET HELP If you are working in a kidnapping hotspot, ask locally for advice about those areas considered too dangerous for a foreigner to visit. Do not set foot in them.

TIME TO ACT In all cases of abduction, the British consul (see page 282) should be contacted for help immediately, once the local police have been informed.

YOU ARE TIED UP

■ **TAKE A DEEP BREATH** When being tied up, try to take a deep breath and expand your chest. When you exhale, the bindings will loosen, increasing your chances of untying them. At the very least, this will make the bindings less tight and more comfortable.

■ **FLEX YOUR MUSCLES** Try to tense your muscles and your fists when your arms are being bound. Hold your wrists as wide apart as possible. Rope is probably the easiest to work loose. Nylon cable ties are the most difficult and will probably need someone else to loosen them. If handcuffed behind your back, the trick is to try to slip your hands under your bottom and to bring the hands to the front of your body.

SURVIVING CAPTIVITY

■ **LISTEN TO THEIR GRIEVANCES** If you know their language, speak to the captors without anger. Listen, do not argue. Challenging behaviour will just antagonise them and threaten your safety. Try to maintain a relaxed and friendly demeanour and try to understand exactly why you have been captured. It may help you to rationalise the whole situation.

■ **TELL THEM ABOUT YOURSELF** Talk to them about your family and your situation. **Anything you can do to bond with them will increase your chances of survival.** Ask for small favours.

■ **STAY MENTALLY STRONG** Be as positive as you can. Give yourself a pep talk. Use your sense of humour. Do maths games, mind puzzles, anything to help you to stay alert. Celebrate any little successes you have. Keep physically fit if you can. It will improve your morale and might aid any escape attempt.

■ **STAY DOWN DURING A RESCUE ATTEMPT** Try to hide or at least stay out of the way during any rescue attempt. Keep down low and stay away from your captors. Protect your head with your hands.

ATTEMPTING ESCAPE

■ **MAKE AN EARLY ATTEMPT** Security experts say that your best chance of escape is in the first few moments of capture. At this point you have the best chance of attracting the attention of bystanders or making a run for it. Only you can decide whether this is a safe possibility.

■ **DO NOT RISK YOUR LIFE** Once captured, plan any escape attempts with great care. If a failed attempt is likely to result in you being killed, it is probably not worth the risk.

■ **DISCERN THEIR PATTERNS** Keep a careful note of when your abductors come and go to try to work out your best escape opportunity. Make a conscious attempt to track time, as your best chance is during the night when your captors will be less alert.

■ **DO NOT RULE OUT THE OBVIOUS** Do not assume that just because a window has a lock that it cannot be opened. Try to find a potential way out that can be concealed while you work on it.

■ **DO NOT ASSUME YOU WILL BE RESCUED** The British government has a specific policy of not negotiating with terrorists, so the chances of a quick release are slim if the abduction is political.

■ **IF YOU ESCAPE** Even if you get away, you might still be confronted by the problem of being somewhere completely unknown, possibly where the people are hostile. Unless you are in desperate need – of medical help, for example – stay hidden until you have worked out who can be trusted.

 TAKE CARE

If gunshots are fired, keep your head down and get to the floor. Roll or crawl to a safe position. Try to get behind any sort of barrier. Stay down until you are sure it is safe.

▶▶See also: **CHILD GOES MISSING ABROAD** pp292–293

under **arrest** abroad

High-profile cases of apparently innocent tourists arrested abroad for being insensitive to local customs or straying into sensitive areas make the news every year. If you are taken into custody overseas, contact the British consul who will help.

WATCHPOINT Never take any photos near border posts, military sites or official installations. You should also seek permission before photographing individuals.

precautions

● Know what papers you need to carry. Many countries expect travellers to carry photo ID at all times. Fail to do so and you could face arrest.

● Read up on local laws in guidebooks or at the Foreign Office website (www.fco.gov.uk). For example, some countries arrest tourists for public drunkenness.

● Take special note of areas where travel is restricted, especially border areas in dispute. Visit these regions and you could be arrested.

● Be aware of national sensibilities. Do not inflame local people by insulting the nation or defacing the flag or currency. In many countries it is illegal to do this.

Do not resist arrest. There will be time later to seek legal advice.

Can the consul help?

The British Embassy, High Commission (in a Commonwealth country) or consulate (outside the capital city) is the place to contact the consular service (see page 282), but do not expect the consul to get you released.

● **THE CONSUL CAN:** Provide a list of lawyers and interpreters, contact your family, make sure medical problems are brought to the attention of the authorities and take up any justified complaints about ill treatment with the police or prison doctor.

● **THE CONSUL CANNOT:** Pay your legal fees, provide legal advice, investigate a crime or get you out of prison or detention. Getting released is an issue for you, your lawyer and the justice system in the country where you have been arrested.

action

■ **INSIST ON YOUR RIGHTS You have the right to contact the embassy or consul if arrested.** Give as much information about your case as you can and ask them to contact friends and family. Travelling companions can contact the consul on your behalf.

■ **GET A LAWYER** The consul will provide a list. Try to enlist help from friends or family to find a good lawyer familiar with dealing with your type of case.

■ **ACT COURTEOUSLY** Never be abusive or violent. It will just make matters worse. Talk to other prisoners to gain information about the local justice system.

■ **DO NOT ADMIT TO SOMETHING YOU DID NOT DO** Say as little as you can to the police if the lawyer is not present. What you say can be used in a trial.

■ **SEEK HELP IN PRISON** Contact UK-based charity Prisoners Abroad (www.prisonersabroad.org.uk) for advice. They will do everything from arranging visits to providing medical supplies. The organisation also has a valuable support service for families of overseas prisoners.

political unrest abroad

Political conditions can change quickly. If you are caught up in unrest, get information fast. Use the internet to get up-to-date news and ask tour officials for advice. Always carry the consular service phone number in case of emergency.

WATCHPOINT Avoid all street demonstrations and protests as they may turn violent. Be especially aware during election periods as this can be a time of political unrest.

precautions

- Before you travel, use the Foreign Office website (www.fco.gov.uk) to check for safety warnings about your destination.
- If you are visiting a place where there is likely to be political unrest, find out the contact details for the British consular service (see page 282).
- Even for a short trip, it is worth registering your journey with the Foreign Office. Sign up for their new LOCATE service at www.fco.gov.uk and the British Embassy will contact you in the event of a major emergency.
- Check your insurance. Most policies include cancellation in the event of war or hostilities; some also exclude travel to certain countries.
- Ask local tourist offices for advice. They should be able to tell you which areas are safe to visit.

action

CAUGHT UP IN UNREST

1 KEEP AN EYE ON THE NEWS Search out local English language newspapers, or their websites if you cannot get a copy. Local papers may be subject to government controls so try to read the foreign media reports on the internet.

2 CONTACT THE CONSUL Phone your embassy, High Commission or consulate. They will give you the latest news and tell you of any evacuation plans.

3 MAKE ESCAPE PLANS Find your best route to the airport or embassy and make sure you leave the building through a safe exit. Check the airport is open before travelling. If you cannot reach your own embassy, head for one of an allied nation.

4 LEAVE AS A GROUP You are much safer in company, so team up with other travellers and make your escape together. That way you are less likely to be singled out in case of trouble.

5 CARRY A BRIBE Situations can change quickly, so get out of the country as soon as you can if unrest turns violent. Carry small amounts of cash, ideally single US dollars divided into small amounts. It can be useful bribe money at checkpoints.

AVOIDING A RIOT

■ **BE CAUTIOUS** Treat all demonstrations with the utmost caution. If you see a protest, walk in the opposite direction or head straight back to your hotel, especially if it turns violent. Do not stay around to watch.

■ **REMAIN INDOORS** If the situation worsens, remain in your accommodation, avoiding windows if there is any rioting or gunfire. Listen to the radio or TV and ask the hotel manager or tour officials for advice.

■ **GET OUT OF THE CITY** Where the violence is localised, you may be safer getting out of the area. Head for the country or the quieter suburbs.

 WARNING
If you cannot escape from a crowd, use your arms to help you to try to stay upright. Many injuries occur when people fall over and are crushed beneath others falling on top of them.

▶▶See also: **CAUGHT IN A RIOT** pp210–211

aircraft emergencies

Flying is one of the safest forms of travel – your chances of being involved in a fatal accident are less than one in a million. But when an emergency occurs on an aeroplane – whether it is a runway problem or severe turbulence, knowing what to do can save lives. It is worth paying attention to safety advice, knowing where exits are and how to use an oxygen mask.

precautions

SAFEST PLACES TO SIT
Airlines insist that all seats are equally safe, but a comprehensive survey of US crash data in 2007 suggested that you are more likely to survive if you sit in the rear of the plane.

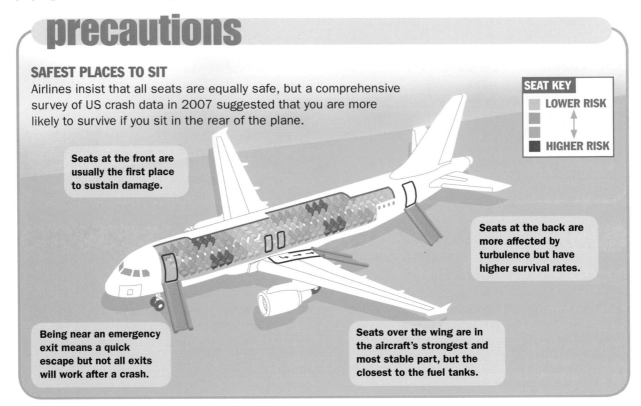

SEAT KEY
LOWER RISK
↕
HIGHER RISK

Seats at the front are usually the first place to sustain damage.

Seats at the back are more affected by turbulence but have higher survival rates.

Being near an emergency exit means a quick escape but not all exits will work after a crash.

Seats over the wing are in the aircraft's strongest and most stable part, but the closest to the fuel tanks.

action

CRASH LANDING

1 ADOPT THE BRACE POSITION Make sure that your seat belt is tightly fastened and your seat is upright. Adopt the brace position: bend as far forward as you can, resting your head against the seat in front of you placing your hands behind your head. Keep your knees back to avoid leg injuries. Put a pillow on a child's lap and hold his head against it.

2 GET TO AN EXIT Stay calm if you can, but expect a mass rush for the exit. The chances are some of the passengers will be going the wrong way – tell them where the nearest exit is and turn them round. Do not take any personal belongings. Take off high-heeled shoes.

3 JUMP ONTO THE SLIDE Do not just sit on the top of the slide – jump into the middle of it. If you hesitate, a member of the crew will give you a push. Keep your arms crossed to minimise the chance of injuring yourself or someone else. Keep your feet together. Run away from the bottom of the slide.

4 INFLATE YOUR LIFE JACKET If the plane has landed on water, wait until you are safely down the slide before activating your life jacket. Get into a life raft and away from the plane as soon as possible as the plane is likely to sink.

GET HELP Your best chance of survival may be to listen to the safety briefing by crew members. Most survivors say that this information proved invaluable during an emergency.

TIME TO ACT Remind yourself of exactly how the seat belt opens. In an emergency, many passengers try to push the centre of the buckle rather than to pull up on it.

FIRE ON BOARD

1 **KNOW YOUR NEAREST EXIT** The smoke from a fire will restrict your visibility so knowing the exact location of the nearest exit is essential. When you take your seat on a plane, **make sure you know which is the nearest exit to you and count and memorise the number of rows of seats to it.**

2 **CRAWL UNDER THE SMOKE** Crawl beneath the smoke towards the nearest emergency exit. The illuminated lights on the floor of the aisle indicate the way. If possible, wet a piece of cloth with water and put it across your mouth and nose to minimise smoke inhalation. Do not attempt to open the exit until the plane is stationary. Once it has inflated, jump onto the slide (see step 3 opposite).

3 **GET WELL AWAY** A major danger with fire on a plane is the possibility of the plane exploding. Get as far away as you can. Do not attempt to go back to look for any travelling companions.

LOSS OF CABIN PRESSURE

1 **RESPOND QUICKLY** Though rare, a loss of cabin pressure is potentially fatal at high altitudes. At 9,100m people can only stay conscious without additional oxygen for up to 30 seconds.

2 **DON YOUR OWN MASK FIRST** Oxygen masks should drop down automatically from panels in the cabin. To ensure that you stay conscious, secure your own mask before helping others, such as children. Do not remove the mask until told to by the crew.

3 **EXPECT A SWIFT DESCENT** Pilots will attempt to bring the plane down as quickly as possible to around 3,000m where the air is breathable, so prepare for the plane to plummet. While this rapid plunge might be frightening, jets are designed to cope with such rapid descents and pilots practise the manoeuvre regularly.

AFTER A CRASH

1 **GET AWAY FROM THE PLANE** Evacuate at least 100m upwind. Planes generally land into the wind so head in the direction that the plane was moving.

2 **GET ORGANISED** When it is safe, do your best to attend to the casualties (see page 12) and reassure those who are uninjured. Ask other survivors what skills they have and tell them how they can help.

AWAITING RESCUE

1 **SALVAGE ALL YOU CAN** If the plane crashes in a remote region, it is likely that you will need to survive for some time before being rescued. When you are certain that it is safe to return to the plane, search for batteries, beacons, anything that can be used for shelter (a life raft perhaps) and food and drink.

2 **SIGNAL TO RESCUERS** The plane's radios may still work, so try them out. Activate any rescue beacons. Also sweep the horizon with mirrors that reflect the sun or with lights at regular intervals.

TURBULENCE

1 **STORE BAGGAGE SECURELY** The greatest danger during turbulence is from objects falling from the overhead lockers. Make sure that everything is correctly stowed and that the locker is shut properly.

2 **WEAR SEAT BELT** It is better to keep your seat belt on at all times. Most injuries caused in turbulence are to people who were not wearing their seat belt.

3 **STAY CALM** Turbulence is one of the leading causes of fear of flying. It is usually harmless and simply a sign of atmospheric changes. Tense muscles heighten the discomfort so try to relax and stay in your seat.

▶▶See also: HIJACK pp214–215

emergencies on board ship

Some of the worst civilian disasters, even in recent years, have involved ferries, with the loss of hundreds and even thousands of lives. But most commercial vessels including cruise ships and ferries do take safety very seriously, with announcements and drills before departure, clearly marked muster stations and well-drilled crew, in case of emergency.

action

SHIP BEGINS TO LIST

■ **GET ON DECK** Listing in a ship may precede a sudden capsize. Your chances of survival are much better if you are on a top deck so that you are not trapped on board and taken down with the ship. Listen to announcements and follow the directions from the crew.

■ **CROUCH DOWN If you are near the edge of the deck, crouch or sit down to ensure that you are not swept overboard.** Wait for the ship to regain an even keel – if it does – before moving about.

FIRE ON BOARD

■ **KNOW THE DRILL** The first warning of a fire will come from emergency announcements and the crew. Follow their instructions carefully. If asked to abandon ship, do not panic. Even the fiercest of fires should leave plenty of time for evacuation.

■ **GET WELL CLEAR** Once in the lifeboats, the most immediate danger will come from burning oil. Move upwind as the oil is likely to be blown downwind.

ROUGH WEATHER

■ **HOLD ON** High seas will cause unpredictable movement of the vessel and slippery walkways. Hold onto handrails, especially on stairs, and avoid being on upper decks. Wear rubber-soled shoes on deck to provide a grip. Close doors firmly to prevent a gust of wind opening them and causing injury.

■ **STAY PUT** Do not move around the ship more than you have to – movement increases the chance of being thrown off balance.

FORCED TO ABANDON SHIP

1 GET YOUR LIFE JACKET If an emergency announcement is made, follow instructions calmly. If you are able, put on as many layers of warm clothes as possible and a final layer of waterproof clothing if available. Move quickly to the appointed place (muster station) according to the evacuation notices.

2 LOCATE YOUR LIFEBOAT Once on deck, await further instructions. A crew member will tell you which lifeboat you will be boarding.

3 BOARD QUICKLY Do not crowd the lifeboat or push to get on, but board as fast as you can. The first person to board needs to be strong enough to help children or any injured into the lifeboat. Most modern craft have engines, flares, several days worth of food and water and basic first-aid supplies.

4 AWAIT RESCUE Newer boats have homing devices so that rescue teams can find you. Stay as near to the wreck as possible as it will increase your chances of being spotted. Do not take off wet clothing as it protects you against heat loss.

■ **COUNTER SEASICKNESS** If you have them, take anti-seasickness pills. Seasickness can cause exhaustion and even hypothermia (see page 46), and threaten your survival.

 TAKE CARE

Follow the safety drill prior to departure carefully so you know the location of your muster station and where the life jackets are kept. If you have a cabin, count the number of doors between you and the exit or stairs and how many stairs there are to the deck, so that you can exit quickly in poor visibility, such as in a fire, or if the boat is listing.

GET HELP Once in a lifeboat, try to say as near to the wreck site as safety allows (unless land is in sight) as this is where rescuers are likely to concentrate their search.

TIME TO ACT If someone falls overboard, immediately shout 'man overboard' and notify a crew member. If possible throw out a marker buoy to mark the spot and point at the victim.

WATCHPOINT Most modern ships are equipped with 'throw-over' inflatable life rafts. Before throwing, ensure it is attached to the boat so you can haul it close to get on.

Lifeboats

Boats carrying passengers, from small charter boats to ocean-going liners, adhere to strict regulations regarding the provision of lifeboats.

● **LIFEBOATS** There is a wide range of traditional large rescue boats that are lowered by davits (small cranes) into the water from a ship. These take up to 150 people and modern versions are often enclosed.

● **LIFE RAFTS** Self-inflating 'throw over' life rafts are packed in cylinders (see right, top) and found on ships, from charter fishing boats to ferries. Larger life raft systems are ejected from ships (if the ship gets into trouble) straight into the water where they inflate to a covered circular raft (see right, bottom). They are often boarded via chutes from the ship's side.

● **FAST RESCUE BOATS** Vessels over 500 tonnes are required to carry a fast rescue boat that is launched in the event of a person falling overboard. These boats can move more speedily than large ships to retrieve a person in the water.

IN THE WATER

■ **COME UP FOR AIR** If you find yourself overboard, a life jacket should bring you up to the surface within a few seconds. If you do not have a life jacket, attempt to swim to the surface then grab anything that floats – driftwood, a cushion, even a plastic bag full of air.

■ **CLING TO WRECKAGE** If possible try to cling to wreckage so that you can pull as much of your body out of the water as possible. The biggest danger is loss of body heat. Most of the loss comes from the head, neck, armpits, groin and chest.

■ **STAY IN A GROUP IF POSSIBLE** If there are two or more of you in the water, huddle together touching chests for warmth with arms around each other. Children should be sandwiched in the middle as they lose body heat more quickly.

ADRIFT IN A LIFEBOAT

■ **MOVE IN CONVOYS** If there is more than one lifeboat or raft, you should tie them together and travel in a convoy. A group of boats is easier to spot.

■ **SAVE WATER** Carefully manage supplies of water and collect rainwater if you can.

■ **SIGNAL TO SEARCHERS** Use a flare gun or a mirror to signal to passing planes.

■ **PUT OUT AN ANCHOR** In rough weather, you should put out a sea anchor to stabilise the lifeboat or raft.

 WARNING

Smokers should never throw cigarette butts over the side of a vessel because they might be blown back onto the ship by the wind, where they could smoulder and cause a fire to start.

▶▶See also: **HYPOTHERMIA** pp46–47 • **DROWNING** pp 250–251

train or coach crash

Bus and train crashes usually happen in an instant and without warning. The passengers on board are likely to be highly distressed and prone to panic, even if they are not injured. But it is possible to lessen your own chances of injury and effectively help others.

action

■ **BRACE YOURSELF** If you have advance warning of a crash, brace yourself against something solid, much as you would in a plane crash (see page 298). Tuck your chin into your chest to protect against whiplash injuries.

■ **EXIT WITH CARE Clamber out carefully – the exit can be the most dangerous part of the crash.** If you are going through a window, you face the danger of jagged shards of glass. You may find yourself having to climb down from a height when you get out of the wreckage, especially if the train or coach is at an odd angle, so beware of dangerous materials impeding your descent.

⚠ **TAKE CARE**
Assess the situation (see below). Exiting from a train crash exposes you to track-side dangers, which could include being hit by other trains or electrocution where there is a live rail. Rail companies recommend waiting until help arrives.

■ **SMASH A WINDOW** If the train carriage is on fire, leave immediately. If you cannot get to a door, break a window. Use the hammers provided. Tap the window firmly near the corner. If the window is double-glazed, you will need to break both panes. Use a bag or heavy object to punch out the glass and make the hole big enough to escape through.

be aware

● On boarding, familiarise yourself with escape routes and the location of safety equipment.
● Keep aisles clear of bags and obstructions.
● In a train, opt for a seat without a table. Airline-style seating in rows is considered safer. Rear-facing seats may give better protection.
● In developing countries, avoid overloaded buses. Never stand if you can avoid it.
● Look at the condition of a bus. If the tyres are worn, for example, it may indicate a careless attitude to safety. If in doubt, do not board.

Helping the injured

Guide the emergency personnel to the most seriously injured. If people are left inside, describe their condition to the emergency services. Do not move a casualty unless he is in immediate danger (see page 12).

ANIMAL ENCOUNTERS

aggressive dog

UK statistics show that hospital treatment for dog bites rose by over 40 per cent from 2004–2008. Some breeds are more likely to attack, and attacks occur more often in urban situations, where people and dogs live in close proximity. Most bites on children are from their own dog. Learn to read a dog's body language and know what to do if faced with an aggressive dog.

assessment

A dog that approaches at a lope, with its head high or low, is probably coming to greet you. If it runs steadily with its head held level, it may be about to attack. Other signs of aggression include:

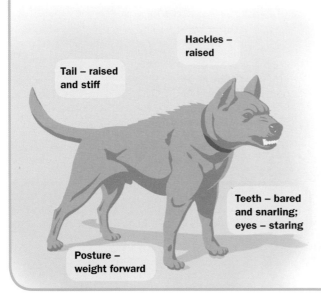

Hackles – raised

Tail – raised and stiff

Teeth – bared and snarling; eyes – staring

Posture – weight forward

 TAKE CARE

● A dog can be very territorial, so try not to trespass on its personal space.
● If a dog sniffs you, stand still and let it confirm that you mean it no harm. It may react defensively to loud noise or if you move quickly.
● Be wary of a dog that is chained up or confined. It may attack anyone it can reach.
● Do not come between a dog and its food or between an adult dog and its pups. Teach children not to disturb a dog that is asleep.
● Do not challenge a dog by staring at it or squaring up to it. Do not smile broadly at a dog, as it may perceive the baring of teeth as a snarl and feel threatened by it.

action

DOG ATTACK

1 STAY AS CALM AS POSSIBLE If you show fear, an aggressive dog will become more confident and more likely to attack.

2 IDENTIFY A PLACE OF SAFETY Look for a car or a building and slowly back away from the dog towards it. Can you call someone for help? Is there anything you can use to protect yourself, such as a chair or is there a piece of furniture you can stand on?

3 DISTRACT THE DOG Give it an alternative target. Throw it a bag or item of clothing. If the ruse works, immediately start to back away slowly.

■ **KEEP STILL** If you cannot escape, stand still, clench your fists and keep your arms by your sides. Turn slightly away from the dog and avoid looking at it directly, but keep it in your peripheral vision. Be patient. A dog usually has a short attention span and will soon go away if you do not challenge it.

■ **PROTECT YOURSELF** If you are knocked to the ground, clasp your hands over the back of your neck and pull your arms to your ears to protect your face. Stay still and the dog will probably lose interest. Fighting back will only aggravate the dog.

 WARNING

Do not run. Running triggers a dog's hunting instinct. It will give chase and you are unlikely to outrun it.

GET HELP All serious dog attacks should be reported at once to the police. A dog that has attacked once is likely to do it again with potentially more serious consequences.

TIME TO ACT If a dog has latched on to its target and you have to act, strike it on the nose. But whenever possible, avoid confrontation and the dog will lose interest in its victim.

DOGS FIGHTING

■ **USE A DISTRACTION TECHNIQUE** Try anything that will distract the dogs long enough to separate them. Throw a blanket over them or throw anything you can find that makes a loud noise near them.

■ **THROW A BUCKET OF WATER OVER THE DOGS** This technique can end a fight, although dowsing the dogs with a hosepipe is even better. A water or CO_2 fire extinguisher can also be effective.

'Wheelbarrow' technique

A technique used by professionals to break up a dog fight is to grab the dogs' back legs to separate them. This should only be tried by someone trained to deal with aggressive dogs.

1 The rear legs of each dog are lifted off the ground, like a wheelbarrow.

2 Both handlers move away so that the dogs are thrown off balance and separate.

3 The dogs are moved in a wide arc to prevent them twisting back and biting. Both handlers move back slowly while moving sideways so the dogs have to sidestep to avoid falling over.

BITTEN BY A DOG

■ **APPLY FIRST AID** (see page 106) Try to stop any bleeding and clean the wounds, but also seek medical advice as soon as possible after a dog attack. Not only is infection common, but the pressure exerted by a dog's jaws can cause internal injuries and broken bones.

■ **SEEK IMMEDIATE MEDICAL HELP** In some circumstances, you should not delay seeking help. Get medical advice immediately if you cannot stop the bleeding, suffer any loss of feeling in the affected limb, or have not had a tetanus injection in the past five years.

 TAKE CARE
● Very small children and toddlers are particularly vulnerable and may not understand the risks or the implications of behaving in certain ways around dogs. If, for instance, they growl back at a dog thinking they are playing with it, they might provoke it to attack. It is important to supervise their contact with dogs at all times. An infant or young child should never be left alone with a dog, even the family pet.
● Teach an older child to ask the owner's permission before attempting to pet a strange dog.
● Certain dog breeds are statistically more likely to be involved in attacks. These include German Shepherds, Rottweilers, Staffordshire bull terriers and Jack Russells, so it is probably worth behaving with extra care around these dogs.

 WARNING
Never attempt to separate fighting dogs by grabbing their collars. You will almost certainly be bitten. When dogs fight they are in survival mode, and they will simply see you as another enemy.

▶▶See also: **ANIMAL OR HUMAN BITE** p106

charging deer

These apparently placid grazing animals may not seem threatening but in some circumstances they can become dangerous. Male deer undergo a change of character in the rutting season and females will attack when they have young to protect. A number of species of deer – including red (the largest), fallow and roe – have been known to attack and even kill people.

be aware

- Even male deer that are tame enough to hand-feed for most of the year can become extremely aggressive as their hormones fluctuate during the mating season.
- **Female deer that are protecting their young can be very aggressive, particularly towards dogs,** who they perceive as a threat to their fawns. Always keep dogs on a lead in areas where you know that deer are breeding. If you see a fawn, do not be tempted to approach it.
- In parts of the world where human habitation has encroached on deer territory, deer have lost much of their timidity towards people. This makes it much harder to predict their behaviour and means they may attack at any time of year.
- Deer kept as pets have no fear of humans and can be extremely unpredictable.

Males in rut

Deer are generally timid but in the autumn mating season, called the rut, stags can become aggressive. During the rut it is advisable to keep away from deer in case you provoke an aggressive response.

Stags make a bellowing sound during the mating season.

action

1 ASSESS THE SITUATION If a deer appears agitated, try to work out why – have you come between it and a female or got too close to some fawns? Whatever the case, move away calmly while watching the deer.

2 GET BEHIND A BARRIER If a deer charges you, try to put some kind of barrier between you and it. Get behind a wall, fence or vehicle.

3 USE A TREE FOR SAFETY If there is a tree you can climb, swing yourself up into its branches. If you cannot climb the tree, try to use its trunk as a protective barrier between you and the deer.

■ **IF YOU CAN'T ESCAPE** Find a weapon or something you can throw at the deer, scream, shout and wave your arms. Make yourself as large, noisy and intimidating as possible.

■ **IF YOU GET KNOCKED TO THE GROUND** Roll up in a ball, use your arms to protect your head and face and try to stay as still as possible to avoid further provoking the animal.

 TAKE CARE

Avoid entering any enclosed area where there are deer. Farmed deer can be as aggressive as wild deer and deer farmers are occasionally gored to death, especially during the rut.

 WARNING

Camera flashes have been identified as a possible cause of deer attacks. Avoid taking close-up photos of them, particularly during the rutting season. If you want to observe them at this time use binoculars or a long lens from a safe distance.

aggressive **cattle**

If you have to walk through a field of cattle, know the signs that warn of danger and what to do if one of the animals attacks. Bulls are among the most dangerous of animals in the UK and cows can trample and crush people to death.

WATCHPOINT Cows with young calves can be more dangerous than bulls. Both cows and bulls are likely to react aggressively to dogs.

assessment

By law, bulls that are kept in fields where there is a public right of way should not be aggressive, but it is still worth knowing the clear signals that tell you an attack is imminent.

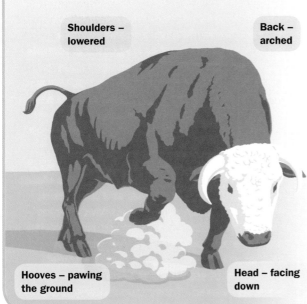

Shoulders – lowered

Back – arched

Hooves – pawing the ground

Head – facing down

⚠ TAKE CARE

● Avoid entering a field where there is a bull, especially if you have children with you. Even if a public footpath crosses it, go round it if you can.
● If it is imperative that you enter a field that has a bull in it, assess the risk before you climb the stile or open the gate. Check where the bull is and what it is doing. Identify your points of exit, and any places of safety, such as a farm building.
● As you cross the field, walk purposefully but do not run. Keep to the field boundary or follow a path that keeps the maximum distance between you and the bull. Be aware of your nearest exit.
● If you are walking with others, stay in a tight group. **Keep children in the centre, shielded by adults.** Before entering the field, agree on who will do what should the bull charge.

action

ENCOUNTER A BULL

1 RECOGNISE THE THREAT A bull may challenge you with what is called the 'broadside threat posture', (see above) where it shows its power by standing or walking sideways-on. If you see this, back away slowly. If the threat escalates, with the bull facing you head on, its shoulders lowered, and its hooves pawing the ground, retreat as rapidly as possible.

2 DO NOT STARE AT THE BULL The bull will walk towards you slowly, twisting its head and roaring with its tongue out. Walk very slowly backwards.

3 THINK TACTICALLY If there are cows in the field, try to put some of them between you and the bull.

4 DODGE A CHARGE Only attempt to outrun the bull if you are close to an exit. Throwing a rucksack or a piece of clothing to one side may provide a distraction, but be ready to side-step or jump out of the way if you have to. Once the bull has passed you, move swiftly in the opposite direction, or towards the exit.

CATTLE APPROACHING

■ **KEEP YOUR NERVE** If the animals approach you, be bold and walk straight through them.

■ **RELEASE YOUR DOG** If you feel in danger, let your dog off the lead and do not appear to protect it.

elephants and rhinos

Both elephants and rhinos can be unpredictable and aggressive. Add to this their sheer size and strong protective instincts where their young are concerned, and their ability to run at over 50km/h. To stay safe when you are around these animals, learn the most effective way to respond if you are being charged and an attack is unavoidable.

action

CHARGING ELEPHANT/RHINO

■ **LOOK FOR A PLACE OF SAFETY** If there is a nearby vehicle, get into it. If not, look for an obstacle to put between you and the animal. Back away slowly, ensuring you maintain eye contact with the animal and do not turn your back on it.

■ **CLIMB A TREE** Look for a tree with branches around head heightand grab a branch. Use your momentum to swing your legs and body up. If you cannot climb a tree, head towards the nearest one that has a thick trunk and stand behind it. In lieu of a tree, sek refuge in a thick bush.

■ **IF YOU ARE CHASED** Do not try to out-run a charging elephant or rhino. Drop a bag or piece of clothing as a decoy. Sometimes, a well-aimed branch thrown at the animal's front feet will cause it to stop. This will give you the chance to find a safer place, for example, behind a large tree.

■ **IF YOU CAN'T GET AWAY** Stand still and face the animal. As it approaches wave your arms wildly and scream and shout as loudly as you can. But be prepared to leap out of the way.

Charge or bluff?

Most elephant charges are bluffs. If the ears are spread and the trunk is up, it is probably a mock charge, and the elephant will stop short. A really agitated elephant will hold its ears flat against its head, and tuck its trunk in. Rhinos will charge towards an unfamiliar scent or sound. They seldom mock charge.

be aware

● Wild elephants are extremely dangerous. If you are observing them, do so from a distance and with a guide or knowledgeable person.
● When driving through elephant or rhino country, take care not to surprise the animals. Be particularly careful at dawn and dusk or where the road is narrow and the bush dense.
● If elephants or rhinos are blocking the path of your vehicle, do not try to edge through or sound the horn. Either turn back, or switch off your engine and wait for them to leave.
● **If you encounter rhinos when on foot, try to stay upwind of them and do not get too close; keep 30–50m between you and the rhinos.**
● Never approach a young elephant or rhino – the maternal bond is very strong and females are extremely protective of their young. A mother will attack anything that is a threat.
● If a herd of elephants is feeding, they are probably relaxed. If they stop feeding and begin showing any signs of irritation, such as shaking their heads, retreat at once.

Female elephants will protect their young with their bodies and even their lives.

aggressive monkeys

Watching wild monkeys can be fascinating but they should never be underestimated. Even when accustomed to people, their behaviour can be extremely unpredictable and they may become very aggressive in an instant, especially if they are hungry and you have food. Like most animals, they may also attack if they feel that their young are threatened.

precautions

- Do not attempt to feed or pet wild monkeys. They may grab at food, jewellery or clothing, which can be the start of an attack.
- Do not show your teeth by smiling or making facial expressions as a monkey may regard this as an aggressive signal. Avoid prolonged eye contact for the same reason.
- Monkeys that are accustomed to receiving food from people, at tourist spots or temples, for instance, may assume that any food that you are carrying is for them. Hide foodstuffs in sealed containers inside your bag or avoid carrying a bag altogether.
- Never get between a mother monkey and her baby as this will arouse her protective instincts and may incur the wrath of the entire troupe of monkeys.

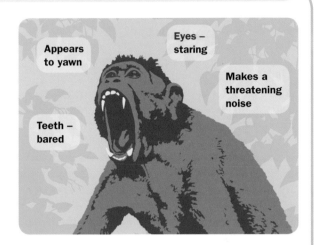

Appears to yawn

Eyes – staring

Makes a threatening noise

Teeth – bared

- If a monkey displays the above signs, it is probably about to attack and you should calmly retreat without showing panic.

action

MONKEY ATTACK

1 GIVE THEM WHAT THEY WANT If a monkey or a troupe are menacing you because they can see that you are carrying food, drop it and retreat. Do not try to beat them off the food. If you do not have any food, show them your open palms to demonstrate that it is pointless to proceed with the attack.

2 DO NOT GIVE WAY TO PANIC Try to stay calm, although screaming and shouting at the monkey may be enough to scare it away.

3 USE A WEAPON If you feel you are in real danger, grab anything that comes to hand – a stick, stone or your belt and use it to repel the monkey. Most monkeys will retreat as soon as they realise that you are not intimidated.

 TAKE CARE

- If you are bitten by a monkey, seek medical help as soon as possible. A monkey bite can be more than a nasty wound. As monkeys are related to humans, they can pass on many serious diseases, such as hepatitis B. A medical practitioner will be able to administer tests to determine whether you have contracted anything serious, and, if necessary, give you preventive medication, such as a tetanus booster.
- Always wash your hands thoroughly after contact with a monkey.

▶▶See also: **ANIMAL OR HUMAN BITE** p106

encountering a **bear**

Although attacks are relatively rare, an encounter with a bear is potentially lethal. If you are planning to go camping or hiking in bear country, such as in the national parks of North America or Canada, make sure you know the best way to coexist safely with bears. In the event of an attack, your life could be saved by knowing the appropriate way to react.

precautions

PLAN AHEAD
● When visiting a national park, or reserve, in bear country, check with the wardens for the best local knowledge of bear behaviour, habits and activity.
● Carry a canister of anti-bear pepper spray (see box, opposite) close at hand. Make sure you know how to use it and practise blindfolded so you will be able to operate it effectively even at night.
● Always travel in groups, the larger the better, and never wander off alone.
● Choose picnic spots with care. Avoid areas where bears are likely to be encountered, such as berry patches, stream sides and stands of whitebark pine. Look for evidence of bears: large droppings, animal prints with claw marks, and any animal carcasses.
● Before cycling in bear country, make sure that your bicycle is fitted with a bell and ring it frequently to alert bears to your presence.

PREVENTION
● In woodland, alert any nearby bears to your presence by talking loudly, clapping or whistling. If a bear knows you are nearby it will normally avoid you.
● Bears are attracted to human food, so if you are planning to camp, take sealable containers for all your edible supplies, and for soaps and cosmetics.
● Keep dogs on a lead or, better still, avoid taking them into bear country.

 TAKE CARE

When camping, do not just lock food inside your vehicle as bears have been known to break into cars and vans. Hang food in sealed containers at least 4m above the ground from a rope tied between two trees, and keep the food at least 100m from your campsite.

recognition

Black bears (*Ursus americanus*) and brown bears (*Ursus arctos*) are both dangerous, but telling one from the other is vital in working out what to do during an attack. Their colour differs widely, so do not rely on that alone. In North America, black bears have killed slightly more people than brown bears, but they are more numerous and tend to have a greater proximity to humans.

Ears – larger, slightly rounded

Shoulders – flat

Nose – straight, 'Roman'

Ears – short, rounded

Shoulders/back – a clearly defined hump

Face – dish shaped

action

BEAR HAS NOT SEEN YOU

1 **DO NOT ATTRACT THE BEAR'S ATTENTION** Stop, and stand still. Make minimal movement.

2 **RETREAT SLOWLY** Revise your route to give the bear the widest possible berth.

3 **NOTE THE WIND DIRECTION** Try to stay downwind of the bear so that it remains unaware of you.

BEAR HAS SEEN YOU

1 **CALL OUT LOUDLY BUT CALMLY** Wave your arms, so that the bear can identify you as human. Bears have relatively poor eyesight, but their hearing and their sense of smell are good.

2 **BACK AWAY SLOWLY** Keep at an angle to the bear's line of sight. Give the bear as wide a berth as possible. Note the wind direction (see above).

BEAR APPROACHES YOU

1 **DO NOT RUN** Running will provoke the chase response and a determined bear will outrun you. It's a myth that bears cannot run quickly downhill.

2 **SPEAK CALMLY TO THE BEAR** Back away slowly at an angle to its line of sight. If the bear continues to approach, stop and hold your ground. Bears frequently bluff charge so try not to panic. If the bear comes to within 5m, use your pepper spray (see box, right) and then retreat.

3 **LOOK FOR A PLACE OF SAFETY** Try to reach a building, car or tree you can climb. If you can, climb a tree up to about 10m above the ground. It's unlikely you will be pursued this high.

⚠ **WARNING**

Pepper spray is an effective deterrent only when discharged as an airborne cloud. It offers no protection when sprayed onto clothing or camping equipment. In fact, some evidence suggests that the residual smell may even attract bears.

BEAR ATTACKS YOU

■ **FIGHT A BLACK BEAR** Throw rocks, hit it with a stick, punch or kick it. Be as aggressive as possible and direct blows at the eyes and nose. If you have pepper spray (see box, below), use it.

■ **PLAY DEAD WITH A BROWN BEAR** Lie face down with your hands clasped across the back of your neck. Use your elbows and legs to make it harder for the bear to flip you over (see above). Wait as long as you can after the bear has left and then seek help.

Bear deterrent pepper spray

Always carry an anti-bear pepper spray in bear country. The spray contains capsaicin, a nontoxic, nonlethal, but highly irritant substance derived from chilli peppers. Pepper sprays are effective from about 4–9m, although wind and rain will reduce their range. Capsaicin causes a temporary, involuntary closure of the eyes and breathing difficulties that may last for 10 to 30 minutes.

1 **POINT THE SPRAY** Direct the nozzle towards a charging bear and spray for a second or so. The bear has to pass through the resulting cloud to get you.

2 **RETREAT** Once the bear breaks off its attack, retreat at once. If the bear manages to make contact with you, take appropriate action (see above).

stingers in the sea

Of the millions of bathers who take to the sea each year, a few are painfully stung. Fast action can reduce some of the discomfort and pain, but with all stings always be prepared to treat for shock (see pages 38–39).

WATCHPOINT Never swim in the sea by yourself. Even minor emergencies can quickly become major ones if there is no one nearby to help or raise the alarm.

be aware

JELLYFISH

● Check with lifeguards for the presence of jellyfish and look for warning signs. Wear protective swimwear to keep bare skin covered.
● The sting of some jellyfish can be excruciating and some can kill.
The most dangerous are the species of box jellyfish found primarily in coastal waters around north Australia and the Indo-Pacific. The jellyfish-like Portuguese man-of-war (right), which floats in warm ocean water worldwide, delivers a very painful, but rarely fatal, sting.

● If you see a jellyfish, leave the water and tell the lifeguard and any nearby swimmers.

WEEVER FISH

● These well camouflaged fish hide just under the surface of the sand with their dorsal spines protruding. They are easily stepped, leant or sat on by accident in shallow water and can inflict a nasty wound.
● Their range is from Norway to north Africa including around the British Isles and in the Mediterranean. They are most commonly found just before or after a low tide. Avoid beaches at these times.

STINGRAYS

● Check if, when and where stingrays occur in your holiday destination, for example, in the Gulf of Mexico stingrays are most common from May to October.
● As stingrays are often found in shallow water, shuffle your feet as you enter the water to avoid stepping on one.
● When snorkelling, avoid sandy seabeds.
● If you happen to catch a stingray when fishing, net it before lifting it into the boat.

SCORPION FISH

● Scorpion fish do not normally attack people – contact is usually accidental because they are so well camouflaged and tend to lie motionless on the sea bed.
● The spines along their backs and the pectoral fins (the ones on either side, just behind the head) do the damage. They are hollow with sacs at the base that contain venom. If you are injured by the spines, it is the venom that causes the painful reaction.
● Although their sting can be extremely painful and the effects may last for 12 hours, it is not usually life-threatening.

action

JELLYFISH STINGS

1 LEAVE THE WATER If you have some, pour vinegar liberally over the stung area or anywhere tentacles adhere. Remove any tentacles from skin carefully – use a plastic bag or a lolly stick, for example. Wash the area in sea water – not fresh.

2 REMOVE ANY REMAINING STINGS Scrape a knife, razor, the edge of a credit card or shell over the skin.

■ **RINSE EYES** Stung eyes should be rinsed with a saline solution then dabbed with a vinegar-soaked towel. Vinegar should not be put on the eyes directly.

■ **GARGLE FOR MOUTH STINGS** Use a solution of three parts water to one part vinegar before spitting it out.

■ **TAKE PAINKILLERS** Take painkillers, such as paracetamol or ibuprofen, to reduce the pain.

BOX JELLYFISH STINGS

1 GET EMERGENCY HELP A box jellyfish sting is life-threatening so call the emergency services at once.

2 SOAK WITH VINEGAR Immediately soak the affected area with ordinary vinegar to help stop more venom being released. Keep the stung area still.

MAN-OF-WAR STINGS

■ **REMOVE TENTACLES** Use tweezers or first-aid gloves to avoid stinging your fingers. Wash with salt water (not fresh). Vinegar should not be used. Rinsing with warm water can ease pain.

■ **TREAT EYES** Rinse eyes with a saline solution. Get medical help at once if your eyes are painful, watering or swollen, or if you have blurred vision after washing.

STINGRAY WOUNDS

1 TREAT THE WOUND Most stingray wounds are to the feet and lower legs and these injuries should first be thoroughly cleaned. A wound to the chest or abdomen requires immediate medical attention.

2 REDUCE THE PAIN Quickly immerse the affected limb in water as hot as you can bear. Soak the wound for 30–90 minutes.

3 DRESS THE WOUND Keep the limb elevated. Take painkillers to reduce the discomfort, which may last two days. Check the wound regularly for infection.

4 GET MEDICAL ATTENTION Even if you have treated the wound, seek medical advice. Parts of the barb may be embedded in the wound and further treatment may be needed.

WEEVER FISH WOUNDS

1 SOAK IN HOT WATER Soak the affected limb in water that is as hot as you can stand for at least 15 minutes. This helps to counteract the effect of the venom and reduces the pain.

2 TAKE PAINKILLERS Weever fish stings are very painful. Mild painkillers, such as paracetamol or ibuprofen, may provide some relief. Some people have also found antihistamines to be helpful.

3 REMOVE THE SPINES If any spines are embedded in the wound, remove them with tweezers after the hot water and painkillers have reduced the pain.

4 WATCH FOR SECONDARY SYMPTOMS If the wound does not seem to be healing, or you experience symptoms such as fainting, dizziness or shortness of breath, seek medical help without delay.

SCORPION FISH WOUNDS

■ **GET MEDICAL HELP** As reactions to venom vary and some spine fragments may be left in the wound, seek medical help as soon as possible. A doctor will give anti-venom if needed and clean the wound.

■ **IF YOU HAVE TO WAIT FOR MEDICAL HELP** Soak the affected limb in water that is as hot as you can stand for 30–90 minutes. Wash with salt water or soap and water. Remove spines with tweezers. Finally, pour clean fresh water over the wound.

▶▶See also: **SEVERE ALLERGIC REACTION** p20 • **SHOCK** pp38–39 • **INFECTED WOUND** p66

shark in the water

In 2008 there were 59 unprovoked shark attacks worldwide (32 off the coast of Florida, USA) with four deaths: two in Mexico, one in Australia and one in California, USA. These figures reveal how rare it is to be attacked – you have more chance of being struck by lightning than being bitten by a shark. But here is what you need to know in the event of a shark attack.

precautions

● When travelling, check the shark safety record of beaches you plan to swim from. If in doubt, stick to beaches with lifeguards or bays protected by shark nets. Florida, Australia, Hawaii, South Africa and California are all shark hot spots.

● Sharks gather where there is food, so avoid swimming near mouths of rivers, fishing boats, or near large numbers of seabirds or seals.

● Stay out of murky water. Bad visibility may prevent you from seeing a shark and increase the chance of a shark attacking you by mistake.

● Avoid swimming near shark-friendly places, such as sharp drops or deep channels between sandbars.

● Do not wear high-contrast clothing or shiny jewellery. Try not to splash. Sharks see contrast well and may associate splashing with a young or injured prey species.

● Swim in groups and stay together. Sharks may attack lone swimmers.

RECOGNISING SHARKS THAT MAY ATTACK

The top three in order of attack statistics are the white (also called the great white), the tiger and the bull shark. The oceanic whitetip has been responsible for the deaths of some involved in mid-ocean disasters.

SHARK NAME	CHARACTERISTICS	
GREAT WHITE SHARK	Pointed snout with many sharp teeth. Long, prominent gill slits. Back blue-grey; underside is pale. Average length 5m. The Great White lives in temperate seas off the coasts of most continents including in the Mediterranean.	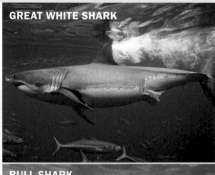 GREAT WHITE SHARK
TIGER SHARK	Back blue-grey, underside pale. Young tiger sharks have bands across their backs, but these fade with age. Average length 5.5m. Found in temperate and tropical coastal waters worldwide and in open oceans.	
BULL SHARK	Back grey, slightly paler beneath. Snout shorter and eyes smaller than great white. Large, pointed dorsal fin. Average length 3.5m. Inhabits tropical and subtropical coastal waters and occasionally estuaries.	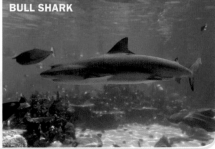 BULL SHARK
OCEANIC WHITETIP	Patchy white tips on most of its larger fins, including the dorsal and tail fins. Back is olive brown to bronze, underneath is light. Average length 3m. It is found in tropical and sub-tropical waters worldwide.	

action

SHARK ENCOUNTER

■ **IF YOU SEE A SHARK** Try not to panic. Alert any nearby swimmers, and then swim towards the shore, a boat or any other way out of the water, as smoothly as you can. Breaststroke is a suitable splash-free stroke. **If a shark is swimming straight towards you, turn to face it.** Tread water so that you are as vertical in the water as possible – most shark prey, such as seals, appears horizontal in the water, so remaining vertical in the water (see above) makes you less appealing to the shark. If you are swimming near a boat, call for help and tread water, watching the shark, until the boat arrives.

■ **IF YOU SENSE A SHARK** If you feel something nudge you or brush past you, leave the water as quickly and calmly as you can before investigating. At times a shark will bump its prey before attacking. Some victims claim not to have realised that they have been bitten until a few moments after an attack.

■ **IF YOU ARE DIVING** Most sharks attack from below so attacks on divers are rare. The best course of action is to stay as calm as possible. Do not display aggressive behaviour as this may aggravate the shark.

SHARK ATTACKS YOU

1 AIM FOR VULNERABLE AREAS If you have a paddle or a diving knife, direct your attack at the eyes and gills. If you have no weapon, use your hands to claw at these vulnerable areas. The snout is also sensitive, but is dangerously close to the mouth.

2 TREAT ANY BITES Try to stop the bleeding by applying pressure directly to the wound. If necessary, swim on your back. Leave the water as swiftly as you can.

3 WARN OTHERS, THEN SEEK HELP Once you are out of the water, warn the lifeguard or other swimmers, then seek medical help.

YOU WITNESS SHARK ATTACK

1 ALERT THE LIFEGUARD If there is no lifeguard or one is not available, do not put yourself at risk. Any rescue is best attempted by boat.

2 GET THE VICTIM OUT Help the victim to leave the water quickly. Staunch any bleeding (see pages 96–97) by applying pressure to the wound.

3 KEEP THE VICTIM AS STILL AS POSSIBLE Wrap the victim in towels to keep warm, in case of shock (see pages 38–39). Call for medical assistance.

 TAKE CARE
If you have been spearfishing and are carrying a catch of fish when you see a shark, let the catch go and slowly swim away from it. Get back in your boat as quickly as you can.

▶▶See also: SEVERE BLEEDING p22 • SHOCK pp38–39 • DROWNING p250–251

facing hippos and crocs

Hippos cause more deaths than any other large animal in Africa; some estimates put the number of people killed annually at more than 100. Crocodiles, too, cause hundreds of deaths worldwide each year. Attacks are avoidable. If you are attacked, keeping a cool head and knowing what to do will greatly increase your chances of survival.

precautions

HIPPOS

- Hippos will attack to protect their young and their territory, and out of fear or bad temper – they are irascible creatures. Always give them a very wide berth both in the water and on land.
- Do not swim anywhere near hippos, and when boating, use your oars to make plenty of noise by splashing and banging on the side of the boat, so that you do not surprise a dozing group.
- At night, hippos graze on land, frequently roaming several kilometres from the river along well-worn tracks. Never place yourself between a hippo and the water.

CROCS

- If you have to go to the water's edge, choose an open spot and never go alone.
- Crocodiles are territorial, especially in the breeding season, so keep well clear.
- Stay away from young crocodiles, as their mothers can be fiercely protective.
- Be especially careful as night falls; this is when these reptiles are at their most active and are much harder to see.
- If you are boating, be vigilant and take turns to keep watch. Do not trail your limbs in the water. Make noise to avoid startling a dozing crocodile.

action

HIPPO ATTACK

■ **FIND A SAFE SPOT** Hippos seldom bluff. If it charges, run straight to the safety of a tree, vehicle or building. **Hippos can run at nearly 30km/h, but cannot turn swiftly**; you might be able to sidestep a charge.

■ **IF A HIPPO CAPSIZES YOUR BOAT** Try to use the hull as a shield between you and the hippo. If a hippo bites you, it may drag you under the water to drown. Use a rock, branch or your fingers to attack its eyes.

CROC ATTACK

1 RUN AWAY Crocs can move quite quickly, but on land 17km/h is their top speed so you should easily be able to escape. Run away from the water and in a straight line. Do not zigzag.

2 RETALIATE If you are bitten in or near water, the reptile may try to drag you under. Scream and fight back. Use any and every weapon to attack the eyes.

3 ATTACK THE PALATAL VALVE If your arm is in the reptile's mouth, try to reach the palatal valve (a membrane that prevents water from entering its throat, see right) behind the tongue. If you can hit it, or force it open, the reptile may release you.

biting insects

If someone has an extreme allergic reaction to an insect bite, the result can be fatal. Even if the person bitten does not have a severe response, many insects carry diseases – some of them serious – so all bites need to be treated with care. To avoid problems, take precautions against being bitten in the first place.

action

INSECT BITES

1 DO NOT SCRATCH Apply calamine lotion, ibuprofen gel or antihistamine cream to reduce the likelihood of infection and swelling, and soothe the itching.

2 WATCH FOR ALLERGIC REACTIONS In extreme cases, a condition called anaphylaxis can occur (see pages 20 and 54–55). Symptoms include wheezing, difficulty in swallowing and faintness. These symptoms normally occur rapidly after a bite. If you experience any of these reactions, get medical help at once.

Insect-borne diseases

Mosquitoes can carry malaria, yellow fever, dengue fever and encephalitis. Ticks may pass on Lyme disease, tsetse flies can carry sleeping sickness and sandflies – found on beaches – leishmaniasis.

TICK BITES

1 USE TWEEZERS Take hold of the tick as close to the skin as possible, and pull gently. Its mouthparts are barbed, but a steady action should pull the tick free.

2 STORE THE TICK If you are in an area where tick-borne diseases are common, keep the tick so that you can have it analysed if you develop any symptoms. A small screw cap covered with cling film or tape makes an ideal impromptu specimen container, or use anything sealable, such as a drinks bottle. Wash your hands if you touched the tick.

3 CLEAN THE BITE Swab the bite with antiseptic, apply antiseptic cream and cover it. Rarely, an anaphylactic reaction may occur (see left). If after a few days it does not seem to be healing, seek medical advice as infection is quite common.

precautions

FLYING INSECTS

● Mosquitoes are most active from two hours before dusk right through until dawn. If possible, head indoors just before the sun goes down.
● Use a repellent. The most effective ones contain DEET, up to a maximum concentration of 30 per cent for adults and 10 per cent for children.
● At night, sleep under mosquito netting or in a room protected by screens. If the screens are open by day, close them and use a mosquito spray to clear the room before you go to bed.
● Treat clothes and mosquito nets with permethrin to repel all types of flying and crawling insects.

CRAWLING INSECTS

● Ticks are active from May to September, so in areas where tick-borne disease is common, avoid prime tick habitats if possible.
● Ticks live in woodland and other well-vegetated areas. They climb up the stems of plants from where they can cling to any passing host. When out walking, wear long-sleeved shirts, long trousers and tuck your trousers into your socks or boots. DEET-based repellents also help.
● Check your skin carefully after a walk. Most ticks are harmless, but remove them quickly to reduce the chances of acquiring an infection.

▶▶See also: **SEVERE ALLERGIC REACTION** p20 • **INFECTED WOUND** p66 • **SWARM OF BEES** p322

venomous **snakes**

Despite their sometimes fearsome reputation, only 15 per cent of the world's 3,000 or so snake species are venomous, with bites that warrant emergency medical treatment. Very few snakes present a serious danger to healthy adults. But snakes will attack when threatened, so the key to safe coexistence with these usually shy and retiring reptiles is respect.

precautions

- Before you travel, check whether the area you are visiting is home to any venomous snakes and, if so, learn to identify them.
- Snakes use the environment to regulate their temperature, and will seek out sunny spots on cool mornings and shady spots in the heat of the day. Be vigilant around areas such as flat rocks and paths, which trap the sun, and in the shade of bushes.
- If you are travelling through an area where snakes are common, keep dogs on a lead and ensure that children walk behind you. Children and dogs are the most frequent victims of snake bite.
- When walking in snake country, wear thick boots. Do not lean against fallen trees and take particular care when collecting firewood.
- Avoid walking in long grass, or use a walking stick to clear the way. Always 'check before you step' and 'look before you reach'.

RECOGNISING VENOMOUS SNAKES

If you are travelling to an unfamiliar area where venomous snakes are common, consult a reliable reference before you arrive. Below is a selection of some commonly encountered venomous snakes.

CONTINENT	DESCRIPTION
AFRICA	**Black mamba** Olive to greenish grey. Lethally venomous and aggressive snake. 2.5–4.5m long. **Cape cobra** Usually yellow or brown, sometimes speckled. Its venom can be fatal. 120–180cm long. **Puff adder** A fat snake, with dark and light bands. 1m long.
EUROPE	**Adder** Usually has a zigzag pattern down its back and a V on its neck. Up to 60cm long. **Montpellier snake** A nondescript greeny grey or brown, has distinctive 'eyebrows'. Average length 2m.
AUSTRALIA	**Common or Eastern brown snake** From pale brown to almost black, sometimes striped or speckled. Average length 1.5m. **Eastern tiger snake** Olive, brown or grey colour, usually with creamy yellow banding. Average length 1m. **Fierce snake** Brown, varying from light to dark and also varies with season and location. Average length 1.8m.
NORTH AMERICA	**Copperhead** Patterned in varying shades of brown. Average length around 76cm. **Common coral snake** Wide red and black bands, divided by narrower yellow bands. Up to 80cm long. **Eastern diamondback** Brown, olive or grey, with a pattern of diamond shapes along its back. Average length 1.7m.
ASIA	**King cobra** Varies from black to light brown or olive, with creamy banding. Average length 4m. **Common krait** Bluish black with white bands. Around 1m.

ADDER

COMMON CORAL SNAKE

KING COBRA

WATCHPOINT Do not try to kill the snake. Attacking the snake will expose you to risk as the snake will defend itself.

GET HELP After you have made sure that you and those nearby are a safe distance away, call the emergency services if you have any concerns that a snake you have seen is dangerous.

TIME TO ACT Although snake bites can be serious, especially for the young, elderly or those in ill-health, a fit adult should have at least two hours to seek medical assistance.

action

YOU SEE A SNAKE

1 STOP AND SLOWLY BACK AWAY A coiled snake can typically reach forward by about half its body length when it strikes, which it may do if it feels threatened. **Do not be tempted to move closer for a better look.**

2 GET PAST IT SAFELY If a snake is blocking your path, detour around it by 10m or more. Move slowly and watch the snake carefully in case it moves.

3 LEAVE THE AREA If a snake is between you and your vehicle or camp, first retreat to a safe distance of 10m or so. If the snake does not leave of its own accord, encourage it to move on by throwing a handful of soil or a few light twigs at it. Aim short of the snake so it will move away from you and the thrown objects, and not towards you.

SNAKE IN THE HOUSE

1 RETREAT IMMEDIATELY If you see a snake in a house or in a holiday home, whether abroad or in the UK, back away to a distance of at least three or four times the snake's length, or if you are not sure how long it is, retreat to a distance of 10m or leave the room, closing the door behind you. Make sure children and pets are safe.

2 MAKE AN ASSESSMENT Try to determine if the snake is a venomous species (see chart, opposite).

3 ISOLATE THE AREA Close doors and windows. Once the snake is secure, keep watch on it and telephone for help.

BITTEN BY A SNAKE

1 GET AWAY Move away from the snake. Do not try to kill or catch it but do take a good look so that you can describe it. A positive ID could save your life when it comes to the administration of anti-venom.

2 STAY AS CALM AS POSSIBLE The faster your heart beats, the faster any venom will be transported around your body. Keep the bitten area as immobile as you can and slightly raised. If you are with someone who has been bitten, do everything you can to keep them calm and keep the bitten limb still.

3 DO NOT ATTEMPT FIRST AID Don't apply a tourniquet or try to cut the wound and suck out the poison. The former can be dangerous and the latter is ineffective. Do not cover the wound.

4 SEEK HELP If you have help and are able to travel, go to the nearest hospital for advice. If you do not have transport or help, or feel immediately unwell, call the emergency services. Describe your injury, the symptoms and your location.

■ **DRESS THE WOUND** If no adverse symptoms appear after 24 hours, the bite may be harmless: the wound can be treated to avoid infection (see page 66).

At the hospital

The heart, blood pressure and breathing will be monitored and pain-relief, anti-allergens and anti-tetanus injections may also be given. In the UK and much of Europe, anti-venom is only administered in severe cases. Most anti-venom is polyvalent – effective against a variety of venoms – so you do not need to know what kind of snake bit you.

venomous **spiders**

Many people have an irrational fear of spiders. In the UK, spider bites are unusual, and although some can be painful, severe reactions are rare. Outside the UK, certain spiders should be shunned at all times as their bites can not only be agonising, but also fatal. Fortunately, most bites can be avoided, and with prompt action can be successfully treated.

RECOGNISING VENOMOUS SPIDERS

If you are travelling in an area that is home to venomous spiders, it is wise to learn to recognise them. This chart describes the most dangerous species that you are likely to encounter.

CONTINENT	DESCRIPTION
AFRICA	**Black (or West coast) button spider** Silky, dark brown or black body. Often marked with white or red. Body up to 12mm. **Six-eyed sand (or crab) spider** Brown, flattened and crab-like, often covered in sand. Body up to 15mm.
EUROPE	**Mediterranean black widow spider** Black, with 13 red, yellow or orange spots on back. Body up to 15mm. **False widow spider** Shiny, dark body with creamy markings and a cream band around the front. Body up to 14mm. **Yellow sac spider** Pale, straw-coloured body. Front legs are longer than the other three pairs. Body 6–8mm long.
AUSTRALIA	**Eastern mouse spider** Smooth, glossy black body with large, bulbous head and jaws. Body up to 20mm. **Redback spider** Females: black body with red/orange stripe. Males: light brown with white markings. Body up to 10mm. **Sydney funnel-web spider** Glossy, dark bodies, black to reddish brown. Body up to 35mm. **White tip spider** Reddish brown bodies with a white tip to the abdomen. Legs are orange-coloured. Body up to 18mm.
NORTH & SOUTH AMERICA	**Black widow spider** Females: shiny black, with red hourglass on underside. Males and juveniles: black or greyish, with white stripes and yellow/orange speckles. Body up to 15mm. **Brazilian wandering spider** Large brown body and legs. Body up to 48mm. **Brown recluse (or violin) spider** Brown or yellowish with 'violin' marking. Has six eyes (not eight). Body up to 20mm.
ASIA	**Chinese bird spider** (Tarantula) Either golden brown with black stripes, or dark brown to black. Body and legs up to 20cm. **Gooty sapphire** (Tarantula) Striking metallic blue coloured body and legs. Body and legs up to 20cm.

BLACK WIDOW

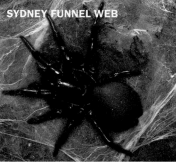
SYDNEY FUNNEL WEB

BROWN RECLUSE SPIDER

 WARNING

There have been rare instances of large venomous spiders entering the UK, in boxes of bananas for example, therefore treat any large or unusual spider with caution and keep your distance.

 TAKE CARE

If you think a spider may be venomous, or you do not want to handle a large spider, cover it with a bucket, add a heavy weight, such as a book or a stone, and arrange for a pet rescue organisation to collect.

GET HELP Medical treatment is a priority. Treat spider bites as seriously as snake bites. Anti-venom and other treatment can be prescribed by a medical professional.

TIME TO ACT With some spider bites, serious pain and other symptoms take up to an hour to manifest themselves. If you think you have been bitten, seek medical help immediately.

WATCHPOINT If the victim of a spider bite is a child under seven or a person over sixty years old, or who has known allergies or heart problems, they are particularly at risk.

action

BITTEN BY A SPIDER

1 DO NOT PANIC Even if you are bitten by a venomous spider, remember that many bites are 'dry', that is, the spider has not necessarily injected any venom. Panicking and rushing about will increase your heart rate and cause any venom to move more quickly through your system.

2 APPLY ICE To ease the pain and reduce the swelling, hold ice cubes in a bag or a pack of frozen peas wrapped in a cloth over the site of the bite.

3 CLEAN THE WOUND Wash the wound with soap and water to remove any traces of venom.

■ **APPLY A PRESSURE BANDAGE IF APPROPRIATE** If the spider that has bitten you is definitely not a recluse spider (see below), you can apply a bandage firmly, but not so tight as to cut off circulation, above the site of the bite. Alternatively, apply a cool compress to ease any pain (see page 106).

■ **RECLUSE SPIDER BITE If you have been bitten by a recluse spider, do not apply a bandage.** You should interfere with a recluse spider bite as little as possible, because the venom from this spider causes tissue breakdown and firm bandaging might increase the tissue damage.

■ **SEEK MEDICAL HELP** Get help from a medical professional as soon as possible. They will be able to deal with any severe allergic reactions and shock, and will administer anti-venom, if necessary. The medical treatment of most spider bites consists of cleaning the wound, administering pain relief, and treatment with antibiotics or even surgery if the wound becomes severely infected.

Catch a venomous spider

The vacuum-cleaner technique works well for a spider up to about 30mm. Keep an eye on it to make sure it does not move out of your sight. Fit the wand attachment to your vacuum cleaner. Turn on the power, but not so near the spider as to alarm it or it may run for cover. Swiftly lower the end of the wand to suck up the spider. Leave the motor running for a little while to ensure that the spider is sucked all the way into the dust bag or reservoir. Take the cleaner outside and carefully empty it into a refuse sack that you can seal and discard.

precautions

If you are in a location where there are likely to be venomous spiders, take these sensible precautions:

● Check shoes and boots before putting your feet into them – spiders like the dark recesses.
● Hang your clothes up and shake out each item before putting it on, especially when you are camping.
● Position your bed slightly away from the wall and check the sheets before getting in.
● Be cautious around places that are favoured by spiders – often dark, shady areas with lots of crevices, such as toilets, around barbecues and swimming pools, garages and woodpiles.

▶▶See also: **SEVERE ALLERGIC REACTION** p20 • **SHOCK** pp38–39 • **INFECTED WOUND** p66

a swarm of bees

When honey bees swarm, thousands take to the air in a blurry, buzzing cloud as they follow their queen in search of a new home. En route they may rest temporarily on a fence post or the branch of a tree. Although most honey bees are not aggressive, encountering a swarm is potentially dangerous, due to the risk of multiple stings.

action

ENCOUNTER A SWARM

■ **IF A SWARM CHASES YOU** Sprint away as fast as you can – you should be able to outrun it. Run to the nearest safe place, such as a vehicle or building.

■ **IF THE BEES ARE CLOSE Shut your mouth and cup your hands over your eyes and nose** as you run to minimise the risk of being stung.

⚠ WARNING

● When running away, do not zigzag – running in a straight line is more effective.
● Do not jump into water, such as a swimming pool. The bees will probably circle the pool for up to 15 minutes, and you risk being stung on the face when you surface to breathe.

STUNG BY BEES

1 REMOVE THE STING
Take it out with tweezers or scrape it out by dragging a blunt knife blade or a credit card across the skin at an oblique angle, working from the sting towards

the sac. Do not rub or squeeze the sting as you may increase the amount of venom you receive.

2 SEEK MEDICAL HELP If you have been stung a number of times, in sensitive areas such as the face, mouth or throat, or experience any symptoms other than swelling and soreness, seek medical help as soon as possible.

be aware

● Honey bees typically tend to swarm on sunny afternoons in early summer, so be particularly vigilant at this time of year. Warn children to take care when climbing trees in case they encounter a resting swarm.
● If you find a swarm resting on a tree or post in your garden do not approach it. Warn others and keep children and pets at a safe distance. Contact your local beekeeping society, who will send someone to collect the swarm safely.
● Do not try to move a swarm on, either by spraying it with water or by shaking the branch it is resting on.
● Do not use lawn mowers or similar garden power tools near a swarm, as the noise and vibrations may antagonise the bees.

Keep at a safe distance from a resting swarm.

⚠ TAKE CARE

The sight and sound of an approaching swarm can be quite frightening, but try to stay calm. Do not wave your arms or swat the bees. Injured bees secrete a pheromone that will incite the rest of the swarm to attack.

▶▶See also: SEVERE ALLERGIC REACTION p20

TECHNOLOGY CRISES

computer freezes or crashes

Some people are completely dependent on computers at both work and home. If your computer suddenly stops working, you may find yourself unable to work or communicate with essential services. But in many cases you can sort out the problem yourself. Work carefully through the reasons why your computer has crashed to get back in action as soon as possible.

assessment

Armed with a little knowledge, you can tackle many minor computer problems on your own. To diagnose more serious problems, you will probably need an expert. Try the simple fixes below to get your computer started, before you call a technician.

TROUBLESHOOTING

PROBLEM	WHAT TO DO
LOCALISED PROBLEM The program you are working on will not respond, but other functions, such as your email, still work.	Software problem **Quit out of the program (see right); make sure Windows is updated (see box); check that the program you are using is up to date. Check that the memory you have is sufficient for all the tasks you want to do simultaneously (see right).**
MOUSE IS NOT WORKING When you move the mouse, nothing seems to move on the screen and/or you cannot see the mouse pointer at all, but the keyboard still works (try the arrow keys).	Check your cables **Check all the cables from the keyboard and mouse are connected in case you have pulled one out by accident.**
SCREEN IS STILL ON BUT NOTHING IS WORKING No programs respond to either the keyboard or the mouse.	Restart **This is a typical system freeze. Note what you were doing when the computer stopped working in case it happens again. Restart the computer (see right), then run your virus protection; check and add more memory if necessary (see right).**
FREQUENT FREEZES If your computer often stops functioning, you may have a serious problem. This could be caused by a virus or because you are asking too much of the machine.	Perform basic maintenance **Go to Control Panel, System and Maintenance and click on Defragment your hard drive. Run your anti-virus software. Reinstall any problematic programs.**
THE COMPUTER IS ON BUT THE SCREEN IS BLANK There is nothing on the screen, or there is a message saying 'No signal received'. This may happen when you first turn on the computer, or when you are in the middle of using your computer.	Check the screen **Make sure the cable from the screen to the computer is securely connected. If you can, connect your screen to another computer. If it does not work, your screen is at fault, not the PC.**
COMPUTER DOES NOT START UP When you press the On button, the computer does not respond at all.	Power supply problem **Check that the computer is plugged in, turned on and there is no problem with the mains supply. If all the above are working, the computer's power supply unit may need to be replaced. Take your PC to a computer repair shop.**
UNUSUAL SOUNDS The computer does not sound as it normally does – maybe the fan is making more or less noise than normal, or the hard drive makes a grinding noise when you first turn on the machine.	Hardware problem **This is probably a hardware problem such as a faulty fan, dust inside the PC or a problem with the motherboard (where the components reside). Contact a repair service.**

action

COMPUTER IS UNRESPONSIVE

1 TRY ESCAPE FIRST Some programs appear to freeze in the middle of a process; pressing the **Esc** key may get it going again. For example, accidentally pressing the **Alt** key activates the menus – press the **Esc** key to release.

2 RIGHT CLICK Try right-clicking the program's button in the taskbar at the bottom of the screen. Click on **Close** from the pop-up menu.

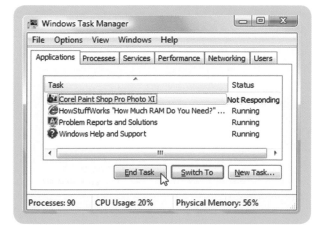

3 CTRL + SHIFT + ESC If right-clicking does not work, press the **Ctrl + Shift + Esc** keys simultaneously. Click on the **Applications** tab to view a list of running programs and their status. You should see the status 'Not responding' against the frozen or crashed program. Click on the non-responsive program to select it and then on **End Task.**

4 CTRL + ALT + DEL If your computer is still unresponsive, press the **Ctrl + Alt + Del** keys to display the Windows options menu. Click the red button at the bottom right to shut down.

5 POWER DOWN If pressing **Ctrl + Alt + Del** does not work, the only course of action left is to switch the computer off. Press and hold down the power switch for at least five seconds by which time you will hear the fan has stopped whirring. Wait for at least 30 seconds and then press the power switch again. Unfortunately, you will lose any work that has not been saved.

INSUFFICIENT MEMORY

1 FIND OUT HOW MUCH MEMORY YOU HAVE From the Start menu, click on **Computer**. The amount of RAM (Random Access Memory) is displayed next to 'Memory' at the bottom of the window. How much you need depends on how you intend to use your computer. Gaming or graphic-design programs may require more RAM, so check the software's requirements. Memory is available online or on the high street. Retailers can advise you what to buy, depending on your computer use, type and model.

2 OPEN YOUR COMPUTER Switch off and unplug the computer. Use an anti-static pad or wrist strap to discharge any static electricity, which could damage the computer and your new RAM, and open the case.

3 SLOT IN THE NEW MEMORY RAM is installed in a series of slots. The memory module has a notch at one end, so that it will only go in one way. Install the memory by placing the module in the slot at 45 degrees and push it down until it snaps into place.

4 CHECK THE MEMORY IS ACTIVE Close the case and switch on the computer. Go back to **Control Panel** and check the increased amount of RAM is shown.

Getting Windows updates

When your computer is connected to the internet, Windows can automatically check for important updates and install them for you just before your computer is shut down.

To set this up, go to the **Start** button and click on **Control Panel, Security, Windows Update** and **Change settings**. Make sure 'Install updates automatically (recommended)' is checked, and set a time to install the updates. Alternatively, make manual choices to control Windows updates. Click **OK**.

▶▶See also: **COMPUTER INFECTED BY A VIRUS** • p326 **POWER SURGE** p330 **325**

computer infected by virus

Computer viruses are constantly mutating and can appear without the user realising. If your computer is attacked it can devastate your work and you may inadvertently spread the virus. Learn to recognise a virus and act quickly to contain it and remove the threat.

be aware

Signs that your computer has been infected by a virus are:

- A virus can be sent by email without the sender's knowledge, so may come from a friend. Check anything suspicious with the sender.
- If you have anti-virus software that has been updated regularly, a message will flash up on the screen warning you of the attack.

- Your computer may run slowly or keep crashing and then restarting.
- You may hear the hard disk whirring when you think the computer should be inactive.
- Dialog boxes and other on-screen elements may look different from usual.

action

1 DISCONNECT Save all open documents, close down all open programs, and disconnect your computer from any networks and from the internet.

2 RUN VIRUS SCAN Run your anti-virus software and, if necessary, run it again to ensure the virus has been dealt with properly, and the computer is clean.

3 RECONNECT EVERYTHING Connect back to your network or router, go to your anti-virus provider's website and check for updates and information. Install updates and run the virus scanner again.

■ **PURCHASE ANTI-VIRUS SOFTWARE** If you do not have anti-virus software, then buy some from suppliers such as McAfee and Norton. You will have to purchase these from a local computer store to save reconnecting. If that is not possible, connect to the internet directly through your router or modem, then disconnect once you have downloaded the software.

■ **INSTALL THE SOFTWARE** Start your computer and install the software. Run the software, then reconnect to the internet and check for updates, then run the anti-virus software again.

for next time...

- Scan all types of media (DVDs, CDs and removable drives) when you insert them. Do not re-use disks from other computers.
- Be alert to email messages with attachments – especially ones with a vague subject line. Delete the email straight away.
- Download files from reputable websites only. Legitimate websites should state that they use anti-virus software to check all downloadable files and programs.
- Ensure your anti-virus software and **Windows Update** (see p325) are configured for automatic updating and to automatically detect viruses.

 TAKE CARE

Make sure that Windows Firewall and Windows Defender are turned on. Check in **Control Panel**, **Security Center** if you are not sure.

Do Macs get viruses?

Although viruses and other malware (malicious software) that attack Macintosh computers are not common, Macs can still be vulnerable. Make sure a Mac has anti-virus software and it is kept up to date. Take the same precautions as PC owners. Note also, that even an iPod and iPhone can now be infected by malware.

internet connection down

Losing your internet connection can be frustrating if you are about to bid for an item on eBay or order almost sold-out tickets for a popular show, but it can cause serious problems if you are using it to access details of flights or other urgently needed information.

assessment

Establish whether the problem is your computer and modem or with your Internet Service Provider (ISP).

Can you connect to popular sites such as google.com and amazon.com?

Yes

Problem is with website you were trying to use.

No

Can you connect to the website of your ISP?

Yes

The problem is probably with your ISP. Call their helpline to check.

No

Are other computers connected to the same modem online? If they are, the problem is with your computer, see right.

Know your modem/router

The lights and labels on most modems or routers are similar to those described below. If you are in any doubt, see your modem's manual. A steady light against the following means:
- **POWER** The power cable is connected and the modem is turned on.
- **STATUS** A steady light means all is well.
- **(A)DSL** Your service is working normally. If it is flashing or off, contact your ISP.
- **WLAN** When flashing, data is being transferred via your wireless network.
- **LAN** When flashing, data is being transferred via your ethernet connection.
- **INTERNET** Internet connection is active.

action

1 SHUT DOWN Close all programs and then turn off your computer. Unplug and remove all cabling. If you have a router, switch this off and remove the cabling. Unplug the phone from the router or modem and from the wall socket. Wait at least 30 seconds, reconnect all cabling and switch everything back on in reverse order.

2 DIAGNOSE AND REPAIR Right-click on your network icon, which is on the right of the taskbar. Click on **Diagnose and Repair**. This opens the **Windows Network Diagnostics** window, which helps to diagnose and repair any networking problems. Follow the on-screen instructions.

3 CHECK YOUR ROUTER If your router has a **Reset** button (see the manual), press it to restore the router to its factory settings. Check the troubleshooting section of any instructions that came with the router. Connect to the router and follow the manual to input your settings.

4 CHECK NETWORK AND SHARING CENTER Click on the **Start** button, **Control Panel**, **Network and internet** then on **Network and Sharing Center**. This displays a map of the route between your computer and the internet. A red 'X' between two icons indicates a break in communication and helps you to locate the problem; if you cannot resolve it, the information will be of use to your ISP.

5 GET ADVICE If you are still having problems and cannot access the internet, call your ISP helpline (check the cost of calls when they answer you). The adviser will talk you through how to check your settings. Be ready to describe everything you have done already, and tell the person the results of the two diagnostics programs you have run.

▶▶See also: POWER SURGE p330

deleted or lost files

It is a common misconception that when you delete a file it is removed from the hard drive of your PC. What actually happens is that the tiny piece of information that points to the location of the file is erased, making the file invisible to the operating system. If the file is still located in the Recycle Bin, it can be restored to its original location.

precautions

● Make regular back-ups (see box, below) of all your important data, in case a file gets permanently deleted from your hard drive.
● Create folders for associated files and clearly label them, for example, 'Family Letters', 'Holidays', 'Household Expenses'. Save your files in these folders to find them easily in future.

Backing up

● **BUY BACK-UP HARDWARE** Before backing up your files, decide on the best way to store them. DVDs and CDs are cheap, but may get lost, broken or corrupted. External hard drives are now reasonably priced and allow you to back up repeatedly.
● **USE BACK-UP SOFTWARE** To back up all of your data files, you can use the Automatic Backup feature that comes with Windows. This lets you choose how often to perform regular back-ups and whether to save the data to an external hard drive, portable media such as a DVD, or a network location. To use this feature, click on the **Start** button, then **Control Panel**, **System and Maintenance** and **Back Up Your Computer**.
● **RESTORE FILES WIZARD** If you have backed up regularly, use the Restore Files wizard to retrieve the backed-up version of your lost file. You can access this wizard in the same way as you set up Automatic Backup.

 WARNING

Certain files and folders cannot be rescued from the Recycle Bin. These include items that were deleted across a network or from removable media such as a CD-ROM or removable hard drive. A warning message is displayed when you delete these items.

action

FILE DELETED

1 GO TO RECYCLE BIN To start restoring a deleted file on your PC or laptop, go to your desktop and double-click on the **Recycle Bin** icon.

2 LOCATE THE FILE A window opens, showing the contents of the Recycle Bin. Next to each item are columns displaying additional information about the deleted files, such as the original location and the date and time the file was deleted.

3 RESTORE THE ITEM To restore an item to its original location, click on it to select it, then click on **Restore this item** from the menu bar above.

■ **RESTORING MULTIPLE ITEMS** To select and restore several items from the Recycle Bin at the same time, hold down the **Control** key and select each item in turn. When finished click on **Restore the selected items** from the menu bar above. All the selected items will now be restored to their original locations on the computer.

FILE IS LOST

1 USE THE WINDOWS SEARCH FACILITY Click on the **Start** button to open the **Start menu**.

2 START THE SEARCH In the **Start Search** box, start typing a word that is part of your lost filename (there is no need to click in the box first). As you type, filenames containing that combination of characters are displayed in the pane above. Hover your mouse pointer over a filename to display its location. Click on a file to open it and launch its associated program. You can now save it to a location where you can find it again, using **Save As**.

FILE OVERWRITTEN

1 LOCATE THE FILE OR FOLDER Click on **Start** and **Explorer**. In **Explorer**, find the file or folder that you have accidentally overwritten with a later version.

2 RIGHT-CLICK ON THE FILE A **Properties** dialog box is displayed. Click on the **Previous Versions** tab. A list of shadow copies – the file as it was at particular points in time – is displayed. You can quickly preview a read-only version of the file to check that it is the version you want. When you have decided which file you need, drag it to a folder or select it and click on the **Restore** button.

be aware

The version of Windows Vista that you are running affects the options for backing up and restoring that are available to you:

● Ultimate, Business and Enterprise versions of Vista have more extensive and sophisticated back-up and restore features.
● If you are using a home version of Vista, you can use third-party software that will give you similar protection. Programs such as Search and Recover, Handy Recovery and Norton Personal Backup are for sale on-line and on the high street. These offer a variety of functions.
● ShadowExplorer is a piece of free software that gives you access to the previous versions of files, so that you have safeguards similar to the more advanced versions of Vista against accidentally overwriting important files.

 TAKE CARE

If you have a generous size of hard drive (200GB or more), only empty the **Recycle Bin** when it is absolutely necessary. You can then go to the Bin when you need a file that you 'deleted' as unwanted.

Lost files on a Mac

If you are using a Mac computer that is running operating system 10.5 or later, a number of options are available for finding lost files, depending on how much you know about the file you have lost.

● **USE RECENT ITEMS** If you know you have recently accessed the file you have lost, click on the **Apple** menu, and then point to **Recent Items** and click on the required application or document.
● **RUN A SPOTLIGHT SEARCH** Click on the **Spotlight** icon – the magnifying glass. This can be found on the menu bar at the top right of the screen, in some applications or in the **Open** or **Save** dialog boxes. Type as much of the filename as you can remember in the search field. Spotlight starts searching as soon as you start typing.
● **SEARCH MORE PRECISELY** In **Finder**, click on the **File** menu and then click on **Find**. In addition to typing the filename, you can also specify the location and other search criteria, such as the type of file.
● **MAKE REGULAR BACK-UPS** To increase your chance of finding lost or deleted files, back up your work regularly. The easiest way to do this is to use Time Machine, part of the operating system. To back up immediately, hold down the mouse button on the **Time Machine** icon – the clock face with an anti-clockwise arrow – in the **Dock**, or open the program from the **Applications** folder, and choose **Back Up Now**. To schedule periodic back-ups, turn on and set up **Time Machine** in **System Preferences**. You will be able to back up weekly or monthly.

power surge

Power surges occur for a number of reasons. Problems at an electricity sub-station, a lightning storm, unexpectedly high demand in your area or faulty domestic wiring can all be culprits – the important thing is to protect your valuable data.

WATCHPOINT An electrical power surge or 'spike' is a temporary (maybe less than one second) increase in the normal UK electrical supply voltage of 240 volts.

precautions

- Buy a surge protector for your computer hardware and sensitive electrical equipment. Make sure it includes a phone-line input socket.
- If you live in an area that is susceptible to power fluctuations and your computer is essential to you, buy an Uninterruptable Power Supply (UPS). If a 'spike' (power surge) or power cut occurs when you are using your computer, this will give you enough time to save your documents.
- Use a power strip with a built-in surge protector for multiple plugs.

A power strip with a surge protector ensures a safe electricity supply.

action

1 DISCONNECT ALL AFFECTED APPLIANCES Appliances that were running at the time of a power surge should be disconnected, tested and, if necessary, reset. Test all appliances, even those that were not running but were still connected to a power supply.

2 CHECK PLUGS Check fuses in the plug of appliances that are no longer working, replacing any that have blown. Use a fuse tester for this.

3 CHECK FUSE BOX Check the fuse box if all appliances on a particular circuit are not working. Switch off the power, take out the fuse and replace with a new fuse of the correct amperage.

4 CHECK MCB UNIT If you have a consumer unit with mini-circuit breakers (MCBs), a switch for the circuit may have tripped and be in the Off position. Push the switch to the On position (normally up).

5 CALL AN ELECTRICIAN If the MCB switch will not stay on, or you have continued problems, call a qualified electrician to check your circuits.

⚠ TAKE CARE

- When working with any electrical appliance or electrical circuitry, **ensure that plugs are removed from sockets and the power is turned off before attempting any repairs.**
- When changing a fuse in a plug, check the fuse rating and make sure that you use the right one. A kettle or a heater normally needs a 13-amp fuse, not a 3-amp fuse, for example.

Effects on computer

- **COMPUTER RUNS ERRATICALLY** You may notice the loss of files or programs, freezing, crashing and other erratic functions. Reinstall your programs. If the PC still performs poorly, consult a computer technician.
- **COMPUTER DOES NOT WORK** Power surges can affect a number of computer components, such as semi-conductors, magnetic discs and circuit boards. The effects can render the computer unrepairable – check with a technician.

liquid spills

At a moment's slip of the hand, your keyboard can easily be covered in liquid from a nearby drink that can render it unusable. Fortunately, the damage may not be irreparable and if it is, a replacement is fairly cheap. While a desktop computer's keyboard is easily cleaned, a laptop keyboard may need repair by a technician.

action

SPILLAGE ON PC KEYBOARD

1 **SWITCH COMPUTER OFF** Shut down the computer immediately and, if it is connected to a mains socket, unplug it.

2 **REMOVE KEYBOARD** Unplug the keyboard from the computer and unplug the mouse if it is connected to the keyboard.

3 **DEAL WITH LIQUID** If you spilled water, turn the keyboard over and let the water drain out. Leave it to dry on an absorbent surface, such as a wad of kitchen paper, for at least 24 hours. If a sticky liquid, such as coffee or cola, is spilled, turn the keyboard over to reveal the fixing screws underneath. Remove these screws and pull the keyboard apart.

4 **DRY OUT** On a flat, clean surface, try to prise the smaller keys off the keyboard with a wide-bladed screwdriver. Do not remove the spacebar, Enter key or other large keys. Use a cotton bud and surgical spirit to remove any sticky residue. Let everything dry for at least 24 hours before reassembling.

Replacing a keyboard

Before buying a new keyboard, note the type of connection the existing keyboard uses, or whether it is wireless. The usual types of connectors are PS/2 (older keyboards) or USB. Having obtained the correct keyboard, simply plug it in (or if it is wireless, install the software and plug in the receiver). If the keyboard does not work, reboot the computer. Most laptop keyboards can be replaced by a technician, or purchase a new USB or wireless keyboard to use with the laptop.

SPILLAGE ON LAPTOP

1 **SWITCH LAPTOP OFF** Shut down the laptop. Pressing and holding the power button for five seconds is quickest. Remove the mains lead, unplug any peripherals and remove the battery. The biggest danger at this time is the device shorting out.

2 **REMOVE EXCESS LIQUID** Blot up excess liquid with a soft lint-free cloth or kitchen paper. Do not use a wiping motion as that just spreads the liquid further.

3 **TURN LAPTOP OVER** With the laptop facing away from you, tilt it from side to side and from front to back in a gentle rocking motion to help the liquid to escape from all four sides.

4 **USE COMPRESSED AIR TO DRY** Make sure that you have removed all excess liquid. Then, if you have one, use a can of compressed air to help to dry the laptop. Alternatively, use a hair dryer on its coolest setting: keep the dryer moving all the time and hold it at least 20cm above the laptop.

5 **LEAVE TO COMPLETELY DRY OUT** Leave the laptop opened in an inverted 'V' shape in a warm area, to completely dry out. Do not leave it in direct sunlight or on a radiator. Wait for 24 hours or longer, making sure the keyboard is completely dry, before reinstalling the battery and peripherals.

for next time...

● Consider purchasing a wet cover protector for your computer keyboard.
● Thin protective skins for laptop keyboards are available for a wide range of different models.

mobile phone

Being unable to make or receive a call or text message is very frustrating, but if you are completely reliant on your phone – perhaps if you are in an isolated area and need to call for help – it is important to know how to restore this lifeline quickly.

assessment

Given the high demands placed on mobile phones, operating problems are likely, but these can usually be solved by simple troubleshooting techniques.

TROUBLESHOOTING

PROBLEM	WHAT TO DO
PHONE ON BUT NOT WORKING If your phone is on and you can see the on-screen display, but nothing happens when you use the keypad, it is likely that the keypad is locked.	**Keypad locked** Press the unlock key and/or enter the unlocking code. The default is often 0000 or the last four digits of your number. To reset it, remove then reinsert the battery, and turn the phone on.
SIM CARD NOT RECOGNISED Phone displays message 'SIM card is not recognised'. The SIM contact points need cleaning and the card seating in the correct position.	**Clean SIM card** Clean the contact points with a cotton bud. If the card is not seated tightly enough against the contact points, wedge it with a small piece of folded paper.
SIGNAL FAULTS The signal display should tell you how good a signal your phone is receiving. This is normally indicated by the number of bars displayed, with more bars signifying a better reception.	**Find good reception** If you cannot get a signal indoors, try going outside or near a window. You may get better reception higher up.
BATTERY FAULTS If your battery loses power very quickly, or gets very warm during use or charging, the battery may need to be replaced. If you are in an emergency situation and the battery is low, you can extend its life until you are somewhere safe (see below).	**Remove battery and check** Remove the cover (usually on the back of the phone) and take out the battery. Check whether it has warped. If you detect these faults, buy a new battery. Carry a charged battery as a back-up.

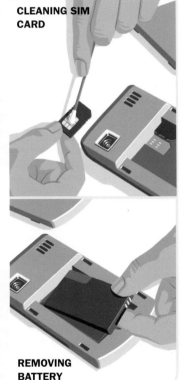

CLEANING SIM CARD

REMOVING BATTERY

Get more from your battery

If you know your battery is low but you need to make or receive a call, turn off the phone until you need to use it. Turn off Bluetooth, vibrate and the backlight. Turn down the brightness and deactivate 3G and any data transmissions.

 **TAKE CARE**

You can normally still make calls to the emergency services, even if the phone's keypad is locked and you have no credit. If you are within Europe but are not sure how to contact the local emergency services, dialling 112 will usually connect you to the appropriate helpline.

READY
REFERENCE

emergency **preparation**

To take effective action in an emergency situation it can help to have specific items to hand. By preparing a kit in advance you can access what you need quickly and easily. Medical, household and driving kits are useful for everyday use. If you're heading to the great outdoors or travelling to a high-risk area, having an emergency kit can be reassuring and potentially life-saving.

♥ medical

first-aid kit for the home
Keep a watertight box containing:
- ❏ Alcohol-free antiseptic wipes
- ❏ Alcohol gel
- ❏ Latex-free disposable gloves
- ❏ Plasters in assorted sizes
- ❏ Gel blister plasters
- ❏ Sterile dressings in assorted sizes
- ❏ Sterile eye pad
- ❏ Triangular bandages
- ❏ Pack of safety pins in assorted sizes
- ❏ Crêpe roller bandages of different widths
- ❏ Elastic bandage
- ❏ Combined sterile dressing and bandage
- ❏ Adhesive tape
- ❏ Scissors
- ❏ Tweezers
- ❏ Digital thermometer

first-aid kit for outdoor activities
When trekking or camping, consider purchasing a pouch travel kit that can easily be carried. The Red Cross travel first-aid kit contains:
- ❏ Plasters
- ❏ Bandages
- ❏ Dressings
- ❏ Disposable gloves
- ❏ Sterile dressings
- ❏ Wipes
- ❏ Safety pins

Useful medication for first-aid kits
- ❏ Paracetamol and paracetamol syrup for children
- ❏ Ibuprofen for adults and children
- ❏ Antiseptic cream
- ❏ Rehydration salts
- ❏ Anti-diarrhoea medicine
- ❏ Antihistamine tablets or syrup
- ❏ Insect repellent
- ❏ Antihistamine cream

finding medical equipment

 First-aid sign used in EU indicates location of either first-aid box or other medical equipment.

 AED (Automated external defibrillator), used if someone has a heart attack. They are often found in shopping centres and other public places, (see page 17).

first-aid kit for the car
It is possible to purchase a first-aid kit that is designed to be kept in a car. A kit from the Red Cross contains:
- ❏ Plasters
- ❏ Triangular bandages
- ❏ Dressing pads
- ❏ Gauze swabs
- ❏ Sterile dressings
- ❏ Adhesive tape
- ❏ Disposable gloves
- ❏ Antiseptic wipes
- ❏ Safety pins
- ❏ Disposable face shield
- ❏ Scissors
- ❏ Tweezers
- ❏ Mylar blanket
- ❏ Note pad and pencil
- ❏ Torch
- ❏ Clinical waste bag

specialist kits
A person who has an allergy or long-term medical condition may be wearing a medical alert bracelet to indicate this (see page 55). He or she is likely to be carrying specialist medical equipment and medication. Someone who suffers from anaphylactic shock will carry an autoinjector (see page 54); a diabetic may carry an insulin kit (see page 58).

household

general purpose tool kit

Keep the items listed below in a durable plastic tool box that is light to carry and allows easy access to each tool. Store the tool box in a place that is quickly accessible. Do not pile other items on top of it.

- ❏ Flat tip, Pozidriv and Philips screwdrivers with large and small heads
- ❏ Electrical screwdriver
- ❏ Hammer
- ❏ Retractable blade knife
- ❏ Tape measure
- ❏ PTFE tape
- ❏ Two adjustable spanners
- ❏ Inspection lamp
- ❏ Wire cutters
- ❏ Pliers
- ❏ Aerosol water repellent (WD40)
- ❏ Petroleum jelly

Ladder safety

Do not attempt to climb a ladder unless you feel totally confident. If you do climb a ladder, ensure it is properly secured at the correct angle – 30cm out for every 1m up the wall. Ask someone to hold on to the bottom of the ladder.

for power failure and replacing fuses

Keep this kit readily available – you will have to find it in the dark:

- ❏ Candles
- ❏ Matches
- ❏ Torch
- ❏ Fuse wire or cartridge fuses if your consumer unit needs them
- ❏ Plug top fuses (3A, 5A and 13A fuses)

emergency plumbing kit

Store small items in plastic bags, clearly labelled. Keep the complete kit in a large box or crate with clear access; drain rods are bulky items so store these in a garage or under stairs.

- ❏ Emergency pipe repair clamp (pipe leaks)
- ❏ Radiator key
- ❏ Slip coupling (pipe leaks)
- ❏ Self-amalgamating tape (pipe leaks)
- ❏ WC flap valve and spare link (faulty WC)
- ❏ Sink plunger (blocked sink, basin etc)
- ❏ WC plunger (blocked WC)
- ❏ Set of drain rods (blocked drains and down pipes)
- ❏ Tap washers (dripping taps)

Fire safety equipment

Knowing the different types of fire extinguishers and when to use them can save lives. The most common extinguisher for use in the home is a dry powder version. Read the instructions when installing and be familiar with how to use it. Keep any extinguisher regularly serviced; once a year is normal. A fire blanket is effective in containing a small fire and most usefully kept in the kitchen.

- **DRY POWDER** (blue label) By far the most common, these extinguishers contain dry powder and are suitable for use on burning solid materials, but also for electrical fires and for those involving flammable liquids (but not cooking oil). It should be at least 1kg in size.
- **FOAM** (cream label) This type of extinguisher contains a spray foam that is ideal for fires involving flammable liquids and can also put out fires involving solid materials but not electric fires (though they are safe if accidentally sprayed on electrical equipment). Minimum 2kg capacity.
- **WATER** (red label) These are limited to tackling fires involving solid materials and should never be used on electrical fires or fires involving flammable liquids. As they send a high-pressure jet, they can be used at a distance on something like burning furniture. Minimum size 5 litres.
- **CARBON DIOXIDE** These are not suitable for putting out fires involving solid materials, but are ideal for flammable liquids (not cooking oil) and for electrical fires, especially with equipment such as computers as they cause minimum damage.
- **FIRE BLANKET** Made from fire-resistant material, it requires no maintenance but can only be used on small, localised fires. Keep it where it is easily accessible in an emergency.

 driving

essential
Keep a torch and reflective clothing inside the car.
- ❏ Torch and spare batteries
- ❏ Basic tool kit
- ❏ Jack and wheel brace
- ❏ Jump leads
- ❏ Duplicate ignition key
- ❏ Warning triangle
- ❏ First-aid kit

useful
- ❏ Owner's manual
- ❏ Tow rope
- ❏ Water repellent lubricant
- ❏ Fire extinguisher (see below)
- ❏ Blanket
- ❏ Petrol can
- ❏ Spare bulbs
- ❏ Spare fuses

when driving in snow and ice
Keep as many items as possible for personal use inside the car to avoid getting wet and cold.
- ❏ Fully charged mobile phone
- ❏ Shovel and long-handled brush
- ❏ High-energy food and drinks
- ❏ A vacuum flask containing a hot drink
- ❏ Warm clothing and blankets
- ❏ Sacking to provide tyre grip in icy conditions

for more extreme conditions
- ❏ Snow chains
- ❏ Can of spare fuel
- ❏ Tow rope
- ❏ Recovery strap for muddy or sandy terrain

Driving abroad
Check what you need in the country you are visiting as legal requirements vary. For overseas driving take:
- ❏ Full UK driving licence, including paper counterpart
- ❏ Vehicle registration document
- ❏ Motor insurance certificate
- ❏ Breakdown cover documents
- ❏ International driving permit when required, such as when hiring cars in some African and Asian countries.

Fire extinguisher for a car

To deal with a car fire, experts recommend a dry-powder extinguisher with a capacity of at least 1.5kg. Smaller models last for just eight seconds, which is probably not enough time to put out a fire. Install the fire extinguisher in an easily accessible place such as under the dashboard or clipped under the driver's seat. Do not keep an extinguisher in the boot.

warning symbols for level crossings

 Level crossing without barrier or gate ahead

 Level crossing without barrier

 Level crossing with barrier or gate ahead

 public

evacuation kit
If you need to make a quick exit from your home, take the following in a waterproof bag:
- ❏ Battery-operated radio
- ❏ Eating utensils
- ❏ Blankets or sleeping bags
- ❏ Passport and valuable papers

for a refuge shelter
For a stay in a shelter for several days, the following will be useful. Pack in a soft holdall or rucksack.
- ❏ Torches and batteries
- ❏ Water (1–2 litres per person per day)
- ❏ Canned foods
- ❏ Milk and beverages
- ❏ Medicine
- ❏ Toilet paper
- ❏ Sanitary towels
- ❏ Nappies
- ❏ Baby food and baby supplies
- ❏ Battery-operated radio
- ❏ Eating utensils
- ❏ Blankets or sleeping bags
- ❏ Passport and valuable papers
- ❏ Games and books
- ❏ To keep finances secure, a note of credit card numbers and bank phone numbers etc.

outdoors

for expeditions

Carry in a waterproof pack, with first-aid kit and torch accessible:

❏ Sufficient food and water for the length of your trip
❏ Iodine water-purifying tablets or water filter
❏ First-aid kit
❏ Head torch and spare batteries
❏ Spare clothes, waterproofs, warm hat, gloves, Mylar blanket
❏ Shelter and sleeping bag
❏ Rope
❏ Fully charged mobile phone and spare battery
❏ Fire-lighting equipment
❏ Lightweight survival bag with thermal insulation can be used as a groundsheet or an improvised tent

when at sea

Keep these essential items in a waterproof sealable pack:

❏ Up-to-date charts
❏ Compass and GPS

Keep a grab bag – a waterproof and watertight pack – prepared ready for an emergency. These items will be essential if anyone needs to evacuate the boat to a life raft:

❏ First-aid kit
❏ Hand-held VHF
❏ Torch and spare batteries
❏ Water and food
❏ Mylar blanket

surviving the desert

Store tools and equipment in a car boot with food, water and a first-aid kit inside the car:

❏ Take twice as much food and water as you expect to need for the trip. In desert conditions allow 5 litres of water per person per day
❏ First-aid kit with extra sun block and Mylar blanket
❏ Appropriate clothing, sunglasses and protective hat
❏ Items to make a solar still (see page 273)
❏ Tools and a spares kit for the car, including a powerful torch, fan belt, radiator hoses, a second spare tyre and a shovel for clearing sand

Essential knots for outdoor emergencies

Knowing just three knots will mean you can efficiently secure a rope or line in emergency situations. Each has its own application.

● **BOWLINE** Use to make a secure loop in the end of a rope, for example for throwing to rescue a drowning person (see page 250).

1 Form a large loop in the end of the rope; make a small loop as shown, with the rope end in front.
2 Pass the end up through the small loop, round the rope and back through the small loop.
3 Pull tight and leave a long tail.

● **HALF HITCH** Use to attach a rope to a post or tree, such as when putting up a tarpaulin for emergency cover for the night (see page 267).

1 Pass end twice round bar, post or tree.
2 Take the end forward over the main rope, around the back, and pass through between the post and rope to form a 'half hitch'.
3 Repeat to form a second half hitch, then push up and pull tight.

● **REEF KNOT** Use to join two ends securely, especially where a flat knot is needed, such as when applying bandages (see page 87).

useful contacts

GENERAL

EMERGENCY SERVICES NUMBERS
UK 999
Textphone users: Freetext 18000
EU 112
Australia 000
New Zealand 111
USA 911

AGE UK
Age UK combines Age Concern and Help the Aged. This name applies from Spring 2010. The individual charities can still be contacted as below.
www.ageuk.org
Age Concern
0800 00 99 66
www.ageconcern.org.uk
Help the Aged
020 7278 1114
www.helptheaged.org.uk

DIAL UK
National disability information and advice service.
St Catherine's, Tickhill Road, Doncaster, South Yorkshire DN4 8QN
01302 310123
www.dialuk.info

HEALTH AND SAFETY EXECUTIVE
HSE Infoline
Caerphilly Business Park, Caerphilly CF8 3GG
0845 345 0055
www.hse.gov.uk

MEDICAL

ALLERGY UK
01322 619898
www.allergyuk.org

ANAPHYLAXIS CAMPAIGN
PO Box 275, Farnborough, Hampshire GU14 6SX
01252 546100
Helpline 01252 542029
www.anaphylaxis.org.uk

ARTHRITIS CARE
18 Stephenson Way, London NW1 2HD
020 7380 6500
www.arthritiscare.org.uk

ASTHMA UK
Summit House, 70 Wilson Street, London EC2A 2DB
0800 121 62 55
UK Adviceline
0800 121 62 44 (9am–5pm, Mon–Fri)
www.asthma.org.uk

BACK CARE
The charity for healthier backs.
16 Elmtree Road, Teddington TW11 8ST
0845 130 2704
www.backcare.org.uk

BRITISH HEART FOUNDATION
Greater London House, 180 Hampstead Road, London NW1 7AW
020 7554 0000 (9am–5pm, Mon–Fri)
Heart Helpline 0300 330 3311 (9am–6pm, Mon–Fri)
www.bhf.org.uk

BRITISH RED CROSS
44 Moorfields, London EC2Y 9AL
0844 871 1111
+44 2071 3879 00 from outside UK
www.redcross.org.uk

DEPARTMENT OF HEALTH
020 7210 4850
www.dh.gov.uk

DIABETES UK
Macleod House, 10 Parkway, London NW1 7AA
020 7424 1000
www.diabetes.org.uk

EPILEPSY ACTION
New Anstey House, Gate Way Drive, Yeadon, Leeds LS19 7XY
Helpline 0808 800 5050
www.epilepsy.org.uk

MENINGITIS RESEARCH FOUNDATION
Midland Way, Thornbury, Bristol BS35 2BS
01454 281811
24-hour helpline:
UK 080 8800 3344
ROI 1800 41 33 44
www.meningitis.org

MIND
Provides information and advice about mental health.
Helpline 0845 766 0163
www.mind.org.uk

MISCARRIAGE ASSOCIATION
Provides support and information.
c/o Clayton Hospital, Northgate, Wakefield, West Yorkshire WF1 3JS
01924 200799 (9am–4pm, Mon–Fri)
www.miscarriageassociation.org.uk

MISSING PEOPLE
24-hour helpline providing advice, practical help and support for missing persons and their families.
0500 700 700

NHS DIRECT FOR ENGLAND, WALES AND N IRELAND
0845 46 47
www.nhs.uk

NHS DIRECT FOR SCOTLAND
NHS24
08454 24 24 24
www.nhs24.com

RoSPA
The Royal Society for the Prevention of Accidents.
RoSPA House, Edgbaston Park, 353 Bristol Road, Edgbaston, Birmingham B5 7ST
0121 248 2000
www.rospa.com

SAMARITANS

Confidential emotional support.
PO Box 9090, Stirling, FK8 2SA
UK 08457 90 90 90
ROI 1850 60 90 90
www.samaritans.org

ST ANDREW'S AMBULANCE ASSOCIATION

St Andrew's House, 48 Milton Street,
Glasgow G4 0HR
0141 332 4031
www.firstaid.org.uk

ST JOHN AMBULANCE

27 St John's Lane,
London EC1M 4BU
08700 10 49 50
www.sja.org.uk

STROKE ASSOCIATION

Essential information for stroke
casualties and carers.
Stroke House, 240 City Road,
London EC1V 2PR
020 7566 0300
Stroke Helpline 0845 303 3100
(9am–5pm, Mon–Fri)
www.stroke.org.uk

HOUSEHOLD

PUBLIC SERVICES

Find local council websites, telephone
numbers and addresses here.
www.direct.gov.uk

COMMUNITIES AND LOCAL GOVERNMENT

Local government information and links
to websites giving advice on subjects
from fire safety to public services.
0303 444 0000
www.community.gov.uk

BAT CONSERVATION TRUST

15 Cloisters House,
8 Battersea Park Road,
London SW8 4BG
Bat helpline 0845 130 0228
www.bats.org.uk

BLUE CROSS

Animal welfare charity.
Shilton Road, Burford,
Oxon OX18 4PF
01993 822651
www.bluecross.org.uk

BRITISH GAS

Emergency number 0800 111 999
Services and repairs 0845 074 4002
www.britishgas.co.uk

BRITISH PEST CONTROL ASSOCIATION

Information on pest control and access
to accredited pest control companies.
1 Gleneagles House, Vernongate,
South Street, Derby DE1 1UP
01332 294288
www.bpca.org.uk

BUILDING REGULATIONS

For advice and information, click on the
'POPULAR LINKS' box in the lower right
corner of this page and select 'Building
regulations'.
www.communities.gov.uk

CATS PROTECTION

Non-veterinary related cat care,
including lost pets.
National Cat Centre, Chelwood Gate,
Haywards Heath, Sussex RH17 7TT
Helpline 03000 12 12 12
www.cats.org.uk

CHARTERED INSTITUTE OF PLUMBING AND HEATING ENGINEERING (IPHE)

To source accredited members.
64 Station Lane, Hornchurch,
Essex RM12 6NB
01708 472791
www.ciphe.org.uk

DOGS TRUST

Dog welfare charity.
17 Wakley Street,
London EC1V 7RQ
0207 837 0006
www.dogstrust.org.uk

ELECTRICAL CONTRACTORS ASSOCIATION

To source accredited members.
ECA, ESCA House, 34 Palace Court,
London W2 4HY
020 7313 4800
www.eca.co.uk

FIRE KILLS

Fire safety information.
http://firekills.direct.gov.uk

MALICIOUS CALLS BUREAU

Specialist advisers are on call
24 hours a day.
0800 661 441

NATIONAL GRID EMERGENCY SERVICES

Gas and carbon monoxide
0800 111 999
Electricity 0800 40 40 90
www.nationalgrid.com/uk/gas/safety

PDSA

Cares for pets of people on low
incomes.
Whitechapel Way, Priorslee, Telford,
Shropshire TF2 9PQ
0800 731 2502 (9am–5pm, Mon–Fri)
www.pdsa.org.uk

PETLOG REGISTER

Helps reunite lost and missing pets
with their owners.
The Kennel Club, 1–5 Clarges Street,
Piccadilly, London W1J 8AB
0844 463 3999
www.thekennelclub.org.uk/petlog

RSPB

Royal Society for the Protection of
Birds. Birds and wildlife advice.
The Lodge, Potton Road, Sandy,
Bedfordshire SG19 2DL
01767 693 690
www.rspb.org.uk

RSPCA

Royal Society for the Prevention of
Cruelty to Animals.
Wilberforce Way, Southwater,
Horsham, West Sussex RH13 9RS
Cruelty line 0300 1234 999
Advice line 0300 1234 555
www.rspca.org.uk

DRIVING

THE AUTOMOBILE ASSOCIATION LTD (AA)

Motoring (UK and overseas) advice.
0800 887766
www.theaa.com

BRAKE

Road safety charity. Helpline for victims
of road traffic accidents and carers.
0845 603 8570
www.brake.org.uk

BRITISH MOTORCYCLISTS FEDERATION
3 Oswin Road
Brailsford Industrial Estate,
Braunstone, Leicester LE3 1HR
0116 2795112
www.bmf.co.uk

THE CARAVAN CLUB LTD
East Grinstead House, East Grinstead
West Sussex RH19 1UA
01342 326944
www.caravanclub.co.uk

CTC
UK's National Cyclists' Organisation.
Parklands, Railton Rd, Guildford,
Surrey GU2 9JX
0844 736 8450
www.ctc.org.uk

INSTITUTE OF ADVANCED MOTORISTS
Road safety charity dedicated to
raising driving and riding standards.
0845 126 8600
www.iam.org.uk

MOTOR INSURERS' BUREAU
01908 830001
www.mib.org.uk

RAC
Motoring (UK and overseas) advice.
08705 722722
www.rac.co.uk

TRAVEL

ABTA THE TRAVEL ASSOCIATION
(formerly Association of British Travel
Agents) Maintains high standards of
trading practice in travel industry.
30 Park Street, London SE1 9EQ
Consumer Affairs 0901 201 5050
(9.00am–5.30pm, Mon–Fri)
www.abta.com

AIR TRANSPORT USERS COUNCIL
UK's consumer watchdog for the
aviation industry.
CAA House, 45–59 Kingsway,
London WC2B 6TE
020 7240 6061
www.auc.org.uk

AMNESTY INTERNATIONAL
The Human Rights Action Centre,
17-25 New Inn Yard, London EC2A 3EA
020 7033 1500
www.amnesty.org.uk

ATOL
Air Travel Organiser's Licencing, run by
the Civil Aviation Authority.
Civil Aviation Authority, ATOL Section,
K3, 45-59 Kingsway,
London WC2B 6TE
020 7453 6700
www.atol.org.uk

CIVIL AVIATION AUTHORITY
CAA House, 45-59 Kingsway,
London WC2B 6TE
020 7379 7311
www.caa.co.uk

EHIC (EUROPEAN HEALTH INSURANCE CARD)
PO Box 1114, Newcastle upon Tyne
NE99 2TL
0845 605 0707
+44 191 212 7500 from outside UK
www.ehic.org.uk

FIT FOR TRAVEL
Travel health information from
NHS Scotland.
www.fitfortravel.scot.nhs.uk

FOREIGN AND COMMONWEALTH OFFICE
Source telephone number and address
of local office before travelling,
especially when visiting areas which
are considered risky for foreigners.
King Charles Street,
London SW1A 2AH
020 7008 1500
www.fco.gov.uk

HOSTAGE UK
Meets the needs of those who fall
victim to kidnapping or hostage-taking
situations.
www.hostageuk.org

INTERNATIONAL ASSOCIATION FOR MEDICAL ASSISTANCE TO TRAVELLERS
www.iamat.org

WESTERN UNION MONEY TRANSFERS
0800 731 1815
+35 3 66 979 2719 from outside UK
www.westernunion.co.uk

CRIME

LOCAL POLICE SERVICES
To find address and phone number of
your local police station.
http://localcrime.direct.gov.uk/

CRIMESTOPPERS
To give information about crime or
criminals anonymously.
0800 555 111
www.crimestoppers-uk.org

ONLINE SCAMS
International source of information on
spoof emails and phishing scams.
www.millersmiles.co.uk

RAPE & SEXUAL ABUSE SUPPORT CENTRE
Helpline 0808 802 999
(12–2.30pm, 7–9.30pm, every day)
020 8683 3311
www.rasasc.org.uk

RAPE CRISIS ENGLAND AND WALES
Find a local support centre.
www.rapecrisis.org.uk

RAPE CRISIS SCOTLAND
08088 01 03 02
www.rapecrisisscotland.org.uk

VICTIM SUPPORT
Victim Supportline, Hannibal House,
Elephant and Castle Shopping Centre,
London SE1 6TB
Supportline 0845 30 30 900
www.victimsupport.org.uk

PUBLIC

NATIONAL EMERGENCIES
Advice on dealing with public
emergencies can be found on the
government website.
www.direct.gov.uk/en/
Governmentcitizensandrights/
Dealingwithemergencies

ENVIRONMENT AGENCY
Includes flood advice and warnings.
National Customer Contact Centre,
PO Box 544, Rotherham S60 1BY
08708 506 506
www.environment-agency.gov.uk

HEALTH PROTECTION AGENCY
Information on health issues.
www.hpa.org.uk

HOME OFFICE
Direct Communications Unit,
2 Marsham Street, London SW1P 4DF
020 7035 4848
www.homeoffice.gov.uk

NATIONAL PANDEMIC FLU SERVICE
0800 1 513 513
www.direct.gov.uk/pandemicflu

OUTDOOR

AVALANCHE-CENTER.ORG
Links to avalanche information and alerts worldwide.
www.avalanche-center.org

MOUNTAIN RESCUE COUNCIL
Dial 999 or 112 and ask for Police, then Mountain Rescue.
www.mountain.rescue.org.uk

NATURAL ENGLAND
Formerly Countryside Agency
Information for countryside visitors.
0845 600 3078
www.naturalengland.org.uk

RAMBLERS
2nd Floor Camelford House
87-90 Albert Embankment,
London SE1 7TW
020 7339 8500
www.ramblers.org.uk

THE ROYAL LIFE SAVING SOCIETY UK
Training and qualifications.
01789 773 994
www.lifesavers.org.uk

RNLI
Royal National Lifeboat Institution.
West Quay Road, Poole BH15 1HZ
0845 045 6999
www.rnli.org.uk

RYA
National body for all forms of boating.
RYA House, Ensign Way, Hamble,
Hants SO31 4YA
02380 604 100
www.rya.org.uk

picture credits

t = top; b = bottom; l = left;
c = centre; r = right.

1 Christian Arnal/Photononstop/Photolibrary; **2-3** Chris Cheadle/All Canada Photos/Photolibrary; **41br** Eaniton/Dreamstime.com; **43cr** Bubbles Photolibrary/Alamy; **48cr** Reuters/Gregg Newton; **52tl** S.White/Fotolia, **br** Robhowarth/Dreamstime.com; **55bl** Mark Clarke/Science Photo Library; **56tl** Andrew Soundarajan/Alamy; **59br** Ian Hooton/Science Photo Library; **63br** Ian Boddy/Science Photo Library; **64tr** istockphoto.com; **77cl** Angela Hampton Picture Library/Alamy; **78c** Banana Stock/Photolibrary; **80br** Westend61/Photolibrary; **115cr** Stephen Gibson/Dreamstime.com; **117tl** Banana Stock/Photolibrary; **122b** Flake/Alamy; **124br** Image Source/Photolibrary; **126tl** Image Source/Getty Images; **127br** Mark Richardson/fotolia; **128bl** Mark Sykes/Science Photo Library; **cr** Michael Blann/White/Photolibrary; **130tr** Astrid & Hanns Frieder Michler/Science Photo Library; **131tr** Roger Coulam/Alamy; **133cr** SusivoutiStock/Alamy; **142tr** Richard Woldendorp/Photolibrary; **148br** Deborah Waters - United Kingdom/Alamy; **153cl** Colin Bowling/Practical Pictures; **156 pic1** Ken Wilson Papilio/CORBIS; **pic2** Aazz1/Dreamstime.com; **pic3** John Downer/Photolibrary; **pic4** Wildlife GmbH/Alamy; **pic5** Mercer/Insects/Alamy; **cr** Manor Photography/Alamy; **158tr** Pat Bennett/Alamy; **165tl** Photononstop/Photolibrary; **167cl** Banana Stock/Photolibrary; **168b** LondonPhotos - Homer Sykes/Alamy; **170b** White/Photolibrary; **177cr** Photofusion Picture Library/Alamy; **178b** Ray Grover/Alamy; **180** Flying Colours Ltd/Getty; **184br** Alistair Laming/Alamy; **186b** Daniel Berehulak/Staff/Getty Images; **189br** Melissa Brandes/Shutterstock.com; **190br** Bronwyn Photo/Fotolia.com; **193t** StockShot/Alamy; **194b** AFP/Getty Images; **196b** Sigurgeir Jonasson; Frank Lane Picture Agency/CORBIS; **197tr** Phil Degginger/Alamy; **198tr** Gary I. Rothstein/epa/Corbis; **199tr** Warren Faidley/Corbis; **200cr** PA Photos; **201t** AFP/Getty Images; **202b** Leo Meier/Corbis; **203tr** Mick Tsikas/epa/Corbis; **208b** Getty Images; **210b** BWAC Images/Alamy; **212tr** Alan Curtis/Alamy; **215t** Thierry Orban/Sygma/Corbis; **216tr** Getty Images; **220tl** Stringer/Getty Images; **222bl** Bubbles Photolibrary/Alamy; **224cl** Ron Chapple Studios/Dreamstime.com; **227tl** Bubbles Photolibrary/Alamy; **228tr** Jochen Tack/Photolibrary; **232tl** Jaubert Bernard/Alamy;

233cl Stuart Pearcey/Dreamstime.com; **237cl** Nordicphotos/Alamy; **239tc** Alvey & Towers Picture Library/Alamy; **242b** Richard Warburton/Alamy; **243br** www.arbil4x4.co.uk; **244b** Fat Chance Productions/Getty; **245br** Motion Picture Library/Paul Ridsdale/Alamy; **247b** Christophe Viseux/Alamy; **256cl** Kingjon/Dreamstime.com; **cr** Scott Eldridge - Eldo Photography/Alamy; **259t** Chris Cheadle/All Canada Photos/Photolibrary; **264b** SCPhotos/Alamy; **267cr** Jeffbanke/Dreamstime.com; **271 pic1** ImageBroker/Imagebroker/FLPA; **pic2** Derek Middleton/FLPA; **pic3** J S Sira/Garden Picture Library/Photolibrary; **pic4** Pixtal Images/Photolibrary; **pic5** Nigel Cattlin/FLPA; **pic6** Werner Bollmann/OSF/Photolibrary; **272bl** Tobias Bernhard/Corbis; **274b** National Geographic Image Collection/Alamy; **275tr** Ashley Cooper/Alamy; **276tc** Peter Titmuss/Alamy; **279t** AFP/Getty Images; **280blt** ABTA Ltd; **blb** ATOL (Air Travel Organisers' Licensing) is managed by the Civil Aviation Authority; **281cl** Robert Adrian Hillman/Dreamstime.com; **bl** Baloncici/Dreamstime.com; **284b** Christian Arnal/Photononstop/Photolibrary; **286b** Esa Hiltula/Alamy; **287tl** Charles Bowman/Alamy; **289bl** Bjanka Kadic/Alamy; **292tr** Mark Lucas/Alamy; **294br** AFP/Getty Images; **296tr** Bongarts/Getty Images; **301tl** Thierry Dosogne/Getty Images; **cl** Leaf/Dreamstime.com; **bl** Pahaoo/Dreamstime.com; **302bl** Jan Remisiewicz/Alamy; **306bl** Terry Whittaker/FLPA; **308br** Drewrawcliffe/Dreamstime; **310bl** Mark Raycroft/Minden Pictures/FLPA; **br** Huan/Dreamstime.com; **311br** www.counterassault.com; **312tl** Norbert Wu/Minden Pictures/FLPA; **tr** Bob Krist/Corbis; **bl** Lawson Wood/CORBIS; **br** ImageBroker/Imagebroker/FLPA; **314tr** Science Photo Library; **cr** Chris and Monique Fallows/OSF/Photolibrary; **br** Ian Scott/Dreamstime; **316br** Rob Henderson/Photolibrary; **317tr** Sebastian Kaulitzki/Alamy; **318rt** John Cancalosi/age fotostock/Photolibrary; **rc** George McCarthy/CORBIS; **rb** Dinodia Images/Alamy; **320tr** Photoshot Holdings Ltd/Alamy; **cr** Esther Beaton/Corbis; **br** James H Robinson/Photolibrary; **322br** Imagebroker/Alamy; **325cr** Creatas/Comstock/Photolibrary; **330tr** Emmeline Watkins/Science Photo Library; **336cr x 3** Crown copyright

index

Page numbers in bold type refer to key entries; numbers in bold italic type refer to illustrations.

WHAT TO DO IN AN EMERGENCY published in 2010 in the United Kingdom by Vivat Direct Limited (t/a Reader's Digest), 157 Edgware Road, London W2 2HR

WHAT TO DO IN AN EMERGENCY is owned and under licence from The Reader's Digest Association, Inc. All rights reserved.

We are committed both to the quality of our products and the service we provide to our customers. We value your comments, so please contact us on 08705 113366 or via our website at **www.readersdigest.co.uk**

✓ **IMPORTANT**

The information in this book has been carefully researched and all efforts have been made to ensure safety and accuracy. Neither the authors nor The Reader's Digest Association, Inc. assume any responsibility for any injuries suffered or losses incurred as a result of following the instructions in this book. Before taking any action based on information in this book, study the information carefully and make sure you understand it fully. Observe any warnings and take care notices.

acknowledgments

Originated by **Creative Plus Publishing Limited**
Project manager Dawn Bates
Development editor Sue Joiner
Writers John Birdsall, Jemima Dunne, David Holloway, Graeme Kerr, Tony Rilett
Editors Sue Churchill, Sue Joiner, Jon Kirkwood, Annette Love, Margaret Maino, Gisela Roberts, Jennet Stott
Design manager Gary Webb
Designers Suzie Bacon, Nancy Dunkerley, Keith Davis

Authenticators Dr Rob Hicks, Dr Viv Armstrong, Mike Lawrence, Michael Buttler, Tom Carpenter (ATOL), Victoria Poland (ABTA), Robert Morgan, Peter and Paul Morrison

Photographers Ruth Jenkinson, Lizzie Orme
Art direction on shoot Emma and Tom Forge
Stylist Jo Rigg
Medical make up Sheree Jewell
Illustrators Tom Connell, Martin Saunders (Beehive Illustration)
Picture research Claire Coakley, Nic Dean
Proofreader Ron Pankhurst
Indexer Marie Lorimer

With thanks to the following organisations for help and advice PDSA, Fire and Rescue Service, Mountain Rescue, National Poisons Society, Royal Life-Saving Society, British Marine Federation, Dr Clive Roberts Wolverhampton University, London Zoo, British Marine Aquarium, Association of Pet Behaviour Counsellors

Vivat Direct Project Team
Editor Lisa Thomas
Art Editor Julie Bennett

For Vivat Direct
Editorial Director Julian Browne
Art Director Anne-Marie Bulat
Managing Editor Nina Hathway
Head of Book Development Sarah Bloxham
Picture Resource Manager Sarah Stewart-Richardson
Pre-Press Technical Manager Dean Russell
Product Production Manager Claudette Bramble
Senior Production Controller Katherine Tibbals

Colour origination Fresh Media Group
Printed and bound in Europe by Arvato Iberia

Concept code UK2223/IC
Book code 400-485 UP0000-1
ISBN 978 0 276 44548 4
Oracle code 250014843H.00.24